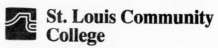

The
Emptiness
Of Japanese
Affluence

Japan in the Modern World

Series Editor: Mark Selden

This series explores political, economic, cultural, and strategic dimensions of Japan's modern transformations, with particular attention to their consequences for the peoples of Japan and the world.

VOICES FROM THE JAPANESE WOMEN'S MOVEMENT
Edited by AMPO-Japan Asia Quarterly Review

THE EMPTINESS OF JAPANESE AFFLUENCE
Gavan McCormack

The Emptiness Of Japanese Affluence

Gavan McCormack

With a Foreword by
Norma Field

An East Gate Book

M.E. Sharpe
Armonk, New York
London, England

An East Gate Book

Copyright © 1996 by M. E. Sharpe, Inc.

Library of Congress Cataloging-in-Publication Data

McCormack, Gavan.
The emptiness of Japanese affluence / Gavan McCormack.
p.   cm. — ("An East gate book.")
Includes bibliographical references and index.
ISBN 1-56324-711-9 (hardcover : alk. paper). — ISBN 1-56324-712-7
(softcover : alk. paper)
1. Japan—Social conditions—1945– 2. Japan—Economic
conditions—1945– 3. Japan—Politics and government—1945–
I. Title. II. Series
HN723.5.M39   1996
306'.0952—dc20   96-4391
CIP
Printed in the United States of America

The paper used in this publication meets the minimum requirements of American National Standard for Information Sciences— Permanence of Paper for Printed Library Materials, ANSI Z 39.48-1984.

BM (c)   10   9   8   7   6   5   4   3   2   1
BM (p)   10   9   8   7   6   5   4   3   2   1

Contents

Photographs follow page 184

Introduction

Part One: Political Economy

Part Two: Identity

Part Three: Memory

Concluding Remarks

List of Figures and Tables

Figures

Tables

Note on Japanese Names

The Japanese convention that family name precedes personal name is generally followed in this book. However, those Japanese who either live in the West or choose to adopt the opposite (Western) convention of personal name followed by family name in their writings in English are identified accordingly. Thus, well-known Japanese scholars such as Tsuru Shigeto and Ui Jun (Professors Tsuru and Ui) are referred to in Western name order when their writings in English are cited but in Japanese name order when reference is made to their writings in Japanese. Uncertainty may be resolved by referring to the Index, where all persons named in the text are listed in alphabetical order according to their family names.

Yen-Dollar Exchange Rate
(Average annual rate, yen per dollar)

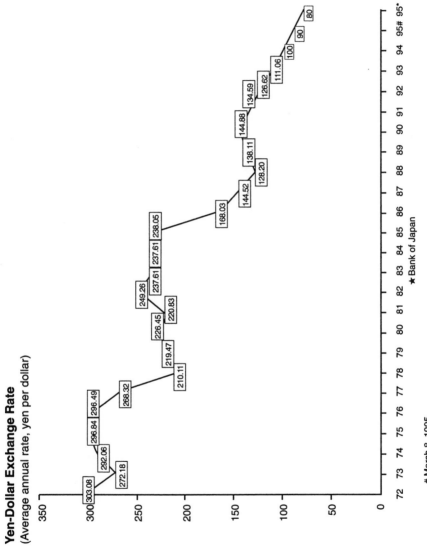

★ Bank of Japan

March 8, 1995
*April 19, 1995

Foreword

During the fiftieth anniversary summer in Japan, a radio report described a "Sunflower Peace Movement" being promoted in one of the metropolitan cities of Japan. The idea was to have sunflower seedlings distributed to citizens at area schools on successive Sundays in late June and July so that by August 15 the city would be full of tall sunflowers proclaiming peace. In Hiroshima, for August 6, an international competition had yielded a new peace song to be premiered by a chorus of young people. Newscasters in the meanwhile wrung their hands after reports of vigorous protests in Australia and New Zealand over the resumption of French nuclear testing in the South Pacific: it did seem, they said, that more should be happening in our own country given that it was, after all, the only country in the world to have been A-bombed. Several politicians campaigning for the upper-house elections in late July embraced the antinuclear issue, thus producing the curious spectacle of newscasters and establishment figures urging an unexcited public to get out and demonstrate.

This was also the summer when the Japan Teachers' Union announced that it was no longer opposing the use of the Rising Sun flag and Kimigayo anthem at school ceremonies. Instead, it intended to cooperate with the Ministry of Education in addressing the problems facing the contemporary Japanese schoolroom. Since its founding in 1947, the JTU was not only dedicated to the economic well-being of its members, but far more saliently in the public eye, committed to vigorous, not to say militant, opposition to rearmament, to textbook censorship, to the reinstatement of "moral" education, to the teachers' efficiency rating system. It lost most of its major battles with the Education Ministry, but it had a clear identity, reflecting an understanding that national politics had both a gross and subtle impact on the classroom. Now that it has shaken hands with the enemy and vowed to cooperate in its agenda, it is difficult to imagine how it will reconstruct a raison d'être. Few tears will be shed over the JTU's plight, but it is a matter of some urgency that there should be no prominent vehicle of organized resistance to the increasingly visible injuries of an educational system ruthlessly harnessed to the needs of the national economy.

Meanwhile, on August 15 itself, Prime Minister Tomiichi Murayama, whose own Social-Democratic Party had surrendered on the flag and anthem a year earlier, delivered a spirited message on "mistaken state policy" as the cause of the suffering brought to other nations by Japan during the last war. His words constituted an unequivocal apology, but they were intended to remain only *words*, unsubstantiated by government compensation to individual victims of that mistaken policy. Most of the overseas media praised Mr. Murayama's performance: The business of apologizing is tedious not only for Japanese leaders but for foreign interests concerned with the business of business, to which end an effective apology has been recognized as useful and probably necessary. Unreported in most accounts, however, was how, on that important anniversary, in response to a reporter's question, Mr. Murayama reinforced the founding myth of postwar Japan by stating that it was established at home and abroad that the emperor had no responsibility for that war. That he felt compelled to respond in this way is as telling a detail as any about the state of Japanese society fifty years after surrender. In any case, Mr. Murayama's apology on behalf of the nation came as an anticlimax to the sorry parliamentary resolution in June. Originally intended as a national apology for Japanese wrongdoing in the Asia-Pacific War, it ended up a bland statement about peace, and one garnering minimal support at that.

Peace, inscribed in the postwar Constitution in an article (no. 9) forswearing war as a means of resolving international disputes, has been an explicit emblem of national identity over the past fifty years. In the earlier decades it showed up in the pairing "peace and democracy"; more recently, it has changed partners to team up with *prosperity*. Thus, recent August 15 addresses at the state memorial service routinely refer to the "peace and prosperity" founded on the people's sacrifice. Japan's defeat and the structures and alignments put in place during the American Occupation have become a world-historical object lesson for responding to the question, what can nation-states do other than wage or prepare to wage war?

They can mobilize the citizenry for prosperity, would be one quick answer from Japan. Prosperity, understood as perpetual development, however, requires ceaseless struggle for global dominance, which in turn implies minute penetration of the everyday lives of citizens. Or, in the succinct phrasing of Gavan McCormack in his remarkable new book, *The Emptiness of Japanese Affluence,* postwar Japan replaced war with the three "C"s of "construction, consumption, and control." McCormack's superbly documented and powerfully argued book shows how it is indispensable to scrutinize this translation of national purpose from the pre- to postwar eras in order to understand Mr. Murayama's August 15 speech, the Sunflower Movement, or the Japan Teachers' Union about-face. As it so happens, none of these specific developments is addressed in the book, but that its analysis makes sense of them is further testimony to its explanatory reach. McCormack's sustained inquiry into a half-dozen aspects of contemporary Japan gives *Emptiness* special distinction amongst the numerous fiftieth anniversary books appearing in English and Japanese. Anyone wanting to know what kind of society Japan has produced in its half-century incarnation as a "peace state" and the implications of its postwar history for the rest of the world will want to read this account from cover to cover.

The book begins provocatively with the Great Hanshin (Kobe-Osaka-Awaji) Earthquake of January, 1995, which turned out to be an unscheduled and all the more momentous test of the material and social resources accumulated by a nation of vaunted wealth and generalized capability. Discussion of the earthquake generates the concerns of the subsequent chapters, lucidly encapsulated in the formulations of the "construction state," the "leisure state," the "farm state," the "regional state," and the "peace state." The penultimate chapter finally turns to an explicit consideration of the legacies of war, wherein forgetfulness has been structured into remembrance. This last is a subject that has been extensively treated in Japan, at least, often by way of contrast to the German example. Taken by itself, McCormack's chapter is arguably the most concise, thorough discussion of unfinished business that is available in English, but its terms are immeasurably expanded by the preceding portrait of contemporary Japan, in turn pointing back to the earthquake and its aftermath as emblem.

In spite of the skepticism, confusion, or outright opposition of many thoughtful—and weary—Japanese, postwar Japan continues to exemplify a society driven by growth for growth's sake, inevitably if unintentionally necessitating subtle and gross disregard for the well-being of its own citizens, and still more fundamentally, short-circuiting the possibility of serious debate about desirable life conditions. McCormack's Cs are a critical echo of other celebrated triplets, such as the "three sacred treasures" (the Imperial regalia of jewel, sword, and stone) of 1954—washer, vacuum cleaner, and refrigerator; the three Cs of 1966—car, "cooler" (air conditioner), color TV; or the three Cs of 1993—career, class, and clever, referring to the desired attributes of the marriageable woman in the wake of the new Crown Princess's example. However seriously one takes these formulas, McCormack's chapters show the enormous effort expended in generating, satisfying, and regenerating new desires as well as the national and global implications of such discipline. How can a society that keeps its citizens so consistently busy, such that even leisure has a frenetic quality (with dire consequences for the environment as the chapter on the "leisure state" so well shows), be expected to have developed the resources for a principled response to the foreign victims of its past actions, whether military comfort women or unpaid and brutalized mineworkers?

Make no mistake: While *The Emptiness of Japanese Affluence* is a critical examination of the dilemmas facing contemporary Japan, it is most emphatically not a work of Japan-bashing. Its scrupulous attention to history and to political economy makes clear that Japan's problems are not the consequence of putative Japanese peculiarities but of specific decisions and processes, on the one hand, and global structural forces, on the other. It is precisely because postwar Japan has been so fabulously successful as to be deemed a model that its actual record requires scrutiny. Its dysfunctions are hardly unique, though they are intensified by the concentration of population harnessed to the motor of growth at any cost. They will be found to be symptomatic of those confronting or soon to confront other so-called advanced societies. Moreover, and also paradigmatically rather than uniquely, Japan's successes are implicated in the exploitation of other sectors of the world.

Another reason it would be fundamentally misguided to identify this book as an exercise in Japan-bashing is that its sources are almost exclusively Japanese, drawn from scholarly, journalistic, and government publications. The book is a sustained argument against any position that would simply equate criticism of Japan with Japan-bashing. That such a claim is too simplistic to be useful should be self-evident, but it is nonetheless repeated, whether disingenuously by parties variously interested in obfuscation, or sincerely, as by some critics of eurocentrism. Whatever the motivation, McCormack shows that the consequence is to impose homogeneity upon Japanese society and to deny an enormous range of Japanese voices. Affirmatively, and most importantly, *The Emptiness of Japanese Affluence* provides unparalleled access in English to the views of Japanese who have thoughtfully and tenaciously resisted the terms of the consensus society. They are mostly respected and relatively well known intellectuals, but we remember that behind them stand the anonymous schoolteachers sustaining Ienaga Saburo's lawsuits against textbook censorship, the housewife activists of the cooperative safe food movement, the doctors who treat foreign laborers, and southeast Asian women caught in the current forms of the sex industry.

This book is indispensable for anyone interested in the implications of extraordinary economic success across the spectrum of social life anywhere in the world and therefore in the tantalizing possibilities of other east and southeast Asian countries. It is incomparably informative, filled with superbly illustrative statistics about contemporary Japan. The clarity and sobriety of Gavan McCormack's prose is particularly effective in conveying the surreal quality of aspects of Japanese life as the archipelago undergoes "resortification," its contours recast in concrete, its parts joined by landfills, and points within melded together as the obsession with speed refines its instruments. Finally, the author's location in Australia, rather than the United States or Japan, is a distinct advantage, yielding benefits of both broad insight and local illustration of global pattern. Some readers are habituated to learning about the disastrous environmental impact of Japanese corporate activity in Thailand or the Philippines. It should also give us pause to learn about the profound consequences of the transformation of Australian cattle herding practices in response to Japanese market "preference."

As we stand at the threshold between the Cold-War order and the twenty-first century, *The Emptiness of Japanese Affluence* exemplifies the thoughtful investigation we all need if we are to proceed with our eyes open, refusing to surrender the vision of a just and humanly livable world.

Norma Field
University of Chicago

Acknowledgments

In writing this book, I have benefited from discussion with many people, and from close critical comment from a few. I may not have satisfied them with the text I have produced or the revisions I have made as a result, but I am grateful to all who have been patient, tolerant, and especially critical with me. I will have forgotten some, but would like to record my debt at least to Aoki Hidekazu, Ronni Alexander, Geremie Barmé, Mitchell Bernard, Dipesh Chakrabarty, Syd Crawcour, Mark Elvin, Norma Field, John Fincher, Jonathan Hutt, Chalmers Johnson, Morris Low, Matsuzawa Tessei, Peter Meyer, Miyamoto Ken'ichi, Nakao Hajime, Hank Nelson, Mark Selden, Sanukida Satoshi, Richard Tanter, Tsuneishi Kei'ichi, Utsumi Aiko, and Wada Haruki. The writing was begun during a three-month visit to Kobe University in 1994, when I was attached to the Graduate School of International Cooperation Studies. I would like to express my appreciation to my colleagues there, especially the head of the school, Professor Serita Kentarō. Thanks especially to my colleagues at the Australian National University, who constitute my everyday working environment of criticism, encouragement, and friendship; to Ian Heyward of the Cartography Unit for help in designing the map on page 27; and to the administrative staff of my division—Dorothy McIntosh, Jude Shanahan, Julie Gordon, Oanh Collins, and Marion Weeks—for their cheerfulness as well as their competence and professionalism. Without them, this book would have taken much longer to see the light of day.

Introduction

Tilting Toward the Millennium: Kobe and Beyond

If the year 1992 was pronounced *annus horribilis* by the Queen of England, there was no doubt, even before it ended, that 1995 in Japan was likewise a *saiyaku no toshi*, an equally awful year, the worst in memory for most people. Economic and political problems had been expected: recession, political instability, corruption, perhaps even another year of unseasonable weather and emergency rice imports. Even before the year began, there had been a sense of anxiety at the prospect of the commemorations that would mark the fiftieth anniversary of the end of the war. But the shocks that were to break over the coming months—earthquake, urban terrorism, and wildly fluctuating currency markets—were unexpected and devastating, loosening or unraveling some strands central to the postwar national identity and sense of purpose, and opening a feeling of uncertainty about the future that had been unknown through the long postwar decades. The agenda for the fifty postwar years—recovery, growth, and attainment of the status of an advanced country—had been clear and accomplished in full measure, but there was no consensus on how to formulate the agenda for the fifty that were to come, and there was a growing suspicion that the priorities of the past fifty might have been fundamentally ill chosen.

It was on a very wet June day in 1962 that I first set foot in Japan, at the port city of Kobe. The war was then already seventeen years past, the last of the Allied occupation forces were ten years gone. All Western foreigners were still assumed to be American, but the signs reading OFF LIMITS or FIFTH AVENUE were already tattered and fading. Recovery from the physical wounds of war was virtually complete, save for

3

the crippled veterans in white who played forlorn tunes on their har-monicas in the subways. It was a drab country, where people were poor and worked long hours, but the income-doubling, high-growth transfor-mation had begun. In the following decades, I returned often to Japan, to live, study, work, and teach. My experience of Japan turned out to coincide with perhaps the most dramatic process of transformation of any country in modern times. When I returned to Kobe in 1994, the sense of change was palpable, although it was much easier to say what had ended than what had begun: The Cold War was certainly over, and the long Japanese struggle to achieve economic parity with the ad-vanced Western countries was also over, but was this, then, the "end of history?" Did Japanese capitalism, so obviously efficient in the world market, represent the way toward which all other developing countries were moving? Was it the whole world's future that I had witnessed coming into being here (and that for me personally constituted my past)? These seemed questions that were worth reflecting upon.

This book is born out of thoughts upon the spectacle of Japanese development, especially in the triangle of Kansai cities—Kyoto, Osaka, and Kobe—in each of which I have lived at various times over a period of thirty-three years. I've set out to reflect upon what it means to be Japanese in this period of postwar transformation. From my Kobe University office in 1994, it was possible to look out over much of the Japanese heartland that lay along the bays of Osaka and Kobe. The spectacle of the frenetic activity, whose pattern and final shape was so elusive, was endlessly fascinating. In 1962, neither I—nor (I suspect) most Japanese people—had much sense of the high-growth miracle that then lay ahead. In 1995, facing the end of the twentieth century, at a moment when much of the mold within which Japan had been con-strained during the long postwar decades had fallen away, it was just as difficult to know what lay ahead. What is certain is that the present portends several alternative futures. This book essays to discern some of the new shapes and directions in which Japan might reorient itself in the wake of the collapse of the Cold War, the attainment by Japan of economic superpower status, and the emergence of Asia as one of the three political and economic foci of the emerging world order. The catastrophe that struck Kobe in 1995 gave added significance to that city as a vantage point.

Three chapters of this book are devoted to aspects of political econ-omy—construction, leisure, and agriculture—with the implications of each for society, politics, the environment, and sustainability. Three concern matters of identity in the broad sense—Japan's relations with other Asian nations and the identity it tries to project to the world. Would the affluent, post–Cold War Japan wish to become an ordinary country, with an ordinary army and a permanent seat on the U.N. Security Council (i.e., an ordinary superpower), or might it choose rather to become the sort of special country whose domestic and international policies were structured around the commitment to pacifism incorporated in its constitution in 1946? It was a choice between embracing the ordinariness of the twentieth century and pioneering what might become the ordinariness of a very different twenty-first.

The question of Japan's identity—contemporary and future—is intimately related to the collective national understanding of its history. The capacity to make a realistic assessment of present problems and to plan for the future rests on the ability to come to grips with the past. For the Japanese, the process of reflection on the experience of modernity and Westernization has to make sense of the enormously destructive cataclysm that was unleashed over Asia two generations ago. Fifty years after the War, how will late-twentieth-century Japan cope with the continuing problem of interpreting, remembering, and representing the past, the soured dreams of the generation of their grandparents? This topic is the focus of Chapter 6.

While this book is about Japan, it was written in the belief that many of the problems dealt with are common to all industrial societies and that Japan, as one of the most successful capitalist countries in history, represents in concentrated form problems facing contemporary industrial civilization as a whole. This is not a study of Japan's economy, or of diplomacy, political parties, the bureaucracy, the education system, the defense forces, or the police. A number of studies, of varying quality, have been written on these subjects. The matters that are dealt with here were chosen because they illuminate the transformations of the past half-century and point to the sorts of issues faced at this turning point, which happens to occur on the fiftieth anniversary of defeat in war. In Japan, the certainties of the Cold War decades already show signs of tattered neglect like those that marked the remaining occupation OFF-LIMITS signs in the early 1960s.

What I have written is also, perhaps to an unusual degree among English-language books about Japan, based upon Japanese sources, materials, and experience. Its basic "problem consciousness" has been formed within the circles of dissenting Japanese scholarship and in the local and national citizens' movement as much as in mainstream academia. It may be that I will be accused of Japan bashing, as I have been in the past,[1] but that would be ironic given that this book is very largely based on analyses written by Japanese scholars, critics, and citizens. What I hope to achieve is to bring issues commonly debated among Japanese people, often in far more passionate and partisan terms than they are here, to an international readership. The thesis of the book is that the prosperous, stable, and economically triumphant Japan of the 1970s and 1980s rested on foundations as insecure as those that the earthquake of 1995 brutally exposed in Kobe. Economic achievement has brought little joy and much anxiety to the people of Japan, and the political, intellectual, cultural, and moral dilemmas facing this nation today are of enormous concern to the whole world. Within Japan, such a position is not at all uncommon; it might indeed even command a majority. It would be a pity if the expression of such views were to be dismissed as bashing simply because they were not written in Japanese.

The early 1990s in Japan were not particularly good years. Many assumptions had been shaken by the events of the post–Cold War, post–Liberal-Democratic Party, post-"bubble," and post-boom economy. The forces of political reform that had welled up and brought the thirty-eight-year long Liberal-Democratic Party hegemony to an end in 1993 seemed exhausted by the attainment of modest electoral reform in 1994. The nation's top bureaucrats were shown to be entangled in webs of corruption such as had previously entwined only politicians and businessmen. The steady escalation of the value of the yen threatened the country's efforts to emerge from recession while simultaneously raising a large question mark over the viability of the country's manufacturing industry. Then, in 1995, came a series of severe shocks to what remained of the national consensus. In January, the heart of the city of Kobe was destroyed by earthquake. In March, commuters in the Tokyo subway system were subjected to a nerve-gas attack, followed shortly afterward by an attempt on the life of the chief of police. Bizarre revelations were made about a doomsday cult that had enrolled some of the country's best young minds, and in April, one of the cult's leaders was stabbed to death in front of the nation's television cameras. On international currency markets, the value of the yen spiraled up and up, while the political leadership was gripped by indecision and impotence. As the outlook darkened and confidence in established institutions faded, comedians were elected to govern the two largest cities. On the shelves of the nation's bookshops, titles about the end of Japan proliferated. The prophecies of Nostradamus were reread, and apocalyptic fantasies gained adherents.

Yet Japan was fabulously wealthy, its GNP (at least at April 1995 exchange rates) more than 80 percent that of the United States, a nation nearly twice its size in per capita terms. Put another way, Japan's GNP was more than double the combined GNP of *all other* Asian nations, including those of the Indian subcontinent. Japan was running a current account surplus at the rate of well over $100 billion per year. With fewer than 120 million people, it was on track to become the largest economy in the world, perhaps even before the end of 1995, thus matching, and exceeding, the highest ambitions, and the wildest dreams, of not only the preceding fifty years but of the century and a half since Japan began to pursue the path of Westernization and modernization.

In 1995, unemployment was statistically insignificant. The nine biggest banks in the world (even before the massive surge in the yen early in 1995) were all Japanese, as were the major trading companies and many of the major industrial corporations. Japanese investment funds flowed in waves that fed the growth of the region. It became the unquestioned chief "goose" behind which formed the ranks of the world's dynamic economies. Japan was the ultimate dragon.

But the shocks of 1995 showed how fragile are Japan's foundations. Kobe was a city characteristic of the new Japan, combining the layers of Japanese industrialization into a scintillating success story: from ceramics, sake, and shipping to steel and petrochemicals, and then to information, fashion, and communications. It was a cosmopolitan, open port city that was pursuing a fresh new identity of style, speed, landfills, and superconsumption. Kobe, as much as anywhere, was a city of the information age. It was also in the vanguard of the whole Kansai region in its efforts to define a new Asian identity and accomplish a thorough integration with its neighboring countries, building upon its long-established Chinese and Korean communities.

In many ways, Kobe was perceived as a model city by the local officials from throughout the country who came to the 1981 opening of the Portopia Expo on Port Island. The city's successes multiplied through the following years. A second manmade island, Rokko Island, was opened in 1992, and the glittering new offshore Kansai Airport and Bayfront Highway were completed in 1994. Kobe's development was conceived and promoted at high political, bureaucratic, and business levels and was supported widely throughout the community—by students, shopkeepers, taxi drivers. By 1995, the local government enjoyed the support of all parties, including the Japan Communist Party. In political and administrative terms, it was possible to see Kobe as a model, showing how all political forces might be co-opted into a united front and all other aspirations merged in the pursuit of economic development, with the local government adopting the role of developer. In other words, it seemed the very embodiment of a social order built on the traditional qualities of consensus and harmony.

All this changed on January 17, 1995. Just before dawn, the city was shaken by an earthquake measuring 7.2 on the Richter scale that has since come to be known as the Great Hanshin Earthquake. It was not as strong as the earthquake measuring 7.9 that destroyed much of Tokyo in 1923 or of earthquakes of similar magnitude that have occurred periodically. However, this one was not

> the "typical" earthquake, caused by the sliding of the Pacific, Asian and Philippines tectonic plates, which meet near Tokyo, over each other at depths of 100 to 200 kilometres underground, triggering widespread horizontal shocks and massive tsunami (tidal waves),

but caused by

> a localised slip fault just 13 kilometres directly below the city producing a vertical shock measured in places at 760 gals (one centimetre per second), the highest ever recorded, four times that of the great Tokyo earthquake of 1923, which killed 140,000 people, mostly by fire.[2]

The Hanshin (Bay Area) expressway, opened amid great fanfare in April 1994, collapsed in seventeen different places. Its supporting pillars toppled like white-anted trees, the concrete peeled away, and the exposed steel reinforcing rods snapped like piano wire. The few early-morning vehicles on the road were plunged into nothingness or left dangling in midair. The tracks of the Sanyo *shinkansen*—the bullet train that linked Osaka with western Japan with 224 trains daily—were torn and buckled. The thin national artery of transport and communications that linked eastern and western Japan was severed.

Kobe's underground railway was blocked by collapsing tunnels; the foundations of the two recently built islands, Port and Rokko, subsided up to two meters into the sea, and the cranes and gantries that were working on and around them collapsed. Liquefaction, the process by which the earth is shaken so violently that its components separate and become a mushy quagmire, was severe on the islands and the newly reclaimed coastal lands where recent urban development had been most intense. The road and rail links from Port Island were severed, so the island was effectively cut off from communication with the rest of the city. The 250 patients of Rokko Island Hospital were left without water or assistance for three days, save what they could scrounge from a nearby hotel.[3] The hospital had been practicing the inventory system known as "just-in-time," which was developed by the automobile industry to minimize holdings of stock, and thus it quickly ran out of essential medical supplies. The major emergency hospital for the city, Kobe Central City Hospital, had been shifted to Port Island in order to free up its former valuable central site for development as a multistory hotel. When the island was cut off by the quake, there was no way for the casualties, or for that matter the doctors, to reach it.[4] A key Hyogo Prefectural police facility, including the emergency command and information operation center, had also been relocated to the island and was likewise unable to function (which appears to have been responsible for the confusion and lack of traffic control in the immediate aftermath of the quake).[5] The city heliport on Port Island was also unusable. The thirty-nine ultramodern container berths that handled 30 percent of the nation's freight were immobilized as all but one of them collapsed.[6] The water mains also collapsed in the quake, and the city had no alternative water-supply system. The absence of authority structures and collapsed or blocked roads made it impossible for the fire brigade to penetrate to the affected areas, so that for days after the quake, fires continued to break out and rage with little or no control, many of them fed by fuel from the oil storage tanks built around the city. These fires caused untold additional damage and an unknown number of deaths.

The last person to be pulled alive from the ruins was rescued on the fifth day after the quake. There is no way of knowing how many others might have been saved but for the delayed, ill-coordinated, poorly planned rescue effort or the fires. The head of the city's water-supply department committed suicide, apparently in despair. Overall, in Kobe and its vicinity, over 6,000 people were killed (and many thousands injured); about one in five dwellings were destroyed; material damage was estimated at between 10 and 20 trillion yen. Three hundred and ten thousand people were made homeless, suddenly plunged back into the world of 1945, where survival, shelter, and sustenance outweighed all other considerations. As in a nightmare, the citizens of the economic superpower watched scenes etched in its collective memory from fifty years before—of a city devastated, its people digging desperately in the ruins for their relatives or belongings, cold and hungry, without food and water. No measurement, whether of human lives or of physical damage, can represent the scale of the catastrophe, much less the shock waves it sent through the society.

When the world reacted with sympathy and showed its desire to help, the bureaucratic response was cold and more concerned with the preservation of its own control, or of the national "face," than with emergency relief. Of sixty-two offers of assistance from foreign governments, only twenty were accepted.[7] The offer to use a U.S. aircraft carrier as a floating refugee camp was refused.[8] Foreign doctors were at first rejected because they lacked Japanese registration; they were eventually admitted on strict conditions. Specialist teams of "sniffer" dogs were held for days in airport quarantine.[9] At a local level, the same behavior was replicated: A man who ran a small tatami factory in the neighboring prefecture of Okayama tried to deliver a load of his mats for the refugees. He was told there was nowhere to put the mats and was sent away.[10]

The Japanese archipelago is, of course, well known as earthquake-prone. Huge sums have been spent on seismic-monitoring research directed toward prediction, although in thirty years, not one earthquake has actually been foretold.[11] Repeated earthquake simulations had been conducted in many parts of the country by the National Land Agency and by prefectural and city authorities, but attention was focused on the conventional tectonic-plate shift threat, and slip faults were ignored. In the established view of the Japan Meteorological Association, the Kobe vicinity was one of the country's eighteen "earthquake-free regions,"[12] but some specialists had taken an opposite view. Fujita Kazuo, head of the Center for Research Materials on Fault Lines and author of a major study on the subject, had tried to draw attention to the web of fault lines in the vicinity of Kobe, warning that the absence of an earthquake within recorded memory should be seen as a sign of danger, not of reassurance.[13] At the 1993 meeting of the Japan Seismological Society, Naka Kō, a Hiroshima University professor, also drew attention to the complex of fault lines beneath the Kansai cities and called for a California-style ban on construction along them.[14] Both were ignored.

The president of Japan's Town Planning Institute, after a study of the Los Angeles quake of 1994, called for a reassessment of the safety standards of Japan's expressways, but the experts in the Ministry of Construction declared that this was unnecessary.[15] Never—not even in the Tokyo vicinity, which all agreed was a high-risk area—had there been any suggestion that buildings, freeways, or railways constructed according to regulations could be vulnerable. In Kobe, therefore, adherence to the regulations governing standards for construction, based on worst-case scenario of a quake registering 5.0 on the Richter scale, was considered adequate. The city was expanding steadily, encroaching on mountain and sea, growing from a population of 1.2 million in 1980 to 1.5 million in 1995, becoming (to use Shimatsu's graphic phrase) "a deathtrap of concrete and neon on a foundation of landfill."[16] Not until the events of January 17 was the scientific-bureaucratic consensus seriously challenged. Shortly afterward, the official assessment was reversed, and Kobe was declared "especially vulnerable to future shocks."[17]

Not only had the experts been wrong, but whatever the nominal standards, they had in many cases been flouted. The industrial and technological superpower had been utterly "Third World" in the engineering of core installations in its heartland. These gerry-built structures were designed and built to allow maximum profit, with minimum sense of professional responsibility or attention to safety. The corruption of the construction industry had become known in general terms during the preceding years (see Chapter 1), but not until Kobe were its lethal consequences made plain. The associations of engineers and experts who had designed and built the buildings, bridges, and columns that collapsed declared themselves struck dumb with astonishment and found themselves fearful to cross bridges built according to their own specifications.[18] In some places, the wooden molds for motorway bridges were found to have been left and the concrete simply poured around them, and in others, only half the specified steel reinforcing bands had been used.[19] Of 143 gas tanks that had been erected in Kobe by Mitsubishi Liquid Gas, 114 (86 percent) were found to have been constructed below the officially prescribed standards, and the land on which they sat subsided in places by up to seventy centimeters.[20] Furthermore, much of the damage was concentrated in the low-lying swamp and waterfront areas or in the new island developments, which had been the very pride of the Kobe City developers.

When the crisis struck, the central government was paralyzed, and the city, prefectural, and national police, fire brigades, water authorities, highways authorities, and Self-Defense Forces were shown to be unreliable.[21] The shinkansen and the expressways that collapsed were supposed to be the distillation of Japan's superior construction technology. Japan's biggest industry was, in other words, either technically unsound, corrupt, or both. While the old Meishin (Nagoya-Kobe) Highway, built in the early 1960s, or the even older Sanyo rail line through Kobe, withstood the shocks, the new ones, built in the heyday of the 1980s and 1990s, and after the privatization of the once-strict Japan National Railways, did not.[22] As for the idea of the two newly built Kobe islands being the embodiment of an information society or information city, after January 1995, it would be some time before such a claim would be revived.

In the wake of Kobe's collapse, many questions were asked. The assumptions that underlay the political economy—not only of the city of Kobe but of late-twentieth-century Japan as a whole—were exposed as suddenly and rudely as the foundations of the buildings, bridges, motorways, and even islands that were torn up by the forces of nature. The questions raised were as severe as they were unexpected. The faith in technology, the trust in the competence of the bureaucracy, the confidence that the authorities would protect people in the event of any crisis, were profoundly shaken. Questions of technology and engineering standards were actually directed toward national identity and direction.

The spectacle of bureaucratic and political incompetence was unforgettable, both as to the confidence with which Kobe had been declared earthquake-free and so was unprepared for the catastrophe that struck it, and in terms of the response to the event itself. As one observer, a journalist who had grown up in Kobe, noted,

> The country that awed Wall Street could barely deliver one rice ball a day to homeless quake victims freezing on the streets. The Self Defense Force that was so eager to go the distance to Rwanda was pitifully late getting a few miles from the Osaka barracks to the town next door [and when they did, they came equipped with hand shovels rather than helicopters or land-moving equipment]. The world's most efficient produc-

tion system—the Kansai-Inland Sea industrial heartland—turned out to be a Rube Goldberg contraption of wires and pulleys that collapsed into one messy tangle.[23]

At a deeper level, novelist and critic Oda Makoto (who happened to live in the adjacent city of Nishinomiya, a major center of damage) observed that the events following the quake exposed the moral bankruptcy of the bureaucracy and the precedence given to engineering and public works while ignoring the forces of nature and the needs of the population.[24] Some went so far as to speak of the defeat of Japan, or of the course of events as revealing the emptiness of the pursuit of growth over life.[25] Others spoke of the disaster as having exposed the contradictions of contemporary Japan at a stroke.[26] A city exclusively devoted to convenience and economic efficiency betrayed the interests of its citizens and sacrificed its weak and poor. Casualties and damage were indeed heavily concentrated in the sectors of the city populated by working-class Japanese, Korean and Chinese workers and their descendants, illegal foreign workers, and Japanese *burakumin* (outcast) communities.[27] The people and communities forgotten in the development policies pursued by the city were those who suffered most when things went wrong. That is what one critic meant when he referred to the disaster as a "discriminatory human catastrophe" rather than a natural catastrophe.[28]

A more detailed critique of the development formula adopted and so vigorously pursued by Kobe is that advanced by Aoki Hidekazu and Kawamiya Nobuo, two young members of a nationwide network of dissenting scholars known as the Japan Entropy Society.[29] In 1994, they published a trenchant critique of the phenomenon of *doken kokka* (construction state) in which they drew attention, in particular, to the fiscal pattern of public-debt financing of massive infrastructural development. The business cycle to which both local and national governments are committed is that of buying, improving, and selling land, a process that is predicated on the continual inflation of the cost of real estate. Further expansion takes precedence over the public interest in public works in Japan, and although considerable private fortunes accumulate, what the public is left with is a massive debt and social infrastructure that is unsafe, inconvenient, and inappropriate to its needs. Kobe City debt, even before the quake, was 1.7 trillion yen (equal to 1.14 million yen per citizen), considerably higher than other comparable cities and amounting to more than five-and-a-half years of revenue.[30] For Aoki and Kawamiya, the quake showed, as if in dramatic fast-forward, the climax of the collapse of Japan's construction state.[31]

Through the three decades of Japan's triumphant economic transformation, skeptical, negative, even (under the circumstances) what might be called heretical, voices continued to be raised. Among the most notable of these were Uzawa Hirofumi, a professor at Chūō University, formerly professor at Tokyo and Niigata universities, whose collected works were recently published (a most unusual distinction for a living, active scholar); and Miyamoto Ken'ichi, head of the Department of Policy Science at Ritsumeikan University in Kyoto. Both had been consistent in their critique of the pattern of development, so when they published their analysis of the Great Hanshin Earthquake, their views were given enormous credibility.[32]

Miyamoto saw the disaster as serving notice of the end of the economic superpower and as a portent of what was likely to happen when the expected quake hit Tokyo.[33] He views Kobe as literally the end of the road of "economism," and foresees the eventual bankruptcy of Japanese technoculture. The thrust of postwar development, according to Miyamoto, has been the concentration of public investment in infrastructure to the advantage of business, rather than the human community as a whole. The result is that cities have been turned into business districts without human communities, and priority has been given to the location of oil-storage tanks and petrochemical plants over considerations of safety. It is the phenomenon others refer to as the replacement of local government in cities like Kobe with municipal-development corporations. Public responsibility for the damages suffered in Kobe was therefore great.

The bursting of the bubble of illusion blown around the city of Kobe by the developmentalist city authorities spelled lessons for the whole country no less profound than those of the bursting of the financial bubble of the 1980s. The question was whether the Kobe model of development, one of the most advanced examples of the general Japanese phenomenon of commitment to, and faith in growth, would be modified but sustained or, perhaps, fundamentally reconsidered.

The stage was set for the contest between technocratic and democratic responses. The technocrats would call for the reinforcement of the nation's structures by the application of massive quantities of steel and concrete, a huge fillip to the already bloated construction industry. Such plans, they argued, would stimulate the Japanese economy's internal demand, thereby easing world-trade tensions, and fall into line with calls for further market deregulation. Their proposal would amount to the "quake-proofing" of cities by enforcing higher standards. They would continue the 1980s developmental agenda of highrises and reclamation, heading toward the realization of the spectacular visions of a triumphalist techno-urban landscape of mammoth buildings and intersecting, multiple-layered, high-speed rail and expressways, linked and made "intelligent" by fiber-optic cables. The alternative solution, which Miyamoto sketched (and which had been a common thread in his many previous essays), would be for a ban on further reclamation of foreshore or bay (as under the Italian Landscape Preservation Law), the revival of the inner city through a partial ban on autos, and the expansion and improvement of the public-transport system. Miyamoto favors neither deregulation on the one hand nor public control in the sense of centralized bureaucracy on the other, but the return of power and autonomy to local communities. Sooner or later, he insists, techno-hubris will have to yield to a quite different understanding of the requirements of a sustainable society.[34]

In a more theoretical vein, Uzawa Hirofumi reiterated his critique of the neglect of the public interest in conventional classical and neoclassical economics. He reasserted his call for the recognition of the rights of what he described as "social common capital," meaning the atmosphere, the sea and rivers, the forests and open spaces. He sees their gradual privatization in the interests of development, especially since the 1960s, as the root of the widespread pollution and environmental illnesses of the 1960s and 1970s, the continuing devastation of so much of the environment and the accompanying structure of endemic corruption.[35] Conventional classical and neoclassical theorists justified the destruction of the foreshore of Osaka and Kobe bays, and the shaving of the adjacent Rokko Mountains (dumped into the sea in the process of reclamation), in terms of market requirements and the growth generated. Such arguments need to be fundamentally reconsidered. In Kobe, the economic gains had been ephemeral, the structural distortions, indebtedness, and social and environmental costs ignored. The scoured environment would take many generations to recover.

Not merely scholars and journalists, but countless ordinary people too, suddenly saw in the light of Kobe the absurdity of conventions of development long taken for granted. Kobe was a typical city in the way it covered up the rivers and streams that flowed through it in the interests of *chisui* (water regulation), filling them with concrete and turning them into closed drains. The lack of water after the January earthquake, whether for drinking or firefighting, or even bathing, was thus a consequence of policy, not nature. Instead of automatically thinking of public works improvement to the rivers and streams by embankment engineering, one forty-six-year-old librarian in Osaka asked, "Why can we not try to coexist with nature and take steps such as planting strong-rooted bamboo along the embankments, letting the pursuit of convenience take second place for a change?"[36]

It remains to be seen whether the Kobe shocks will serve to shift Japan from the treadmill track of growth, consumption, and waste, onto the very different track of sustainable development. The mosaic of slip faults in the Kobe/Osaka vicinity is duplicated by similar patterns throughout the archipelago, and the pattern of intensive development of reclaimed lands, filled-in estuary, bay, and waterfront sites is common. While the threat of a conventional earthquake stemming from shifts in the tectonic plates is in no way diminished, much of Japan hitherto thought immune from threat must, like Kobe, now be reclassified.

Two of the largest current and future projects in the Kobe area are the Akashi Straits Bridge (due for completion in 1997) and the Kobe Airport. Both lie almost astride the fault lines that caused the 1995 catastrophe. Throughout the country, the past several decades have been a time of intense development of low-lying seafront and river estuary lands, complemented by the creation of manmade islands. These newly created lands, which include Disneyland and the Makuhari *Messe* (convention) complex just outside Tokyo, have been built over similar fault lines on precisely the type of land that collapsed from liquefaction in Kobe.

Projections of an earthquake in the Tokyo area have never contemplated the possibility of the collapse of facilities such as highways, bridges, railway lines, or modern high-rise buildings, or the liquefaction of lands around or under major new installations. Now this has to be taken into consideration. In the past 400 years, there have been forty-one earthquakes directly beneath the Tokyo region, but none since 1894, a quiescence that can only seem ominous after Kobe.[37] The safety of existing installations and structures, and the implications of planned ones, have to be fundamentally reconsidered. As for the likely consequences of a Kobe-scale earthquake beneath a nuclear power plant or, say, near the controversial nuclear-waste facility in Aomori Prefecture, the public will be bound to wonder whether the judgment of the authorities, shown in so many other respects to be disastrously wrong, should be trusted.

As the shock gradually wears off, however, the likelihood that these lessons will be learned and applied diminishes. Entrenched political, bureaucratic, and corporate interests have long stressed a commitment to technocratic solutions: tighter bureaucratic controls, higher standards, more materials, massive reinforcement of the nation's infrastructure (in order to quake proof everything), plus a National Emergency Law to allow centralized authority to suspend the law and mobilize the military (Self-Defense Forces). While many thousand of its citizens were still subsisting in refugee camps, Kobe City was preparing to use the rubble from the disaster as "filling" for the construction of phase two of Port Island and for the base of the planned Kobe Airport, while pitching its plans for recovery around the hosting of a Kobe Leisure World 2000 to mark the end of the century.[38]

The Japanese government has pledged to spend astronomical sums over the next few years in the name of public works (the construction of more freeways, high-speed railways, airports, river-blocking barrages, nuclear-power plants) in order to increase the absorptive capacity of the national economy and thereby reduce the surplus. The social forces that would resist such formulas are certainly stronger than ever before, but they are ill-coordinated and face a highly articulated and ramified system of commitment to continued growth at any cost. All that can be said with certainty after Kobe is that the case for continuing to do all these things will be a little less obvious. More people will question the need to go on razing mountains, blocking rivers, felling forests, and filling in seas, and they will want to know why these things must be done and at what cost.

But there are other omens. The outcome of the local government elections of April 1995 was a political earthquake, triggered by growing tension between the frozen surfaces of political structures and the seething subterranean discontent of people fed up with corruption, arrogance, and remoteness of the political-bureaucratic system. The candidates of consensus, pursuing traditional high-cost electoral campaigns and supported by virtually all of the established parties, were resoundingly defeated. Moderate reformists, promising to clear up and rationalize and modernize the system, were likewise rejected. Instead, power over the city of Tokyo was entrusted to a television personality and comedian, Aoshima Yukio (his best-known role: Nasty Gran), who had scarcely even bothered to campaign. Aoshima had concentrated on three promises: refusal of support for the planned bailout of two credit unions that had collapsed amid massive excesses and evident high-level corruption; the drastic revision of two enormously expensive projects that had been central to his predecessor's regime—the planned World City Expo—Tokyo 1996 (which he would cancel), and the eight-trillion-yen waterfront development scheme (see discussion in Chapter 1). In Osaka, another television personality was triumphant: Isamu "Nokku" Yokoyama, best known for his role as Knock in the three-comedians routine of Knock, Hook, and Punch, and for his ability to impersonate an octopus. He had campaigned by cycling around the city, sticking up his own posters, and socializing in bathhouses.[39]

The result of the 1995 local elections was a body blow, perhaps even a death knell, for traditional Japanese politics. Money and organization did not work as planned. Analysts could only agree that the outcome showed the depth of alienation from the established, increasingly indistinguishable political parties steeped in the manipulation of interest, collusion, backroom deals, money politics, corruption, and subservience to the bureaucracy, and their disappointment that the post–Cold War, post–Liberal-Democratic Party hegemony (from July 1993) had brought no change. It may yet turn out that this strange electoral result signaled even more, however, and will amount to the first shots in a Japanese cultural revolution. It may be pointing to an order struggling to be born as much as to the collapse of one that was entrenched. These might turn out to be not just reform local governments, such as had held power in Japanese cities for more than a decade from 1967, but the embodiments, or the avatars, of a different value system.

Affluence has brought little sense of fulfillment to the people of Tokyo and Osaka. Although they are supposed to be the richest burghers in the world, their lives seem profoundly empty and alienated. In rejecting the candidates who symbolized work, accumulation, and progress (the corporation-centered social and political order), they may in a sense be seen as turning against progress, rationalization, and modernization. They are seeking a new direction. There could be no more symbolic focus for these concerns than that of cancellation of the World City Expo, meant to mark the culmination of the Japanese celebration of growth and modernity that was at a peak in the Expo at Osaka in 1970.

The significance of the 1995 elections will not be confined to the two cities, since it is well understood that Tokyo and Osaka blaze the trail for the rest of the country. Tokyo, for example, has an annual budget of 12 trillion yen, larger than China or Spain and almost equal to that of the United Kingdom, and there are 200,000 civil servants in Aoshima's new administration. Both Aoshima and Yokoyama have plenty of experience in national politics, having performed honorably, if not in a particularly distinguished fashion, for more than twenty years as independents in the House of Councillors. Whether they succeed in controlling their own bureaucracies is problematic. It remains to be seen if they will have success in tapping the resources of enthusiasm and creative energy in the citizenry so that they may overcome the cynicism and despair that led to the rejection of the old political order. The uproar from corporate and bureaucratic circles that faced Aoshima over his cancellation of the World City Expo—Tokyo 1996 showed the sort of opposition he would face and was only the first of many battles that will have to be fought.

The pressures are enormous. Neither Aoshima nor Yokoyama appear to have any organization or any policy prescription other than that of maximum consultation, empowerment, and devolution. Although long-suffering citizens evidently hope that they might empower local communities, that is a tall order. To begin the process of restoration of local autonomy—what reforming politicians have long talked about as *chihō bunken*—would be to reverse the direction of one hundred years of centralization and modernization and to remake the map of national politics.

It is Ohmae Kenichi, an opponent of Aoshima in the 1995 Tokyo election, who has been most closely associated with the call for political decentralization, but any presumption for political reform must include this perspective, and Ohmae's prescription for the division of Japan into eleven self-governing regions, a "United States of Japan" by 2005, has much to commend it.[40] If Aoshima and Yokoyama do what others promising reform in the past have always done—fail and betray their promise so that the bureaucracy and bureaucratic priorities are restored—the social consequences in terms of widening nihilism will be unpredictable.

Beyond all these upheavals in the political, economic, social, and even (in Kobe) the physical order, an optimist might say it is just possible to discern, however dimly, the outlines of a green, democratic, republican, internationalist, and pacifist Japan. This new order would be characterized by the gradual emergence of a different type of development model that would boast of zero growth, the restoration of a bruised and scarred environment, and the creation of multiple, self-sustaining regional economies. The people would produce, store, and transport what they need in terms of basic food, housing, and clothing largely from locally available resources, using a minimum amount of energy. This would reduce the hours of work (and extend those of play), actually turn work into play, and expand the opportunities for social intercourse and artistic and cultural creativity. In such a Japan, identities suppressed, denied, or still only faintly glimpsed might attain full and free expression: the regions (the non-megalopolitan bits of Japan) might regain their voice; multiple lines of communication might be opened between Japan and its adjacent Asian region; and the corporate and bureaucratic accents in which Japan commonly communicates with the world might be broadened too so that the voices of the many dreamers, visionaries, and open-hearted "volunteers" of ordinary metropolitan Japan could also be heard.

In the lobbies, meeting halls, bars, and coffee shops of late-twentieth-century Japan may be heard plenty of voices agreeing on the basic outlines of such a program. This book is written in the faith that people have the basic common sense to see through the servitude of institutions that exploit or demean them and will continue to aspire to create a sensible, decent, humane world. It is dedicated to the countless ordinary Japanese people who have shared with me some of their disquiet and some of their aspiration for a very different twenty-first century future. They introduced me to one or another corner of Japan in which values quite different from those of the hegemonic corporate or bureaucratic Japan are preserved and celebrated.

For those who would see, the seeds of many different possible futures are sprouting in Japan. Which will strengthen and grow to maturity, and which will weaken and die, will be determined by the struggles that will ensue over the years that span the end of the century and the millennium.

Notes

1. Haga Tōru, "Nichibunken," *Bunka kaigi*, November 1993, p. 1; Gavan McCormack, "Kokusaika, Nichibunken, and the Question of Japan-Bashing," *Asian Studies Review*, Vol. 17, No. 3, April 1994, pp. 166–72.

2. Murray Sayle, "Shock Treatment," *Sydney Morning Herald*, February 11, 1995. The quake actually seems to have been centered approximately 30 kilometers offshore from Kobe, at a depth of some 20 kilometers beneath the adjacent island of Awajishima.

3. William Dawkins, "Quake Survivors Struggle to Pick Up the Pieces," *The Australian*, January 26, 1995.

4. Uchihashi Katsuto, "Poruto airurando de nani okotta ka," *Sekai*, April 1995, pp. 97–103, at p. 98.

5. Ibid. See also Aoki Hidekazu and Kawamiya Nobuo, "Hanshin daishinsai de taoresatta mono," *Jōkyō*, April 1995, pp. 97–109, at pp. 103–4.

6. Sayle, "Shock Treatment," 1995.

7. Peter Hartcher, "After-shock of Anger with a Bungling Bureaucracy—Tokyo Observed," *Australian Financial Review*, January 30, 1995.

8. Eric Talmedge, "Japanese Quake Evacuees Grill Bureaucrats on TV," *The Australian*, January 30, 1995.

9. Ben Hills, "Murayama Slammed over Quake Bungle," *Sydney Morning Herald*, January 24, 1995; Robert Guest, "Elite British Rescue Team Ignored in Quake City," *Daily Telegraph*, January 31, 1995; Aoki and Kawamiya, "Hanshin daishinsai," p. 103.

10. Otsu Ikuo, "Munō na kanryō to hikui doboku gijutsu" (letter), *Shūkan kinyōbi*, April 7, 1995, p. 30.

11. Ben Hills, "Epidemic Fear as Bodies Rot in Kobe," *The Age*, January 23, 1995.

12. "Fear of Trembling," A Survey of Earthquake Engineering, *The Economist*, April 22, 1995, p. 4.

13. Fujita Kazuo, *Hendō suru Nihon rettō*, Iwanami shinsho, 1985, (especially the map and analysis at p. 127).

14. Aoki and Kawamiya, "Hanshin daishinsai," p. 101.

15. Ibid., p. 101.

16. Yoichi Clark Shimatsu, "After the Earthquake, an Economy Built on Quicksand is Exposed," *Los Angeles Times*, January 20, 1995.

17. "Fear of Trembling," April 22, 1995.

18. Honda Katsuichi, "Hanshin daishinsai," *Shūkan kinyōbi*, February 3, 1995, pp. 7–13.

19. Sayle, "Shock Treatment," 1995; Aoki and Kawamiya, "Hanshin daishinsai," April 1995, p. 99.

20. Aoki and Kawamiya, "Hanshin daishinsai," April 1995, p. 104.

21. Chikushi Tetsuya, "Nihon no haiboku," *Shūkan kinyōbi*,, January 27, 1995, pp. 8–9.

22. Aoki and Kawamiya, "Hanshin daishinsai," April 1995, p. 99.

23. Shimatsu, "After the Earthquake," January 20, 1995.

24. Oda Makoto, "Jinsai no naka de okori, kangaeru," *Shūkan kinyōbi*, January 27, 1995, pp. 10–11.

25. Chikushi, "Nihon no haibaku," January 27, and Hayakawa Kazuo, "Saigai mubōbi toshi Kobe wa ko tsukareta," in *Shūkan kinyōbi*, February 3, 1995, pp. 14–17.

26. Honda Katsu'ichi, "Hanshin daishinsai," *Shūkan kinyōbi*, February 3, 1995, p. 7.

27. Sayle, "Shock Treatment," 1995.

28. Honda, "Hanshin daishinsai," February 3, 1995.

29. Aoki Hidekazu and Kawamiya Nobuo, "Nihon doken kokka ron," *Chūkyō daigaku kyōyō ronshū*, Part 1, Vol. 35, No. 1, 1994, pp. 29–88, and Part 2, Vol. 35, No. 3, 1995, pp. 19–64. See also Aoki and Kawamiya, "Hanshin daishinsai," April 1995.

30. Uchihashi, "Poruto airurando," April 1995, p. 102.

31. Aoki and Kawamiya, "Hanshin daishinsai," April 1995, p. 109.

32. Uzawa Hirofumi, *Uzawa Hirofumi chosakushu—atarashii keizaigaku o motomete*, 12 vols., Iwanami shoten, 1994.

33. Miyamoto Ken'ichi, "Toshi keiei kara toshi seisaku e," *Sekai*, April 1995, pp. 86–96.

34. For another succinct recent statement, see Miyamoto Ken'ichi, ed., *Chikyū kankyō seisaku to Nihon no kadai*, Iwanami bukkuretto No. 368, March 1995.

35. Uzawa Hirofumi, "Nijūisseiki 'atarashii keizaigaku' no kanōsei," *Ekonomisuto*, February 14, 1995, pp. 84–99.

36. Hayashi Michiyo, "Saigaiji no kawa no jūyōsei," *Shūkan kinyōbi*, March 10, 1995, p. 2 (letter).

37. Tsukada Hiroyasu, "Omoni o oite, tōkimichi o," *Sekai*, May 1995, pp. 144–54, at p. 145.

38. Ibid., p. 105.

39. See Ben Hills, "At $20bn, He's a Real Party Pooper," *Sydney Morning Herald*, April 29, 1995; Yamanoue Reiko and Yamamoto Masao, "Kōyaku wa Aoshima chiji no seimeisen," *Aera*, April 24, 1995, pp. 6–9, and Yamawaki Ayako, "Naniwa no jōshiki 'boke wa kashikoi'," ibid., pp. 10–11; Shindō Muneyuki, "Tōitsu chihōsen," *Shūkan kinyōbi*, April 21, 1995, pp. 8–10.

40. Richard McGregor, "Tokyo Candidate Battles the Bureaucrats," *The Australian*, February 7, 1995.

Part One
Political Economy

1

The Construction State: The Pathology of the *Doken Kokka*

Production and Need

In order to satisfy people's many needs—for food, shelter, work, recreation, and so on—the capacity to produce goods has to be expanded; that is what modernization is about, and Japan has been outstandingly successful at it. However, the mere expansion of productive power does not in itself assure that human needs will be met; it merely makes that possible. Having escaped the bonds of the traditional, undeveloped economy, and unlocked the secrets of growth, the question remains of how to channel that growth so that human needs are met. Such needs may be left unsatisfied even in an economy of unrestrained expansion or indiscriminate productivity.

Japan had shown a genius for multiplying productivity, but in the 1990s, there were growing signs that it was still struggling to find an answer to this particular problem. The problem is profoundly political, but at the same time it is a moral and philosophical issue. While it confronts Japan in its most acute form, it is a problem of modern industrial civilization as a whole, and the Japanese failure, or success, in coping with it has huge significance. It is at root the problem of establishing social control over the forces of production.

A Kansai View

Early in 1994, the slopes of Mount Rokko, overlooking the shores of Osaka Bay between Osaka and Kobe, constituted a nice vantage point from which to observe and reflect upon where Japan was going. Was this indeed the Japan that had been plunged into the depths of unprecedented recession? A panoramic vista of construction spread across the horizon. Ships—a steady flow of liners, containers, barges, tugs, tankers—steamed in and out of the bay, passing by Port Island and Rokko Island—both island cities in their own right (known sometimes as Future Cities or Marine Cities of Culture), both built recently on reclaimed land. So far as the eye can see in either direction, the scene is punctuated by cranes—mute, startled giraffes standing frozen along the shoreline. Winding along the shore, also on reclaimed land, and visible for much of its eighty kilometers, is the Hanshin Expressway, opened to traffic at the beginning of April. From Port Island adjacent to Kobe, it passes Rokko Island, Phoenix Project on Amagasaki Bay, Technoport Osaka, Cosmosquare, Harbor Light 21 Project, Izumi Otsu Bay Phoenix Project, to Rinkū Town and out the causeway to Kansai International Airport (opened in September 1994).

The airport is a remarkable technical and engineering feat. The 511-hectare island on which it stands was built in eighteen meters of water, on a base so soft and unpredictable that it subsided half a meter in the three months before it opened, and was expected to continue subsiding at a rate of about half-a-millimeter a day for up to fifty years, thus requiring the services of highly skilled engineers to monitor the thousands of adjustable jacks on which it all rested.[1] It was built on the sea, 3.75 kilometers offshore, because the existing Osaka Airport had been swallowed by urban development and considerations of noise, not to mention safety, ruled out expansion of existing facilities. The construction of a twenty-four-hour airport was a central element in the plan to usurp Tokyo (and its notoriously inconvenient airport at Narita) as hub of the national and regional economy. The cost was horrendous: about fifteen trillion yen, or five times as much as the Tokyo International Airport, with an additional three trillion yen needed to build additional runways.[2] Opened in September 1994, it was expected to play a central role in galvanizing the economy of its surrounding region.

Along the Osaka shoreline, the outline of the office towers that are going up around Cosmosquare may just be discerned. They include the World Trade Center Building and Asia and Pacific Trade Center (or Exotic Oasis O's, evidently to be known simply as "Oz"), which constitute Japan's largest commercial complex. Like the airport, it offers international communications and commercial facilities on a twenty-four-hour-per-day basis. In June 1994, the world's largest dinosaur exhibition opened here. Beyond Osaka and the airport, although just

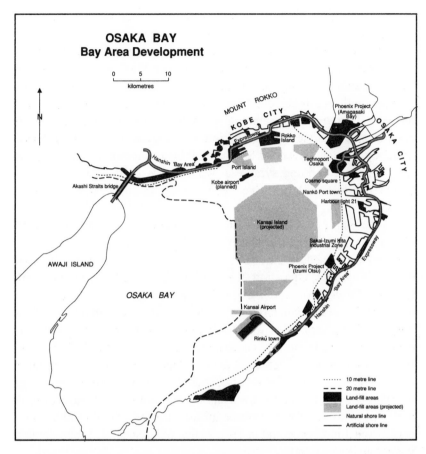

around a point and therefore not visible from Rokko, lies Wakayama City, which also boasts a Marine City and hosted a World Resort Expo in the summer of 1994.

Turning to the west, although also just out of sight, lie more focal points in the emerging transport and communications infrastructure: Linking Honshu just west of Kobe with the island of Awaji will be the Akashi Straits Bridge, 3,910 meters long and due for completion in 1997. It will feature the longest suspension span in the world (1,990 meters) and will cost an estimated 610 billion yen.[3] Awaji Island will also be linked directly to Wakayama, at the eastern end of Osaka Bay, and to Shikoku Island via the Onarutokyo Bridge. Each one of these bridges and tunnels is a major engineering feat, and the circuit they create will integrate this vast region and give it rapid international connection with the world. Awaji and Shikoku will, in effect, cease to be islands.

Just inland from Osaka, Kansai Science City, a new cultural metropolis, takes shape, centered around Keihanna Plaza (named after the Chinese readings of Kyoto, Osaka, and Nara). This is to be a "model city that will combine scientific research with an attractive city and residential environment, making it a vibrant, international center for cultural and lifestyle studies and industrial development." Its International Center for Advanced Studies will host scholars from around the world for research and symposia, while in Osaka itself the U.N. Research Institute of Innovative Technologies for the Earth opened in 1994.

As the Kansai region of western Japan (incorporating the cities of Kyoto, Osaka, Kobe, and Nara) gradually shifts its center of gravity out onto what used be the sea, it declares an identity in which internationalism, culture, education, the environment, and leisure are central. It is all a far cry from the heavy industrial base on which the economy of the region rested since the 1960s. Kyoto city celebrated the twelve-hundredth anniversary of its foundation in 1994, coinciding with the airport opening, while Kansai was orienting itself toward the twenty-first century as both a center of ancient Japanese culture and tradition and a dynamic center of business, research, and international exchange to rival Tokyo (a core for the Asia-Pacific region). Already Kansai, with a population of twenty-three million, boasts a GNP of about seventy-two trillion yen, equal in 1994 to that of Canada, and considerably greater at 1995 exchange rates.

This region was for long Japan's hub. The historic contrast between the Kansai area as commercial center and the Kanto district surrounding Tokyo as political and bureaucratic center manifests itself via language (dialect), cuisine, values, and culture, and is so deep-seated as to be proverbial. The substance of the new identity the Kansai region began to forge in the 1980s and 1990s deserves serious attention, as do the likelihood of its being accomplished, as well as its compatibility with the region's past, and the interests of its populace.

Though specific to the Kansai region, much that is underway is also representative of developments in Japan as a whole. Common characteristics include the priority given to speed on the one hand, and to pushing back the barriers of the sea of the other. Speed has been a key concern—obsession is scarcely too strong a word—of developers for at least thirty years. The new Kansai Airport is accessible from downtown Osaka in about forty minutes and from most places in a radius of several hundred kilometers within a couple of hours. If the new generation SST passenger planes projected for the early twenty-first century come into service, it will then be about three hours away from the major capitals of the world, and if the projected mag-lev connection from Tokyo is installed, then the capital will be just one hour away. The new transport systems will bring sites of Japan's ancient, medieval, early modern, and modern history within easy access of its present and future, making possible the construction of a "zone of regional economy and culture as rich in variety as a stained glass window."[4]

The area around which this wave of development is rising is the one that has been the focus of national development plans since the 1960s—the Inland Sea. Before development began, the vista here was one of white sands and green pines along a chain of fine sandy beaches where the children of Osaka and Kobe swam, fished, and played. Although reclamation for industrial purposes (which means filling in the sea and developing the sea-front), began here in the 1960s, for hundreds of years a process of gradual encroachment of the river estuary had been underway. In the 1990s, 95 percent of the shoreline of the bay is artificial, and the tiny pockets of beach, such as Suma (famed from ancient literary texts such as the *Manyōshū*) fight a losing battle against developers.[5] The claims about forging a new identity that would be compatible with ancient cultural identity and with natural and environmental harmony have to be examined in the light of such trends.

The scale of investment in these developments is huge. According to the official Osaka Bay Area Development Grand Design, published by bureaucratic and business promoters in 1988, the cost will run to 15.8 trillion yen for the main 150 projects involved, or to about thirty-five trillion if all related projects were included.[6] This plan was the basis for the Osaka Bay Special Regional Development Infrastructure Law, which was passed by the National Diet in December 1992. A homogeneous pattern of development was integrating 160 kilometers of the coast around Osaka Bay, including Awajishima Island, but extending beyond to Shikoku Island and a vast hinterland.

The context for this transformation of the bay, continuing unabated from the years of the bubble through those of the recession, has been Kansai business's search for a response to the problems of changing industrial structure. The advantage it once enjoyed in manufacturing, especially in heavy and chemical industries, has been eroded due to the high yen and competition from newly industrializing Asian neighbor countries. Around the shores of the Inland Sea, with Osaka as the hub, is concentrated 58 percent of Japan's steel-making capacity, 40 percent of its oil refining, 35 percent of petrochemical refining, 63 percent of copper refining, and 76 percent of lead-refining capacity.[7] But since the late 1980s, Japanese industry hollowed out rapidly as the comparative advantage once enjoyed by heavy industry and the chemical-manufacturing and -refining sector eroded. By 1988, according to a study by the Osaka Center for Science and Technology, 1,300 of the 7,000 hectares of industrial land in the Osaka Bay area were lying idle.[8] The strategy devised by leading Osaka business circles to meet these problems was to revive Kansai's regional economy through effecting a strategic switch away from its traditional strengths and into "soft" information and cultural industries. The airport was to be the center of the structural transformation, projecting Osaka as the embodiment of a new Kansai (and Asian) lifestyle, that would be based on leisure, consumption, entertainment, fashion, and information.

However, the softness of the Bay Area's post-Fordist future would be firmly grounded in a hard base of construction and civil engineering, whose technology and capital would help confer other significant long-term competitive advantages on Kansai, thus helping to compensate for the decline of its traditional industries. The 1992 Law, a major piece of national legislation, will help overcome objections based on environmental grounds or upon the constraints written into previous laws, such as the Seto Inland Sea Environmental Protection Special Measures Law of 1972. The choice of a solution to current excess capacity by greatly adding to it was bold; only time will tell whether it was economically, or environmentally, wise.

It might be thought that such a scale of works would be enough to satisfy most ambitions, but it appears to have only whetted them. Plans for an *additional* new airport to be built off Port Island in Kobe are moving toward formal ratification. They call for construction of another 300-hectare island three kilometers offshore (or eight kilometers from Kobe's central Sannomiya district) to be completed in 2003.[9] In November 1993, JAPIC (Japan Industrial Projects Council, the representative body for some 215 development and financial groups, headed by Saitō Eishirō) announced the plan to put a much larger (1,000-hectare) island into the bay. This would be double the size of the just-completed airport island; to be called Kansaijima (Kansai Island), it would cost 5.5 trillion yen, and should be completed by the year 2030. Set among other recently completed and projected islands, it would serve as an international communications center. A little later, it was revealed that the Osaka prefectural government had plans to fill the entire bay to a depth of fifteen meters, thereby extending the land by a further 4,600 hectares. It seemed to take the view that such expansion would be necessary by the year 2010 for continuing development.[10]

What had seemed an idle and ridiculous fancy when first gazing out over the unfolding spectacle of bay development from Mount Rokko early in 1994 had in this light to be considered a real, long-term possibility. While the early landfill work done around the bay had been in shallow waters up to ten meters, the technology utilized in the recent airport construction was capable of dealing with depths of up to eighteen meters. Therefore, should the current position be adopted, it is only one further step to the twenty-meter line, which would then cover about one third of the entire bay area. At present rates of development, both actual and projected, Osaka Bay could disappear within the next hundred or so years. The now fresh and new Port Island and Rokko Island could be overtaken and find the seas gradually retreating from them, leaving perhaps a network of canals linking them to a receding shoreline. Wakayama would come much closer to Kobe, since it would no longer be necessary to go around the bay to reach it—one could simply drive straight across.

The vision of turning the whole of the area around the cities of Kyoto, Nara, Osaka, Kobe, and Wakayama, plus the islands of Awaji and Shikoku, into a vast, "intelligent" city that would be somehow both "pastoral"[11] and yet also a twenty-first-century megalopolis, is widely shared and rarely questioned.[12] Regional pride and sentiment is a powerful force helping to disarm opposition, and advertising promotion plays heavily on the theme of a distinctive (superior to Tokyo) Kansai identity, which would also claim to be essentially "Asian." Since the citizens' group that campaigns for the preservation of the bay has a reported membership of 250,[13] the prospect for blocking bureaucratic and corporate momentum intent on this particular form of development does not seem strong.

Since the 1960s inaugurated high-growth in Japan, the pace of development in this region has been phenomenal. "Breathtaking," if not "breakneck," are terms that come to mind. What is argued here, however, is that three decades of drastic change has induced a certain giddiness or intoxication, in which reflection on why such growth was undertaken in the first place and where it was expected to lead has become difficult. The social consensus of the 1960s was of the need to work, accumulate, invest, develop, and grow, as a means to achieve a decent, happy, fulfilled, and creative life. The question in the 1990s is whether a subtle change has not been worked so that growth and development have become the ends, rather than the means to the ends. Facing the turn of the century, it seems appropriate to question the imperative of growth and to attempt to see what long-term processes are at work. The custom of certain North American Indian tribes, notably the Iroquois, of considering the likely consequences of their acts to seven generations into the future is perhaps the sort of long-term perspective that is commonly neglected in modern industrial societies. It would certainly be appropriate to take such a view when considering where Japan might be headed in the coming millennium.[14]

Planning and Public Works

Civil engineering and construction have long been at the heart of the Japanese political economy. From premodern times, land reclamation and irrigation works were carried out, often on a large scale and requiring considerable mobilization of labor.[15] Although it is Japan's largest industry, it does not make such an impact outside the country as does manufacturing, and it has therefore been relatively little studied. Through the decades of Japan's postwar high growth, this sector played a pivotal role, and because of the centrality of public works, the links between the contractors, bureaucracy, and government were always close. The industry in which 75,000 contractors employed close to two and a half million people in 1960[16] grew to have half a million contractors employing more than six million people in the early 1990s.[17] Manufacturing industries, by contrast, were gradually shrinking as a proportion of the national economy in the transition to postindustrialism, and in 1991, employed only 4.8 million.[18] The construction industry comprises a small number of general contracting (or *zenekon*) firms at the top of the pyramid, who make up only 0.2 percent of the total, while the other 99.8 percent consists of tiny subcontractors who actually carry out the work.[19]

In 1993, a staggering 31.8 trillion yen of public investment went to the construction industry. Given total public expenditure for the year of around seventy-three trillion, that means 43 percent of the national budget went to construction.[20] If private housing and civil-engineering construction are added in, the total construction expenditure rises to ninety trillion yen and the proportion of GDP to around 19.1 percent. By comparison, the United States spends just fifty-four trillion yen (approximately $500 billion) on its public works (although its land area is about twenty-five times greater than that of Japan).[21] In other words, Japan outspends the United States on construction by a ratio of 2.6:1, or in proportion to relative land area, 32:1.[22] Incredibly, Japan spends more on public works than the United States does on defense, and was doing so even at the height of the Cold War.[23]

Why? The answer is not that Japan's mountainous lands need much more civil engineering than do other countries, but that during the long period of one-party rule in postwar Japan, a collusive system of exploiting the public by massive corruption evolved, sometimes called the *doken kokka* or construction state, in which construction is incidental to the reproduction of power and the distribution of profit. It became a massive welfare system, with beneficiaries numbered in the millions, an incubus on the state and society comparable to the mafia in other countries. As the term military-industrial complex was sometimes used in the United States to characterize the core structure of its Cold War political economy, the term doken kokka is equally descriptive of Japan, and the end of the Cold War has so far done little to weaken Japan's construction state.

The system works like this: the Ministry of Construction allocates contracts to firms that belong to officially recognized cartels (*dangō*). These firms are assured regular contracts and do not have to worry about competition. The prices, initially inflated, allow generous profit margins, even after the creaming off of a levy, usually between 1 and 3 percent, which goes to maintain the political system at local and national levels. In due course, the construction companies provide comfortable sinecures for retiring bureaucrats from the ministry, or help in campaigns to elect such men to the National Diet or Local Assemblies, thereby sealing the magic circle of shared business-bureaucratic-political benefit. Prime ministers, until very recently, simply bought office, and once in office they had to "feed the troops," while ordinary members too needed large sums of money to run their constituency affairs.

The system is one of collusion (*yuchaku*) between political bosses, businessmen, bankers, bureaucrats, and occasionally gangsters, who rub shoulders and exchange bundles of cash. Politics in the conventional sense is irrelevant. It is the business of the politician to serve as broker, articulating the interests of various social groups, not as the advocate of policies or ideas. The corruption generated by this system was at the heart of the political crisis of 1993.

Where construction concrete is poured, and what it is poured for, is therefore incidental in the functioning of these circuits for transferring public funds into private or political party purposes. But if the pouring of concrete in a particular project is incidental to the process of serving the social and political interests of the many stakeholders in the system, it is not, of course, irrelevant to citizens and state, and it has had a very major effect on both the physical, moral, and political environment of Japan.

Collusion, price fixing, and bribery have long characterized this industry. When sudden light was cast on the inner workings of the system in 1993 and 1994, it was learned that 1 percent of all public works contracts of up to two or three billion yen, and 0.5 percent in cases of contracts for sums of more than ten billion yen, had been going in gifts to politicians.[24] A large contract could thus bring its political patrons a benefit worth two to three hundred million yen, or even up to one billion yen. Given the scale of the public-works budget, this means that more than 300 billion yen annually was being diverted from the public to political or private ends. This illegal—indeed criminal—system spread a net that embraced many of the most respected figures in Japanese society. What is usually referred to as organized crime is quite a different field of activity, although the underlying principle differs not one whit. These collusive links between politicians, bureaucrats, and business leaders were at the heart of the Japanese political crisis of the early 1990s.

The system of structural collusion was perfected in the 1970s by Tanaka Kakuei, who in turn was succeeded by Takeshita Noboru and then Kanemaru Shin. The Ministry of Construction came to be recognized as the citadel of the Tanaka faction. The award of public-works contracts to appropriate general construction firms set up the flow of funds into Liberal-Democratic Party (LDP) coffers and thus helped to pay for electoral and other political costs, both central and local. The system thus created came to be known as the doken kokka.

By its workings, astronomical sums have been appropriated into circuits from which many benefited. While the momentum of growth was maintained, Japan's reputation as a great power was enhanced, and trade frictions with the G7 member countries eased. Massive civil-engineering projects were favored: bridges, tunnels, highways, railways, and airports. The circuits through which the construction state functions ensure that sufficient largess has been spread locally to hold in place the ruling party's support network, with some funds in "rebates" and kickbacks for the party's central apparatus. Politicians are valued for their ability to bring work, money, and jobs to their electorate, and money to their party. The cost of being a politician in Japan far exceeds that in any other country, by a factor of more than four according to one estimate, and a politician commonly needs a couple of million dollars (hundreds of million yen) a year to run constituency affairs.

Because of this structure of collusive corruption, construction costs are much higher in Japan than elsewhere. That is why, for example, it costs four times as much to build a road in Japan as in Germany, and nine times as much as in the United States.[25] It is also the reason why Japanese construction is not internationally competitive.

In this system, the expansionist drive and the determination of construction goals and priorities is done by the industry, stemming from its need to expand and replicate itself rather than in response to social forces expressing community needs. Aoki and Kawamiya characterize this system as a "*potlatch* construction economy," from the American Indian term for "a ceremonial festival at which gifts are bestowed on the guests and property destroyed in a competitive show of wealth."[26] In a similar vein, another Japanese economist likened the process to the construction of the Egyptian pyramids—market considerations and social need being equally irrelevant to both.[27] The concrete world that results is the kind that best suits the imperative of profit and corporate accumulation, but the objects constructed were incidental to the process. Any enhancement of the quality of people's lives is likewise incidental; frequently, that quality was instead diminished.

In good times, the bureaucrats ended their careers with a descent from heaven into lucrative sinecures in the construction companies, ensuring the permanence of the relationships; in bad times—and the 1990s turned bad—all the members of the magic circle, except the still-serving bureaucrats, started to go to prison.

Kanemaru Shin, commonly known in Japan as "The Don," was the most powerful politician in the country before his arrest on March 6, 1993, and subsequent indictment for tax evasion. Bars of gold, bundles of cash, and sheaves of securities, along with masses of documents, were discovered in his safe. Among the documents was a list of major (zenekon) construction firms with the details of the amounts of their political contributions. During June and July of the same year, there followed a series of arrests of top political and business leaders:

The Mayor of Sendai
The Governor of Ibaraki Prefecture
The Governor of Miyagi Prefecture
The Chairman, President, and Managing-Director of Hazama Construction Company
The Chairman, Vice President, and Managing-Director of Shimizu Construction Company
The President and Vice President of Taisei Construction Company
The Vice President of Kajima Construction Company
The President of the Japan Federation of Construction Organizations
Senior executives of Shimizu Construction, Nishimatsu Construction, Mitsui Trading Company

As a climax, Nakamura Kishirō, former Minister for Construction, was arrested on April 1, 1994, and charged with "influence peddling."[28]

The arrest of such prominent figures was enough to make 1993–94 an unusual period. Much that had been long known to insiders in the construction industry, and suspected by outsiders, was confirmed. Although few were particularly surprised at the offenses, there was surprise at the indictments, not least among the corporate chieftains arrested, some of whom had only recently hired senior retiring prosecutors as legal advisers.[29] The general public's response to the arrests was not so much surprise as disgust. Everyone knew that the system was rotten, and it was assumed that the web of corruption exposed in relation to the construction of dams, universities, hospitals, government offices, new railway lines, sports centers, and liquefied natural gas (LNG) installations in two provinces was in no way unique.

Of those arrested, Nakamura Kishirō was bright, ambitious, and the first postwar-born politician to reach cabinet rank.[30] Governor Takeuchi Fujio of Ibaraki had ruled for eighteen giddying years of growth in his prefecture, an enthusiastic supporter of Tanaka Kakuei's vision of a restructured archipelago, the model of a successful politician in his proven ability to bring public-works projects to his district. Ishii Tōru, mayor of Sendai, had been chairman of the Japan Association of City Mayors since 1991.

The executives arrested controlled some of Japan's biggest companies. Shimizu, with 1992 annual sales of 2.16 trillion yen and an operating profit of 132 billion, was Japan's largest corporation and had been accustomed to allocating an annual budget of two billion yen for gifts to politicians (including eighty top national politicians on a list headed by Kanemaru). All the top zenekon companies followed the same practice, and the National Tax Agency reported an unaccounted flow of at least thirty-eight billion yen from them in 1991 and 59.5 billion in 1993.[31]

Ironically, the group of LDP politicians who left the party in 1993 to form a new political grouping, Shinseitō, or Japan Renewal Party, and who subsequently constituted the center of the new Hosokawa Government, contained the main heirs and associates of Tanaka, Takeshita, and Kanemaru. The task of reforming the political system thus fell to those deeply embedded in it. Politicians, the construction industry, and the bureaucracy were bound in an iron triangle of benefit and influence: The construction companies gave money to the politicians of the so-called "construction tribe" and collected votes on their behalf, and were allocated a share of construction work determined by the bureaucrats of the Ministry of Construction; the bureaucrats allocated contracts to friendly companies at a prearranged tender figure (the designated-tender system), and eventually stood for election (in which case they would enjoy the support of the Kanemaru electoral machine). In 1994, 111 out of 511 former Ministry of Construction bureaucrats were found to have celebrated their retirement from public service by floating down from heaven on silken parachutes to land in pleasant and lucrative positions either directly in the big zenekon corporations or in related semipublic bodies.[32]

Kanemaru's effort, cut short by his arrest, was to rationalize the premodern and personalized system and turn it into a modern one of extraction of a fixed levy, in effect a tax. He established procedures for all companies that belonged to dangō (specifically, for those in the Associations of Construction Companies) around the country to be levied an appropriate sum annually in accordance with the scale of the works they did, thereby reducing (but not eliminating) the specific job-related payments. The revenues thus raised were not strictly private, but used to finance the Liberal-Democratic Party. Apart from the sums levied in this way—between 1 and 3 percent of annual sales—other levies were made in relation to particular contracts. They were known by various sobriquets, such as *manjū* (dumpling), understood to be one million yen each, or *kōhī* (cups of coffee), understood to be either fifty or one hundred thousand yen each.[33]

The system of doken kokka ensured that competition would be avoided, and so costs were regularly forced up. Cossetted against the operations of the market, the construction industry grew from around 80,000 companies in 1960 to 500,000 by 1985.[34] The interests of citizen taxpayers were consistently trampled on. After long deliberations, the Fair Trade Commission decided in April 1994 not to take criminal proceedings against the dangō, and the likelihood that administrative measures—for example, instructions that the dangō be dissolved—will be successful in reforming the system seem slight.[35]

If the Fair Trade Commission was a toothless hound, then some critics began to suggest that it was time for the laws relating to organized crime to be brought into play against the construction industry.[36] Other models, such as the Australian Independent Commission Against Corruption, also seemed worth considering. Public anger at influence peddling and corruption has yet to lead to the demand for a general and thorough reform of the system, and prosecutors are concerned with particular acts rather than their structural context. The role played by the construction business in Japan, not only the terms on which the business is done but the general nature of the business, is infrequently questioned. In April 1994, prosecutors announced that their investigation was closed. Those who found themselves in prison as a result could feel with some justice that they had been picked out as ceremonial scapegoats to allow the system, suitably refurbished, to survive.

Financing Public Works: The Bottom Line

It is bad enough that taxpaying citizens are in this way innocent victims of a high-level extortion racket, but the reality is even more pernicious. Not only do citizens pay an involuntary, secret, and illegal levy on every project and on the public-works industry as a whole, but to a large extent the money is extracted both from tax-based regular state income and also from special deficit bonds, and the accumulated deficit has risen to an astronomical sum that weighs even more heavily on the shoulders of citizens. Though the Japanese government is supposed to be the model of fiscal rectitude, in contrast to its profligate counterpart in the United States, the reality is very different. The U.S. government's complicity in the savings and loan scams of the 1980s was matched by the Japanese government's involvement in the construction scam and the fiscal steps it took to finance it. The outcome in both nations is prodigious debt, although Japan's is owed by its government to its own citizens.

As of December 1994, the Japanese government was indebted to the tune of nearly 300 trillion yen in deficit bonds (three trillion dollars at the 1994 rate of exchange, or about six times the official cost estimate of the savings and loan scam in the United States), virtually all of it accumulated in the post-1973 period as part of recession recovery public works that evolved into Tanaka's "Reconstructing Japan" and the many other grandiose projects that followed. However, if other hidden debts and the debts of local governments and public corporations are included, the sum reaches 380 trillion, and if that were to be repaid at a rate of 5 percent interest it would amount to 1,000 trillion yen (approximately eight million per person). As Aoki and Kawamiya comment, there are only two ways in which such a sum could be paid: hypertaxation or hyperinflation.[37]

Almost 16 percent of Japan's tax revenues—a substantially greater figure than in other industrial countries, as Table 1.1 makes clear—must now go to pay merely the interest on this accumulated debt—nearly sixteen cents in every tax dollar in other words—and any sudden rise in that interest rate would have crippling effects.[38] Rather than take urgent steps to reduce and eliminate that debt, however, it is almost certain that the Japanese government will continue to spend profligately on public works through the mid-1990s. The problem will be not only meeting demands by the United States to have the construction business conducted henceforth on a level playing field in which foreign companies can compete equally but of actually finding projects capable of justifying such huge outlays. Sky-piercing build-

Figure 1.1 **Japanese Governmental Debts Balance and Gross Domestic Product, 1970–94** (Figure by Aoki Hidekazu)

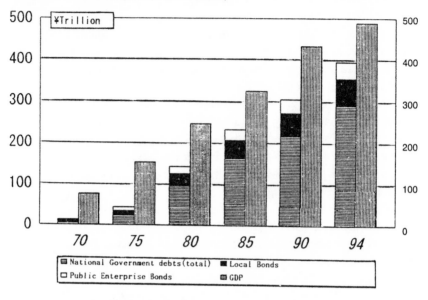

Figure 1.2 **Interest Payments on National Debt** (Figure by Aoki Hidekazu)

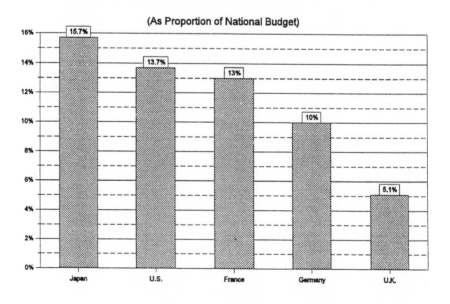

Figure 1.3 **Long-Term Debt Balance of the Central Government** (Figure by Aoki Hidekazu)

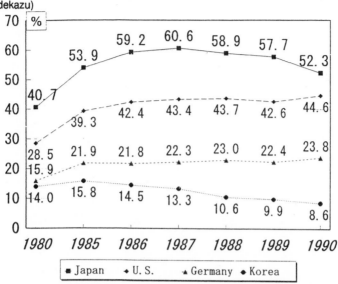

ings, sea-filling islands, river-blocking dams, and island-linking bridges and tunnels will certainly be put forward in the attempt.

The U.S. demand to stimulate the economy will be cited as a warrant for taking such steps, and the golden circuit linking the construction industry, the Ministry of Construction, and politicians will continue to need oiling. In the structural impediment talks with the United States in June 1990, Japan's LDP government promised that it would spend around 430 trillion yen on public works before the end of the millennium. It is remarkable that a vast expenditure of this kind, perhaps without precedent or parallel, could be undertaken by a sovereign government in response to external pressure, with but minimal and marginalized opposition.[39] Though well behind target in October 1994, the figure was increased by a further 200 trillion as part of the ten-year Public Works Investment Basic Plan (1995–2004). The basic plan did not indicate where the money was going to come from, although the answer was inescapable: further debt.[40] Even that, according to some, was too modest and should be further expanded, indeed virtually doubled, to 1,000 trillion yen.[41] The scene is certainly set for a dramatic public-works-sector investment-led economic recovery. Its allocation was increased in the 1994 budget by 29.6 percent.[42] To come anywhere near meeting the official end-of-century target, that

Figure 1.4 International Comparison of Construction Investments (Figure by Aoki Hidekazu)

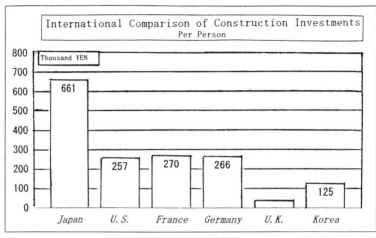

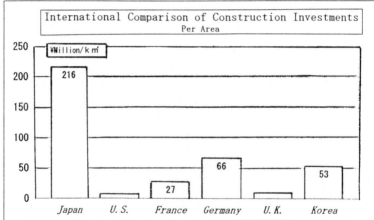

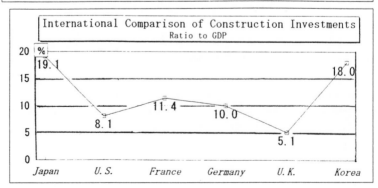

will have to be greatly increased again hereafter. The treasury is, however, not only empty, but full of IOUs accumulated from the profligacy and corruption of the long LDP era. The public works being undertaken in 1994 were more than 90 percent financed by deficit bonds.[43] The reform focus of the post-LDP governments, even the socialist-led Murayama administration (1994–   ) was confined to the electoral system, not to the structural roots of the corruption that led to the downfall of the LDP in 1993. To guide the economy out of bubble and recession into the safe waters of recovery and stable growth, the tiller is being entrusted to precisely those who sailed it into the whirlpools of the late 1980s. The term construction state, used here to describe this complex, is designed to focus attention not only on construction and public works as Japan's major industry, but also to the collusive circuits that link bureaucrats, politicians, and business in a web of influence peddling and corruption. Having evolved during the Cold War years, the construction state is in some respects akin to the military-industrial complex in Cold War America (or the Soviet Union), sucking in the country's wealth, consuming it inefficiently, growing like a cancer, and bequeathing both fiscal crisis and environmental devastation.[44]

The pressure building from the spiraling tracer of the fault lines beneath this extraordinary fiscal system concerns ultimately not only Japan but the entire world, yet it is as little appreciated as was the import of the fault lines that until 1995 lay dormant beneath the city of Kobe. It is true that the debt is domestic rather than foreign, much of it being funded from the collective savings of ordinary Japanese people held in the nation's Post Office Savings Account Fund (the world's largest financial institution by far), but the instability and untenability of the system is no less for this. Furthermore, the reverberations of the failure of Hyogo Bank in 1995 made it increasingly likely that the prodigious debts of Japan's private banking sector—with officially forty trillion yen but more likely seventy or eighty trillion in non-performing loans—would also eventually have to be met by the public, the taxpayer. Deutsche Bank's Kenneth Courtis reckoned an infusion of thirty-five trillion in public funds would be necessary to save the banking system.[45] In the past, debt of such scale has been liquidated by war, which simply eliminated the people's savings, or by dissolution and privatization, as in the case of the chronically debt-ridden Japan National Railways in 1983 (although in that case, the thirty-seven-trillion-yen debt remained in the hands of a specially created public body and was accumulating interest).[46] Simply rolling over debt of this scale, snowballing it, so to speak, and passing on the problem to future generations, cannot be continued indefinitely. Increases in indirect taxation, however politically indefensible, will increasingly be necessary, and can be represented as welfare taxes to cope with an increasingly aging society, but the scale of the problem is already such as to have become not susceptible to any gradual, remedial measures. Ultimately, perhaps, it has come to resemble nothing so much as the frog described by the early-twentieth-century novelist Natsume Sōseki which inflated itself to try to become a cow, with inevitably fatal effects.

Planning: The Zensō

1950 Law

The construction-and-public-works sector of the economy is characterized by very high levels of planning and control. Comprehensive plans for the development of the country as a whole have been adopted and revised periodically since the first Comprehensive Law for the Development of the National Land of 1950 (*Kokudo sōgō kaihatsuhō*), which underwent major revisions with what became known as the first to fourth Comprehensive National Development Plans (*Zenkoku sōgō kaihatsu keikaku*, or *Zensō*) in 1962, 1969, 1977, and 1987. These revisions have themselves been supplemented or modified by additional legislation or official statements of future vision such as the New Industrial Towns and Industrial Facilities Regional Development Promotion Law (1963), the "Follow-Up" Law to the third Comprehensive Plan (1983), the Outlook for Japan in the Twenty-first Century (1984), the Technopolis Law (1983), Capital Improvement Law (1985), Resort Law (1987), and Regional Base Cities Law (1992).

Water Engineering

Dams. Water engineering, including dam construction, various kinds of river works, and coastal land reclamation, played the central role in plans adopted in the 1950s and 1960s. Although this process was launched under the 1950 plan, it continues in the 1990s, and the problems of dams and reclamation are therefore considered here as a whole.

The bulldozer was introduced into Japan in the 1950s, its capacity astounding and delighting Japanese engineers and feeding their faith in technology.[47] The Tennessee Valley Authority (TVA) was one closely studied model for the integration of regional and agricultural development, water regulation, transport, and electrical power generation.[48] However, while learning from it, the Japanese planners chose not to follow it in two significant respects. The idea of local empowerment was strong in the Knoxville-based TVA, but was ignored in Japan, where priority was given to the supply of the electricity to developing industries in the cities. In contrast to the TVA, which had supplied power to local areas at prices about half the national average, Japan simply concentrated on the supply of cheap power to urban industry. Electrical power was thus supplied to industry at prices about one-third of those operating in West Germany.[49] In other words, Japan adopted the technology of comprehensive dam construction and hydropower generation, but primarily as a means to strengthen urban industry. The areas designated in 1950 as special regions for development gradually became backward and depopulated, while heavy industry and chemical manufacturing flourished. This national strategy was widely supported and seemed obvious and necessary at the time, just as it has seemed obvious and necessary to rapidly industrializing countries ever since. In retrospect, it becomes much more open to doubt that this was the only or the best way. Furthermore, once embarked on the process of filling in the coastline and straightening and concreting (or damming) the rivers, the momentum generated by continuing and successful accomplishment created vested interests and a dynamic process difficult to arrest.[50] From time to time, criticism is leveled at the process on economic or environmental grounds. Awareness of the problems of silting, loss of water quality due to reduced water flow, environmental damage, or danger from collapsing walls or earthquake has slowly grown. Red tides, indicating general environmental malaise, occurred at eighty-one dams in 1992.[51] In the fifty years since the end of the war, 1,000 dams were built and as of 1995 an additional 400 were either under construction or planned. The existing dams were, however, clogged by well over a billion tons of silt. Though the dams were the central achievement of the postwar doken kokka, and the major contributing factor to the huge national debt, most were useless, possessing a steadily shrinking capacity to serve the purposes of water conservation and regulation for which they were built.[52] Some—such as those on the Kurobe and Tenryū rivers—were 40 percent silted, while the Sakuma Dam in Shizuoka Prefecture, after thirty-five years of operation, was one-third silted up.[53] The phenomenon is far from new. As early as 1951, the scientist Nakatani Ukichirō pointed to the fact that the Yasuoka Dam on the Tenryū River was 85 percent silted up only fifteen years after its construction.[54]

This growing problem was simply not anticipated when the dams were constructed, as the head of the engineering and construction section at Kansai Electric Power Company admitted in 1994.[55] The experiment in 1994 with a new type of dam wall, which included a built-in sluice gate to allow release of the accumulated muck on the dam floor, was hastily abandoned when devastating environmental consequences were reported.[56] There is no known technical solution, and in due course, all of Japan's dams are bound to be filled up and rendered useless, leaving the problem of huge, unstable blocks of mountain soil, concrete, and muck astride the country's rivers. Perhaps they could be blown up, causing temporary devastation but in such a way that the river might regenerate, but no one knows. This is an ecological nightmare to which Japan is only beginning to wake. Ironically, in many cases, payment of the debt accumulated to pay for constructing the dams will continue long after the dams themselves have become useless.

By 1994, the only free-flowing river on the main island of Honshu was the Nagara. Flowing through the three prefectures of Aichi, Mie, and Gifu, the river is one of the richest ecological treasures in Japan, host to more known species than any other river in the country.[57] The idea of damming it to provide water for industrial purposes as part of a projected installation of heavy-industry and chemical plants on the shores of Ise Bay goes back to 1960, but local opposition was very strong.[58] The dam's location near the mouth of the river is a highly prized fishing site, noted for the *ayu* (sweet fish) and *satsuki-masu* (trout that swim out to the ocean and then back to fresh waters to spawn), and is crucial to the fishing industry for up to 100 kilometers upstream. After money was poured into the region to buy fishing rights from local fishing cooperatives or to improve the local infrastructure, eventually the purpose of water control (flood prevention) was added to the original idea of industrial use in 1968, and the decision to dam it was adopted at the cabinet level. Again, however, it was successfully blocked for two decades by objections from local fishing and environmental groups.

In the summer of 1990, Kitakawa Ishimatsu, Minister for the Environment in the second Kaifu Cabinet (July 1989 to December 1990), came to see the project as both unnecessary and environmentally damaging. However, having made up his mind to issue an order temporarily suspending work, he faced both implacable opposition from his own ministry, which feared the consequences of attracting the hostility of the ministries of Construction and Finance, and open threats from Deputy Prime Minister Kanemaru, who warned him that persistence in opposition would mean the end of Kitakawa's political career.[59] As the project proceeded, the Ministry of Construction agreed that there would be no use for 90 percent of the water that would become available upon its completion.[60] In 1993–94, when the long dominance of the Liberal-Democratic Party finally ended and the reform cabinet of Hosokawa Morihiro came to power, a further effort was made to stop the dam. Igarashi Kōzō, the socialist who was appointed Minister for Construction, was known as a committed opponent of the project. He called on Prime Minister Hosokawa to undertake a thorough review of all large-scale public works planned under the preceding LDP governments. Again, however, opposition from within the ministries thwarted him, and after only eight months, the Hosokawa government collapsed.[61]

This is a project to which Japan's main scientific community, nature and environmental groups, and the media are opposed. It was denounced by the well-known conservative philosopher Umehara Takeshi as something that offered "one hundred harms and not one single benefit."[62] This Ministry of Construction project best exemplifies the corrupt and collusive system described above, having been originally approved by Mr. Kanemaru and the construction contracts given in characteristic dangō fashion to the Kashima and Taisei construction companies.[63] In 1994, despite this, and despite the fact that the original rationale for the dam—industrial water—had been completely abandoned, the works proceeded toward completion. By the end of 1992, 184 billion yen had been spent, thirteen giant pillars straddled the river, the sluice gates were tested, and the outcome seemed to be all but settled.

Although plans for massive increases in dam construction were adopted in the 1960s and 1970s, on the assumption of a continuing and growing need for water for industrial purposes, the transformation in the country's industrial structure that followed meant that much of the planned extra capacity, as in the Nagara case, became redundant. Yet water works is an area in which the collusion between bureaucrats and the construction industry is particularly strong, and the growing excess capacity has not deterred the construction program.[64] This is also the case in Hokkaido, where the Nibutani Dam, nearing completion on the Saru River, is not only redundant because of the abandonment of nearly all of the planned Tomakomai East industrial estate, but is being constructed at a site claimed as sacred by the aboriginal Ainu people.[65]

However, challenges to the long hegemony exercised over the country's rivers by the Ministry of Construction are becoming more and more frequent. In tiny villages, such as Kitōmura (population 2,300) on the Nakagawa River in the mountains of Shikoku, entire communities were uniting around their mayor and local Assembly in opposition to the Ministry of Construction's plans for dam construction in their locality, and intense efforts were being devoted to the pursuit of a strategy for a dam-free future.[66] The head of the hydrological section at Japan's Geological Survey, Ishii Takemasu, described the dam-construction business as a matter of political expedience: "The construction companies, politicians, and elite bureaucrats—all three elements are conspiring to stuff Japan with dams."[67] The contemporary scientist and environmentalist Ui Jun, long a trenchant critic of the idea of damming all rivers, argues persuasively for a thorough reappraisal of the practice of water control. Other voices are beginning to be heard that call not only for the suspension of one or another new project but for the demolition of dams and the revival of the country's once magnificent rivers.[68] Such voices can be expected to grow into a new social movement in the years remaining to the end of the century.

Coastal Land Reclamation. The process of coastal land reclamation got underway around the beginning of the seventeenth century in Japan, but proceeded at a generally slow tempo through the 300 years of the Tokugawa, during which an estimated 3,000 hectares was reclaimed, with little ecological damage resulting.[69] The pace of change remained slow through the years to the end of the war in 1945. In 1953, the Bay Area Infrastructure Promotion Act established a system of nationally planned coastal reclamation. The Ministry of Transportation was empowered to issue permits for reclamation projects, with the actual execution in the hands of provincial authorities, who in due course could sell the lands thus created to private developers as factory sites. The cost of creating land was about half that of purchasing comparable farm land. By 1960, a total of 2,321 hectares had been reclaimed, but the tempo increased rapidly during the high-growth decade that followed. During the 1960s, a further 24,957 hectares was reclaimed. Massive expansion was planned for the 1970s, with that figure supposed to rise to 40,000 hectares during the first five years of the decade, but the oil shock and ensuing reconsideration of industrial strategy saw the figure reduced to 12,512.[70] During the high-growth 1960s, extensive works were carried out around Tokyo, Nagoya, the Seto Inland Sea, Toyama, Oita, and Kagoshima, as well as Osaka. Five hundred kilometers of the Seto Inland Sea coastline was concreted over.[71] So far as Osaka Bay is concerned, 5,600 hectares was reclaimed in the forty years to 1990, including three-quarters of the ecologically precious shallows that once covered one eighth of the entire bay.

Neither the continuing recession in the early 1990s, nor the transition to a post-LDP political era, was going to make any difference to the construction state and its assumptions and interests. The last act of the Hosokawa reform government, in April 1994, was to issue the go-ahead for construction of a 401-hectare container-port island in Hakata Bay in Kyushu, designed to reinforce the role of Hakata as an international port city and information and research-and-development base. The approval was rushed through just after the press conference at which the Hosokawa resignation had been announced, and hours after receipt of the opinion of the Minister of the Environment urging the case for registration of the region under the Ramsara Convention* because of its importance as a habitat and migratory route of countless birds (including a number of rare and endangered species, such as the black-faced spoon-bill, Chinese heron, crested little grebe, and black-headed gull). With the loss of so many other sites, the tidal flats of the bay had become a major refuge in the autumn and winter period, attracting up to 60,000 birds a day en route between Siberia and Australia-New Zealand. Despite the strength of domestic and international opposition to the project, work began in July 1994 and was scheduled to continue until the year 2003.[72]

Japan's four main islands have a coastline 18,919 kilometers long, but by 1984, only 46 percent of that remained in its pristine, natural

---

*1971 international convention for the protection of the world's water birds and their habitats.

state.[73] In the decade that followed this survey, development proceeded at a greatly accelerated rate, and obviously the resort developments of the late 1980s have greatly shrunk the few remaining segments of natural coastline. Of Osaka Bay, only a tiny 2 percent, at its eastern and western extremities, remains in its natural state (more or less), free of reclamation or development. When a periodic stocktaking of the country as a whole was undertaken early in the 1990s, it was found that apart from the loss of natural coastline, 40 percent of all Japan's tidelands had also disappeared due to landfill and the construction of roads and other works.[74]

First Zensō, 1962

The 1960s was a decade of miraculous economic growth, characterized by the advance of the heavy and chemical industries and the flourishing of the so-called "heavy, thick, long, and big" industries (*jū-kō-chō-dai*), as steel, ships, and petrochemicals came to be known. The first "Zensō" (1962) was conceived at the time that the income-doubling policies of the Ikeda Cabinet had been adopted and the high-growth era was dawning. It projected the evening out of discrepancies in wealth and development between urban and rural districts by the dispersal of *kombinat*, or strategic concentration, of key industries—basically petrochemicals, steel, aluminum, and the like—to the regions. A series of sites was selected for new cities, each to have a projected population of one million. Every prefecture became involved in the struggle to gain endorsement under the plan, and as much was spent in lobbying as had been allocated for expenditure in the first year of the program itself.[75] Fifteen sites, and a further six "provisional" locations, were named. Only two of the fifteen, South Okayama Prefecture (Mizushima) and Oita (in North Kyushu), were successful in attracting investment as new industrial towns. Ultimately, it was these two, and Kashima (in Chiba Prefecture, near Tokyo), that eventuated as kombinat cities. Even in these, a government report of May 1981 showed that only 30 percent of the targeted industrial output had been reached.

Originally conceived as a fifteen-year plan, by the time it was completed, the assumptions on which it had been based had collapsed; steel, ships, and petrochemicals were no longer the stars of the technological revolution, and cities like Oita, whose fates had been tied to them, were already entering decline.[76] The burden of the attempt to induce investment—by infrastructural spending—helped deepen the fiscal problems of those who failed.[77] A different set of problems awaited the successful, and litigation over the problems of illness and environmental pollution caused by the absence of constraint on these industries continues in the courts today. In many cases, sites set aside for development that did not see construction in the 1960s were later revived and proposed as potential sites for resorts.

Studies of the fate of the new industrial towns and regions show that, apart from the pollution-related social and environmental costs, actual economic benefits to the regions (as distinct from the city-based corporations) were small. In the case of the Sakai-Kita Izumi Waterfront kombinat, located within Osaka Prefecture on the shore of Osaka Bay, Miyamoto's research team calculated that, while they accounted for more than 41 percent of the electrical power used and the pollutants generated in all industry, they contributed only 7.8 percent of the surplus value added, 1.7 percent of employment, and 1.6 percent of corporate taxes paid.[78] The output was commonly either further processed elsewhere, within the large corporate system (rather than by the creation of new linkages with local entrepreneurs), or exported. A prominent business leader, returning for a visit to his home town and seeing the extent to which its development was externally induced, with most benefits flowing out to corporations based in Tokyo, described what was happening in Mizushima as a "colonial style of development."[79] By 1970, even the president of the Sakai Chamber of Commerce and Industry was opposed to any expansion of existing facilities.

In March 1994, the Okayama District Court held that Kawasaki Steel and seven other companies had been responsible for emissions of sulfur dioxide, nitrogen dioxide, and other pollutants that caused chronic bronchitis, asthma, and emphysema. The order to compensate forty-one residents for health damage occurring between the late 1950s and the 1970s amounted to a judgment against the policies of the state under Zensō. Following twenty-two years after a similar judgment in the Yokkaichi case, it precedes judgments in other cases concerning Osaka and Yokohama. There, residents are demanding not only compensation, but also restitution of their lost environment, the removal of concrete from the foreshore and the relocation of a freeway (underground, or somewhere out of the way).[80]

The Yokkaichi petrochemical kombinat began full-scale operations in 1960 on the shore of Ise Bay, close to Nagoya City. At the time, it was the largest such plant in the Asia-Pacific region. By autumn of the same year, some 1,000 people were suffering from asthma in the adjacent villages; school classes had to be conducted with windows closed because of the smell, and various unusual ailments and illnesses were reported. In 1963, when the government finally moved to impose restrictions on the output of smoke, the standards it imposed were still below prewar levels; atmospheric pollution and "Yokkaichi disease" (asthma) continued to spread.[81]

In retrospect, perhaps the most significant transformation effected in this period was the welding of the major Tōkaidō cities of Tokyo, Yokohama, Nagoya, Kyoto, and Osaka into a single mammoth unit (a megalopolis) as a result of the introduction of new transport technologies, especially the bullet train, or shinkansen, which in 1964 reduced the travel time between Tokyo and Osaka from six hours and fifty minutes to three hours and ten minutes (further reduced, in 1992, to two-and-a-half hours). Whether people would have preferred to continue enjoying the comfort and relative leisure of the old expresses was impossible to judge, since that service was withdrawn. Since 1994, the person who wishes to travel from Osaka to Tokyo by non-shinkansen train (thereby avoiding the special express charges) finds that it takes longer than it did thirty years ago.

By 1980, after decades of planning for regional development, 8.4 million people were found to be living in depopulated (kasochi) areas. This amounted to 44 percent of the nation's land, or 34 percent of all towns and villages in the country. Like the prewar planners, whose failure to address the problem of the villages had produced great social unrest and suffering, so the postwar planners failed to pay serious attention to the specific needs of different regions. Although development and growth-oriented policies undoubtedly differed enormously, in that the standards of living of urban and rural people alike were raised rapidly in this period, the consequences of regional depopulation and environmental decline only became evident slowly.

Regional-development policy in the 1960s reinforced the priority of central, industrial, and urban needs over regional, rural, or agricultural interests. Though some manufacturing functions were gradually relocated to the provinces, the process of centralization of planning, control, research, information, and services in the metropolitan centers, especially Tokyo, was overwhelming. When local government elections returned reform administrations in some regions in the 1970s, the newly elected officials found that they had actually little power to initiate reforms of substance. Their main role (as Hosokawa Morihiro, the governor of Kumamoto, and later prime minister, frequently complained) was to preside over a branch office controlled from Tokyo.

During this turbulent decade of development, the concentration of available resources in the quest for capital accumulation and expansion gave Japan the character that was sometimes described by observers in other countries as "Japan Inc.," or as the "capitalist developmental state,"[82] and by critics within Japan as the *kigyō kokka*, or business state, or even as "true state monopoly capitalism."[83] While public-works expenditure for the decade totaled 33.7 trillion yen—about equal to the whole expenditure for the period from 1868 to 1945, but equal to a mere year's expenditure of the mid-1990s—the resources were committed overwhelmingly to infrastructure to support economic growth rather than to improving the social infrastructure.[84]

The decision to become an automobile society, and in due course the greatest auto exporter in the world, was not made democratically, but it had enormous consequences. When I first arrived in Japan in 1962, the annual output of autos was about half a million (481,000 in 1960), the public-transport system was quite good, and no one really needed a car. By 1970, however, the annual output of automobiles was 5.2 million, and by 1985, it reached 12.3 million. Output dropped thereafter to its present level of between nine and ten million annually, of which about half are exported. The Japan that had a mere 3.4 million automobiles in 1960 had sixty-five million by 1993—and 5,400 kilometers of expressway. Apart from the severe pressures on its own environment, and the growing frictions with its trading partners, there are other costs. About 20,000 people die every year on Japanese roads (700,000 dead between 1945 and 1991, plus countless more injured).[85] While battlefield casualties of such scale would have caused enormous social and political turmoil, little attention is paid to this issue, since these are victims of the impersonal forces of modernization. For forty years, investment in roads topped public-works spending. Nearly three trillion cubic meters of concrete was poured during the period 1975 to 1993, enough, as Aoki laconically notes, to spread an 800-meter-wide, ten-meter-thick strip of it all the way from Tokyo to Nagoya.[86] Again in the 1994 budget, the lion's share of the public works appropriation, three trillion yen, or about ten trillion if local and regional expenditure is taken into account, was to go to road construction.[87] Generally speaking, the private auto has been an unnecessary, intrusive, wasteful, and massively destructive force in Japan, despite its contribution to miraculous GNP growth.[88]

Second Zensō, 1969

The vision of the second Zensō, sometimes known as *Shin Zensō* or new Zensō, was best articulated in the famous plan by which Prime Minister Tanaka Kakuei proposed reconstructing the Japanese Archipelago.[89] The scale of the plan was such that it envisioned a total investment of between 450 and 550 trillion yen over twenty years (as against a grand total investment since the Meiji period of 140 trillion) to achieve a multiplication of the national GNP by a factor of five.[90] It projected an organic nation, in which control functions were exercised, and culture, education, and services concentrated, within the Tokaido belt along the Pacific coast from the Tokyo area to North Kyushu. Big industrial and tourism sites were to be located in the northeast and southwest, and the whole would be linked by a high-speed network of information, transport, and communications. Mega-industrial sites, projected to be about 10,000 hectares in area and on a scale twice that of Kashima, were designated for Mutsu-Ogawara in Aomori Prefecture in Northern Honshu and for Shibushi in Kagoshima Prefecture, as well as several other sites.[91] The plan assumed that Japan would import 600 million kiloliters of oil per year, about half the total available on the world market. It was designed, probably, to emulate the income-doubling plan of the 1960s, and was predicated on growth continuing at something like 9 percent per annum.[92] Tanaka assumed a continuation of existing trends, and he showed an almost obsessive belief in the superiority of the large-scale, and an Olympian lack of concern for the interests of local communities.

However, these massive projects were stalled by a combination of the wave of speculation it fed, especially in land, rising popular resistance, and a shrinking economic outlook following the oil shocks of 1973. The idea of regional development by means of developmental bases (a uniquely Japanese notion), so much promoted in the 1960s and 1970s, thereafter vanished without trace (except in some countries attempting to follow a Japanese model).[93] Within Japan, major designated sites, such as Mutsu-Ogawara in Northern Honshu, having been left high and dry by the planners of the second Zensō, eventually found little alternative but to host huge oil storage facilities in the 1980s and the Rokkasho-village nuclear reprocessing and waste facilities in the 1990s.[94]

Third Zensō, 1977

Welfare and environmental considerations became more difficult to ignore from the third Zensō (1977). It is not that faith in development had weakened among bureaucrats and corporate executives, but that they came under greatly increased public pressure to face the social and environmental consequences of their policies. The major litigation cases in the courts about the consequences of previous decisions—especially in relation to the Minamata disease (poisoning caused by organic mercury effluent from chemical plants, both at Kumamoto and at Niigata), the Toyama *itai-itai* disease, caused by cadmium poisoning, and the Yokkaichi disease (an asthma caused by industrial emissions, particularly sulfur dioxide, in the atmosphere), and the rising citizens' and residents' movements around them played the key role in this reconsideration. Although popular pressure was not strong enough to force any major change of direction, environmental assessment, nature preservation, and the provision of educational, welfare, and cultural services were given some attention in industrial location planning, and the need to restrict the flow of population to the cities was recognized, at least in theory.

In the late 1970s, a different form of development gradually emerged. The age of "heavy, thick, long, and big," centered around the materials-based heavy and petrochemical industries, gave way to its opposite: the high-tech and electronic age of the "light, thin, short, and small" (*kei-haku-tan-shō*). But the underlying conviction of the way to proceed did not change: In place of the materials-processing bases of the earlier period came the information-processing bases, the technopolises.

The technopolis was part of the Ministry of International Trade and Industry (MITI) solution to the problem of regional development. First proposed in the Commerce and Industry Policy Vision for the 1980s as part of a Japanese counterpart to Silicon Valley in the United States, the idea was to establish high-tech, usually information-related, industries (and especially integrated circuit [IC] plants) in regional towns, taking advantage of their supply of cheap land, labor, and (in the case of IC plants) clean water. The High-tech Industry Concentration Regional Development Promotion Law (1983) was a ten-year plan under which education, research, and manufacturing were supposed to become concentrated in a dynamic interrelationship within new satellite cities of between 40,000 to 50,000 people that would grow in the vicinity of existing mother cities of about 200,000 to 300,000 people.

The effect of this prescription too was to increase the dependence of the regions on Tokyo since, with few exceptions, whatever was established in the regional centers remained subject to the metropolitan authority of the larger corporate entity, especially in managerial and technological matters. Thus arose the phenomenon described by Sasaki as "technopolis without brains."[95]

After a fierce competition, comparable to that unleashed in the 1960s over their designation as new industrial towns, the twenty-six regions eventually chosen faced a huge fiscal burden in attempting to provide the necessary infrastructure to satisfy the corporations they wooed. Moreover, by the late 1980s, their comparative advantage withered as the high yen and the pressures of international competitiveness led to the relocation of much high-tech manufacturing offshore, especially in continental Asia. Eventually, even MITI recognized that the best formula for the economic development of the regions was to pursue local initiatives for the development of local resources.[96] Even in the "successful" technopolises, plan targets were not met, technology transfer did not occur, and high-tech pollution of the local water left an uncertain legacy.[97] The record in relation to the third leg of the plan for regional development, the resort, is dealt with in Chapter 2.

During the 1980s, belief in technological solutions to environmental problems grew: confidence in large-scale engineering projects reached new peaks as the strategy of placating international trade competitors by boosting domestic demand (*naiju kakudai*) simultaneously inflated domestic demand, satisfied (at least momentarily) the Americans, and served major domestic interests (i.e., filled the coffers of both the Liberal-Democratic Party and the construction lobby). In the longer term, it helped blow out the bubble that crippled the economy at the end of the decade and drove the LDP to excesses that nearly destroyed it too.

Fourth Zensō, 1987

The fourth Zensō (1987) articulated the vision of the government of Nakasone Yasuhiro. It was supposed to promote the equal development of the country by arresting the growing imbalance between extreme unipolar centralization in the Tokyo area and decline of the regions, to respond to the needs of the information age, and to facilitate Japan's internationalization. Instead, this long-term plan (for the period 1987–2000) heightened the gap between Tokyo and the regions and concentrated even more of the high-tech information functions in the capital. Through what was referred to as reliance on the dynamism of the private sector (*minkatsu*), the fourth Zensō sparked speculative land inflation, which intensified the gaps between Tokyo and other areas,[98] spread environmental pollution, and severely damaged the national economy. The domestic economy was awash with the trade surplus and capital gains from the revalued yen, and it was stimulated to a frenzy by the low-interest-rate policy. The boom in urban-land speculation that had gathered force during the so-called urban renaissance of 1985–87—when Tokyo land prices rose by an average 300 percent[99]—was extended throughout the entire country from 1987 by the effects of the fourth Zensō and the Resort Law. This Zensō envisaged an investment of 1,000 trillion yen between 1986 and the turn of the century in the provision of basic infrastructural amenities to the entire country. The public input was to come from the freeing of public assets, especially land, to be complemented by private investment in transport, housing, communications, information technology, and urban redevelopment. The transformations wrought under the Resort Law in much of regional Japan provide the best case study in the workings of the fourth Zensō principles. It is significant that the governors of the three prefectures supposed to benefit from the Nakasone policies became vociferous critics: the governors of Hokkaido, Oita, and Kumamoto (the latter, Hosokawa Morihiro, was prime minister from 1993).[100]

The term "intelligent city" came to mean a place in which the provision of communications and information facilities was coordinated by means of advanced (usually fiber-optic cable) technology that channeled information to and between "intelligent buildings"; incorporation in city planning from the initial stages was obviously the most desirable mode. In practice, the degree of intelligence seems to have borne a close correlation to the level of corruption in local administration, as was revealed when the zenekon scam was brought to light in the early 1990s.[101]

Regional planning, from the early postwar period and through the four phases of Zensō, has been characterized by ambitious, impractical, desktop bureaucratic projects for reorganizing the country. The utopian rhetoric within which the prescriptions were couched cannot conceal their failure to address the problems of sharpening polarity between the great megalopolis of Tokyo to North Kyushu on the one hand, and the rapidly depopulated countryside and mountain and coastal villages on the other. Their obsessive focus on growth, neglect of social and environmental considerations, and promotion of large Tokyo (or Osaka) controlled mega-industrial groupings at the expense of regional, locally grown development was so thorough and complete that such planned development may take as long to redress as it took to accomplish. The questions of what the economic growth attained means to the residents of the megolopolises, and the consequences for the long-term future of the country as a whole, have to be considered further.

The effect of the accumulated failings of Japanese regional development policy was reinforced by steps taken from the mid-1980s under the Nakasone government to ease international trade pressures by boosting demand in the domestic economy. The various Maekawa Report policies stressed slogans of minkatsu (revitalization through reliance on the private sector) and *naiju kakudai* (expansion of domestic demand). In practice, this meant pump priming through large-scale infrastructural and public-works spending. The channels through which the projects were organized were those characteristic of the construction state.[102]

National Capital Plans

Among the big-ticket projects that proliferated in the early 1990s were many schemes to redevelop the national capital. The rise of Tokyo to its present size and national importance began with extensive civil engineering and reclamation projects in medieval and early modern times. Much of present-day Tokyo, including the Imperial Palace, Hibiya Park, the National Diet, and the Ginza, is built on land reclaimed at various times since the early seventeenth century. During this period, there were as many as 3,000 ships, each ferrying 100 men between Edo and Izu, where they collected heavy stones for reclamation and castle construction. Work continued through the 1930s, was suspended during World War II, and resumed again in 1948 with the first Bay Improvement Five Year Plan.[103] The 1960s saw a sudden increase in activity, and with the era of mass consumption came mass waste, much of which was dumped in the bay, gradually building up into what became known as Dream Island and New Dream Island. In the 1980s, however, incremental and piecemeal adjustments to the bay gave way to comprehensive, integrated qualitative plans for its transformation.

The future of the city was vigorously debated, especially under Suzuki Shun-ichi, who became governor in April 1983. The idea of a Metropolitan Waterfront Subcenter Project, when first broached in 1982, was to develop a neglected segment of the city's old waterfront so as to provide residential and recreational facilities where city residents could live in more exuberant (*ikiiki shita*) style.[104] But the proposed site—448.4 hectares of which 213 could be earmarked for development—situated only between five and seven kilometers from Tokyo Station, soon became caught up in debate over the desired future of the capital. The idea of moving the capital either eastward to somewhere like Sendai, or westward toward Nagoya, thus avoiding excessive concentration of the political, bureaucratic, business, and cultural functions of Japan in a single site, attracted many proponents. Suzuki strongly opposed the idea, evidently believing it would lead to a weakening of the country's economic drive. The Waterfront Subcenter Project became the focus of plans to resist the move by redeveloping the capital. This implied further expansion and a deepening of the existing problems of the city, and it was a significant factor in helping stir the speculative land fever in Tokyo that spread across the whole country in the late 1980s.

The modest prospect of enhanced residential and recreational facilities was overtaken by a grand scheme for a futuristic Tokyo Teleport Town, one-and-a-half times the size of Tokyo's bustling Shinjuku district and home to 3.6 million people,[105] divided into separate and distinctive residential, commercial, business, and cultural zones linked by huge (eighty-meter-wide) symbolic promenades (rivaling the Champs Elysées) at ground level, and ten-meter-wide skyways high above the ground.[106] The cost of the project gradually grew from original estimates of between three and four trillion yen, to eight trillion yen, and by late in 1991, to a staggering ten trillion yen. Although the project flourished under the dual sponsorship of Governor Suzuki and Deputy

Prime Minister Kanemaru, the political crises that shook Japan during the early 1990s saw Kanemaru thoroughly disgraced. However, backed by a powerful promotion body on which six national ministries are represented, his works outlived him, and in 1993, 640 cranes and 30,000 workers engaged in basic site construction of Teleport Town continued to work around the clock.[107] The works were being conducted under the aegis of the forty-three large general construction (zenekon) companies that were understood to have contributed to Liberal-Democratic Party funds and therefore be at the heart of the "structural corruption." This did not seem to constitute a fatal encumbrance in post-LDP times.

However, the scale of the project was such that in the recession of the early 1990s, its progress was slowed, and its wisdom and economic sense increasingly questioned. Critics questioned its relevance to actual social needs, its extravagance, and also its economic viability. (With Makuhari Messe just completed, did Tokyo need yet another International Exhibition Center?) Even without the Waterfront Subcenter, it was estimated that available commercial space in Tokyo would exceed demand by some 1,000 hectares, or sixty times the space available in the Kasumigaseki Building, by the end of the century.[108] As of July 1993, the average occupancy rate of newly opened buildings in Tokyo was 60.8 percent, in parts of Shinjuku as low as 32 percent, and in certain buildings no more than 11 percent.[109] As construction proceeded, it seemed that all chance for decentralization had been lost. Tokyo had become a megalopolis of thirty million people living within a radius of fifty kilometers.

By the mid-1990s, much of the bloated excess of the late-1980s bubble had melted away. However, one big project that remained, at least nominally, was the Tokyo Frontier Expo. In April 1990, Governor Suzuki advanced the idea of a major international event that would be held on the Waterfront site of the projected Teleport Town, across Rainbow Bridge from central Tokyo, and would rank with the Tokyo Olympics of 1964 and the Osaka Expo of 1970 as a major international attraction. The Frontier Expo was supposed to suggest lifestyles of the twenty-first century, which would push back the frontiers of the geofront (deep underground), the space-front (high in the sky), and the waterfront.[110] Because the public response was lukewarm, and corporate enthusiasm difficult to arouse in the recession, the project, which was supposed to open in 1994, was postponed. It was revived as World

City Expo Tokyo '96—Urban Frontier, which was scheduled to run from March to October 1996. It was announced as an expo that would focus on the problems of cities—population growth, housing, leisure, traffic, environment, and welfare—presenting in distilled form a Japanese vision of the city of the next century. After a groundbreaking ceremony in October 1994, work proceeded on the many pavilions that would make up what seemed to be essentially a huge theme park. There would be exhibitions on the history of Tokyo (featuring nineteenth-century streetcars); a contemporary linear motor (or magnetic-levitation) vehicle; an Ecology Plaza, a space station (courtesy of NASA); reconstructions of world cities, from Turkish rock houses to Indonesian grass houses; and a Wonder City devoted to the latest virtual-reality fantasies.[111] A conference on the subject of world cities was to be cosponsored by the United Nations as part of the exposition. Twenty million visitors were anticipated, well over a trillion yen was spent, and over forty countries had committed to participate.

All told, in the early 1990s, there were about forty major projects underway around Tokyo Bay, including the Trans-Bay Highway (to be constructed between 1989 and 1996 at a cost of about 1.13 trillion yen, and including a 9.8-kilometer stretch of tunnel under the bay),[112] the new Tokyo Airport (at Haneda, costing 1.15 trillion yen, for completion in 1995); the Minato Mirai 21 or 21st Century Port City at Yokohama (a 186-hectare development of hotels, museums, conference center, and offices, to cost a total of more than two trillion yen by the year 2000), the Makuhari New City, and a new Research and Development City at Kazuza. For the trans-bay bridge, the hills of Bōsō in Chiba Prefecture were being leveled to produce 900 million cubic meters of earth (about twelve times that required to build the Suez Canal).[113] About one-fifth of the bay that had existed in 1868 was gone.[114]

Architects have been prominent among visionaries of a new Tokyo. In 1960, Tange Kenzō conceived of the city as built along three axes—city (old Tokyo), capital (the Marunouchi-Kasumigaseki area), and international (the waterfront). In the 1980s, Kurokawa Kisho proposed extending the capital by constructing a 30,000-hectare island within Tokyo Bay and cutting a swath of canals and freeways in and around the city.[115] Five million people could be relocated on the island, and another million in a new city, Bōsō New Town, which would be built at the Chiba end of the bridge. The estimated cost of realizing his vision amounts to $2,450 billion (around 300 trillion yen, or in other terms a sum twenty times greater than the cost of the Apollo space program) over thirty-five years. The island construction projects would require a staggering 8,400 million cubic meters of fill, 125 times the scale of Suez.[116] Kurokawa, whose ideas found strong political support in Japan during the Nakasone government years and after, uses the 1990's most overworked slogan, "*kyōsei*," meaning "symbiosis," or quite literally, "living together," to describe his vision.[117]

There were also plans for construction of a second expressway link between Tokyo and Osaka (for construction between 1993 and 2002 at a cost of eight trillion yen) and a mag-lev train (to cut the time of the 500-kilometer journey from Tokyo to Osaka to about one hour) by the early twenty-first century. When one reads of Japanese interest in the theoretical possibilities of transport in vacuum-sealed tunnels deep underground reaching such speeds that it would be possible to reach Osaka in about one minute, or New York in an hour, it is impossible to dismiss them as science fiction.[118]

Transportation of goods within the vastly expanded Tokyo area could be facilitated by the construction of a network of seventy- to one-hundred meter deep transport tunnels. A second freeway link is also planned (for completion between 1993 and 2002, at a cost of about eight trillion yen), and new bullet train lines are being constructed in various parts of the country (with 1.4 trillion yen to be spent on them by 2001). Other plans, so far only on drawing boards, envisage sinking much of the Tokyo commuter rail network (the Yamanote and part of the Chūō lines) deep underground to free up space for redevelopment,[119] and building other islands in various locations, such as one, imaginatively entitled Japan Sea Acropolis, to go in the seas between Japan and Russia and Korea.[120]

Despite the recession of the early 1990s, visionary plans for transforming the city continued to be drawn up on the planning boards of the major construction companies. While the tallest building in the world at present is the Sears Tower in Chicago (443 meters), and the tallest in Japan is Yokohama's Landmark Tower (296 meters), Kajima and Obayashi were both working on designs for an 800-meter (200-story) Dynamic Intelligent Building, to be known as DIB–200 (Kajima) and Millennium Tower (Obayashi). One of the architects described the DIB–200 as "a pleasant place for a population equivalent to that of a middle-sized town."[121] More ambitiously, Takenaka was working on a 1,000-meter-high Sky City 1000, which would accommodate 35,000 residents and 100,000 office workers in "a synthetic, yet totally comprehensive environment which will unite both urban functions and nature with the goal of developing the vertical utilization of urban space."[122] Shimizu, with plans for TRY 2004, a building two kilometers high and covering a ground area of about eight square kilometers, and Taisei, with its grandiose construction X-SEED 4000, shaped like Mount Fuji and exceeding it in height by several hundred meters (so that dwellers in the penthouse suites would be able to look *down* on the sacred mountain), recognized that their ambitions would probably not be realized till the mid-twenty-first century.

The ambition to become the "highest" was not confined to Japan. Hong Kong seemed likely to claim the title of world's tallest building if it completed a planned 480-meter structure by 1998, while Kuala Lumpur is planning a 450-meter Twin Tower construction, and Chungking a 517-meter one, presumably for the early twenty-first century.[123]

These grand tunneling and nature-transforming construction projects would extend the perimeters of the already huge megalopolises of Tokyo and Osaka, shrinking what pockets of nature still remain in their vicinity and contributing in substantial measure to global warming by their erection of huge edifices of steel, glass, and concrete. Tokyo now has no natural coastline left at all, while its adjacent prefectures of Kanagawa and Chiba have 6 and 2.9 kilometers respectively (in sum, 1.2 percent of the 753-kilometer coastline around Tokyo).[124] Tokyo Bay, once a rich trove of marine and aquatic life,[125] is "threatened with extinction . . . its waters will become a vast aquatic dump for the refuse of industrial civilization."[126]

The residents of a megalopolis such as Tokyo were ill-served by the neoconservative policies of the late 1980s, which wrought as much environmental and economic damage as they were subsequently found to have done to the moral and political fabric of society. As speculative fires raged around the inner city lands, fed by banks, bureaucrats, and corporate greed, the salaried middle-class masses were driven farther into the suburban fringes, their working day stretched by hours of commuting each way, and deprived of any real prospect of ever owning a home. Some five million people were living in cramped wooden apartments measuring less than the recognized minimum of fifty square meters.[127] The possibility of achieving any symbiosis with nature, other than within the controlled atmosphere of the great entertainment or shopping complexes, shrank. Tokyo residents enjoyed an average 2.6 square meters per head of urban park lands, compared to 30.4 meters in London, 37.4 in Bonn, 45.7 in Washington, and 12.2 in Paris,[128] and the remaining green spaces, currently designated agricultural, would be threatened by a new wave of development if the deregulation being recommended at high-level advisory committees is adopted.[129]

There is a further dimension, increasingly serious as development and population growth continues unabated in the Tokyo region. It is the atmospheric effect known as heat island. Because of the combined consequences of constant heat emissions from autos, air conditioners, and the like, the heat-retaining qualities of concrete, the greenhouse effect from carbon-dioxide emissions, and the diminution of vegetation, Tokyo is heating up at a rate more than ten times the world average.[130] According to the Environment Agency, tropical nights (when the August night temperature does not fall below twenty-five degrees centigrade) increased from an average of 2.6 in the 1920s to 13.6 in the 1980s;[131] central Tokyo is on average about four degrees warmer than it was in premodern times, and the temperature in areas of central Tokyo (such as Shinjuku or Shinagawa) rises to as much as eight degrees above that in suburban districts such as Hachioji.[132] Furthermore, the hotter the city becomes, the more people seek respite by buying air conditioners. Heat pollution is an inevitable consequence of the megalopolis phenomenon.

This suggests that the concentration of population, amenities, and facilities in the capital area is approaching an untenable scale. Indeed, as the environmental and energy specialist Saitō Takeo puts it, Tokyo is becoming uninhabitable.[133] And, while the Japanese government pledges its support for finding solutions to the problem of global warming, and to the idea of a sustainable economy, it has yet to address the contradiction between that goal and the commitment to the policies of expansion and growth.

As this chapter was being revised for publication, however, two events occurred that may have the effect of causing a radical rethinking on current directions: the earthquake in Kobe on January 17, 1995, and the election in April 1995 of a Tokyo governor who vowed to scrap the scheduled World City Exposition '96, which he described as "a mistake from the beginning . . . just throwing the taxpayers' money away," and to also scale down the waterfront project as a whole, turning it into "a park or a forest."[134] Of these two events, one was an example of the physical constraints on the construction state, and the other pointed to a growing intellectual grasp and political will to seek a path beyond it.

Development, Democracy, and Direction

At the heart of the Japanese growth during the 1980s was a contradiction that slowly became manifest in the 1990s. Since entering upon the tasks of modernization, industrialization, and catchup with the West in the late nineteenth century, successive generations of Japanese people toiled in the belief that its sacrifices would make life better and easier for the next. Capital had accumulated and technology refined to the point where, in the 1990s, the world turned to Japanese engineers for advice on tunneling, bridge building, and island building instead of to the Scots, the Germans, or the Americans.

Undoubtedly, the Japanese development of recent decades has shown an extraordinary vigor and a Promethean energy, expressed in ideas of lopping off mountains, filling in the seas, and exploring the deep geo-front, akin perhaps to that which marked the launching of Crusades and the founding of empires in other times. Yet too much of the energy, capital, and skills of the Japanese people had been appropriated, mobilized, and focused in a political economy of exploitation, both human and material, that ultimately exhausted both the people and their environment.

Despite great accomplishments, Japanese expansion has outrun the social and political structures necessary to determine social priorities and needs and has begun to threaten the fragile ecosystem. Neither the tempo nor the direction of recent Japanese development is sustainable. The authors of the recent NHK (Japan Broadcasting Corporation) study reached the sober conclusion that the great technical accomplishments, such as the Tokyo Bay and Osaka Bay bridges, and the islands and tunnels, were prodigiously expensive, and even the engineers responsible for them doubt that they could or should be replicated. The new islands are extremely vulnerable to any rise in the oceans due to global warming or to any earthquake (as was tragically illustrated in January 1995). Other worsening environmental problems stemming from the untrammeled growth of recent decades include the disposal (legal or otherwise) of excavated earth and waste-construction materials, both being generated on such scale that there was simply nowhere to put them.

Although the basic infrastructural unity of the Japanese islands—bridges, tunnels, rail, and road, etc.—is now accomplished, and would be little improved by further grand nature remodeling, the real and growing need is for imaginative projects designed to undo some of the damage to the environment: begin *de*concreting the rivers and coast, demolishing some of the dams, restoring some of the rivers to their natural course. Lake Biwa, the country's largest lake, is currently in a perilous state after decades of virtually indiscriminate development, and might cost something like two trillion yen to restore. A social consensus might be formed around the objective, however, as not only would it generate much local employment, but would also stimulate the economy and in so doing rebuild the conditions for viable, sustained prosperity.[135] Careful long-term planning is necessary, but, as I have shown, periodic attempts to devise such a plan in the past have not only failed but done great harm.

One of the more philosophically minded of Japan's postwar corporate leaders, Matsushita Kōnosuke of National-Panasonic, once advocated a 200-year national project for the construction of a new island that would involve leveling 20 percent, or 75,000 square kilometers, of Japan's mountains and dumping them in the sea to create a fifth island about the size of Shikoku. He argued that only the containment and focusing of Japan's energies in some such gigantic project at home could create the sort of national unity and sense of purpose that formerly had come from war.[136] Had Matsushita, writing in 1976, lived to see the depth of friction created internationally by Japan's untrammeled expansion in subsequent years, he would undoubtedly have seen in it further justification for his plan. However, Matsushita's vision of the Japanese people being mobilized to level mountains and fill in the sea lest the force of their impact on the outside world provoke uncontainable anti-Japaneseness, or even lead to war, is a fundamentally impoverished one. In preferring to tie the Japanese people to the treadmill of endless (and meaningless) growth rather than face the possibility of constructive, imaginative engagement with the world, it is even suggestive of despair, reminding one of that army of the "Grand Old Duke of York" that was once marched up the hill and then down again.

In contrast to the grand and supremely confident kyōsei vision of men like Kurokawa are the voices from nonmainstream Japanese society—academics, philosophers, local activists, artists—who are scathing about the failures of three decades of planned regional development in Japan.[137] Fundamentally critical of the hubris of the nature-remaking schemes pursued in Japan over the last several decades, they are skeptical of the idea that Japan has become a prosperous country as a result. They warn that implicit in those grand plans lurk environmental catastrophe, social rootlessness, and irrelevance to actual needs.[138] Instead, these new voices of conscience urge more modest visions of regional sufficiency and autonomy (including food); a shrunken apparatus of central government; and preservation of existing rural, mountain, and coastal communities rather than their displacement by gigantic development corridors of teletopias and green cities. They would turn villages into places in which people would want to live, rather than expand the cities without limit.

They too on occasion employ the word kyōsei to encapsulate their prescription,[139] indicating the existence of a struggle to determine the content of the term, similar perhaps to the struggle in the 1930s to determine what would be the content of the closely related term kyōzon kyōei (coexistence and coprosperity). The attraction of the term, which, though translated as symbiosis, literally means living together, may be its association with an order of community and nature that is widely seen as past, but that exercises a powerful pull on the imagination such that it continues to feed nostalgic longings or to be naively projected into utopian dreams of the future.

What was visible from the slopes of Mount Rokko in 1994 was therefore both old and new: The centrality of construction and public works had been a feature of the Japanese state since Meiji (and earlier). The structural nexus between the reshaping of nature on a massive scale in Osaka Bay and the political corruption that had plagued Japan for a decade and more was plain, yet the political reforms of 1994 did not begin to address it. Furthermore, the pious sentiments about sustainable development and harmony with nature professed by the Japanese delegates to the Rio Conference in the summer of 1992 had not begun to weigh against the insistence on growth at all costs. Even if Japan were to be forced permanently to a low-growth trajectory of, say, 1.4 percent GNP annually, that would mean an economy that doubled in fifty years, quadrupled in 100, and multiplied by 1,000 over the course of 500 years.[140] Such a long-term course would be absurd. Zero growth is the only serious option for humanity and its environment. The attainment of such a stable society may be post-poned during a transitional phase of uncertain length during which resources will need to be transferred on a massive scale to the poor countries of the South in order to achieve the necessary social and economic development. Moreover, there exists the pressing need to rectify damage that has been done to the natural environment caused by the distorted development of recent decades in the advanced countries such as Japan, a process that will require huge investment in the immediate future. The zero-growth orientation is, however, seen as the rankest heresy in the circles of the "wise men" of Tokyo and Osaka.

While Osaka Bay was the fullest flowering of the construction state, it was also site for Japan's most determined effort to cope with a form of capitalism for which there was as yet not even an agreed name, a third generation, post-1945 capitalism. In place of the "heavy, thick, long, and big" (jū-kō-chō-dai) age of heavy and chemical industries in the 1960s, and the "light, thin, short, and small" (kei-haku-tan-shō) miniaturized, electronic age that succeeded it in the 1970s and 1980s, would come an era that in the minds of the burghers of Osaka and Kobe would be one of "beauty, sensitivity, play, and creativity" (bi-kan-yū-sō), in which fashion, tourism, resorts, leisure, and so on would be central. Much of the new Bay Area development (and quite a bit that preceded it) helped to give the Kobe area especially a theme-park atmosphere, "with its faux Italian villas that house boutiques, tanning salons and beer halls, the ultrafast shinkansen bullet trains, the all-female Takarazuka revue and the church-like wedding halls,"[141] not to mention the tinsel-town island developments and the funicular cars stretching up into the mountains behind, with their Swiss farm and British golf course. One of the major developments planned in Kobe is the Leisure World, designed to rival Tokyo's Disneyland, which is scheduled to open on Port Island in 1997 and to attract millions of visitors to experience life in the world's great cities (at their peak)— Rome of the first century, Chang-an of the eighth, New Orleans of the 1920s, etc. The Aquarian World of theme parks and playgrounds was thus the latest conduit for the expansion of the hard-engineering-based construction industry.

The optimistic view of these developments would be to see in them a groping, however confused and contradictory, toward the zero growth future, and a new political economy based on the principles of the humanization of work, the maximization of creative and leisure opportunities, and the rendering of everyday life itself into art.[142] But the pessimistic view would be to see in them the continuing fetishistic pursuit of formulas for new "growth" through the generation and manipulation of the desire to consume.

In 1994, Japan was still in recession. The way out of previous recessions, in 1973, 1979, and 1985, had been to combine increased exports with expansion of domestic demand by public-works spending. Export expansion was unthinkable in the international circumstances of 1994.[143] When the prosecutors in April 1994 signaled an end to their investigations into construction industry corruption after token arrests and indictments, the likelihood was strong that the response to both domestic and Western (especially American) pressures to stimulate the economy would be more pump priming by the traditional method of increased public-works spending. The same bureaucratic planning agencies that for forty years had promoted one after another harebrained notion for the balanced development of the national lands would be invited to come up with further schemes. Their only previous accomplishment was the unprecedented concentration of wealth and power in the coastal corridor between Tokyo and North Kyushu—with 40 percent of the population of the nation in the three megalopolises of Tokyo (Kanto), Nagoya (Chubu), and Osaka (Kansai).

Deliberations did indeed begin early in 1995 toward the preparation of a new, fifth Zensō or Comprehensive National Development Plan, to set the guidelines for national development for the years up to 2010. In fact, if early reports are correct, it would seem that thinking was proceeding along well-established tracks, with plans for the construction of 14,000 kilometers of roadway, a series of new high-speed rail and sea links and airports, a network of East-West cross-archipelagic bridges and tunnels, and perhaps a new, or second, capital. When Japan endorsed the Uruguay Round agreement of GATT at the end of 1993 (see Chapter 3), the domestic deal put together by the coalition government under its socialist premier involved a payment of just over six trillion yen to "help farmers adjust to foreign competition."[144] Most of it, in practice, would go to revitalize the circuits of the construction state, building bridges and roads, and draining paddy fields. Several trillion yen more were then appropriated for the postearthquake reconstruction of Kobe, a process of reinforcement of bridges, tunnels, and buildings that would last until well into the next millennium. After the recession, scandals that exposed and for a time seemed to threaten the construction state, and after the profound questions raised by the earthquake itself, it was back to business as usual; a new boondoggle was in the making.

There can be little prospect of the underlying problems being addressed unless the grossly uneven and inequitable pattern of development that resulted from the various plans for the comprehensive development of Japan's lands is recognized, and the fiscal crisis of the state and the structural corruption it has fed or produced recognized. Out of the political chaos and indecisiveness that prevailed in the mid-1990s, it was perhaps too much to look for a vision appropriate to the new millennium. Until politicians with the wisdom of Iroquois tribal elders emerge in Japan, the structures described in this chapter are therefore likely to continue.

Notes

1. NHK, Technopower Project, ed, *Kyodai kensetsu no sekai*, 4 vols., Vol. 3, *Kaijō kūkō: shinka to no arasoi*, p. 210. See also Chris Falvey, "Airport Set to Rank with World's Most Inefficient," *The Australian*, July 5, 1994, p. 9, and Itagaki Yuka, "Naru ka 'Ajia no genkan,' " *Aera*, May 16, 1994, pp. 30–35.

2. Itagaki, "Naruka," 1994, p. 33.

3. This construction project will consume 200,000 tons of steel and 1.4 million cubic meters of concrete (Sano Shin'ichi, "Tōkyō-wan ni nagekomareru yamayama," *Aera*, December 15, 1992, p. 8).

4. Onishi Masafumi, President of Osaka Chamber of Commerce and Industry, in "Kansai kūkō e no dai dōmyaku," *Asahi shimbun*, April 2, 1994.

5. Sanukida Satoshi, "Bei eria hō ni tsuite," Osaka-wan shinpojiumu, ed., *Osaka-wan no hon*, 1993, pp. 60–71, at pp. 68–69.

6. I am most grateful to Professor Sanukida for his advice on these matters, and learned greatly from his articles. Sanukida Satoshi, "Osaka-wan wa ima" in ibid at pp. 28–40; "Osaka wan bei eria tokubetsuhō," *Sekai*, March 1993, pp. 180–81; and "Bei eria hō ni tsuite."

7. Shigeto Tsuru, *Japan's Capitalism: Creative Defeat and Beyond*, Cambridge, Cambridge: Cambridge University Press, 1993, p. 130.

8. Sanukida, "Bei eria hō ni tsuite," p. 62.

9. *Kōbe kūkō nyūsu*, no. 5, March 28, 1994.

10. "Suishin 15 mētoru made umetate sōtei," *Asahi shimbun*, March 3, 1994.

11. A term favored by the Ministry of Construction. See the two-page feature advertisement in *Asahi shimbun*, April 2, 1994.

12. "Osaka-wan gururi daihenshin" (Total transformation of Osaka Bay), *Asahi shimbun*, May 5, 1992.

13. "Suishin suru 15 mētoru made umetate sōtei," *Asahi shimbun*, March 3, 1994. (Petitions expressing opposition, however, attract many thousands of signatures.)

14. I owe the Iroquois reference to Jean Chesneaux, writing in *Le Monde Diplomatique*, November 1993, who in turn was referring to Ignacy Sachs, "Une terre en renaissance, les semences du developpement durable," Le Monde Diplomatique, ed., *Savoirs 2*, Paris, October 1993.

15. Hajime Matsuzaki, *Construction Industry Unionism in Japan*, especially Chapter Seven entitled "Early History of Construction Industry and Unionism," unpublished doctoral thesis, University of New South Wales, 1995.

16. Yoneyama Shōzō and Kiuchi Takashi, *Kensetsu sangyōron*, Tokyo, Toshi bunkasha, 1983, pp. 23, 35.

17. Nihon keizai shimbunsha, ed., *Bijuaru—Nihon no sangyō*, 1994, pp. 114–15.

18. Matsuzaki, *Construction Industry Union in Japan*, Chapter Eight, p. 5.

19. N.a., "Zusetsu kōkyō jigyō," *Sekai*, December 1993, pp. 47–53, at p. 53.

20. "Kōkyō tōshi 510 chō en ni," *Nihon keizai shimbun*, June 15, 1994. (This is the Ministry of Construction estimate, difficult to analyze because it comprises various budgetary items: not only the specific item of public works but also a significant proportion of "regional tax allocation" and "public finance and investment.") For a perceptive and thorough analysis of the fiscal dimensions of Japan's construction state," see Aoki Hidekazu and Kawamiya Nobuo, "Nihon doken kokka ron," *Chūkyō daigaku kyōyō ronshū*, Vol. 35, No. 1, 1994, pp. 29–88.

21. Tahara Sōichirō, "Shakaitō daijin nani o kaeta ka," *Shūkan bunshun*, May 5–12, 1994, pp. 44–57, at pp. 46–47.

22. Aoki and Kawamiya, "Nihon doken kokka ron," pp. 43–44.

23. Chalmers Johnson, "Nihon wa shihonshugi-chū saidai no ochikobore shika nai," *Sapio*, April 28, 1994, p. 22. (U.S. defense expenditure at the height of the Cold War in 1989 amounted to $315 billion.)

24. Ishikawa Masumi, "Konken seiji," Rinji Zōkan *Sekai*, No. 594, April 1994, pp. 132–35, at p. 133 (offering this proportion as an *Asahi shimbun* estimate).

25. Ochiai Nobuhiko, *Nihon no shōtai*, Tokyo, Za Masada, 1994, p. 224. Building costs in Japan are also estimated to be about two to three times the U.S. figure, while labor costs are about one half (Takahashi Ei-ichi, "Nihon no kōkyō jigyō wa takai," *Tōyō Keizai*, October 30, 1993, pp. 18–19).

26. Aoki and Kawamiya, "Nihon doken kokka ron," p. 33. Definition from *The Macquarie Dictionary*, 2d rev. ed., 1987.

27. Sawa Takamitsu, quoted in Teruoka Itsuko, Nakamura Tatsuya, and Nishikawa Jun, "Kakudai keizai kara seijuku keizai e," Rinji zōkan *Sekai*, No. 694, April 1994, pp. 263–78, at p. 268.

28. For a convenient recent summary, Tahara Sōichirō, "'Kokuei zenekon' ni dangō ga kireru ka," *Shūkan bunshun*, April 28, 1994, pp. 48–53. In December 1994 the mayor of Kita-Ibaraki was arrested on corruption charges connected with golf-course construction. He subsequently committed suicide while in detention, and his successor as mayor was also arrested in March 1995 (Jiji Press News, "Kitaibaraki mayor arrested on bribery charges," March 2, 1995).

29. Nakazato Noriyasu, "Zenekon 'oshoku rettō' o tsukuriageta 'amakaduri' ni mesu," *Views*, November 24, 1994, pp. 45–48.

30. Itō Keiko, "Kanemaru hizōkkō eikō to tenraku," *Aera*, March 21, 1994, pp. 9–11.

31. Zusetsu kōkyō jigyō, cit, and for 1993, Matsuzaki, *Construction Industry*

Union in Japan, Chapter Eight, p. 19 (quoting *Nihon keizai shimbun*, December 30, 1993).

32. N.a., "Amakudari no kensetsu kanryō 111 nin kōteki hōjin o keiyu," *Asahi shimbun*, May 4, 1994. See also Murata Takanori, "Dēta ban—Nihon kensetsu fuhai chizu," *Tōyō Keizai*, August 14–21, 1993, pp. 16–17.

33. Tahara, "Kokuei zenekon," p. 51.

34. See table in Mamiya Jun, "Kensetsu fuhai no kōzō," *Tōyō keizai*, August 14–21, 1993, pp. 6–9, at p. 9.

35. Tanaka Akira, "Kōseii wa kokuhatsu taisei tsukure," *Asahi shimbun*, April 19, 1994.

36. Sataka Makoto, "Zenekon no taishitsu masaka ni 'bōryokudan,' " *Views*, November 24, 1993, p. 49.

37. Aoki and Kawamiya, "Nihon doken kokka ron," p. 29.

38. Mizutani Kenji (vice president and chief director of Tokai Research Institute), "Nichibei dōjidai hasan ga sekai kyōfu o yobiokosu," *Bart*, No. 9, May 9, 1994, pp. 30–32, at p. 32. (Mizutani notes that the U.S. repayment rate on interest on its debt is only 13.7 percent of budget outlays.)

39. Kuno Osamu, *Kuno Osamu sekai o mitsumeru*, Jiyū Kokuminsha, 1995, pp. 83–84.

40. Aoki Hidekazu and Kawamiya Nobuo, "Hasan ni mukau Nihon no ruiseki zaisei akaji," *Chūkyō daigaku kyōyō ronshū*, Vol. 35, No. 3, 1994, pp. 19–64, at p. 37.

41. Noguchi Yukio (Hitotsubashi University), "Nihon keizai no bijon: kokusai de kōkyō tōshi zō o," *Asahi shimbun*, May 3, 1994.

42. Aoki and Kawamiya, "Nihon doken kokka ron," p. 32.

43. Ibid., p. 57.

44. Ibid., p. 81.

45. Vikram Khanna, "Long way to go to revive Japan's economy," *Business Times*, Singapore, September 22, 1995.

46. Aoki and Kawamiya, "Nihon doken kokka ron," pp. 33–34.

47. Ui Jun, "Kinsei no ekoroji shisō no nagare" (Trends on ecology in Japan since the seventeenth century), *Okinawa daigaku kiyō*, No. 9, March 1992, pp. 30–44.

48. For a convenient summary, see Miyamoto Ken-ichi, *Kankyō to kaihatsu*, Tokyo, Iwanami, 1992, pp. 65–85 passim.

49. Miyamoto Ken-ichi, "Kokudo sōgō kaihatsu no 30 nen," *Sekai*, August 1992, pp. 169–76. (Reproduced in slightly revised form as "Kokudo kaihatsu to kōgai," in Rinji Zōkan *Sekai*, No. 594, April 1994, *Kiiwādo sengo Nihon seiji 50 nen*, pp. 98–101.)

50. On a very recent trend away from the concreting of rivers, known in Europe as "near nature engineering" (with the implication of "back to nature"), and in Japan as "more nature engineering" (*tashizengata kōhō*), see NHK, Vol. 1, *Suiatsu to tatakau damu unga*, 1993, pp. 244 ff.

51. *Mizu shigen hakusho*, quoted in Tsuchida Keiji, "Kankyō fukugen ni shin hōritsu no seitei o," *Asahi shimbun*, March 29, 1994.

52. Ueno Hideo, "Damu ni mirai wa nai," *Sekai*, August 1995, pp. 217–24, at p. 217.

53. Ishikawa Tetsuya, "Kurobegawa Dashidaira damu haisa mondai," *Shūkan kinyōbi*, April 29, 1994, pp. 36–41, at p. 39.

54. Tajima Kazuo, "Damu keikaku minaosu jiki da," *Asahi shimbun*, March 17, 1994.

55. Ibid.

56. Tada Minoru, "Sengyōshi wa uttaeru," *Shūkan kinyōbi*, No. 28, June 3, 1994, pp. 38–42.

57. Honda Katsuichi (interviewing Omori Katsuyoshi), "Nagaragawa no kakōseki kensetsu," *Asahi shimbun*, October 13, 1991.

58. For a convenient, detailed chronology of plans for the river, 1959–93, see Amano Reiko and David Brower, *Nagaragawa kara Nippon o miru*, Tokyo, Iwanami Bukkuretto, No. 313, 1993, pp. 10–13.

59. Momose Toshiaki, "Kankyōcho chōkan o dōkatsu shita Kanemaru Shin," *Tōyō keizai*, August 14–21, 1993, pp. 11–14.

60. Naoya Sugio, "Opposition to Nagara Dam building up," *Japan Times*, January 6, 1992.

61. "Yuragu kanryō shinwa," Part 3, *Asahi shinbun*, March 29, 1994.

62. Quoted in Amano and Brower, "Nagaragawa kara Nippon," pp. 3–4.

63. *Asahi shimbun*, June 25, 1993, quoted in ibid., p. 16.

64. One-third of officials of the Water Resource Development Corporation (Mizu shigen kaihatsu kōdan) proceed after retirement to take up positions in construction companies or consultant firms closely connected with the dam business (Baba Shin, "Damu kanren kigyō e OB 3 wari amakudari," *Asahi shimbun*, May 23, 1994).

65. A court case by two Ainu plaintiffs to prevent the appropriation of their land for dam-construction purposes was launched in May 1993, based on the inherent right of the indigenous people to preservation of their culture ("Ainu seek to halt dam construction," *Japan Times*, March 29, 1994).

66. Ueno, "Damu ni mirai," pp. 217–19.

67. Peter Hadfield, "The Revenge of the Rain Gods," *New Scientist*, August 20, 1994, pp. 14–15.

68. See, for example, the series on the Shimanto River in Shikoku by Tada Minoru in *Shūkan kinyōbi* commencing April 22, 1994, subsequently published as *Shimantogawa o aruite kudaru*, Tsukiji shoten, 1995.

69. Jun Ui, *Industrial Pollution in Japan*, Tokyo, United Nations University Press, 1992, p. 71 (and see table of rate of reclamation from 1600 at p. 72).

70. Tsuru, pp. 102–3.

71. Ibid, p. 130.

72. Matsumoto Satoru, "Kokusaiteki ni mo jūyō na higata o, naze 'jinkōjima' ni umetateru no," *Shūkan kinyōbi*, February 3, 1995, pp. 48–49. See also Reiji Yoshida, "Boondoggle, Bird Threat Seen in Hakata Port Projects," *Japan Times*, October 27, 1994.

73. According to this survey, 565 kilometers of natural coastline had been lost in the preceding five years (*Kankyō hakusho, zōsetsu*, 1994, p. 372).

74. "Higata" (Tidelands), *Asahi shimbun*, September 6, 1992.

75. Miyamoto Ken-ichi, *Kankyō to kaihatsu*, Tokyo, Iwanami, 1992, p. 189.

76. Shinobu Ohe, "Future City Planning: The Japanese Experience and the

MFP," in Gavan McCormack, ed., *Bonsai Australia Banzai: Multifunctionpolis and the Making of a Special Relationship with Japan*, Sydney, Pluto, 1991, pp. 84–102, at p. 94.

77. Tessa Morris-Suzuki, "MFP and the Japanese Developmental Model," in ibid., pp. 123–37, at pp. 128–29.

78. Miyamoto, *Kankyō to kaihatsu*, 1992, pp. 190–91 (and Table, p. 191). See also Miyamoto Ken-ichi, ed., *Daitoshi to kombinat Osaka*, Tokyo, Chikuma, 1977.

79. Miyamoto, *Kankyō to kaihatsu*, p. 191 (quoting Ohara Sōichirō, president of Kurashiki Rayon, on Mizushima).

80. Editorial, "Kokudo seisaku ga sabakareta," *Asahi shimbun*, March 24, 1994.

81. Miyamoto, *Kankyō to kaihatsu*, pp. 198–99.

82. Chalmers Johnson, *MITI and the Japanese Miracle: The Growth of Industrial Policy, 1925–1975*, Stanford, Stanford University Press, 1982, p. 316.

83. Ui, *Industrial Pollution in Japan*, p. 3.

84. Miyamoto, *Kankyō to kaihatsu*, p. 182.

85. Sugita Satoshi, "'Jidōsha' wa kempō ihan da," *Shūkan kinyōbi*, February 11, 1994, pp. 27–38, at p. 32. Official police estimates put the figure at 453,000, but they include only those who died within twenty-four hours of an accident.

86. Aoki Hidekazu, "Kankyō hakai to zaisei hatan kara nukedasō," Kyōdō kumiai keiei kenkyūjō, ed., *Kenkyū geppō*, July 1995.

87. Saitō Ichirō, "Tanaka kara Nakasone made no michi," *Aera*, March 21, 1994, pp. 14–15.

88. One of the few voices consistently critical of the "automobilization" of Japan has been the economist Uzawa Hirofumi. See his just-published collected works: *Uzawa Hirofumi chosakushū*, 12 vols., Iwanami shoten, 1994, especially Vol. 1.

89. Tanaka Kakuei, *Nihon rettō kaizōron*, Tokyo, Nikkan kōgyō shimbunsha, 1972. (In English as *Building a New Japan: A Plan for Remodelling the Japanese Archipelago*, Tokyo, translated by Simul International, Simul Press, 1973.)

90. Miyamoto, *Kankyō to kaihatsu*, pp. 193–94.

91. For an analysis at the time, see Jon Halliday and Gavan McCormack, *Japanese Imperialism Today: Co-Prosperity in Greater East Asia*, London and New York, Penguin and Monthly Review, 1973, pp. 176–78.

92. Nakamura Takafusa, *Lectures on Modern Japanese Economic History 1926–1994*, Tokyo, LTCB, International Library Selection, No. 1, 1994 (English translation of *Shōwa keizaishi*, Iwanami, 1986), pp. 248–49.

93. For a chart of how the theory worked, as against how it was supposed to work, see Miyamoto, *Kankyō to kaihatsu*, p. 187.

94. Shimada Kei, "Nuclear Curse—A Report from Rokkasho-mura," *Ampo: Japan-Asia Quarterly Review*, Vol. 25, No. 2, 1994, pp. 33–36.

95. Masayuki Sasaki, "Japan, Australia and the Multifunctionpolis," in McCormack, ed., *Bonsai Australia*, pp. 138–51, at p. 142.

96. "Committee for Consideration of Technopolis 2000 Plan," a MITI report, quoted by Sasaki, ibid., p. 145.

97. Ibid. For a table of the targets and achievements of the Oita and Toyama

technopolises, see especially pp. 146–47, and on Kumamoto, see Morris-Suzuki in ibid., at p. 130.

98. Tokyo land prices rose by 85.7 percent in the year from July 1986 to June 1987, as against an average rise for the country as a whole of 9.7 percent (Miyamoto, *Kankyō to kaihatsu*, p. 231).

99. Miyamoto Ken'ichi, "Nihon kankyō hōkoku—Rizōtohō o kangaeru," *Asahi jānaru*, November 10, 1989, p. 53.

100. Ohe, "Future City Planning," p. 98. And see Hosokawa Morihiro, "Matohazure no 'seikai saihen' rongi," *Gekkan Asahi*, April 1992, pp. 8–31.

101. Ohe, "Future City Planning," p. 98, for comment on one "intelligent city" in Ibaraki Prefecture.

102. For a further analysis of this phenomenon, see my "Pacific Dreamtime and Japan's New Millennialism," *Australian Outlook*, Vol. 43, No. 2, August 1989, pp. 64–73.

103. NHK 1993, Vol. 1, pp. 156–60.

104. Suda Harumi, "Mujun ga shūchū suru rinkai fukutoshin keikaku," *Sekai*, February 1991, pp. 348–54, at p. 349.

105. Okabe Yūzō, "Rinkai 10 chō en purojekuto sei-kan-zai yuchaku no kōzō," *Sekai*, December 1993, pp. 82–100. See also the same author's *Dokyumento—Zenekon yuchaku 10 chō en purojekuto—rinkai fukutoshin keikaku,* Akebi shobō, 1993.

106. Takashi Onishi, "The Waterfront Subcenter Project—Hopes for Area Transport," *The Wheel Extended: A Toyota Quarterly Review*, special issue, 1993, pp. 4–5.

107. Okabe, "Rinkai 10," p. 86.

108. Suda, "Mujun ga shūchū," pp. 350–52.

109. Okabe, "Rinkai 10," p. 100.

110. Okabe, *Dokyumento*, pp. 162–78.

111. Hitoshi Fukui, "World City Exposition Tokyo '96," *Asahi Evening News*, Supplement, November 23, 1994, p. 7.

112. Sanō, "Tōkyō-wan ni," pp. 6–10

113. Sanō, "Tōkyō-wan ni," p. 6.

114. Sanō, "Tōkyō-wan ni," 1992, p. 7.

115. Kurokawa Kisho, ed., "21 seiki e no teigen: Tōkyō to chihō no kyōsei" (Proposal for the 21st century: Tokyo and the regions living together), *Lightup*, April 1992. This is a convenient resume of the more substantial text by Kurokawa and "Gurūpu 2025": *Tōkyō kaizō keikaku no kinkyū teian: 2025 nen no kokudo to Tōkyō* (Urgent proposal for a plan for reshaping Tokyo: Tokyo and the national lands in year 2025).

116. Ibid.

117. See also Kurokawa's *The Architecture of Symbiosis,* New York, Rizzoli, 1988.

118. "Kansei ressha," in Jiyū kokuminsha, ed., *Gendai yōgo no kiso chishiki*, Tokyo, 1993, p. 573 (New York to Los Angeles in less than two minutes, according to the calculations at MIT in Boston). A Swiss consortium was reported in 1994 to be beginning a feasibility study on an "underground high-speed magnetic levitation (maglev) train system" that would be pressurized and able to travel at 500 km per hour, not in a vacuum but in a tunnel with reduced atmospheric

pressure (*Financial Times*, "Fast Train Has Swiss Up in Air," *The Australian*, September 20, 1994).

119. A Kumagai plan, which it reckons could be done for about $80 billion ("Chika 100 mētoru ni JR sen," *Asahi shimbun*, June 15, 1988).

120. A Tobishima Corporation idea: a 3.14 square kilometer island at estimated cost about $250 billion (¥33 trillion), to be built over fifteen years and accommodate between 50,000 and 100,000 people ("Floating Island Proposed by Tokyo Firm," *Japan Times*, September 6, 1991).

121. Bill O'Neill, "Cities in the Sky," *New Scientist*, October 2, 1993, pp. 22–24.

122. Ibid., quoting from the Takenaka brochure.

123. Nakasaki Takashi, "Shinka suru chō kōsō biru," *Aera*, April 25, 1994, pp. 42–43.

124. Sanō, "Tōkyō-wan ni," p. 7.

125. Kevin Short, "Tokyo Bay: Crabs and Concrete," *Japan Environment Monitor*, Vol. 2, No. 3, July 1989, pp. 1, 6–7, 16.

126. Yasuda Yasoi, "Tokyo On and Under the Bay," *Japan Quarterly*, 35, 2, April-June 1988, p. 124.

127. "Watakushi wa usagi ja nai," editorial, *Asahi shimbun*, May 22, 1994 (1.4 million households of average size of four persons).

128. Miyazaki Isamu, *Sekai keizai zusetsu*, Tokyo, Iwanami shinsho, 1994, p. 195.

129. According to Miyamoto (*Kankyō to kaihatsu*, p. 233) the three main cities of Tokyo, Nagoya, and Osaka had a total of 37,000 hectares of such "agricultural" land.

130. Ueno Hideo, "Tōkyō hōkai," Part 4, "Netsu osen," *Sekai*, August 1993, pp. 144–149, at p. 145 (seven degrees centigrade per 100 years as against world average of 0.7 degrees).

131. Quoted in Okabe, *Dokyumento—Zenekon yuchaku*, p. 81.

132. "Tensei jingo," *Asahi shimbun*, September 6, 1992.

133. Ibid.

134. Ben Hills, "At $20bn, He's a Real Party Pooper," *Sydney Morning Herald*, April 29, 1995; see also Yamanoue Reiko and Yamamoto Masao, "Kōyaku wa Aoshima chiji no seimeisen," *Aera*, April 24, 1995, pp. 6–9.

135. Tsuchida Keiji, Secretary of the All-Japan Council for Rivers, Lakes and Swamps, "Kankyō fukugen no shin hōritsu no seitei o," *Asahi shimbun*, March 29, 1994.

136. Matsushita Kōnosuke, "Watashi no kokudo baizōron," *Bungei shunjū*, May 1976, pp. 136–42, translated as "Doubling Japan's Land Space," *Japan Interpreter*, Vol. 11, No. 3, Winter 1977, pp. 279–92.

137. Miyamoto Kenichi, "Kokudo sono kaihatsu no 30 nen," *Sekai*, August 1992, pp. 169–76.

138. Perhaps the best-known are Miyamoto Kenichi, Uzawa Hirofumi, and Murota Takeshi of Ritsumeikan, Chūō and Hitotsubashi Universities respectively. See, for example, Uzawa Hirofumi and Murota Takeshi, "Jizokuteki kaihatsu to keizaigaku no yakuwari," *Ekonomisuto*, March 10, 1992, pp. 82–88; Miyamoto Kenichi, "Shūchū hōka o abita Nihongata uotafuronto kaihatsu," *Gekkan Asahi*, June 1991, and, also by Miyamoto, "Kankyō hozon

no wakunai de keizai o hatten saseyo," *Ekonomisuto*, March 17, 1992, pp. 24–31.

139. See, for example, Tsuchida Takashi, *Kyōsei no jidai*, Jushinsha, 1981; Hanazaki Kōhei, *Aidentiti to kyōsei no tetsugaku*, Chikuma shobō, 1993; and Uchihashi Katsuto, *Kyōsei no daichi*, Iwanami shinsho, 1995.

140. Oonoki Yoshinori and Fukuma Koji, "Zero seichō no susume," *Aera*, January 3–10, 1994, p. 58.

141. Yoichi Clark Shimatsu, "After the Earthquake, an Economy Built on Sand Is Exposed," *Los Angeles Times*, January 20, 1995.

142. See Tsuru Shigeto, " 'Seichō' de wa naku 'rōdō no ningenka' o," *Sekai*, April 1994, pp. 84–98, at p. 96. (Here I have slightly reworked, rather than directly translated, Tsuru's words.)

143. Itō Mitsuharu, "90 nendai fukyō wa kōkyō tōshi de wa sukuenai," *Sekai*, December 1993, pp. 56–70, at p. 56.

144. Hasegawa Hiroshi, "Tsukamigane 6 chō en wa yami no naka," *Aera*, December 26, 1994, pp. 16–19.

2

The Leisure State: Work, Rest, and Consumption

Toward a "Sensitive" Capitalism

It is well known that Japan is an economic superpower—the world's greatest asset country[1]—with the biggest per capita GNP, the biggest aid budgets, the biggest banks, and many of the biggest corporations in the world, and the center of the most dynamic sector of the world-trading system.[2] But can it be assumed that, because Japan is economically resoundingly successful as a nation, its people are correspondingly happy, wealthy, and enjoying the fruits of that success? It is true that consumer income has risen, so that it soars like a statistical Mount Fuji over the surrounding region (and most of the world). A kind of wealth is certainly reflected in the conspicuous consumption that absorbs the energies of Japan's people. Prosperity means that sixty million cars clog the highways; one-third of the world's tuna catch and two-fifths of its shrimp pass through Japanese stomachs; one-quarter of the world's tropical timber is imported; millions of ordinary people take overseas holidays every year.[3] In terms of life expectancy, literacy, years of schooling, and personal income, Japan ranked number one in the world from 1990 to 1993, and remained number three even after that.[4]

These are impressive figures, but they have to be put in perspective. In measuring standards of living, it would be foolish to ignore availability of gourmet foods, the amount of overseas travel, the level of ownership of cars and electronic gadgetry, but one would expect such things to follow general satisfaction of the more essential needs—for housing, urban infrastructure (transport, water, sewerage, leisure and welfare facilities, quality of environment). On comparative tables, Japan matches or surpasses the advanced industrial countries of Europe and North America only in per-capita income, television sets, and electronic equipment (although length of life, in which Japan is ahead of the rest of the world, should be added).[5] Nomura Research Institute notes that Japan is well behind countries like the United States and Germany in terms of living standards, and it is likely to remain so.[6] In December 1990 the average price of a fifty-seven-square-meter apartment in Tokyo was 80 million yen, or twelve times the average Tokyo resident's annual income; metropolitan housing was forty times oversubscribed.[7] By another measure, the average anticipated life earnings of a college graduate are just enough to buy a one-room apartment in Tokyo.[8] Three or four hours daily commuting to work, a couple of rooms in a high-rise apartment, in an environment saturated with images of affluence that mock their reality, is the common expectation. As they enter the workforce, young people are skeptical of claims that Japan is a "livelihood great power." As they contemplate their estimated life earnings, they know at the start of their career the virtual certainty of ultimate relative poverty. If people were a little slow in the 1990s to respond to the message that it was their patriotic duty to increase their consumption of foreign goods in order to help reduce Japan's massive foreign-trade surplus, it was hard to blame them.

While corporate prosperity is real, incomes high, and the shops filled with goods, the prospect is not uniformly bright. Capitalism has always developed unevenly, but at a time when its productive capacity excites unalloyed admiration worldwide, its contradictions in highly developed Japan deserve close attention.

Japan steered its economic course with remarkable agility through the oil shocks and consequent economic restructuring of the past two decades. It led the way in the transition from a base in the modern heavy and chemical industries of steel, ships, petrochemicals, and so forth, to the postmodern or information-society industries characterized by high-technology and services. More recently, it pioneered the shift into leisure industries, a move that has broad implications for economic and social policy. The range and quality of recreational facilities available in Japan has vastly increased.

Paradoxically, the massive increase in physical amenities is out of all proportion to people's needs or capacity to enjoy them. The leisure market is huge—seventy trillion yen a year in 1990, and still rising fast—but at the same time, the average Japanese work year remains virtually unchanged from the mid 1970s—between 200 and 500 hours more than elsewhere in the industrialized world, and roughly on a par with Europe during the period of postwar economic recovery in the early 1950s.

Although the official figure for hours worked was 2,080 (in 1991), as compared to 1,943 (United States), 1,902 (Britain), 1,582 (Germany), and 1,682 (France),[9] other estimates put the real figure as high as 2,617 hours for men and 2,409 hours for women.[10] The discrepancies partly stem from uncertainty over how to treat something rather whimsically known as "voluntary overtime" (*sābisu zangyū*), a category unknown in other countries, which refers to the number of hours of unpaid extra work that employees are compelled by a combination of moral and other pressures to undertake. In any case, the discrepancy between hours worked in Japan and in other advanced industrial countries—Japan's competitors—is striking. Market, and market share, do not correlate solely with hours worked, but nevertheless, they are important factors and have been a matter of concern to European and American trade negotiators with Japan for over a decade. A survey of conditions in the automotive industry, as of 1990, found a very marked discrepancy between the average for Japanese workers, 2,275 hours, and that for workers in the French and German auto industry, where most companies ranged between 1,650 and 1,750 hours, and some as little as 1,548 hours (BMW in Regensburg), an astonishing 727 fewer hours than their Japanese competitors.[11] Fewer than 20 percent of Japanese workers enjoy a two-day weekend. Overtime, at an average of 190 hours per year, has *increased* since 1986, and annual paid leave in Japan amounts, on average, to nine days, as against nineteen in the United States, twenty-four in the United Kingdom, twenty-six in France, and twenty-nine in (West) Germany.[12] During the period 1975–90, hours of work for male Japanese workers in their forties rose by 40 percent, while their hours of sleep shrank by 23 percent.[13] The revision of the Labor Standards Law to establish a forty-four-hour work-week (in 1991), then a forty-hour week (in 1994), and the adoption of a five-day week for civil servants (in 1993), must make some impact on such figures, but it will be limited by the fact that two-thirds of the workforce is employed in small- and medium-sized enterprises not covered by the legislation. In many cases, a fifty-five-hour work week remains common, and the desperate efforts of small businesses to maintain their competitiveness despite the soaring yen means that this will not easily change.[14] The contrast with Japan's international competitors remains strong, with some major European manufacturers moving in 1994 to introduce a twenty-eight-and-a-half-hour working week and a three-day weekend.[15]

If the social organization of labor in Japan, as shown by these details, looks quite distinctive, it is because of the specific historical circumstances from which it emerged. Three layers of influence were particularly strong: firstly, the prewar authoritarian and hierarchical tradition of mobilizing labor for service to company and state, in which the forces of social democracy were crushed even as they were born (reaching its climax in the wartime total mobilization system); secondly, the defeat and neutralization of the militant labor movement that had emerged in early postwar Japan in the period from the late 1940s to about 1960, a process that ensured that the Cold War role that Japan had to play would not be "subverted" and that provided the labor discipline necessary for economic recovery and growth; and the major reverses suffered during the administrative reform process of the 1980s by the formerly powerful public-sector unions, especially in the railway sector with the privatization of the National Railways.

The system that was gradually constructed, and that commonly came to be thought of as *the* system of Japanese labor relations, featured three key elements: lifetime employment, promotion by seniority, and enterprise unionism. They were not absolutes, nor were they elements deducted from some ineffable quality of Japanese culture, nor (from a 1990s perspective) would they prove eternal. Feeding upon and reinforcing each other, these three processes helped ensure the dynamism of Japan's growth, creating an engine whose competitive strength was (in the words of the economist Sawa Takamitsu) like that of Ben Johnson in the Olympic Games, attributable to its running on the equivalent of "dope." [16] The stress on efficiency and productivity could be carried to obsessive lengths because the economic structure, nominally a free market, was actually a "market simulating sham," with the result that Japan was becoming "the world's orphan."[17] But, in due course, this finely tuned motor of growth and market expansion, described by Chalmers Johnson as one of "adversarial trade," created drastic imbalances, and in turn such upheavals in the currency markets, that in 1995, a 20 percent appreciation of the Japanese yen threatened to force many small, and some not-so-small, Japanese businesses to the wall.

The critic Sataka Makoto has written extensively about this quasi-military, expansionist dynamism of Japanese business. He argues that postwar democratic reforms had considerable impact on the family, education, and other areas of Japanese life, but that the company remained out of bounds. As the weight of the company in Japanese society as a whole grew from the 1960s, its undemocratic values began to spread and to devour those areas of Japanese life that had been democratized.[18] When the Aum Supreme Truth cult burst into sensational prominence in 1995 with its sarin chemical attack on the Tokyo subway, and its apocalyptic plans for chemical, biological, and nuclear armageddon were subsequently revealed, Sataka analyzed the cult not as a bizarre and inexplicable phenomenon but as *characteristically Japanese*—closely resembling the structure of high-tech corporations such as Toyota, Hitachi, Matsushita, etc., in its stress on the rituals of initiation, purification, secret teachings, and mind control techniques designed to achieve the assimilation and subordination of the will and intellect of the individual to the corporate purpose.[19] In the 1990s, reform of the structure of the Japanese corporation had become urgent.

However extreme such sentiments may sound, the sense of crisis is widely shared. The Japanese company, and "companyism," the successful solution to the problems of one age, had become in itself a problem.[20] The thrust of the analysis by Sataka and Sawa was echoed in the assessment made by some of the country's most powerful and respected business leaders and by prominent figures in the labor movement. Morita Akio, chairman of Sony Corporation and vice-chairman of Keidanren (the Japan Federation of Economic Organizations), described Japan as being "in desperate need of a new philosophy of management, a new paradigm for competitiveness, a new sense of self."[21] His prescription was for substantially reduced working hours, increased wages, improved dividends, and much greater corporate social and environmental sensitivity.[22] Until Japan proved ready to redefine itself, he added, "It cannot hope to be accepted on the same stage as Europe and North America." He implied that the obsessive, even fetishistic, pursuit of efficiency and productivity was no longer tolerable.

Meanwhile, the general secretary of the Confederation of Japan Automobile Workers' Unions described his industry as suffering from a triple burden: exhausted and overworked workers, unprofitable enterprises, and Japan-bashing from the outside. "Unless we change," he said, "the Japanese automobile industry will collapse."[23] A similar call for transition to a softer, more conciliatory engagement with its own people and with the world, placing less weight on market share or profit, was enunciated by Hiraiwa Gaishi, chairman of Keidanren and head of Tokyo Electric Power Company.[24] Hiraiwa called for kyōsei, symbiosis. The term had been used before, but since around 1992, it has become central to prescriptions for reform. The government-funded think tank, the National Institute for Research Advancement (NIRA) was given the problem of how to realize kyōsei in practice.[25] Keidanren chose as its 1992 orientation the quest for kyōsei with foreign countries and the righting of "the evils of a company-centered society."[26] The Economic Planning Agency's twelfth five-year plan, released in July 1992, projected a vision of Japan transformed "from an aggressively competitive corporate culture into a consumer-oriented society where the quality of life takes precedence over the quantity of production."[27] Unlike previous plans, this one adopted as a mission the generation of a whole new philosophy of life, offering the vision of Japan as a "livelihood great power," meaning a "society with a simple lifestyle in a beautiful natural environment, in which each and every person would be able to experience affluence and leisure, and be given equal opportunity to realize a multiplicity of values."[28] The crisis was recognized as of such dimension that (according to Kaku Ryūzaburō, the chairman of Canon, Inc.) even the education system needed to be fundamentally revamped so that it would emphasize "creativity, ingenuity, morality and ethics," qualities that he obviously felt were little-valued in the existing society.[29]

What this meant was that the hardworking, accumulating, unquestioningly obedient, and almost ascetic corporate cipher that powered the economic miracle in Japan had become a positive embarrassment to his creators ("his" because the phenomenon was almost wholly male). Nothing could more eloquently convey the shift at work than the sponsorship by MITI of a project entitled Research Group on Sensitive Business, which in 1994 published *Modernization's Forgotten Things: Toward a Society Rich in Sensitivity*.[30] Members of the Research Group included executives from major media, publishing, pharmaceutical, tobacco, fashion, construction, and film companies, together with a few academics and the heads of traditional schools of flower arrangement and tea ceremony. Featuring on its cover a lush, tropical forest scene suggestive of the bounty of a luxuriant mother nature, the volume lacks any coherence in the normal sense, having neither analytical framework, hypothesis, or conclusion. Instead, it features vague assertions about the contrast between the mentality of the monotheistic West and the pantheistic East, the desirability of recovering the "Oriental" primacy of spiritual values that was sacrificed in the quest for modernity, along with technical discussions of the mental processes of Balinese religious rituals, brief reference to the phenomenon of brain washing, the drug problems of contemporary society, and the issue of stress management. Perhaps the core of the project is the note that "consumer needs for 'sensitive values and experiences'" had grown, with the implication that MITI was still playing its traditional role of identifying new market opportunities and helping Japanese business to benefit from them.

Despite this profound ambiguity, it would be difficult to imagine a government-sponsored project in any other country devoted to the promotion of sensitivity, and the sponsorship of this project by MITI, the bridge of the flagship of world capitalism, was enough to show how far Japan had traveled in thirty years. When Chalmers Johnson concentrated upon the institution in his classic 1982 study, MITI was the main temple of the capitalist faith in Japan and the center of the national quest for productivity and market share; now it was engaged on a much more ambiguous and uncertain project.

These concerns, and this new vision, were prompted, not so much by any organized social movement, or by the pungent criticisms of Sawa or Sataka (and many others), as by fear that the rising wave of hostility toward Japanese aggressive economic expansion in Europe and North America might otherwise prove impossible to contain. The program is best seen (at least for the time being) as strategic and instrumental, its spokesmen themselves major architects or builders of the system in which they now find basic flaws. Only time would tell whether substantial changes would flow from the new business-bureaucratic consensus around kyōsei, or whether it would become rather an ideological instrument of obfuscation, a term of utopian fancy akin to the slogan coprosperity that was advanced in an earlier age to mask unresolved contradictions within the system. Criticism of capitalism was nowhere to be heard, and the deep religious faith in continuing economic growth remained unshaken.

The bureaucratic and business elite is conspicuously schizophrenic on this point, because relaxing or slowing down have long been interpreted as symptoms of the "English disease" or the "advanced-country disease," and therefore are to be avoided at all costs. In the 1990s, it is true that Japan is gradually becoming more and more insistent on the commitment to reduced working hours, more leisure, etc. But the idea that this might somehow be associated with a zero-growth GNP, or that the dynamism of modern Japan be somehow sacrificed, remained anathema. Therefore, leisure, resorts, and "sensitive" consumerism have to be seen as a new growth area of the late twentieth-century economy rather than the way to a nongrowth future.

Although availability of leisure time seems scarcely to match that of facilities, the need for recreation is clear, not only on the basis of reward for contribution to achievement but evidently also on the basis of physical need. Ministry of Health and Welfare figures show a four-fold increase in the general rate of ill health in the community between 1955 and 1985, with high blood pressure and nervous disorders marked by much greater increases.[31]

Hypertension as a medical phenomenon increased by more than four times in the three high-growth decades from 1960.[32] Stress in extreme form, leading to the phenomenon of sudden death from over-work (karōshi), became a widely noted social phenomenon.[33] "Volunteers," who literally work themselves to death for the corporation, are the contemporary avatars of the wartime kamikaze, having managed to internalize the same spirit of total sacrifice of self for the good of the larger collective (messhi hōkō). The number of victims is obviously difficult to specify, since few of the bereaved families make any official claim and fewer still gain official recognition, but many reckon the figure might be as high as 10,000 per year.[34] When the Economic Planning Agency conducted a survey in 1988, it found that 58.5 percent of those polled responded that their level of leisure, or time and space to do their own thing (yutori), was inadequate.[35] Measured in comparative terms, Japanese workers are more dissatisfied with wages and general conditions than employees in the United States, Britain, Germany, Australia, or Singapore.[36] Furthermore, despite the common view that Japanese workers are uniquely dedicated to their work, most want shorter hours.[37] Had they time to think about it, most would be happy to raise their hands in favor of a life of sensitivity and affluence.

Under these circumstances, it seems obvious that reduced working hours, decentralization of population, and facilities for cheap relaxation in natural surroundings are called for. Some moves have indeed been made in this direction, but corporate Japan has also sought high-tech and ingenious solutions to stress: special kinds of chewing gum; meditation chambers (one hundred PSY Brain Mind Gym Relaxation Salons opened across the country in 1990); womb-like Refresh Capsules, equipped with tape facilities that allow one to be completely immersed in the environment of "murmuring brooks, singing birds, and gently breaking waves," or biofeedback devices that measure and adjust the rhythms of the mind.[38] However, a real contradiction remains between the injunction to consume more, enjoy, and become sensitive (universally represented as passive and receptive behavior) on the one hand, and the call to creativity, to make and exchange things on the other. Characteristic of the organized, institutional Japanese, response to the problem thus far has been the peculiar institution known as the resort.[39]

The Resort Boom

The "resort state" of contemporary Japan evolved in a very specific national and international context. As the huge Japanese trade surpluses began to build up during the early 1980s, Japan faced pressures to prime its domestic pump and to promote imports. At the same time the discrepancy between life in Tokyo and the megalopolis along its eastern seaboard, and the rest of the country, particularly rural Japan, was growing more serious. Large stretches of rural Japan were becoming semideserted refuges for the old. Attempts to achieve a comprehensive development of the national lands under the various Comprehensive National Development Plans, or Zensō, had been conspicuously unsuccessful; agriculture was in profound recession, with the rice support price being steadily reduced from 1986; and stockpiles of rice were consuming huge subsidies. Other rural industries were also in crisis, especially from the consequences of trade liberalization. Japan's nationally owned forest enterprises were sinking into a fiscal bog, burdened with a cumulative deficit for the period 1975–88 of over 800 billion yen and a long-term debt of nearly 1.9 trillion yen built up over the same period.[40] The administrative reform principles of the 1980s insisted that they pay their way, leaving no alternative to the removal of barriers to the development of national lands and the active promotion of resort. In short, farm, fishing, and mountain villages throughout the country were suffering from debt, depopulation, aging,

and isolation, and were demoralized over the constant shifts and abandonment of one after another national policy. "Resortification" seemed
to be the answer.

With the massive appreciation of the yen following the Plaza agreement of May 1985, the crisis deepened. The old-style export industries
of steel and ships were shaken, manufacturing went offshore rather
than to the regional bases designated under the various plans, and
agriculture was again sacrificed to the imperative of expanded imports.
Under the prescription enunciated by the Maekawa Report of April
1986, huge infrastructural, urban-development, and land-release programs were undertaken. Reliance on the private sector (minkatsu) was
the watchword. Awash with the trade surplus and capital gains from
the revalued yen, the domestic economy was stimulated to frenzy point
by the low-interest-rate policy. An urban land speculative boom gathered force during the so-called "urban renaissance" of 1985–87, when
Tokyo land prices rose by an average 300 percent.[41] That boom was
extended throughout the entire country from 1987 by the effects of the
Comprehensive National Land Development Plan (Zensō; on which
see Chapter One) and the Resort Law. The transformations wrought
under the Resort Law in much of regional Japan provide the best case
study in the workings of the Zensō principles.

There could be no clearer example of the mismatch between the
perceived need for relaxation and communion with the natural order,
and the policies adopted in practice, than this 1987 Law. Relaxation,
along with freshness, greenness, and "my life," was incidental to what
happened. The expansionary thrust of Japanese capitalism shifted to a
higher gear. The Resort Archipelago formula devised by Prime Minister Nakasone Yasuhiro created a huge new market and fed fierce expansionary pressures, which involved not only the established real
estate and development companies but also trading companies, hotel
chains, railway companies, insurance companies, banks, shipbuilders,
and finance groups. In the Green Japan Plan Phase Two, published in
July 1988, resorts were described for the first time as "a new basic
industry for Japan."[42] When Nakasone spoke of his ideal for Japan of
"peace, freedom, and verdant greenery,"[43] it should be understood that
what he meant was the things described in this chapter: a land of
chemicalized golf courses, expensive marinas, toll expressways that
penetrated the deepest mountains, and resorts that multiplied the ideology and aesthetics of Disneyland, where culture meant consumption.

The passage of the Resort Law was marked by a political and bureaucratic consensus at the highest level; tax breaks were generous, various financially attractive packages of incentives were offered, and administrative procedures were simplified. Not only was the area of land involved far greater than during the ill-famed "Remodeling the Japanese Archipelago" years of the Tanaka government in the mid-seventies, but legal and administrative measures then adopted to protect national parks and the mountain and coastal environment were watered down or abandoned in the name of what was described as a Human Green Plan.

This meant a proliferation of golf courses, ski facilities, and luxury hotels, virtually all of which were, in the late 1980s, tied to the heart of the bubble of speculation and corruption. The contributors to the MITI study in 1994 were loath to spell out whether their vision of the "sensitive society" was one achievable through the clubhouses and greens of Japan's burgeoning golf world. Certainly their role in the relief of corporate stress was considerable.

The legislation specified reliance on the abilities of private entrepreneurs to ensure the comprehensive provision of sporting, recreational, educational, and cultural activities in areas possessing good natural conditions. Though passed as national legislation after only the most perfunctory debate, it had an immediate and remarkable effect. Towns, villages, and prefectures throughout the country entered into such intense competition to be designated as resort areas that, as of December 1991, around 20 percent of the entire land area of Japan was designated for resort development (7.5 million hectares, as against 5.5 million for agriculture).[44] The construction of homogeneous and nouveau riche resorts, drawn to identical Tokyo design, commonly entailed encroachment on either public or community assets, whether forest, coastline, river, or catchment area.[45]

Ski resorts, golf courses, and marinas sprouted like autumn mushrooms after the Resort Law. They rejoiced in suggestive names such as "Mie Sunbelt Zone," "Aizu Fresh Resort," "Snow and Green My Life Resort Niigata," "Gunma Refresh My Life Resort," "40 Degrees Longitude Seasonal Resort Akita," "Nagasaki Exotic Resort," and so on. For the island of Kyushu, for example, 26.7 percent of the land was incorporated in plans for 135 resorts with an estimated investment of about 300 billion yen, including 100 golf courses and ten Disneyland-style "space-world" theme parks.[46] As for Okinawa, the poorest prefecture in Japan, all seventy of its islands were declared a tropical resort, and efforts were launched to increase the annual tourist intake from 2.4 million yen to Hawaiian levels of about 6 million yen by the end of the century.[47]

Golf

In Japan, golf is almost synonymous with resort. Administrators in the depopulated villages and rural districts of Japan came to believe that, while there was no future in agriculture or forestry and fisheries, there might be in resort development. Although there were only 100 golf courses in Japan in 1955, the numbers grew rapidly during the years of the Tanaka government, and again explosively during the late 1980s following the Resort Law. By 1994, there were about 2,000 completed courses,[48] and at least 1,680 square kilometers, or 1/115th of the country's narrow, mountainous lands, were devoted to the game, with many other courses either under construction or planned.[49] The Japan Golf Association estimated there were about 13 million golf players (out of around 50 million worldwide), and they were overwhelmingly male.[50] There is no real parallel for the phenomenon in other advanced industrial countries, although the forces driving it in Japan are now also expanding rapidly throughout the Pacific region, making especially rapid inroads into the "land-cheap" countries of communist southeast Asia. The American mode of development is followed—flattening the environment, removing hills or even the tops of mountains, scouring natural foliage, and applying massive quantities of chemicals.

The frenzied quality of Japan's 1980s golf boom has also spread, with Korean and Taiwanese businessmen, in particular, having become active proselytes for the golf cause, to the extent that they were reported to be enthusiastically playing on Vietnamese minefields, "apparently unable to wait for the course to be finished and all the mines to be defused."[51] Protest movements were spreading from Hawaii to Malaysia, not only on ecological grounds or because of the culture of corruption that is frequently associated with the game, but often because of displacement of tribal peoples or the felling of forests. The economic, social, and environmental implications of the Japanese golf phenomenon are worthy of attention, and the question of whether and to what extent the need for relaxation and leisure is met in the simulated, sanitized world of the clubhouse and green has to be asked.

How do golf courses get built? In 1990, capital costs for an eighteen-hole course in the Osaka vicinity were estimated to be about 20 billion yen, so if 1,000 members could be subscribed at an average of 40 million yen, there would already be a 100 percent profit. Such profit was often realized before a course even opened. The value of club memberships, as tradable commodities, rocketed in the late 1980s, appreciating by about 400 percent between 1982 and 1989, and by an additional 190 percent during 1989.[52]

A course under construction in Chiba Prefecture, just outside Tokyo, in the so-called Golf Course Ginza area, had a capital cost of 7 billion yen. The company concerned planned to put up 80 million yen and enroll 1,400 members. This enrollment would be done in several stages, membership being limited at first to a group of several hundred at a special charter rate of about 3 million yen per person and gradually increasing through subsequent tranches to about 10 million yen. The initial investment of 80 million yen would yield a return of 3 billion yen.

Since the average membership on the Osaka exchange in 1990–91 was around 40 million yen, or four times what the last ones in this venture had to pay, golf played a key role in feeding the speculative bubble. Catering to those who aspired to the exclusive,[53] million-dol-lar-membership country clubs (*okukan*) proliferated, with prices ranging up to 400 million yen plus, enough to buy an *entire golf course* in many countries. One of the many attractive features of the golf-club corporate assets deriving from membership fees is that, technically, such monies were regarded as merely temporarily deposited funds and were therefore not taxable.[54]

A similar analysis can be made for ski-course developments. At the beginning of the 1990s, there were between six and seven hundred of these, also expanding rapidly.[55] However, as golf and ski resorts had been at the center of the bubble, the consequences of its bursting (after 1990) were inevitably drastic, and the cost of membership in the most expensive golf courses slipped from around 400 million yen to 120 million, while the development of new courses was frozen.[56]

The economic and social consequences of this type of development were serious, particularly in terms of the built-in potential for corruption. The politicians, bureaucrats, and local or national men of power and influence who were enrolled as charter members of a country club, at highly discounted rates, had a vested interest in seeing that the permits for fast-track construction were secured and local opposition defeated. Politicians, needing a hundred million yen or more a year to run their political machines, were enthusiastic, especially since the Supreme Court in 1982 took the very narrow view that, although memberships could be traded and used as collateral for bank loans, they were not valuable securities, so that there could be no issue of bribery involved.[57] Had all the new courses that were on the drawing boards at the end of the 1980s been built, each with two to three hundred charter members, the web of vested interest, whether or not technically one of corruption, would be spun over an influential section of the population, perhaps 300,000 people.

Land-price inflation had far exceeded growth rates in the real economy, while at the same time driving it. Through the 1970s, while Japan's GNP increased fivefold, its land assets grew tenfold, a disproportion that continued to widen during the 1980s.[58] The real-estate industry, employing about 790,000 people, was able to generate an operating surplus almost on a par with manufacturing (which employed nearly 15 million).[59] Its exponential growth out-performed all other sectors of the economy.

Not only was there no net addition to real national wealth or welfare in this, the reverse may be true if one considers the burden for millions of ordinary people whose lives were outside the vicious circles of speculation. For them, escalating land prices constituted a nightmare. In the late 1980s, a piece of land of about 100 square meters in central Tokyo could have been exchanged for a castle in Europe or a modest-sized island in Canada or Australia. The situation in Japan was probably without historical precedent, although England before the Glorious Revolution of 1688 comes close.[60] Land constituted 65 percent of Japan's national wealth, against comparable figures of 25 percent for (West) Germany, 33 percent for the United States, and a mere 2.5 percent for the United Kingdom.[61]

Responsibility for the processes was too complex to be attributed to a few corrupt men; it proceeded because it was driven by complex economic forces. The problem of land-price inflation is central. Though Japan's commodity-price inflation level has long been among the lowest of industrial countries, the rate of land-price inflation in the 1980s had no parallel (and few, if any, precedents). In a sense, Japan was operating a dual currency system: the yen on the one hand, and "land currency" (*doka*) on the other, the latter being linked to the real-estate market and to political interests. The relationship between the two was articulated by bank credit issued against land or stock securities.[62] The scale of inflation of Japan's land and stock values over the twenty years to 1990 was remarkable.

However, the madness of those years could not last. In due course, Toshiyuki Inamura, who, as director-general of the Environment Agency in 1986 and 1987 had presided over the first stages of the resort boom, was arrested in December 1990 for evading taxes on approximately 2.8 billion yen profit generated on stock dealings from companies actively involved in development.[63] Subsequently, several provincial governors and the heads of major construction companies were also arrested (see Chapter 1).

Between January and October 1990, stock prices on the Nikkei Index plunged 48 percent, a loss equivalent to twice the Third World's outstanding debt, or more than four times the estimated $500 billion cost of bailing out America's savings and loan industry.[64] Land prices, too, floating in a sea of debt, began to sink, and credit started to dry up as financial and other institutions faced the trauma of the bursting of the biggest speculative bubble seen this century. As golf had been a major focus of the speculative fever, so it played a central role in its collapse and was a focus of many of the corruption cases that came before the courts thereafter. By 1995, there was still no sign of recovery in this important index, and the average price of a membership in one of the country's leading 530 courses stood at a mere 26 percent of its 1990 peak.[65] This savage deflation continued to have large social and political consequences.

As the Tokyo money spread over the countryside, it infected the whole country with the vices of speculation and inflation, exacting as heavy a price on the social and moral values of local Japanese communities as did (in many cases) the resorts themselves of the physical environment. In short, the golfing phenomenon was driven by supply-side pressures rather than increased demand, money and corporate greed were the core phenomena, and recreation incidental.

The International Dimension

Much of the expansion into the tourism and resort industries around the Pacific rim was financed from the castles of money built around the redoubts of golf in Japan. By the early 1990s, there were over 200 overseas Japanese courses, as well as many hotels and other resorts.[66]

The Japanese offer to buy all the private courses in the Sydney, Australia, area becomes understandable against this background.[67]

As Japanese economic influence spread, naturally the patterns of the Japanese domestic political economy were reproduced through a widening regional and global sphere of influence. Whether in Australia, Hawaii, Malaysia, or Thailand, land-price inflation was a conspicuous consequence of the golf boom. Throughout the 1980s, the level of capital flowing out of Japan into tourism and real-estate development around the region grew steadily, stimulated by the accumulation of trade surplus, the inflation of domestic land and stock assets, and the availability of cheap credit (commonly around 4 percent) against the collateral of land. In 1990, Japan's outflow of direct foreign investment funds to the world ($44.1 billion) surpassed that of the United States ($31.7 billion) and Britain ($31.8 billion).[68] In aggregate terms, too, Japan seemed likely to become number one in the near future.

By the end of the 1980s, as a result, many of the first-class hotels, golf courses, and luxury hotels and apartment buildings in places like the Australian Gold Coast and Hawaii were in Japanese hands. Japanese funds flowed into the Gold Coast area at the rate of over $1 billion per year during the 1980s, until half the property in the central business district was reported to be under Japanese ownership.[69] Large projects for marinas, golf courses, luxury apartments and hotels were also under way in North Queensland (with Cairns sometimes seen as a Daikyo company town), Western Australia, and northern New South Wales. In Hawaii, there were sixty-eight existing golf courses as of 1992, and 100 more planned, half of them Japanese owned and run.[70] In Malaysia, the number of golf courses doubled to about eighty during the 1980s, and was expected to double again by the end of the century; many of the courses were being built by Japanese companies and for Japanese demand.[71] Some of the more extravagant schemes, including a resort on the east coast of Johor that was to feature a replica of the Tokyo ski dome, and a plan to build an Acropolis, with a Disneyland-style theme park, golf courses, and a Japanese retirement village on top of Penang Hill, were blocked in the early 1990s by a combination of the collapsed bubble in Japan and a strengthening environmental movement in Malaysia.[72] In Thailand, the same pattern was occurring, though the tempo of development was faster, with the number of courses expected to rise from eighty-six in 1991 to over 300 within the next few years.[73]

In Southeast Asia, the rapid expansion of the opposition movement, whose conferences and campaigns, such as "No Golf Day," attracted considerable publicity, probably helped slow the rate of expansion. Still, the golf business, as the "fastest-growing type of land development in the world,"[74] "a multi-billion dollar, multi-national industry, including developers, hotel chains, tour operators, airlines and, not least, course designers and makers of golfing wear"[75] was making inroads into new areas: Vietnam, Laos, Burma, China, and India. Not only did it carry with it well-recognized problems from Japan, such as chemical pollution, destruction of forest, conversion of agriculturally productive lands, speculation, corruption, social polarization, and exploitation of women, but also some new ones—neocolonialism (since the development was heavily for the benefit of rich foreigners) and encroachment on the lands of tribal and minority peoples and on ecologically sensitive areas rich in biodiversity (such as rain forest).[76]

As the bubble burst at the end of the 1980s, however, and asset prices began to fall, the broad speculative band that had grown around the golf business in Japan itself was quickly shed, and many fingers were burned. *All* Japanese-owned courses in the United States went into the red, and 70 percent of them were put on the market at greatly reduced prices.[77] The giant construction firm of Shimizu had to write off 80 billion yen in overseas losses, and Kajima lost 66 billion on its Australian investments alone.[78]

The Japanese company EIE, which in the late 1980s bought up hotels and other resort property in the Pacific region for a total portfolio of over one trillion yen—including a university, an exclusive resort, and major hotels worth around 200 billion yen in Australia, making it that country's biggest foreign investor—was put into the hands of its bankers in early 1991 and declared bankruptcy in 1994, its sustaining mechanism of high leverage and low-interest–capital availability having broken down. Its expansion had been fed by massive borrowing on the slightest of collateral. Much of the money vanished into investment in exclusive golf and other speculative resort developments, and in 1994, two credit unions, Tokyo Kyōwa and Anzen, both of which had lent huge sums to EIE, also were liquidated when they were unable to meet debts of 110 billion yen.[79] One former minister, as well as many other prominent politicians—"the head of the Tokyo tax office . . . , the former head of the Government-owned Long Term Credit Bank of Japan (EIE's biggest lender), three of the top men at the Ministry of

Finance, even a former governor of the Bank of Japan"[80]—came under investigation for various suspected corrupt and illegal connections with EIE and its flamboyant president, Takahashi Harunori. Japan's leading corporations had invested in the Takahashi operation in its heyday. Takahashi was indicted early in 1995. Confidence in the nation's financial institutions and in the highest echelons of the bureaucracy was further undermined as the details of yet another scandal unfolded.

Environmental Impact

In the long run, however, it is the environmental impact of the golf boom that may be the most serious. Economic circumstances may cause many of the rash of resorts currently being built to collapse, sooner or later, but the swathes of the Japanese countryside cleared for development will not quickly recover. A golf-course development needs a site of about 100 hectares, preferably in undulating countryside with good access to major population centers. By the 1980s, there were no such sites left free of housing or agricultural development in Japan. Consequently, as environmental scholar Yamada Kunihiro describes it,

> much golf-course development has occurred in forested areas at the foot of mountains. Developers clear-cut the forests and use bulldozers to level off hilltops and fill in valleys. In this way, golf-course construction is tantamount to the destruction of forests, pure and simple. Even though 67 percent of Japan's total land area is covered by forests, its forest products self-sufficiency rate has fallen to only 30 percent.[81]

According to an official of the Ministry of the Environment, by 1987, 5,000 hectares of forest were being cleared annually for golf construction.[82] The environment suffered complex wounds from the felling of 1 percent of Japan's forests for golf and related development.[83] This included the giant forest trees of Shiretoko in northern Japan, felled to try to achieve solvency for the Forest Agency.[84] The diminishing of forest cover accelerates the greenhouse effect, while the reduction of Japan's domestic timber reserves also stimulates an increased reliance on imported timber, and therefore depredation of Third World forests.

The green quality of the mountain and coastal resorts promoted under this scheme is deceptive. Japan's environment is very wet and humid, and control is only achieved at a price. In the case of a golf course, greenness is achieved by the application of three to four tons per year of herbicides, germicides, pesticides, coloring agents, organic chlorine, and other fertilizers, including chemicals that are carcinogenic or cause various health abnormalities.[85] This rich brew, three times the intensity of what the most chemically minded farmer would apply to vegetables, ultimately drains off into rivers, ponds, swamps, lakes, or the sea.[86] The Naoki Prize–winning author, Takahashi Osamu, describes the hills of Chiba Prefecture adjacent to Narita Airport as resembling defoliated Vietnam—and likely to take as long to recover.[87] At the end of the 1980s, the Ministry of Health found 950 places where the quality or quantity of water had been adversely affected by golf-course development.[88]

The Japan Ecological Association has expressed profound concern at the damage being done to nature in the name of leisure, particularly at the encroachment on national parks. The denuding and remolding of mountains for ski purposes also causes landslides, and the association estimated that a single development might be responsible for the loss of the equivalent of between 100 and 200 ten-ton dump-truck loads of soil into surrounding rivers in a year.[89]

The natural environment in narrow, mountainous Japan is severely threatened by the development of recent decades. The causes are more complex than simply the golf-led onslaught, but there is no doubt that the resort boom played a considerable role. Widespread damage has been reported not only to sea, river, forest, and mountain, but to animal, bird, insect, and marine life. Already, according to the Environment Agency, 628 of Japan's wildlife species and 899 of its wild plants are on the brink of extinction. Among the threatened fauna are the Satsuki trout of the Nagara River, the Iriomote wildcat of Okinawa, the crested ibis of Sado Island, the mud-skipper (or *mutsugoro*) of Ariake Bay, the striped owl, the otter, and the snow goose; among threatened flora are the fringed orchid and the primrose.[90] One experienced biologist reckons that Japan faces a pending biological disaster and that "virtually one-quarter of all vertebrate populations in Japan can be regarded as at risk."[91] He adds the black and brown bears to the list. The last crested ibis died in its mountain sanctuary in 1995. Further transformations of the environment of rural and mountain Japan, such as envisaged under the 1987 Resort Law, could have catastrophic consequences.

The island territory of Okinawa, seized by the United States in 1945, was only returned to Japanese jurisdiction in 1972. The occasion was celebrated by the convening of the Okinawa Marine Expo on the theme of the role the sea might play in the future of humanity, but within two decades, over 80 percent of its coral was dead, its best beaches privatized, and its fishermen reporting drastically reduced catches.[92] Even the famed blue coral of Ishigaki Island, described by the International Union for the Conservation of Nature in 1988 as the oldest and largest colony in the northern hemisphere, was slowly asphyxiating from the impact of soil runoff caused by uncontrolled development (including various road and other "improvement" works) and a spreading "crown of thorns."[93] To meet the anticipated demand for water of future development, all the rivers of Okinawa were to be dammed, which was expected to wreak havoc on their upstream ecology and hasten the silting of their mouths.[94] Greed, and the reluctance to invest in appropriate engineering or to control agricultural (including chemical) wastes, was gradually stifling the life of the tropical seas that had been the focus of the original tourism development.[95]

However, opposition forces gradually developed, and, by 1994, GAG'M (Global Anti-Golf Movement) was formed. GAG'M claims already to have blocked the construction of some 300 courses in Japan and is growing into an international movement.[96] The major newspapers have all taken critical positions, and the Japan Bar Association passed a resolution calling for the Resort Law to be repealed. A comprehensive set of revisions to the law were proposed by the then-Japan Socialist Party leader, Doi Takako.[97] The combination of broad-ranging opposition and recession forced the shelving of many projects, though it would not be clear until the economy recovered what the eventual outcome would be.[98]

Theme Parks

The Japanese predilection for theme parks is notable. It dates back to the Osaka Expo of 1970, which was heavily modeled on the New York World's Fair of 1939–40 (whose Future City Panorama bears strong resemblance to the Tokyo district of Nishi Shinjuku in the 1980s).[99] The phenomenal success of Tokyo Disneyland (founded in 1983 and host to 140 million visitors in its first decade) first gave permanent form to the celebration of consumption over production, marking in tangible form the social and economic transformation accomplished by the income-doubling 1960s. In any case, in the 1980s, the theme park became a quintessential Japanese-style resort feature. Elements from it were incorporated in the design of department stores and shopping complexes, and even the underlying principle in the design of some cities, especially cities such as Kobe. Included are places such as Gluck Kingdom in Hokkaido, which re-creates settings of the Grimm brothers' fairy tales; the Russian village in Niigata; the Venice of Japan, known as Garasu-no-sato, in Hiroshima; the Spanish Costa del Sol at Kure near Hiroshima (and Shima Spain Village in Mie Prefecture); the Canadian World at Ashibetsu in Hokkaido.

Much in the resort boom was ephemeral, speculative, or corrupt, and some developments were all of these things. But there were exceptions, none more remarkable than Huis Ten Bosch (often Anglicized as House Tempos), the recreation of medieval Dutch life on a 152-hectare site of windmills, tulips, and canals on Omura Bay in Nagasaki Prefecture. This is, in a sense, a theme park, but it is much more besides, and conveys a strong sense of permanence. It amounts to the foundation of a new type of city, reflecting a set of values contrasting somewhat with those of Disneyland or other theme parks. Its founders claim that it is being built to last 1,000 years, and that, as the building of the city of Kyoto in the eighth century was modeled on that of T'ang China's capital at Ch'ang-an so, in the future, Huis Ten Bosch may come to be seen as the first of a new type of postindustrial urban development, drawing upon European models but certainly no more Dutch than Kyoto is Chinese, and creating in the process a city that Dutch people can only look upon with astonishment.[100] Its founder, Kamijika Yoshikuni, evidently likes to think of the project as symbolizing a merger of the ecological and the economic.[101]

To construct only the first stages cost 225 billion yen. Concrete and steel, both modern materials, were avoided in favor of brick and stone. Holland became, for a time, the world's leading brick exporter as it geared up to supply twenty million specially fired bricks for construction of buildings that include replicas of Queen Beatrix's palace and of the offices of the East India Company, together with the Hotel Europe, which embodies the pinnacle of opulence (as well it would have to, to secure patrons at the 34,000 yen minimum charged for a night's accommodation in 1994).[102] Winding through the city is a six-kilometer network of urban canals, built to a scale three times the size of its Dutch equivalent and far more carefully tended.[103] The water supply comes from the sea and is treated for desalination, then is returned to the sea after use in the town gardens. What the whole project represents is still hard to say, but the claim to be pioneering ecological town planning, with emphasis on the needs of the coming "aging and leisure-oriented society of the twenty-first century," is not easily dismissed. The harvest festivals, the jovial, red-faced "Dutch" men and women who eat cheese and drink beer, sing and dance, or drive horse-drawn carriages through the streets, and the reconstructions of medieval Dutch life, may not last, but the urban infrastructure will, and there is certainly more free space and less manipulative control here than in Disneyland or other such resorts.[104] It has been enormously expensive to build, but will leave something much more solid and interesting than other resorts. It has also been successful, despite the recession in which it was launched, drawing 3.86 million visitors in its first year.[105] A second phase, to complement the initial museums, hotels, palaces, museums, canals, harbor, and shops with "ordinary" housing is planned.

In a slightly different vein, but also massively successful and probably equally suggestive of social and cultural trends, are Sea Gaia at Miyazaki in Kyushu and La Port Ski Dome SSAWS in Funabashi City outside Tokyo. At Sea Gaia's Ocean Dome, one can enjoy a Hawaiian-style tropical beach resort in a totally manufactured environment complete with palm trees, an (absolutely clean) beach of crushed marble, with mechanically produced waves up to 2.5 meters (and even "tube-riding," if desired), in an environment that is never too hot or humid, too cold, or too . . . anything at all.[106] The water is not from the nearby sea, and therefore not salty, but chlorinated, and the (artificial) volcano of Bali Hai erupts every fifteen minutes. At SSAWS (which stands for "Spring, Summer, Autumn, Winter, Snow"), it is possible to ski throughout the year on artificial snow, but on a 500 meter slope and at levels up to advanced, inside a huge dome that is kept throughout the year at a constant minus two degrees centigrade.

Places like Huis Ten Bosch, Sea Gaia, and SSAWS aspire to become resort centers, and in due course actual resort cities for visitors from throughout the region. If the success of their early (recession) years is anything to go on, that is, indeed, what they seem bound to become. They seem also certain to set regional (and world) trends in resort-style development.[107] Huis Ten Bosch seems already to be well on the way to becoming an East Asian Nice or Riviera-style resort, and many other cities will try to emulate it. However superficially Western, it is impossible to avoid the feeling that in the unlikely settings of Huis Ten Bosch or Sea Gaia, a fresh and cosmopolitan Asian sense of identity may be emerging.

But, even if it should turn out that new cultural hybrid developments are emerging in Western Japan, where the confrontation with European cultures began more than 400 years ago, European-American hegemony remains in the capital area. Disneyland, which continues to attract 10 million people annually, is described by the critic Yoshimi Shunya as a central cultural symbol of the new Japan. This "Happiest Place on Earth," which is gradually being replicated in the shopping malls and exhibition centers of the 1990s, allows visitors to consume the prepackaged American symbols of fantasy, love, and adventure passively, while depriving them of opportunities for spontaneous festivity and human interaction.[108] Yoshimi sees this as a fulfillment of the promise of Orwell's *1984*.[109] Another critic, Asada Akira, describes the Disneyland phenomenon as infantile.[110] It is indeed worse, since it involves the sanitization of myth and the exclusion of the real world to eliminate violence and sexuality, "to deodorize the real, the raw, the natural" (as Mita Munesuke puts it)[111] and to present an adult fantasy of infancy in which *kawairashisa*, or cuteness, is predominant. The manmade spaces of such worlds represent in concentrated form the hyperreality of contemporary Japan.

Yoshimi concludes his analysis of the phenomenon by locating it both in the real and in the inner world:

> The "opulence" enjoyed by many Japanese people today is the product of countless expropriations and displacements against nature and against the Third World. It is something to which we possess no legitimate right and moreover we know this. All that we can choose to do in this situation is to strive as far as possible not to see that which we are continually rejecting, and to immerse ourselves in the "kingdom of dreams and magic." And by effectively operating a mechanism of "oblivion" rather than of "succour" this "kingdom" increasingly dissolves the interior into multiple fragments, trapping people's gaze in variety and oscillation.[112]

However, there are two qualifications to this. At least some of the developments of "Resort Japan" are not simply extensions of the Disneyland phenomenon but, potentially at least, new and distinctive. And secondly, all these developments, whether Huis Ten Bosch, Sea Gaia,

SSAWS, or Disneyland, may serve to protect the real or natural environment. If they attract millions of people, they may (as a UNESCO report noted) have:

> kept millions of people away from *other* [italics added] destinations where they would probably have done much more harm. . . . Despite their totally artificial character, there is no doubt that they provide the kind of tourism that people want and do so at a fraction of the environmental and cultural costs of today's charter flights and resort hotels around the world.[113] (italics added)

The Japanese resort boom of the 1980s is not in itself unique, although the scale of the phenomenon, the speed of its growth, the obsession with luxury, and the gulf between 1980s style resort life and traditional resort life may be more exceptional. The Japanese people have long been inveterate travelers and pilgrims, curious and gregarious explorers within their own country. Hot-spring resorts flourish, some of them with a history of over 1,000 years. But prosperity came suddenly to Japan in the 1980s, and the extension of the consumer market into the realm of daydreaming and anticipation (which, as Urry notes, is central to "the dialectic of novelty and insatiability at the heart of contemporary consumerism"[114] and tourism) was a sudden quantum leap.

Perhaps it is not surprising that, when the daydreams of the workaholic generation that had grown up in the drab and narrow world of the corporation came suddenly to be realized, they were found to be dreams of space, material (consumer) affluence carried to the nth degree, and ready and safe access to the wealth and mysteries of the world. Ironically, however, the experience of such dreams could only occur within the strict rules and constraints of dream, for a few days a year. Its force depended on its very remoteness from the everyday world, which indeed it helped to sustain as its mirror image.

Prescriptions from Below

In contrast with the pattern of such "resorts" that were basically imposed by political and business forces from Tokyo on the regions in accordance with the 1987 Act, one remarkable experiment of a quite different kind was made in 1988 to empower local communities.

Under the Takeshita government, all the 3,268 local governing villages and towns in the country were given a "one-off" grant of 100 million yen, which they were to spend, in whatever way they thought fit, toward invigorating their communities. It was the first, and only, experiment in highly centralized Japan in leaving things entirely to unfettered local discretion. The idea built upon local initiatives from the early 1980s, such as the One Village, One Product movement and the *Nihon-ichi* (Number One in Japan) movement under which, for example, one village in Kumamoto Prefecture, in Kyushu, had built the longest stone stairway in the country (3,333 steps up a mountain), thereby attracting enormous numbers of curious visitors, while others had built the biggest waterwheel in the country, or the biggest stew pot (six meters wide and able to hold enough to feed 30,000 people), or the biggest drum, the biggest sand clock in the world, or a 460-meter-long bench by the seaside simply for people to sit on.[115] The Takeshita initiative sparked a remarkable outpouring of ideas, over 50,000 in all, notable for their range and variety, and their reflection of local values, customs, and aspirations.

Perhaps most famous was the town of Tsuna, in Hyogo Prefecture, which used its money to buy a sixty-three-kilo lump of gold that it then put on display. This was so successful that on weekends, the streets leading in and out of the village were blocked with tour buses, and in the three years from 1989 to 1992, over a million people made the pilgrimage. The fishing town of Naka Tosa in Kochi Prefecture commissioned a sculpture of a bonito fish in pure gold. Eigenji in Shiga Prefecture spent its money on a massive program of planting maple trees (though local objections on grounds of extravagance forced them to reduce the scale of the program somewhat). Misei (which means "beautiful stars") in Okayama strove to build its reputation as the best place in Japan for viewing the stars (and, inter alia, passed an edict forbidding the use of neon lights in the village), while Moriyama in Shiga Prefecture spent the money on cleaning up its river, building a "mountain," and planting appropriate trees and shrubs to attract fireflies for which it was once renowned. Besshiyama in Ehime, the smallest village in Japan, population only 300, looked to revive itself as the center of *matsutake* (Japanese mushroom) cultivation. Other ideas included building the biggest scarecrow in the world (28.8 meters high) in Yamagata Prefecture; raising rhinoceros beetles (*kabutomushi*) in Fukushima; establishing a goat herd to produce cheese in

Ibaraki; attracting as many varieties of butterfly as possible in Saitama; developing a whale-watching industry in Ogasawara; cultivating "trees that will never be chopped" in Yamagata; creating a World Plum Park of 1,500 plum trees (of 350 varieties) in Hyogo; reviving charcoal making (valuable now for water purification as well as cooking, and an example of a local initiative in ecotourism), turning an old house into an inn, with a restaurant and facilities for meetings and lectures in Okayama; and concocting a local brandy out of 105 varieties of date in Chiba.[116] As villages struggled to articulate their identity in such ways, capitalizing on their exotic, almost foreign quality in relation to urban Japan, the transmission of social knowledge from village to town—in things like "woodcrafts, dyeing, pottery-making, cloth-making, straw sandal making, paper-making, bamboo-making—as well as various forms of cultivation"[117]—became a modest growth industry.

These ideas of local development, bizarre or quixotic as some of them may sound, point to a diversity and modesty that contrasts sharply with the prescriptions issuing from bureaucrats in Tokyo or think tanks associated with the resort or construction industry. Were the so-far vague ideas of political reform through decentralization and the restoring of power to local communities to be implemented, this experiment suggests that there is a fund of energy and originality at the local level that could, given the chance, lead to their revival. The village that invested in the lump of gold may have been most deeply affected by the bubble mentality of the time and may not have gained much of enduring value from its investment, but in general their proposals are characterized by their remoteness from the vain and extravagant world of the bubble.

In much the same spirit of insistence on local autonomy and locally generated development as was revealed in these plans, the idea of building barriers to prevent interference (or subversion as some would see it) by outside bureaucratic or capital forces in their communities has been gradually gaining force. Yufuin, near Beppu in Kyushu, was very successful as a semi-traditional (hot-spring) resort that branched out, establishing itself as a center for music and art so successfully that it was drawing over three million visitors a year in the late 1980s.[118] To protect its own autonomy and its environment from the threat of outside, Tokyo-style resort development, Yufuin established its own charter of development (in September 1990), with provisions for strict control over projected development by means of environmental assessment, community consultation, and provision for water, waste, and general environment protection.[119] One of the centers of the local defense movement at Yufuin is a local inn, built into its environment around courtyards and gardens, not more than a couple of stories high but humming with activity like a medieval monastery, a proud center of local cultural and artistic life, and employing 100 local people, from teenagers to senior citizens. The contrast between the world represented by such institutions—common enough among local inns and traditional hot-spring resorts throughout the country—and the standardized high-rise resort hotel, dedicated to extravagant (gourmet) consumption or golf, and sealed off from its local environment, is profound.[120]

Two other examples may be cited: The small town of Kuma (population 8,000), in Ehime Prefecture (Shikoku), faced with the common problems of an aging population and the decline of a traditional agricultural and forestry base, chose to redevelop its agricultural sector by shifting to production of market vegetables (stressing organic production methods) and to develop a modest local resort that featured mountain cabins, camp villages, and bird-watching parks rather than luxury hotels, adding new elements such as a concert hall and art gallery and a planetarium (for which the dark skies surrounding the town constituted a significant comparative advantage);[121] and the island village of Zamami (population 853) about forty kilometers west of Naha in Okinawa, which attracts 55,000 recreational divers per year. Accommodated in simple pension-style fashion, tourists are escorted around the coral in local waters and enlisted in attempts to eliminate the threatening crown of thorns. Outside capital is not involved, and further expansion is not wanted since it would not benefit the local people and would be likely to threaten the delicate environment in which they live.[122]

"Enrich the Country, Impoverish the People"

While the human stock of both urban and rural Japan were disoriented and swept up in vast dislocating transformations occasioned by the inflation of the capital stock, these changes sowed alienation and unrest, eroded political and economic morality, and devastated the heritage of people received from their ancestors in trust. Those who know Kawabata Yasunari's classic novel *Snow Country*, with its opening lines, "The train came out of the long tunnel into the snow country. The earth lay white under the night sky," or who were ever able to go through that tunnel into the Snow Country, would be astounded today at the high-rise vistas that now confront one in the hot-spring village of Echigo Yuzawa.[123] It received 7.2 million visitors in 1987, its land price rose by a factor of ten in the three years to 1989, and it was virtually swallowed by Tokyo, 167 kilometers distant.[124]

Land inflation also drove ordinary people to commute farther and farther to work. Deprived of any prospect of owning a home in the city itself, over 20 percent of the Tokyo workforce commutes for more than three hours per day.[125] Symptomatic of the failure to solve this problem is the rise of what may be known as "reverse" resort lifestyle, where *furusato* (home village) is redefined as the place outside Tokyo where one leaves one's family during the week to live in a capsule hotel (or equivalent) in Tokyo, returning at weekends to the "Resort Mansion."[126]

As homogeneous and nouveau riche resorts drawn to identical Tokyo design proliferated in the Japanese islands, local interests or peculiarities were swallowed up and negated; the natural environment that originally justified the siting of the resort facilities undermined; and environmental damage, whose ultimate costs—including economic costs—are incalculable, spread; social morality was undermined and communities divided as speculative virus spread and eroded the ethic of work and production that brought Japan success in the first place.

The "resortification" of Japan had undoubtedly succeeded in boosting growth, stimulating the construction business, and oiling the gear wheels of corruption, but it failed as a strategy to invigorate declining local communities, relieve their isolation and chronic aging profile, or to provide facilities to meet the needs of the Japanese people as a whole for relaxation and recreation. In the long run, it may turn out that even the macroeconomic gains were illusory or counterproductive and that the resort strategy merely camouflaged a failure to resolve basic problems of urban and rural work, environmental protection and enhancement, housing, and food, while the growing wave of Japanese investment in the resort and tourist industries of the whole Pacific region probably did little to alleviate trade pressures.

Resolution of these problems will not be easy. The tide of golf courses, ski resorts, and marinas that now rises over the land is striking for its irrelevance to the needs and problems of local communities, many of whom now see the whole process as a contemporary form of enclosure movement, in which public land, forests, mountains, and beaches are enclosed by private interests for corporate profit. While corporate Japan thrives, they say, the people suffer. Hence the recently coined slogan: *fukoku hinmin* (Enrich the country, impoverish the people). It is a phrase that points to the poverty at the heart of affluence.

Japanese commentators commonly agree on certain elements of an alternative prescription.[127] The regions will only be invigorated by finding solutions to their problems that are locally driven, arising from and responding to local needs, and based upon strong institutions of local self-government that have the power and the will to control external interventions by big (Tokyo) corporations and bureaucrats. Small developments, rooted in agriculture, the arts, crafts, or various low-cost, nonintrusive activities, would be given precedence under such a prescription. The forests and mountains, home to the ancestors of local communities, would be protected, and the fields and seas that are the source of their basic livelihood respected. The speculative virus would be resisted like the plague, while the stressed workers and residents of the megalopolis could take rest and recuperation in close proximity to the natural world. Ultimately, only a Japan that moves to overcome its frenetic restlessness and to deepen its democratic and ecological ethos along such lines will be able to resolve the stresses and frictions in its relationship with the outside world.

Notes

1. "Assets" here defined as balance of foreign assets (government and commercial) over liabilities. The Japanese government in May 1995 reported that the figure for Japan was $688.9 billion, as against $210.3 billion for Germany, with the United States registering a *negative* figure of $555.7 billion. "Taigai junshisan Nihon 4 nen renzoku sekai-ichi," *Mainichi shimbun*, May 26, 1995.

2. For other recent analyses of the significance of Japan's rise, see my "Pacific Dreamtime and Japan's New Millennialism," *Australian Outlook*, Vol. 43, No. 2, August 1989, pp. 64–73; "Capitalism Triumphant? The Evidence from 'Number One,' " *Kyoto Journal*, Spring 1990, pp. 4–10; and "The Price of Affluence: The Political Economy of Japanese Leisure," *New Left Review*, No. 188, July-August 1991, pp. 121–34.

3. Murai Yoshinori, "Hakyoku ni itaru kaihatsushugi to kajō shohi," *Keizai seminā*, No. 422, 1990, pp. 12–16; and *Ebi to Nihonjin*, Iwanami 1988.

4. "Nation slips in index of human development," *Japan Times*, June 3, 1994.

5. "Nichibei kankei, 6," *Asahi Shimbun*, March 29, 1990, p. 3.

6. Japan rates 58 to (West) Germany's 79, the US's 80, the UK's 53; quoted in Takagake Yūji, "En pāwa no seijigaku," *Ajia Keizai*, September 1989, pp. 80–98, at p. 94.

7. Paul Waley, "Rabbit Hutch Life Holds Seeds of Social Fracture," *Japan Times*, December 9, 1990.

8. Shigeto Tsuru, *Japan's Capitalism: Creative Defeat and Beyond*, Cambridge, Cambridge University Press, 1993, p. 169.

9. Enno Berndt, " 'Nihon-teki keiei' kara no dakkyaku," *Ritsumeikan keieigaku*, Vol. 33, No. 3, September 1994, pp. 1–37, at p. 34 (using Japan Productivity Council statistics).

10. Yasumaru Yoshio, "Rekishi kenkyū to gendai Nihon to no daiwa," *Sekai*, January 1994, pp. 23–35, at pp. 26–27.

11. Berndt, "Nihon-teki," p. 35. (I have calculated the Japanese total by averaging the figure given for the five Japanese auto companies.)

12. Wataai Yumi, "90 nendai no yoka shijō," *Nihon keizai shimbun*, July 5, 1990, p. 27.

13. According to a survey conducted by NHK, quoted in Yasumaru, "Rekishi kenkyū," p. 27. Another estimate is that the working hours of men aged about 30 rose during the 1980s so that 60 percent of them worked more than 50 hours, and 20 percent more than 60 hours per week (Shimada Haruo, "The Desperate Need for New Values in Japanese Corporate Behavior," *Journal of Japanese Studies*, Vol. 17, No. 1, Winter 1991, pp. 107–21, at p. 115).

14. Philippe Pons, "Japanese Ponder How to Stop Work," *Guardian Weekly*, April 12, 1992.

15. Enno Berndt, "Atarashii shijō o sōzō suru rōdō kankyō to wa," *Jitsugyō no nihon*, May 1994, pp. 42–3.

16. Michitoshi Takabatake and Takamitsu Sawa, "Japan Acts as Role Model," *Japan Times*, January 1, 1992.

17. Sawa Takamitsu, "Koritsu shijō de wa jiyū shakai no koji ni," *Mainichi shimbun*, April 7, 1992.

18. Sataka Makoto, *"Kaisha kokka" o utsu*, Kyoto, Kamogawa Bukkuretto No. 64, p. 14.

19. Sataka Makoto, "Oumu shinrikyō to kigyōkyō wa kami hitoe," *Shūkan kinyōbi*, July 7, 1995, p. 35.

20. Nagano Kenji, "Kaishashugi" no shizuka na hōkai," *Sekai*, February 1992, pp. 44–51.

21. "Morita Shock: A New Paradigm Needed for Japanese Management," *Japanese Business Today*, Vol. 60, No. 3, March 1992, pp. 40–42.

22. Morita Akio, "Nihongata keiei ga abunai," *Bungei shunjū*, February 1992, pp. 94–103.

23. Quoted in Totsuka Hideo, "Building Japan's Corporate Society," *Ampo— Japan-Asia Quarterly Review*, Vol. 25, No. 1, 1994, pp. 11–19, at p. 16.

24. Tsuji Yōmei, "Burokkuka suru sekai keizai," Part 16, *Asahi shimbun*, April 27, 1992. (All three of these English terms were used by Hiraiwa as he struggled to articulate what he meant.) See also Anthony Rowley, "Ease up, Japan," *Far Eastern Economic Review*, August 6, 1992.

25. Tsuji, "Burokkuka suru."

26. *Asahi shimbun*, editorial, February 7, 1992.

27. Anthony Rowley, "Kinder, Gentler Japan," *Far Eastern Economic Review*, July 9, 1992.

28. Keizai kikakuchō, *Seikatsu taikoku gokanen keikaku—chikyū shakai to no kyōzon o mezashite*, July 1992.

29. Robyn Williams, "Corporate Ethic under Canon Fire," *The Australian* (Higher Education Supplement), August 18, 1993.

30. Ministry of international Trade and Industry, ed., *Kindai ni wasuremono—kansei yutaka na shakai o mezashite*, Tokyo, Kyōdō tsūshinsha, 1994.

31. From 37.9 per 1,000 in 1955 to 145.2 per 1,000 in 1985. Satō Makoto, *Rizōto rettō*, Iwanami shinsho 1990, p. 157. Japan Hospital Association figures show rates of community health continuing to decline, especially in the Osaka-Kobe area, through the decade of 1984–94. Reuter, "Hospitals say health of Japanese declining," Tokyo, August 23, 1995.

32. Kōseishō, *Kanja chōsa*, 1990, in Asahi shimbunsha, *Japan Almanac 1995*, p. 211.

33. Teruoka Itsuko, *Yutakasa to wa nanika*, Iwanami, 1989, p. 142 ff. (Teruoka also includes an excellent general discussion of the phenomenon of stress.)

34. The U.S.-based International Educational Development Inc. estimates 10,000 per year, a figure that in Japan itself is not controversial, and may be too low. *Japan Times*, February 19, 1992. See also Louise do Rosario and Anthony Rowley, "A Dying Breed," *Far Eastern Economic Review*, August 3, 1992, pp. 55–56.

35. Quoted in Satō, *Rizōto rettō*, p. 157.

36. Survey conducted by Flinders University (South Australia) and the International Survey Research Corporation (Chicago), reported in *Nihon keizai shimbun*, November 7, 1991. See also Riaz Hassan, "Attitudes of Employees: 1991 International Norm Comparisons." (My thanks to Professor Hassan, of Flinders University, for a copy of this unpublished paper.)

37. According to the Labor Ministry survey, 61.7 percent. *Asahi Evening News*, November 11, 1991.

38. J. Waish and Mizuho Toyoshima, "All in Your Mind," *Look Japan*, April 1990, pp. 30–31. (Also various advertising materials.)

39. On resorts in general, see the following: *Gekkan Jichiken*, Vol. 31, No. 361, October 1989, "Kizutsuku Nihon rettō"; Satō Makoto and NHK "Ohayō jānaru shusaihan," *Dokyumento-rizōto*, Nihon hyōronsha 1989; Satō, *Rizōto rettō*; Yamada Kunihiro, *Gorufujō bōkokuron*, Shinhyōron 1989, and in English, "The Triple Evil of Golf Courses," *Japan Quarterly*, July–September 1990, pp. 291–97; *Nōgyo kyōdō kumiai*, Vol. 426, August 1990, special issue, "Dō suru-rizōto kaihatsu." Also in audiovisual materials: NHK Kyūshū supeshiaru, "Kuzureyuku rakuen-Okinawa no shizen wa ima," August 1989; and NHK dokyumento supeshiaru, "Rizōto rettō," July 1990.

40. Fujiwara Makoto, "Katsute naki shizen hakai e no michi," *Sekai*, June 1990, pp. 131–43, at p. 140. On the general rural and fishing industry crisis, the NHK film material is evocative.

41. Miyamoto Ken'ichi, "Nihon kankyō hōkoku—Rizōtohō o kangaeru," *Asahi jānaru*, November 10, 1989, p. 53.

42. Satō, *Rizōto rettō*, pp. 171–72.

43. "Blueprint for the 21st Century," speech to Forty-second Session of the United Nations General Assembly, September 21, 1987, *Speaking of Japan*, December 1987, pp. 26–32.

44. Satō, *Rizōto rettō*, 1990, p. 123; Hayashi Ryōji, "Kankyō hakai no rizōto hō o haishi seyo," *Ekonomisuto*, January 21, 1992, pp. 54–57, at p. 55.

45. One percent of Japan's forests was felled for golf construction by the end of the 1980s. Yamada Kunihiro, "The Triple Evil of Golf Courses," *Japan Quarterly*, July–September 1990, p. 235.

46. Satō, *Rizōto rettō*, pp. 3–4. For a table of projects to December 1991, see "Zenkoku no rizōto kōsō," *Ekonomisuto*, January 21, 1992, pp. 62–63.

47. *Sekai*, June 1990, p. 223 (quoting *Ryūkyū shinpō*). On Okinawa and Kyushu, see also Kyūshū bengoshi rengōkai, *Rizōto kaihatsu hikari to kage*, Fukuoka, 1991, pp. 38–40.

48. Fumiko Fujisaki, "All Bets Off at Slumping Links," *Japan Times*, April 20, 1994.

49. "Kuni o mushibamu Nihon no gorufujō," *Nōsaido*, January 1992, p. 114. There are an estimated 25,000 golf courses worldwide covering an area as large as Belgium, 14,000 in the United States and 3,000 in the United Kingdom as against the 2,000 in Japan (Genevieve Fox, "How About Bunking Off for the Day?" *The Independent*, April 28, 1994).

50. Ibid. 23.6 percent of men and 2.6 percent of women were counted as players.

51. Ibid.

52. Satō, *Rizōto rettō*, p. 132. Also NHK, dokyumento supeshiaru, 1990.

53. Satō, *Rizōto rettō*, p. 131. Also NHK, dokyumento supeshiaru, 1990. Both sources refer to a Kumagai development on the Bōsō peninsula (in Chiba Prefecture), where a profit of 17.3 billion yen was anticipated for a zero (sic) initial capital outlay.

54. Satō, *Rizōto rettō*, p. 125.

55. "Nihon seitai gakkai rizōto ni keishō," *Akahata*, December 13, 1989, p. 12. Also various articles by Honda Katsuichi in *Asahi jānaru*, April and May 1990.

56. Fujisaki, "All bets off."

57. "Rizōto kaihatsu," *Nihon keizai shimbun*, January 14, 1990.

58. Ibid, p. 136 (and see tables on pp. 136–37). See also Yukio Noguchi, "The Bubble and Economic Policies in the 1980s," *Journal of Japanese Studies*, Vol. 20, No. 2, Summer 1994, pp. 291–330, at pp. 292–93.

59. Satō, *Rizōto rettō*, p. 146.

60. Christopher Wood, "Japanese Finance," special supplement to *The Economist*, December 8, 1990, p. 3.

61. Ibid., p. 138.

62. Satō, *Rizōto rettō*, p. 128.

63. Various Japanese media reports, December 19, 1990, and subsequent.

64. Christopher Wood, "Japanese Finance," special supplement to *The Economist*, December 8, 1990, p. 3.

65. Peter Hartcher, "Japanic! Putt Options Sink to a Nine-Year Low," *Australian Financial Review*, March 21, 1995.

66. Satō, *Rizōto rettō*, p. 132.

67. Abe David and Ted Wheelwright, *The Third Wave: Asian Capitalism and Australia*, Sydney, 1989, p. 153 (quoting the *Daily Mirror* of January 13, 1989).

68. "Chokusetsu tōshi—Nihon Eibei nuki sekai ichi," *Asahi shimbun*, December 21, 1990.

69. *The Australian*, June 16, 1990.

70. Gen Morita, "Golf Courses Threaten Hawaii Lifestyles," *Resources* (Consumer Union of Japan Newsletter), No. 80, January–March 1992, pp. 1–2.

71. Gwen Benjamin, "Japanese Golf Boom Alarms Malaysians," *Japan Times*, January 5, 1992.

72. Ismail Kassim, "Zoo Row Puts Spotlight on Golf and Condo Projects," *The Straits Times*, October 7, 1991; also Lincoln Kaye, "Look to the Hills," *Far Eastern Economic Review*, August 22, 1991, and Doug Tsuruoka, "Malice in Wonderland," *Far Eastern Economic Review*, October 10, 1991.

73. NHK TV, "21," September 1, 1991.

74. Anne Platt, "Toxic Green: The Trouble with Golf," *World Watch*, May–June 1994, pp. 27–40.

75. Tony Allison et al., "Rough Justice," *Asia Magazine*, April 15–17, 1994, p. 26.

76. "GAG'M Update No. 2," May 1994, Chiba, Penang, Bangkok, Hawaii, and Bedford (England), GAG'M coordinating networks.

77. Matsuo Takashi, "Beikoku de hatan suru Nihon-shiki gorufu shōhō," *Tōyō keizai*, March 14, 1992, p. 20.

78. Henny Sender, "No Going Back," *Far Eastern Economic Review*, September 15, 1994, pp. 74–75.

79. Yamamoto Atsuko, "Takahashi Harunori-shi wa kamoku na dai-shakkin-ō," *Aera*, February 27, 1995, pp. 6–9.

80. Ben Hills, "Scandal exposes Japan Inc," *Sydney Morning Herald*, April 5, 1995.

81. Yamada, "The Triple Evil of Golf Courses," p. 292.

82. Hideki Minamikawa, quoted in Platt, "Toxic Green," p. 38.

83. Yamada, 1990, p. 235.

84. Honda Katsuichi, *Asahi jānaru*, December 15, 1989.

85. Yamada, "The Triple Evil of Golf Courses," p. 292; also Yamada, 1989, passim.

86. "Tsukaisute ōkoku (6) nōyaku o nagasu gorufujō," *Asahi shimbun*, December 20, 1989, p. 10.

87. See "Rizōto tokushū" (special issue on resorts), *Sekai*, June 1990, p. 60.

88. Satō, *Rizōto rettō*, pp. 163-64; NHK dokyumento supeshiaru, 1990; Fujiwara Makoto, "Katsute naki shizen hakai e no michi, pp. 131-43.

89. Satō, *Rizōto rettō*.

90. "Protection of Wildlife," editorial, *Mainichi Daily News*, January 1990, p. 2.

91. Mark Brazil, "The Wildlife of Japan: A Twentieth-Century Naturalist's view," *Japan Quarterly*, July-September 1992, pp. 328–38.

92. NHK, dokyumento supeshiaru.

93. Yamazato Setsuko, interview, Shiraho, Ishigaki, December 1989. Also Noike Motoki, "Sango no umi o kowashi, nōka o kurushimeru 'tochi kairyō' jigyō," *Shūkan kinyōbi*, June 24, 1994, pp. 28–33.

94. Satō and NHK "Ohayō jānaru shuzaihan," 1989, p. 30.

95. Matsutaka Akihiro and Ui Jun, "Shizen yutaka datta shima no fukō," *Shūkan kinyōbi*, June 17, 1994, pp. 50–53; "Yamu sango—riku no kaihatsu ga eikyō Ishigakijima," *Asahi shimbun*, November 15, 1994.

96. GAG'M, 1994.

97. Udagawa Hideo, "Hatan shita rizōto," *Tōyō keizai*, March 14, 1992, pp. 8–14, at p. 10.

98. For a list of "stalemated" projects: "Kishimu rizōto rettō," (report by special team), *Asahi shimbun*, May 25, 1992. (See also "Tenkan no rizōto," *Nihon keizai shimbun*, April 17, 1992.)

99. Yoshimi Shunya, *Hakurankai no seijigaku*, Chūkō shinsho, 1992, p. 234 ff.

100. Kaminogō Toshiaki, *Hausu tenposu monogatari*, Purejidentosha, 1992.

101. Quoted in ibid., p. 46.

102. Cameron Hay, "Dutch Resort Has No Trouble Staying Afloat in Recession," *Japan Times*, May 17, 1994.

103. Kaminogō, *Hausu tenposu*, p. 79.

104. Impression gained on this author's visit in November 1994.

105. This was only the first stage of the projected "Nagasaki Exotic Resort" development, and a city of 150,000 people was projected in due course for the environs of Huis Ten Bosch.

106. The design and construction is by Mitsubishi Heavy Industries, marking a growing shift away from its heavy reliance on ships and weapons (Saitō Ichirō, "Mitsubishi gurūpu no shisan 100 chō en pāwa," *Aera*, July 20, 1993, pp. 26–28).

107. For a nicely illustrated introduction, see Kikuo Arai, "Taking the Outdoors Indoors" (with photographs by Tadasuke Akiyama) in *Pacific Friend*, Vol. 21, No. 6, October 1993, pp. 2–9.

108. Yoshimi Shunya, "Yūenchi no yūtopia," *Sekai*, September 1989, pp. 293–306, at p. 306. This essay is reproduced, with notes, under the title "Shimyurākuru no rakuen" in Taki Koji and Uchida Ryūzō, eds., *Zero no shūjigaku*, Riburopōto, 1992, pp. 79–136.

109. Yoshimi Shunya, *Hakurankai*, p. 256.

110. Asada Akira, "Infantile Capitalism and Japan's Post Modernism: A Fairy Tale," in Masao Miyoshi and H.D. Harootunian, eds., *Post-Modernism and Japan*, Durham and London, Duke University Press, 1989, pp. 273–78, at p. 275–76.

111. Mita Munesuke, "Reality, Dream and Fiction: Japan 1945–90," *Journal of Pacific Asia*, 1994, No. 1, pp. 121–33, at p. 131.

112. Yoshimi, "Hakurankai," p. 306.

113. Bernd Von Droste, Dana Silk, and Mechtild Rössler, "Tourism, World Heritage and Sustainable Development," *Kyoto Journal*, No. 24, 1993, pp. 5–8 (reprinted from the July–December issue of the UNEP journal *Industry and Environment*).

114. John Urry, *The Tourist Gaze: Leisure and Travel in Contemporary Societies*, London, Newbury Park, California, and New Delhi, 1990, p. 13.

115. Okubo Keiji, "Muraokoshi ni kono te ano te," *Aera*, October 27, 1992, pp. 50–51.

116. For a list of 241 such projects, see "Himo-nashi bōnasu 1 oku en chie o shibotte machiokoshi," *Asahi shimbun*, December 21, 1991. Other examples drawn from "Go nenme no furusato sōsei," *Asahi shimbun*, April 23, 1992,

"Furusato sōsei natta ka nai ka," *Asahi shimbun*, May 20, 1993, and Asako Murakami, "Charcoal helps revive Iwate village," *Japan Times*, November 9, 1993.

117. John Knight, "Rural *Kokusaika*? Foreign Motifs and Village Revival in Japan," *Japan Forum*, Vol. 5, No. 2, October 1993, pp. 203–15, at p. 208.

118. Nakatani Gentarō, Mizoguchi Kunpei, and Kihara Keikichi, "Hontō no rizōto wa nani ka—Oita-ken Yufuin o tazunete," *Kōgai kenkyū*, Vol. 21, No. 2, Autumn 1991, pp. 2–9, at p. 9.

119. Oita-ken Yufuin-machi, "Uruoi no aru machizukuri kankei jōrei," Kyūshū bengoshikai rengōkai, *Rizōto kaihatsu hikari to kage*, Fukuoka, 1991, pp. 202–5.

120. For a detailed study of Yufuin, see Suzuki Shigeru and Kobuchi Minato, Eds., *Rizōto no sōgōteki kenkyū*, Kyoto, Kōyō shobō, 1991, pp. 206–18.

121. Takahashi Saya et al., "Kuma-chō no chiiki sangyō shinkō seisaku—sono tokuchō to kadai," Ehime-ken jichitai mondai kenkyūjō, *Ehime no jichi*, No. 68, April 1993.

122. Matsutaka Akihiro, in Matsutaka and Ui, "Shizen yutaka," p. 52.

123. See, for example, the photos in *Sekai*, June 1990, pp. 30–31, or in the film footage in Satō and NHK "Ohayō jānaru shusaihan," 1989, pp. 27, 32.

124. Satō, *Rizōto rettō*, p. 114.

125. Ibid., p. 20. Also NHK, dokyumento supeshiaru, 1990.

126. A vision defined by Prime Minister Takeshita in December 1987, quoted in Satō, *Rizōto rettō*, p. 21.

127. See for example, Miyamoto Kenichi, Yokota Shigeru, and Nakamura Kojirō, *Chiiki keizaigaku*, Yuhikaku bukkusu 1990, pp. 339 ff; and, for a union response to the problem, Zen Nihon jichi dantai rōdō kumiai, *Atarashii jidai no kuni-chihō kankei*, October 1989, pp. 52–57.

3

The Farm State: GATTing Japan

Introduction: Corn Laws–Rice Laws

The world is slowly awakening to a sense of gathering material crisis of population, resources, and environment. As the end of the Cold War signaled the revision of the basic structures by which Japan had for long related with the world on political and strategic terms, so its global economic linkages were simultaneously shaken by fundamental revisions of the General Agreement on Tariff and Trade (GATT) system and the introduction in 1995 of the World Trade Organization (WTO). Neither the political nor the economic was one-dimensional, for what, at one level, was a matter of market and monetary value was at another one of fundamental social and moral value, impinging not only on the material "whatness" or "howness," but also the moral "whyness" of life. Beneath the manifold forms of global material crisis impinging on Japan lay a crisis of values.

The existence of protected agricultural markets in Japan (and other East Asian states that are major industrial exporters) has become increasingly anomalous under the free-trade agenda of GATT, and the particular butt of criticism from major agricultural exporters such as the United States and the European Economic Community. Since Japan depends on GATT for open export markets for its industrial and service exports, its resistance in the farm sector became more and more difficult to sustain. Late in 1993, when the Japanese government agreed to allow a partial opening of its rice market under the so-called Uruguay Round negotiations of GATT, it was a profoundly symbolic concession. The defenses of a core sector that had been preserved in isolation from the world economy, the most purely Japanese enclave, had fallen, and it was assumed that the processes of rationalization and internationalization that have marked other sectors of the economy would now penetrate agriculture and food distribution. The restructuring of the Japanese food market could be expected to mean increasing dependence on imported foodstuffs, a greater role for international (and Japanese) agribusiness, and a diminished one for both the small-scale family farm and local supply and distribution networks, and a radical transformation of the Japanese landscape.

The Uruguay Round negotiations were prolonged, having begun in 1986, and the concession to the proposal drafted by Arthur Dunkel in 1994 was only the last of a series of concessions, but it concerned rice, and that alone gave it incomparable symbolic impact. Could Japanese rice farming survive? If Japan ceased to be a rice-growing and rice-consuming culture, then what would it be? If Japan, having attained wealth and power in the world, could not feed its own people and instead exposed future generations to an unprecedented vulnerability, was not the achievement of the present generation somehow hollow? Doubts and anxieties about fundamental questions of identity, survival, and meaning lay beneath the superficially economic terms of the debate.

Political leaders had repeatedly pledged that not one grain of foreign rice would be admitted to Japan, so when they backed down in 1993, it was both controversial and humiliating. When the Japanese government accepted the principle of an open market, there was certainly no social consensus supporting such change. Even those few who did support it tended to be of the reluctant kind that saw the concession as essential to avoid breakdown of the Uruguay Round negotiations and severe recriminations from the international community as a result. Some took comfort in thinking of the agreement as very modest in character, since under the Minimum Access Formula, imports would be held to an annual agreed-upon proportion of domestic needs for six years, rising gradually to 8 percent of the rice market (about 800,000 tons), followed by gradual further opening under a tariff system from the year 2001. Others, however, hailed it as an historic opening, comparable to the repeal of the corn laws by which Britain had abandoned agricultural protection and adopted comprehensive free trade policies in 1846.[1] The liberalization of the Japanese rice market would signify a comparable, confident, and responsible opening to the world by the late-twentieth-century power of Japan. As Funabashi put it, "To internationalize this sacred staple would not only internationalize the mythic essence of Japan, it would also revolutionize political culture, which has been founded for the last forty years on rice protectionism."[2] Other prominent figures, from agricultural economists such as Hayami Yūjirō to advocates of political reform based on priority to urban consumers such as Ohmae Kenichi, also agreed that drastic agricultural reform, and moves toward a fully open market, were both desirable and necessary.[3]

The apparent success of the East Asian countries, especially Japan, in coping with the international market economy is held by the proponents of the global market to prove the wisdom of their case, showing, in other words, that what seemed to work in manufactured goods would also work for agricultural produce. A free and greatly enhanced flow of commodities and services around the world is confidently expected to follow from the ratification of the Uruguay Round of GATT. There are, nevertheless, grounds for doubting whether faith in the free market will be matched by its ability to solve the immense problems already outlined. As in all transitions from a protected to a free market, it is the powerful states (and anticipated beneficiaries) that have been most enthusiastic. In contrast to its enthusiasm about playing a positive role in constructing a new *political* world order in the United Nations, Japan was notably reluctant about the GATT formula for a new *economic* world order, at least insofar as it concerned the agricultural sector. It yielded in the end, despite fierce domestic opposition, only because resistance would have exposed it to an unacceptably high degree of international isolation and recrimination, especially from the United States. The same was true of the other East Asian industrial states, especially Taiwan and South Korea.

The analogy with nineteenth-century Britain and the appeal to Japan to exercise an open, responsible contemporary world citizenship are persuasive, but this chapter argues that responsible citizenship in the late-twentieth-century world context might call for a quite different response. The Japanese decision needs to be seen not only in terms of free trade *versus* protection, or of the tensions within the G7 (or indeed within the G2 of the United States and Japan), but also in the context of changes in the world environmental and population balance, shrinking global agricultural acreage, and declining harvests, and within the political as well as economic dimensions of the North-South relationship.

Whatever long-term assessment one makes of the prospects, and opinions differ widely, the cycle of production, distribution, and consumption of food is being rapidly integrated by global market forces. Ratification of the GATT agreements of 1993 will further reduce the barriers between local and global networks and expand the dominant (first-world) pattern of production. Being heavily reliant on capital-, chemical-, and machine-intensive techniques, gradual elimination of small producers, and expansion of scale, increased monocropping, and production for global (often remote) markets, proves advantageous for those with maximum market purchasing power. Whether agriculture and food can be treated as just a commodity, like toothbrushes and autos, is the question.

Food, Population, and the Malthus Nightmare

Contemporary thinking on these matters remains firmly rooted in classical political economy. The optimists look to the workings of the principle of comparative advantage enunciated by David Ricardo to adjust competing and unequal interests within the market, and argue that it is natural for Japan, with its advantage in the production of autos and computers, to import food. Pessimists pursue the insights of the early-nineteenth-century English clergyman Thomas Malthus, who focused attention on the limits of the economic system, particularly on the perceived contradiction between the geometric progression by which human population was expanding and the arithmetic progression by which the forces of production, and therefore the resources upon which populations depended, expanded. For Japan, they argue, reliance on world-market forces in this sector would be stupid and shortsighted. Where neoclassical, free-market economists remain confident of the market's continuing capacity to respond and regulate pressures upon it, critics are much more likely to align themselves with specialists in the natural sciences, especially the life sciences, who look to the indicators of the failing health of the system as a whole, and to signs that the self-regulating capacity is not functioning. The prospect that so alarmed Thomas Malthus at the beginning of the nineteenth century has now become much more plausible.

World population, perhaps 200 million at the time of Christ, reached 500 million during the lifetime of Columbus, then doubled to one billion by 1830, doubled again in the one hundred years to 1930, again in around forty-five years to 1975, and passed the five billion mark in

1987. A careful review of the alternative population scenarios concludes that the figure in 2030 could be either eight billion or eleven billion, depending on fertility and mortality variables.[4]

The phenomenon of doubling at shorter and shorter intervals is exponential, or, as described by one demographer emphasizing the rate of the climb, "super-exponential."[5] Not only is the rate increasing, but the absolute numbers involved have increased explosively. Such accelerating, geometric progression is obviously not sustainable over the long term, and while the question of what the long term is may be debated, the implications for humanity grow more serious as the graph rises. In the current phase of the twenty years between 1990 and 2010, world population is expected to increase by a figure approximately equal to the entire world population of 1900, with 94 percent of the increase to be in the developing countries. If the U.N. experts' prediction of a mid-twenty-first-century world population of ten billion is realized, it would mean virtually doubling the figure of the early 1990s.[6] Some senior U.N. officials believe that at current levels, the world has already become "a full-occupancy planet," with particular concern for "supplies of fresh water, of sea fisheries and surface soils."[7] Seventeen percent of the earth's soil is degraded and (during the 1980s) 1 percent of its tropical forest was being lost yearly, not to mention the ongoing phenomena of global warming, the hole in the ozone layer, rising sea levels, expanding deserts, vanishing species, etc. This is the world that our grandchildren will inherit.

Already one billion people are chronically malnourished.[8] While the richest one-fifth of the world's people, mostly living in the relative comfort of the North, consume 83 percent of the world product, the poorest one-fifth, mostly living in the South, consume a mere 1.4 percent of it.[9] The present industrialized countries will account for a steadily diminishing proportion of world population in the coming decades, from 22 percent in 1990 to around 14 percent in 2030.[10] Food production, which needs to triple up to the mid-twenty-first century, is actually shrinking, as land is taken out of crop production and turned over to urban or industrial purposes, or suffers salination, loss of nutrients, desertification, or other degradation. The volume of water available per world inhabitant is only one-third of what it was in 1970. Rivers, lakes, and underground aquifers show signs of depletion and degradation, and 40 percent of the world's people lack access to proper supplies of drinking water. It is difficult to view with equanim-

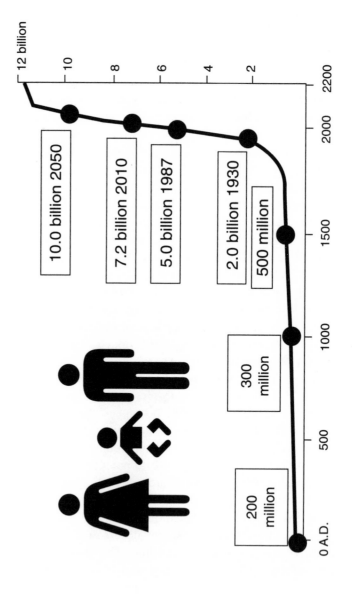

Figure 3.1 World Population Growth

ity this pattern of a resource base that shrinks in quantity and deteriorates in quality, as water, soil, and air suffer degradation and the biodiversity of botanical and zoological species is threatened, while the pressures of population grow in unprecedented proportion. Recent studies conclude that "by every conceivable measure, mankind is ecologically abnormal,"[11] that a "malignant ecopathological process"[12] is underway, or that "we have already entered this natural catastrophic phase in the evolution of the human species."[13]

However, optimists remind us that the Club of Rome, in its famous report of 1972 on "The Limits to Growth," predicted famine in Asia, and that, instead, the decades that followed the Green Revolution brought a massive increase in productivity that lifted vast numbers of people above the survival line and created a burgeoning new middle class across Asia. The average income in the developing world doubled in the decades after 1960; absolute-poverty and infant-mortality figures declined dramatically, while literacy and life expectancy grew.[14] Despite the stark impression of the population- and food-trend statistics, there is, therefore, inveterate optimism in some quarters, and a tendency to dismiss as crude Malthusian determinism any talk of limits. In this spirit are the forecasts of *The Economist,* which looks forward to the market of "a billion consumers" in Asia,[15] and the *Far Eastern Economic Review,* which concludes its assessment by saying, "Though much remains to seat everyone at the banquet of prosperity, we now know what works: free peoples trading freely with one another."[16]

If the sanguine predictions for the future are inclined to issue from economists—at least those who believe the free market is capable of achieving miracles—most scientists are more sober. Thus, early in 1992, the U.S. National Academy of Sciences and the British Royal Society issued a joint warning that:

> If current predictions of population growth prove accurate and patterns of human activity on the planet remain unchanged, science and technology may not be able to prevent either irreversible degradation of the environment or continued poverty for much of the world.[17]

One of the most eloquent spokesmen for the pessimistic view is Lester R. Brown of the Worldwatch Institute. He believes that:

> When the history of the late twentieth century is written, the 1990s will be seen as a decade of discontinuity—a time when familiar trends that

had seemed likely to go on forever, like smooth straight roads, came to abrupt bends or junctures and began descending abruptly.[18]

The output of coal, the production of steel, the harvest of grain, and the catch of fish, all of which had been steadily growing for decades (and indeed, with the exception of steel, since the advent of the Industrial Revolution), began to turn downward, even as the upward spiral of population growth continued inexorably. Grain output is perhaps the most crucial. Growing on average at around 3 percent per year in the period from 1950 to 1984, it outstripped population growth and allowed much improved nutrition for countless people, but since 1984, the rate of increase was pared to around 1 percent, which meant an actual per capita decline. In 1991, world grain production registered its largest every year-to-year drop, by 84 million tons.[19] Specialists in the World Hunger Project calculate that "the planetary ecosystem could, with present agrotechnologies and with equal distribution of food supplies, *sustainably* support no more than 6 billion people even if they all lived off a vegetarian diet—and the 1993 global population is already 5.5 billion. If humans . . . gained 25 percent of their calories from animal protein, as is the case with most people in North America, the Earth could sustainably support only 2.8 billion people."[20]

Fish production also began to decline in both absolute and per capita terms in the 1990s, and according to the U.N.'s Food and Agriculture Organization (FAO), "All 17 of the world's major fishing areas have either reached or exceeded their natural limits, and . . . 9 are in serious decline."[21] By 1993, the overall world catch had declined some 7 percent from its all-time high in 1989.[22] Not only are catches down, but the mangrove nurseries are being pushed back, coral reefs are under threat, and marine animals, such as whales, penguins, seals, and dolphins are carrying in their bodies increasing concentrations of farm chemicals.[23] Across the world, carbon-dioxide emissions are steadily rising and, only a few years after the U.N.'s Special Conference on the Environment and Development held in Rio de Janeiro in June 1992, the prospect of meeting the emission standards set there is receding, bringing closer the likelihood of average world temperatures increasing by between two and four degrees by mid-century and causing a drastic reduction in agricultural yields in some of the world's most productive areas.[24] In other words, the food-population balance is already most delicately poised and headed toward unprecedented crisis.

Table 3.1

Growth in Food Production and Natural Resources, 1950–92

	Rapid Growth Period		Slow Growth Period	
	Year	Percentage rate	Year	Percentage rate
Major Food Products				
Grain production	1950–84	+2.9	1984–92	+0.7
Soy bean production	1950–80	+5.1	1980–92	+2.2
Meat production	1950–86	+3.4	1986–92	+2.0
Fish catch	1950–88	+4.0	1988–92	−0.8
Major Agricultural Resources				
Crop cultivation area	1950–81	+0.7	1981–92	−0.5
Irrigated area	1950–78	+2.8	1978–92	+1.2
Fertilizer use	1950–84	+6.7	1984–92	+0.7

Source: Tokoro Hideo, "Shokuryō wa jiyū bōeki ni najimanai," in Iba Mikako and Furusawa Kōyū, *Gatto—Jiyū bōeki e no gimon*, Gakuyō shobō, 1993, pp. 21–35. Note that although grain output rose slightly, by 0.7 percent per annum, between 1984 and 1992, in per capita population terms, this represented a shrinkage of 6 percent.

China, the world's most populous country and scene of a remarkable economic boom in the early 1990s, is losing one million hectares of cropland per year under industrialization and is converting more of its grain to livestock feeding to accommodate the dietary requirements of an expanded urban middle class.[25] The Worldwatch Institute predicts that China's grain production will fall by at least 20 percent between 1990 and 2030, and its grain import needs will far outstrip the world capacity to supply.[26]

In the context of the long-term prospect of deepening crisis of population versus resources, the GATT/WTO position (or the small group of advanced countries that dominates those bodies) is that free trade provides the answer. The market will solve it. That is, however, a dogmatic, rather than a scientific, proposition.

Hunger and deprivation in the contemporary world is not absolute, however absolute it is for those who experience it. The problem is that distribution is far from equal, and the adherents of market faith offer little assurance that the global market will handle this problem better than the semiglobal one of today. In this integrated market, the interests of the rich will obviously have precedence, and it is possible that polarization may intensify as the expanded global middle class insists on its right to consumption patterns that are closely tied to a high-protein diet, especially to increased consumption of meat. Since it requires approximately seven kilograms of grain to produce one of beef (four in the case of pork and two for poultry),[27] the unequal contest between wealthy and poor consumers is likely to intensify as the market opens and the gap between supply and demand widens.[28]

The Food-Dependent Superpower

However reluctantly Japan agreed to seat itself at the Uruguay Round "banquet" table in 1993, it had nevertheless, long before GATT, shown the way to the rest of the world in terms of its commitment to dependence on world-market forces. Few countries could compare with Japan in commitment to an open-door policy on food imports even prior to the 1993 moves on rice. Japan's self-sufficiency rate in terms of the capacity to supply its people with food from domestic sources has declined steadily. In 1960, it met 82 percent of the grain needs and 79 percent of calorie requirements from domestic sources, but by 1990, only 29 and 47 percent respectively.[29] Among the industrial countries, its pattern of a deliberately chosen high level of food dependence is highly distinctive. Britain, once in a similar position, deliberately reversed its dependence, so that by 1988, it had become 105 percent self-sufficient in cereals (while France, West Germany and Italy were at 222, 106, and 80 percent respectively).[30] Japan was unquestionably the world's number one food-importing country, even before moving to liberalize its rice market. In 1989, for example, it imported twenty-seven million tons, or 11.4 percent, of the world's traded grain total of 236 million tons.[31] In that same year, it imported 84 percent of its corn, 71 percent of its sorghum, 75 percent of its soybeans, 55 percent of its wheat, 43 percent of its beef and veal, 38 percent of its poultry meat, 98 percent of its citrus, and 43 percent of its cotton from the United States alone.[32] Food imports in 1991 amounted to 4.6 trillion yen (approximately $34 billion), more than was spent on oil.[33] Japan also regularly imports around one-quarter of the world's traded marine products, including one-third of its tuna and two-fifths of its shrimp, and is an increasingly important importer of meat (imports of which rose fourteen times between 1983 and 1988). Beef imports, rising at 20 percent per year during the period of quotas in the 1980s, continued after liberalization to register a further steady, if slower, increase.[34] The Japanese pet-food market alone is worth 200 billion yen (roughly $2 billion) annually.

Postwar Japanese governments have drastically diminished the security of people's livelihood in the sense of choosing an extraordinary degree of vulnerability to market forces beyond their control. Curiously, this dismantling of internal defenses was accompanied by a heightened rhetoric about food security and ran parallel to a stubborn insistence on conventional, military security, such that the alliance with the United States was the core of all postwar Japanese strategic thinking. Japan eventually grew to boast of the second-greatest military budget in the world. The choices have been deliberate, but the context within which they were made, like so much of the basic institutional structure of modern Japan, was the Cold War. The basis of the present, small-farmer system was laid out by the U.S. occupation (1945–52), which undertook a redistribution of agricultural land ownership, ended tenancy, and removed the powers and privileges of the old landowning class. These early changes unleashed a burst of productivity, but the system of small, independent ownership gradually rigidified. Attempts at further reform such as the 1961 Basic Law on Agriculture, which envisaged doubling the average minimum farm size to two hectares and reducing farm households to 2.3 million, failed.[35] The political will was never mobilized to achieve anything so drastic, in large part because the electoral base of conservative political party rule was heavily rural and opposed to reform. The advent of the high-growth, income-doubling policies of the 1960s ushered in a steady decline in the farming population. Millions moved into the cities, while those who remained were transformed into part-time farmers, whose major income came from elsewhere, commonly (as in the sector described in Chapter 1), the construction state. By the early 1990s, there were 4.25 million farmers (14 percent of the population), but 88 percent of them (3.76 million) were part-timers.[36] Among rice farmers, 83 percent were still working allotments of less one hectare.[37]

The Japanese market was insulated from the world under the Food Control Law (1942), a wartime measure that, despite revisions, in the mid-1990s provided the basic framework of governmental regulation of the production, distribution, and sale of rice. Imports were banned, and the Agriculture Ministry's Food Control Agency bought rice directly from farmers and sold to consumers at subsidized rates through specially licensed retailers. Through the postwar years, the differential between domestic and world prices widened to between six and ten to one. As a "rice mountain" began to accumulate behind protective barriers in the late 1960s, the Agriculture Ministry turned from encouraging production to attempting to limit it, and, year after year, designated acreages were removed from production under the system known as *gentan* (zoning regulations that allowed conversion of agricultural lands to other purposes within the various Comprehensive National Plans). Influential reports, such as the 1986 Maekawa Report (by an advisory committee headed by Maekawa Haruo, former governor of the Bank of Japan, to Prime Minister Nakasone on how to achieve an internationally harmonious industrial structure), declared that sectors of the economy that were high-priced but characterized by low productivity, such as coal and agriculture, should be converted to import industries.[38]

The stagnation of the domestic agricultural system within its protected and controlled confines was matched by dependence on food imports, which had begun in the context of the postwar food crisis and continued as Japan became locked into place as the world's largest and most profitable market for U.S. agricultural surpluses (wheat, corn, soybeans, etc.).[39] The huge imbalance in the general bilateral trade that followed upon Japan's encroachments in the 1970s and 1980s on U.S. markets for industrial goods led to and fueled U.S. demands for remaining barriers to be swept away. Swept away they were, in one sector after another, up to citrus fruits and beef (1991). Then, the final citadel of rice faced the assault launched in the form of the Dunkel draft around which the whole GATT system was debated in 1993.

By 1993, Japan faced a crisis by reason of external market-opening pressures, but adding to those pressures was the fact that the agricultural sector had been brought to the brink of collapse by fifty years of bureaucratic state control. Demoralization was rife over vacillating government policies; rural depopulation was chronic; fields, especially in remote and hilly countryside, were being abandoned under the gentan (by 1994, the number of abandoned fields amounted to 600 thousand hectares, or approximately 20 percent of the country's agricultural acreage);[40] the farmers themselves were rapidly aging (more than half of them being over sixty in 1990); and faith in farming as a way of life was fading so rapidly that only 1,700 young high-school graduates throughout the country were opting for it as a way of life,[41] leaving only 6.5 percent of farming households with the prospect of an heir.[42] More people were employed in the construction industry than in agriculture, and more land was designated for resort development than for farming. With or without GATT, Japanese agriculture was in a serious plight.

The combination of external market opening (however initially gradual) with the encroaching force of other markets—seeking to convert agricultural land to resorts, motorways, or urban or residential development—is such as to raise very large questions. Whether Japanese agriculture would be able to make the adjustments necessary to survive into the new century was far from clear. Pure Ricardian economists (with whom Japanese bankers like Maekawa and agricultural specialists like Hayami would have to be counted) argue that overall productivity in Japan would rise if agriculture ceased altogether, and that the minimum viable size for a rice farm should be between five and ten hectares (i.e. up to ten times greater than the current average size).[43] In 1992, Hayami wrote, "The most important contribution to the international community that Japan can make at this critical juncture would be to take the lead in accepting the Dunkel draft."[44] For him, the abandonment of a sector in which comparative advantage was slight (if not negative) appeared rational and beneficial. Following earlier structural adjustments that had led to the progressive scuttling of textiles, parts of the heavy and chemical and shipping industries, and indeed (under the high-yen pressures of post-1985) of manufacturing in general, agriculture should not be allowed immunity from market laws. Since Japan had been the major beneficiary of the free market during its decades of expansion, the gesture of freeing up its own farm sector might seem a small price to pay, and the opposition to be irrational, romantic, even atavistic.

The 1942 system of control certainly seemed to have reached a point of no return; it was undermined by the rapid spread of a black market[45] and the defiance of producers and consumers alike, as well as by foreign pressures. Whether there was a way to reform successfully and thereby survive was problematic, but several paths, not necessarily consistent, were being explored: expansion of scale by consolidation of uneconomic holdings to allow capital-intensive and machine-intensive farming methods to the point of international competitiveness (competing with the American/multinational food industry on its terms); organic farming, often by cooperatives hoping to combat lower imported-food prices by offering the intangible factors of safety and health at a market premium (competing by stressing difference);[46] or a concentration on the protection of lands not capable of being sustained on pure market criteria but of such noneconomic value as to warrant special public subsidy, such as remote, mountainous, or environmentally sensitive lands, while allowing market criteria to operate in general (drawing a line between market and nonmarket sectors). In any event, the nexus of conservative political hegemony based on rural patronage had been undermined by the combination of post–Cold War environment and the adoption of a political reform package concentrating on electoral reform. Only in the 1990s did change in the agrarian structures therefore become possible, and the way was cleared for either extinction or real reform.

Holes in GATT

But there are a series of doubts about the GATT formula. First, is it actually a free market that is at issue? While Japan and other countries adding their signatures to the agreement commit themselves to open markets, it was far from clear that the agricultural superpowers, especially the United States and the European Economic Community, would commit themselves to ending production or export subsidies. In fact, the United States, although it entered GATT as champion of free trade, is actually the bastion of neoprotectionism. Within GATT, the United States enjoys the remarkable privilege of a series of exemptions (known as the Nathan exemptions) under which its domestic market for a range of commodities, from peanuts to dairy products and cotton, is protected. Contrary to the general view, the U.S. agricultural market is *more* protected than the Japanese.[47] Furthermore, the U.S. policy of guaranteed prices and subsidies to boost exports of corn, rice, tobacco, and other commodities in order to recover the world cereal markets it used to dominate in the early 1970s is well-established. Under the so-called Export Enhancement Program (EEP), the United States pushed back its competition, especially from Europe, and expanded its share of the world grain market from 31 percent to 46 percent. It also pushed back the share of its ally—the true free market competitor, Australia—from 20 percent to 10 percent.[48] The agricultural sector, which accounts for 10 percent of U.S. exports, receives 80 percent of federal export aids, and the *New York Times* estimates the gross sum of payouts at about $50 billion per year.[49] By 1987, for example, it was through subsidies amounting to $17 per 100 pounds, that U.S. multinational agribusinesses had been able to push down the price of unhusked rice per 100 pounds (approximately 45 kilograms) from approximately $8 to below $4, thereby achieving an export price of approximately $80 per ton below Third World production cost, or about $140 per ton below even American production cost.[50] Contrary to established wisdom, this would suggest that U.S. agriculture is inefficient, wasteful, and unsustainable, and that if energy and environmental costs were factored into U.S. prices and subsidies eliminated, competitiveness would be drastically eroded.

Both labor-intensive agricultural producing countries, such as India, and unsubsidized agricultural exporters, such as Australia, are hard put to cope with such competition, which can scarcely be described as free. Prominent Third World advocates describe it as a concerted assault on the agriculture of the Third World likely to lead, in due course, to famine.[51] It is even misleading to refer to nation-states as units somehow representative of their people or of a collective national interest that is to be advanced by the freeing of agricultural trade, since agribusiness interests are highly autonomous, and in the case of grain, just four giant U.S.-based corporations control 90 percent of the world trade.[52] Whatever else it may be, it is hard to think of GATT as a truly multilateral and democratic institution.

There is a further set of issues. The workings of the food market in nonrice sectors presumably indicate the trends that can be expected from rice "liberalization." Japan's status as a food-import-dependent great power is established, and its impact on the agrarian economy of the region is already profound. Because it is a rich country, its purchases of food serve to stimulate foreign-market restructuring, reduce stocks available on local markets, and force up prices. The growing industry of production, processing, preservation, and transport of the fresh products of the farms, oceans, and forests of Asia to the Japanese consumer is highly energy intensive. As monocropping and orientation toward distant markets spreads, the local consumer often is deprived of traditional foods, or forced to pay in Manila or Djakarta prices appropriate in Osaka or Tokyo. Perhaps if there was a point at which the market ought to be resisted *in principle*, this was it, and on this issue Japan might stand firm and appeal to universal criteria of humanity and civilization in opposition to market rationality. Yet the political and bureaucratic perception was the reverse, and any appeal for rice to be exempted from the workings of GATT was assumed to be totally unacceptable to the international community.

Secondly, whatever one may say about free trade in manufactured goods or services, is a free-market system in food desirable? Virtually every country possesses the ingredients required to produce food— soil, water, seeds, seasonal changes, people—and the social life in all cultures has evolved its distinctive patterns of adjustment to local environs through collective involvement in the seasonal cycle of work— planting, tending, harvesting, exchanging, and consuming the fruits of the local soil, rivers, and seas. A structure that encourages them to abandon all that goes with their traditional food culture and rely instead on a market rationality that drives them to depend on production and supply organized by remote multinational agribusinesses is not necessarily superior.

The New World countries (U.S., Canada, Australia, etc.) enjoy a significant comparative advantage in terms of scale, and have been able to deploy their advantages to substitute capital, machines, chemicals, etc., for much of the labor-intensive phases of the agriculture of the Old World. There is a world of difference between a 100-hectare Californian rice field, planted and sprayed by helicopter, water levels laser adjusted, rarely touched by human hand, and a Japanese paddy, mostly of less than a single hectare, commonly closely nurtured by generations of a single family and integrated in a social and community life built around the rituals of the agrarian cycle. It is not obvious that the enforcement of free competition between them is either necessary or desirable.

In the new world order, the economic (GATT) instruments, by privileging multinational agribusiness over small farmers, point in a different direction from those international instruments concerned with political, social, or ecological rights. To the extent that the restraints on the global food trade are removed, not only are the poor turned into beggars at the banquet of the rich, but in many cases their labor is diverted from production for their own needs to production for the international market, while they themselves are left to consume the leftovers and crops little valued at that level. An increasingly capital-intensive, large-scale mode of agricultural production will require increased inputs of energy per output unit to produce, and also to transport, store, and distribute. It will tend to encourage the kind of rational-shaped production unit—large, square fields devoid of obstacles to mechanized production (including trees)—that maximize short-term productivity and convenience but induce long-term degradation, including loss of topsoil and salinization. The substitution of machine for human labor will intensify the depopulation of rural communities throughout the world, thus adding to the phenomenon of concentration of people in megalopolises, with their escalating material problems of pollution and waste, not to mention their human and social problems of employment and meaningful existence. Although free market globalization sounds like a modern and progressive path, it involves preference for a mode that in many ways is nonsustainable over a way that is both demonstrably sustainable and (in a world in which the problem of providing meaningful employment for citizens is increasingly vexing) also satisfying and labor-intensive.

The GATT issue, superficially commercial, is therefore deeply political and social. Among the most trenchant critics have been the French. Bernard Cassen writes:

> . . . the globalization of the flow of merchandise, services, and capital, the delocalization of production, the power of giant businesses whose center is at once everywhere and nowhere, in short all the declensions of free exchange, constitute . . . threats against democracy. . . . In other words, the more a political entity is economically "open," the more it thereby becomes dependent on foreign markets for its exports and for "strategic" imports in all high-technology sectors, and the more it loses all control over itself and its "governability" becomes problematic.[53]

Cassen's position is that GATT is a profoundly flawed institution that has evolved separately from, and in significant respects at odds with, the spirit of the rest of the family of U.N. organizations and conferences, such as ILO, UNESCO, the Rio Conference of 1992, and the UNDP. The consumer may, as he puts it, have a financial interest in purchasing "socks made by prisoners in China, carpets hand-woven by children in India, Japanese vehicles that are cheaper in Copenhagen than in Osaka, and counter-seasonal fruits grown in Africa to the detriment of food-producing (*vivrière*) cultures." In similar terms, the American consumer advocate, Ralph Nader, says that "this trade agreement is driven by the mission of global corporations to pit one country against another in order to get the lowest cost, the most permissive laws and least restrictions on what they need to do."[54] Advocates of the new order rest, at bottom, upon their faith that agriculture, like the auto or textile industry, should be reformed so that its work-force is slashed, costs minimized, and productivity and profits maximized. The ideology of free exchange is blind to democratic, social, cultural, or ecological considerations, being as well served by atomized, alienated consumers as anything else, and the liberal catechism that is preached in GATT is silent on questions that concern the citizen, such as the social cohesion of his/her own society and responsibilities toward less-privileged peoples.

Fundamental reform is necessary. The end of social justice and the rights of individuals and communities to survive and make a decent living are more important than the abstract pursuit of "market" autonomy. GATT should be radically reformed so that social, ecological, and cultural provisions, along with provisions directed at the equitable readjustment of North-South relations, are incorporated in it and given compelling force.[55]

The principles that would have to underlie such a reform are clear, their basic point being that environmental, social, and cultural costs should be assessed by some agreed-upon international standard before free trade is implemented in food, and that countries that internalize the social or environmental costs of production should not have to compete against those that do not. One such proposal for fair trade lists six necessary principles:

1. The life-cycle of the product or produce (i.e., the internalizing into the product price of any costs to the environment or to future generations);
2. The polluter pays;
3. Guaranteed wages and assured safety for workers (including the right to collective bargaining);
4. Safeguarding against possible future health or environmental damage;
5. Democracy of procedure (including openness of information);
6. Public interest and scientific data (ultimately the public interest of the communities in the countries concerned to be protected).[56]

Were these preconditions for fair trade to be met, it could safely be also made "free." The agribusiness interests that are promoted by the U.S. government and bureaucracy do not necessarily coincide with the interests of the dwindling community of small U.S. farmers, but the voice of the latter is rarely heard outside the country. Its unhappiness with GATT seems to match that of small farmers elsewhere. The November 1991 Joint Communiqué of the (U.S.) National Family Farm Coalition and the European Small Farmers' League declared that the GATT negotiations "should allow all countries, including the Third World, to produce enough healthy food to nourish their own population."[57]

It is no coincidence that Japan and France, two countries that had managed (at least until recently) to accomplish the transition to capitalism without destroying their farming communities, should have been at the forefront of the recent movement to resist the World Trade Order. The critique advanced by one very articulate Japanese farmer that GATT/WTO is bound to lead to the "deagriculturalization" of much of the Third World in order to serve the short-term interests of U.S. agribusiness, and that this effect of the proliferation of nonagricultural countries is a recipe for disaster, would be widely shared.[58] In the end, however, the governments of both countries missed the one opportunity to forge a common cause and a common front between Europe and Asia. Made to feel that it would be akin to terrorism to disrupt GATT, since to do so might lead to a trade war and economic recession, and facing an American-imposed ultimatum, all opposition collapsed, and the agreement was adopted in December 1993.

Irrespective of the outcome of the December 1993 GATT world-trade agreement, the Japanese influence on the structure of the East Asian economy will continue to be huge, reflecting the disproportionate might of the Japanese economy as a whole, and its consumption patterns will continue to shape the pattern of the regional economy. But the common perception that Japan has been the most successful country in history, its economy a miracle, and its prosperity and lifestyles models to be replicated, needs to be scrutinized with care. From this perspective, it constitutes both model and countermodel: model in the sense of the ecologically sound traditional practices now being placed on the chopping block by GATT and WTO, and countermodel in the mainstream consumerism of contemporary society, its dedication to maximization of alienated and wasteful consumption, unequal distribution, and depletion of nonrenewable resources, and environmental degradation. In a word, unsustainability. Sadly, it is the elements described here as countermodel that exercise the greatest force. Widely interpreted as being the model, these patterns threaten, like Japanese patterns of leisure and consumption generally, to spread rapidly and without limit throughout the region.

Regional Patterns: Japan, Southeast Asia, and Australia

The general patterns of Japanese prosperity are discussed in other chapters. Here the focus is confined to the impact of its consumption patterns on the region, particularly Southeast Asia and Australia. These are the two areas that, with the United States and China, play the largest role in supplying Japan with all sorts of food, and, in the future, are expected to add rice to the existing range.

Despite the enduring and perhaps intractable difficulties in areas such as work, housing, and commuting in contemporary Japan, few would deny that in terms of food and drink, Japan has reached levels of mass affluence and abundance rarely approached in history. Japanese supermarkets, hotels, and restaurants offer the gourmet delights harvested from the world's oceans, forests, and farms, and Japanese consumption patterns have become incomparably splendid. Tourism, both domestic and foreign, projects images of luxury and gourmet delights (gourmet being an adjective that attaches itself to desirable experiences and expectations, almost as peace and hope did once for the first postwar generation). One-time luxuries have become daily staples. To take only one example, a bottle of Johnny Walker Black Label whiskey, 10,000 yen through the 1960s and early 1970s, could be bought for around 2,000 yen in the early 1990s. Many other items had undergone a similar transformation. It was a remarkable change for a people whose staple diet had long consisted of rice, pickled vegetables, and fish. But the Japanese people were increasingly being fed on fantasy, and similar images of success and the good life were being implanted among countless millions outside Japan. They may be accomplished for a few, but only at a cost of deepening social polarization and the waste of precious resources. Even among the beneficiaries of the "new food order" being created, the Japanese people themselves, there are increasing fears that the diet of success is creating serious new health problems, especially complex and so-far inexplicable allergies.

The general Japanese dependence on imported foods—from grain to fruit, vegetables, marine products, and beef—has already been mentioned, but the social and ecological implications of the raw statistics need also to be appreciated. How has the market been working in respect to a few of the basic items on the Japanese table—vegetables, beef, wheat, pork, and shrimp? Even from the 1970s, the process of

reorganizing agriculture into monocultural, agribusiness-type special-
ized farming had already been carried to a high degree in certain
sectors. In the Philippines, about 55 percent of farming acreage was
devoted to export crops, including bananas and pineapples for the Japanese market.[59] In the *endaka,* or high-yen phase that followed 1985,
the restructuring of agriculture and fisheries to maximize Japanese yen
or hard-currency income and to satisfy the Japanese gourmet boom
gained momentum. It has been characteristic of the global food industry for decades that "more and more land in the UDCs [underdevel-
oped countries] is devoted to greater and greater quantities of luxury
food products that fewer and fewer people, proportionally, can af-
ford."[60] However, the Japanese appetite gradually extended from such
relative luxuries as shrimp and beef to common items—from chicken
and pork, to wheat and beans, to onions and asparagus and oranges—
that came to be imported in ever-growing quantities. By 1991, not only
half of Japan's beef but half of its onions were being imported. Factories in Thailand and Indonesia were set up to process carrots, beans,
cabbages, onions, asparagus, and cucumber. Even the supposedly
healthy and quintessentially Japanese ingredients of *furusato* (village)
products, such as those that constitute the *sansai* pickle, are imported,
including the bracken (*warabi* and *zenmai*), bamboo shoots, and mush-
room-type fungi (*takenoko* and *kinoko*). The stalls selling *soba* (buck-
wheat) noodles on railway platforms (and countless other places) are
dependent on imports from as far away as Turkey and Tasmania for
their product, which is 80 percent imported (China being the largest
supplier). Japanese cats, once fed on leftover rice with a few shavings
of dried bonito, developed an appetite for cans of tuna and bonito from
Southeast Asia. Perhaps a half a million people came to be employed
in Southeast Asia in the production of shrimp for Japanese consumption, to meet an appetite that increased by nearly 500 times in the years
from 1960 to 1990 (from about a half a million to 286 million tons).[61]
The mangrove forests of Southeast Asia have been and continue to be
pushed back, with severe ecological consequences and drastic depletion of traditional fish stocks, to accommodate the industry.[62] In Thailand, for one example, the mangrove forests were virtually halved,
from 350 thousand to 180 thousand hectares, in fewer than thirty years
from 1961 to 1989, with a similar pattern occurring in the Philippines,
Malaysia, and Indonesia.[63] As for pork, Taiwanese producers moved to
take advantage of the market opportunity, and the numbers of pigs

grew to between 700,000 and one million, with about half the output being destined for the Japanese market. The effluent from a single pig is estimated to equal the waste of one person; with their wastes flowing untreated into the rivers of Taiwan, these piggeries have therefore created ecological havoc.[64] The ecological costs do not constitute part of the price paid by Japanese consumers, but eventually will have to be paid by Taiwanese taxpayers and citizens.

From the late 1980s, China rose rapidly as a major food supplier for Japan, so that by 1993, it surpassed suppliers such as Taiwan and Australia and was second only to the United States. In contrast to the major (U.S.) supply of large-volume wheat, beef, and various agricultural raw materials such as corn, China was providing large quantities of frozen, pickled, and processed vegetables. Yet the outlook for the early twenty-first century is that of a China gradually transformed into a food-importing power, driven by population growth, a burgeoning middle class demanding a grain-fed, meat-based diet, and loss of agricultural lands due to urban and industrial development, spreading erosion, salinization, soil decline, and acid rain. The temporary suspension of exports of corn and wheat in 1994, and of soybeans in 1995, was a pointer to this transformation.[65] For China to achieve a per capita grain consumption level equivalent to, say, South Korea, would require around 600 million tons of cereals per year—four times the amount now traded on the world market.[66] Japan's rising levels of dependence on China as a food supplier, understandable in market terms, was difficult to defend in terms of long-term national interest.

Since the 1960s, Australia has had a symbiotic relationship with Japan, supplying a high proportion of the minerals and energy materials on which its industrial achievement was based, as well as an important segment of the food imports of wheat, barley, sugar, fruits, fish, and beef. Very unusually, and in particular contrast with the United States, the bilateral balance of the Japan-Australia trade is heavily in Australia's favor. In the 1980s, beef and rice became important sectors of the food trade, the former a major beneficiary of the market opening adopted in 1992, and the latter anticipating major benefits to flow from the partial market opening adopted in 1993.

The Japanese beef market grew enormously during the 1980s, and by the early 1990s Australia was supplying over 40 percent of it. Traditionally, however, Australian beef was from grass-fed, free-range cattle, and as such it occupied the lower levels of the market because of the Japanese preference for marbled, grain-fed beef. To meet this preference, the Australian industry began restructuring. Where there had been fewer than 200,000 head per annum produced (slaughtered) during most of the 1980s, by 1994, that figure had risen to 650,000 on about 400 feedlot properties, producing more than A\$500 million in export revenue.[67] Exports to Japan were growing at 25 percent per year.[68] Much of the increase was accounted for by Japanese-owned production bases that were established from the late 1980s in anticipation of beef liberalization.[69] But no sooner had production been greatly expanded than the drought of 1994 struck, and the booming export sector suddenly found itself dependent on imported grain from the United States and Canada to survive.[70] The expansion process had favored the gigantic, highly commercial, agribusiness operations, and as a result sharpened the polarization between them and the proprietors of the traditional family farms. It also created major environmental problems, since the intensity of the feedlot farm was such that each beast produced 10 tons of waste per year.[71] Put another way, a feedlot operation of, say, 40,000 head of cattle produces the effluent equivalent of a city of the size of Canberra.[72] The waste is either heaped to dry in the sun or diluted with water, but in either case, much of it leeches or flows back into the environment, breaking down only very slowly. The steady decline in the ecology of inland river systems, marked by a recurrence of tides of blue-green algae, is compounded by the addition of such nutrient-rich waste. Because water is such a scarce commodity throughout inland Australia, its diversion to dilution of feedlot waste is an extravagance that can be ill afforded. If the environmental consequences were factored into calculations of the economics of the Australia-Japan food trade, the terms would look much less advantageous than they might at first appear.

The principal objection to the feedlot industry, however, is that it actually *reduces* the food-production capacity of the country by tying an increasing proportion of land to production of food for the elite markets of Japan (and the United States). Though traditional, free-range cattle are not in competition with humans, feedlot cattle are. The preference for the most energy-intensive, high-calorie, high-cholesterol, wasteful, and environmentally least sustainable forms of cattle farming, to serve the most elite sections of the world market, is indicative of a retrograde direction taken as Australian rural policy focused narrowly and exclusively on market economics. Yet the force of the Japanese market was well-nigh irresistible.

Grains have long constituted a major export commodity from Australia to Japan. The Australian grain-producing lands are located in the main along a thin strip of land between the east and west coasts and the dry interior. With a total area of a million square kilometers, the area of France and Spain combined, the irrigated region lying along the Murray-Darling river basin in southeastern Australia, overlapping the states of Queensland, New South Wales, Victoria, and South Australia, is one of the most productive and export-oriented agricultural areas. Its annual agricultural production in the early 1990s was about A$10 billion, and 80 percent of its wheat, 97 percent of its wool, and 50 percent of its beef was exported.[73] The environment of the region is delicate and beleaguered. According to rural sociologist Geoffrey Lawrence, it suffers "salination, acidification, deteriorating soil structure, loss of topsoil through erosion, weed growth, water turbidity, destruction of wetlands, species decline and pollution through agrochemicals . . . [with] rising salt levels in both irrigated and dry-land farming systems."[74] The soil-formation rate in the region is so low as to be generally considered to be zero, so that for each ton of grain produced, about thirteen tons of topsoil are lost, amounting to a loss of about fifty tons per hectare per year.[75] Current farming practices are causing reduced yields and decline of the rural environment. One rough estimate is that it would cost around A$1.6 billion to address existing environmental problems.[76]

In many respects, the problems of this Australian farming region are typical of the degradation caused by current farming practice throughout key agricultural zones worldwide. Topsoil loss per year according to region is estimated at: 1.7 billion tons (United States), 2.5 billion tons (Russia), 4.3 billion tons (China), 4.7 billion tons (India), out of a world total of twenty-six billion tons. Since the world grain crop is about 1.6 billion tons, and grain production accounts for about one-half of those lands, a rough calculation indicates that about eight tons of topsoil is being lost for each ton of grain produced.[77] About 40 percent of U.S. agricultural lands are already affected to some degree by topsoil loss, and on a worldwide scale, an area of some five million hectares, equivalent to the combined area of Kyushu and Shikoku, is being devastated every year.[78]

The growing poverty of the earth is reinforced by the social and relative poverty of the farmers, who are driven by debt, low incomes, and low world prices for their product, to press harder upon their resources.[79] In Australia, the unprecedented drought of 1994 across much of the country merely accentuated that trend. Giant dust storms swept millions of tons of soil from the parched grazing lands out across the southern cities, eventually dumping it in the ocean. Scientists reiterated what should have been obvious: "Existing systems of food and fibre production are unsustainable."[80] A radical restructuring of the rural economy is necessary, but it is hard to conceive of a way toward accomplishing it within the constraints of the free-trade regime that GATT is promoting. A state role is bound to become more, rather than less, necessary in the future. One idea in this direction is that of the well-known economist and environmentalist H. C. Coombs: that "enterprises engaged in agriculture, pastoralism, forestry, fishing, or other resource uses capable of depleting the productivity of the land or seas concerned should be subject to a similar regeneration tax."[81]

The combination of fiscal pressures and increasing market specialization leads to further degradation of the "agro-ecosystem." As the role of multinational agribusiness interests, or of foreign (often corporate) owners, in decisions on land use increases, an intensification of such pressures may be expected, for it would be too much to expect remote or multinational foreign owners to promote the sort of long-term ecological recovery policies that the Australian environment so desperately requires. Nor are the occasional, politically inspired gestures such as tree-planting campaigns likely to be the answer, necessary as they are. Instead of hasty attempts to harness the land to satisfy remote, external demands, a radically different approach to the resuscitation of a failing and heavily stressed environment is called for. A starting point might be that the only obviously sustainable agriculture for the Australian continent is the one that has been sustained for many generations—of native animals such as kangaroos, who tread lightly upon the earth and whose meat is virtually cholesterol-free and requires almost zero inputs of labor and capital to farm, and new industries based on native essential oils, grains, flowers, and plants. Such moves might help restore degraded soil and water systems, as well as be financially viable.[82]

There is perhaps one exception to this somber picture of the Australian agricultural environment and its relationship with Japan. Rice production is a relatively recent Australian rural industry whose output is almost entirely exported. It boasts the lowest chemical and fertilizer input levels in the world and a complete absence of natural predators.[83] Around 2,000 farmers are engaged in mixed farming, in which rice is grown in rotation with other crops, on average fields of fifty to sixty hectares. Although their production costs and producer price are about one-tenth of that in Japan, these are marginal producers. Output in the early 1990s was about one million tons per year, and in the Japanese emergency of 1993, 200 thousand tons were exported. However, restrictions on the availability of irrigated water in the rice-growing region and commitments to other long-term export markets are such that there is little possibility of that figure being much increased in the future. U.S. pressures will also, most likely, work to hold down the exports of Australian rice, as they did during the 1980s, when U.S.-subsidized exports forced Australian rice sales down from 720 thousand tons in 1982 to below 400 thousand tons late in the decade.[84] So the output of Australian rice will play a minor, but probably not environmentally deleterious, role in the bilateral relationship.

The peculiarity of world rice farming is that the traded proportion of the world crop is tiny (around 3 percent),[85] and the major producing countries (China, India, Indonesia, and Bangladesh), which account for 70 percent of world production, basically consume their own crop, while the United States (1.5 percent of world production) and Thailand (4 percent of world production) account for 20 and 40 percent of exports respectively.[86] In the 1980s, the agrarian sector in the United States was increasingly characterized by the domination of agribusiness and a vigorous push to open the world (and particularly the rich Japanese market) to its product.

The Japanese defenses were simultaneously weakened in 1993 by the combination of an extraordinary failure of the domestic crop (due to unusual weather conditions), which left no alternative, at least in the short term, to large rice imports, and political changes that drastically undermined the significance of the rural vote-gathering machine and therefore the political importance of the rural sector. It was this combination of circumstances that made possible the GATT concessions of December 1993. The imports of 1993 (two million tons) were exceptional, five times greater than would begin under the Minimum Access Formula the following year. But the outcome raised expectations (in the United States, Thailand, and Australia), inflated markets (in poor rice-consuming or -importing countries), and fed a crisis mood (among

Japanese farmers). It also sowed confusion among Japanese bureaucrats and politicians. When the massive imports of 1993 turned into a glut, and 1994 produced a bumper harvest, the depth of the problem was again shown.

Peculiarities of Japanese Agriculture

Whatever the long-term prospects for the farmers of Japan, there are some striking qualities that distinguish its agriculture from that of the major food-exporting countries. The most remarkable is that rice production in Japan is environmentally *beneficial*, a quality shared with some other East Asian mountainous and monsoonal countries, but very different from the agricultural powers. Japan's heavy rainfall (annual precipitation of around 1,800 mm. or 71 inches), mountainous terrain with steep gradients, and seasonal temperature variation have been developed creatively by many generations. Paddy agriculture has positively created what is commonly thought of as Japan, in the sense that the flow of humus-rich sediment from the mountains that cover most of the country was captured and turned into paddy fields by a complex system of irrigation developed over the centuries.[87] Productivity for rice grew by about fivefold in the 1,300 years since rice agriculture was established across the Japanese islands.[88]

Far from being a resource-poor country, Japan thus possesses "enormous ecological resources" and conditions for agriculture that are "almost ideal," "producing the most advantageous flow of water to foster mountain forests, croplands, and paddy fields."[89] During the postwar decades, it is true that fertilizers, insecticides, and pesticides were used liberally, and even with abandon, but the farm system was not intrinsically dependent on them. It is estimated that production levels of about 75 percent of current levels could be maintained if chemicals were abandoned and traditional, complex farming practices, including nutritional recycling, were reintroduced (as many farmers are attempting to do).[90] By contrast, the modern system of farming, U.S. or Australian style, is best understood as "an agro-industrial system for the conversion of fossil fuel into food . . . for each calorie of food the system harvests, it burns about 2.5 calories of fossil fuel."[91] The soil is progressively impoverished by cropping and must either be artificially replenished or eventually lost. Japan contrasts sharply with this, in that the work of farming serves to enrich and replenish the environment

Table 3.2

Rice Productivity and Population Change in Japan, ca. 729–1974

Period	Paddy area[a]	Tonnage[b]	Kgs per hectare	Population[c]	Kgs per capita
729–806	1.05	1.06	101	3.7	287
1532–1615	1.05–2.0	1.8–1.85	150–177	22.3	81–83
1716–48	1.63	3.15	193	26.5	119
1830–44	1.55	3.00	194	27.0	111
1878–87	2.56	4.77	186	37.4	127
1908–17	2.99	7.94	265	50.9	156
1938–42	3.15	9.53	302	73.2	131
1959–65	3.10	12.38	399	93.4	143
1971–74	2.62	11.70	448	107.9	109

Source: Adapted from Andō Kōtarō, *Nihon kodai inasakushi kenkyū*, Nōrin tōkei kyōkai, 1959, by Yoshida Takehiko, *Suiden keishi wa nōgyō o horobosu*, Nōsan gyoson bunka kyōkai, 1978, p. 78.
[a]In million hectares.
[b]In million tons.
[c]In millions.

naturally, and the impoverishment of Japan's environment occurs in proportion to the degree it is *not* farmed. Because of the heavy rainfall, even if agricultural chemicals are applied, the regular flooding of the paddies prevents the leaching of nitrogen from the fertilizer into the soil, and, whatever is not broken down is flushed into surrounding seas, a pattern quite unlike that of drier counties such as the United States or Australia.[92] In short, considerations of the economics of the rice-growing system need to take account of the other roles performed by the national system of water flow associated with it: The paddies and their water canals hold a staggering 8 billion tons of water,[93] which serves not only the purposes of agriculture but also water conservation, flood prevention, landslide prevention, soil-erosion prevention, biodegrading of organic wastes, and improvement of air quality.[94] A survey conducted by the Mitsubishi Research Institute for the Japanese government found that land and environmental functions of rice paddies were worth twelve trillion yen per year, three times the total value of the rice produced.[95] If the international free market dictates that Japan's rice is noncompetitive and its rice industry is gradually wound down, who will pay such costs?

In short, Japan is ideally suited to rice cultivation. That does not mean that its farmers could compete, in purely market terms, against, say, Californian agribusiness producers, but it does mean that Japanese agriculture, to the extent that it reverts from fossil fuel-based inputs to nutrient recycling, can be both highly economical and indefinitely sustainable. In contrast to American (or, to some extent, European) agriculture, in Japan productivity increases in proportion to the labor input. The GATT principles of economic rationalism are heedless of such considerations. This point was rarely made during the GATT negotiations because even the Japanese government and bureaucracy chose not to base the case for exclusion from GATT on universalist, ecological, and environmental considerations, but instead stressed "cultural identity" and "food security."[96] In the worldwide quest for ecologically sustainable forms of rural economy, the Japanese case is a positive model, and the Australian and American, negative models. Like its peace constitution, it is something to which Japan's public spokesmen commonly attach little value, but in the longer-term perspective, it may be much more precious than, say, its auto or shipbuilding industries.

The Japanese Model

It is in the context of Asia as a whole that the problem of Japan's contemporary economic success stands out in sharpest relief, both in terms of what it has attained and what it holds out by way of a model to be pursued by other countries. As Japan has turned itself into an unprecedentedly food-dependent country, systematically stripping away one after another dimension of the capacity to feed and nourish its people in the single-minded pursuit of industrial exporting greatness, it demonstrates a faith in the continuance of an open and surplus world food market that looks increasingly shortsighted and that contrasts sharply with the long-term perspective that is often said to characterize Japanese corporations. The industrial and economic restructuring that followed the Plaza Agreement of 1985 lowered every defense, in terms of food, while investing heavily in weapons, which many commentators agreed were totally useless for defense but necessary to placate American trade pressures. At this level, the problem of whether Japan has found an answer to the question of the meaning of life looks problematic.

There is no question that Japanese living standards, predicated on

the assumption of an ability to continue to monopolize a vastly disproportionate share of the region's food resources, are not only unsustainable, but enshrine a culture of profligacy and waste.[97] There is not
room in the world for two countries to consume as Japan does. As
world agricultural acreage continues to shrink, will Japan be allowed to
continue feeding its people with the fruits of around twelve million
hectares of foreign soil (about three times its own acreage), even if the
farmers who labor to feed them, and the citizens of whatever country it
is, themselves go hungry? In terms of "ecological footprint," the term
developed to refer to the "optional carrying capacity or environmental
space (by which we may judge how much a region depends on the rest
of the world), or the human appropriation of net primary production
which, if calculated for different regions and countries of the world,
would show how some of them live beyond their own biomass production, while others live below this," it is clear that Japan is shod in
giant's boots.[98] Even if Japanese consumption patterns were sustainable, in a fortress Japan, they could not be extended to the region,
much less to the world. The Japanese vision of success and prosperity
in the long run can only sharpen the contradiction between it and its
neighbor region, quite the obverse of the ideal of *kokusaika* (internationalization) in which politicians, bureaucrats, and many ordinary
people believe.

Insofar as it is generally agreed that the late-twentieth-century world
faces two crucial problems—the deteriorating environment and the
widening economic gap between North and South—the trajectory of
Japanese development is set on a course designed to compound both.
Of course it is far from being unique in this, but the fact that few other
countries have managed to combine the modern (high-tech, industrialization) with the preservation of the premodern (village-based farms)
focuses attention on the choices it now makes. There is, too, a profound sense of unease in Japan about the character of the new world
order in the making. The priority to consumption over creation, waste
over preservation, extravagance over simplicity, all point to problems
to be overcome rather than to any element of a solution. Sooner or
later, the flow of resources, especially food, from poor countries in the
South to rich countries in the North, Japan foremost among the latter,
is bound to become a political issue. The trajectory charted by the
Japanese Agriculture Ministry, in line with the course mapped out by
GATT, calls for the advanced countries to retain (and increase) their

per capita grain consumption in the years to the end of century, and to retain precisely the same differential between their consumption and that of the people in the South as existed in 1988, even though the population of the South will, by then, make up just under 80 percent of the people on the earth.[99] This prospect raises large moral questions, but also has implications for security (military policy), since the prediction is as much threat as promise—the threat to continue monopolizing the diminishing resources of earth and sea, and the will to defend the system that makes it possible to do so.

The crisis facing agriculture in Japan predates the GATT restructuring of the 1990s. Rooted in the sort of industrialism, economism, and GNPism that have always been ready to sacrifice agriculture to some other end, it has also been shaped by four Cold War decades of deliberate prioritization to U.S. interests, especially U.S. farm interests, and it has been exacerbated in recent years by the pressures on the world trading system created by the very success of the Japanese industrial-export sector. The project to open world markets to free trade in food has simply brought all the existing contradictions to the head. Japan's controlled food system, which had grown into a colossal, self-serving and -perpetuating, bureaucratic machine that was parasitical of farmers rather than serving their interests, is collapsing.

Debate about what alternative there might be to the GATT–World Trade Organization is only beginning. The greatest obstacle is the belief that the world to which we have become accustomed will continue without drastic change, that GNP will continue to grow without limit, the world economy will remain open, and food will stay cheap and readily available. Whatever growth may occur in the economy, however, the ecosystem does not expand, and ultimately it imposes absolute limits on the economy. As Bruce Rich, environmentalist and lawyer, recently observed in his study of the World Bank, "Economic growth in its current form has reached the point where it has unleashed an almost unimaginable impoverishment through the destruction in a short time of most of the human worlds and a significant proportion of the life forms that have evolved and survived on earth. Assumptions about growth and efficiency vis-à-vis the GNP have not begun to factor in environmental or energy considerations, much less in social or cultural considerations or the global considerations of equity and justice between North and South."[100]

Within Japan, pessimism about the prospects for agriculture in the

WTO is common. There are groups of farmers in various parts of the country who believe in their capacity to adapt to a "borderless" world, but they are few.[101] Prosperity in late-twentieth-century Japan has been achieved at the cost of stripping away the defenses of future generations and making them vulnerable to unpredictable future world food markets. It has involved building Japan into a relationship with its neighbor countries that combines domination and dependence, contradiction rather than cooperation. Japanese consumption patterns are unique (although only in the sense of being the most representative of the "advanced-country syndrome") and cannot be reproduced anywhere else. Increasingly, Japan's overconsumption (*hōshoku*) is achieved by taking food out of the mouths of the poor and hungry, compensating by greed and gourmet fantasies for the failure to meet the aspiration for social and personal fulfillment. The rising wave of agricultural imports not only ruptures and distorts the food policies of the region, but also threatens virtually all Japanese producers. At current rice price support levels, which are certain to be cut further, only 2 percent of farmers were expected to be able to survive.[102]

The combination of GATT/WTO pressures on the one hand, and the escalating yen on the other, drives Japanese distribution networks and trading companies to "outsource" their supply by shifting production offshore to neighbor countries, where the market is everything and environmental and human rights considerations count for much less than they do in Japan itself. The official, *shokkansei*, food price-support system, and the quasi-official *nōkyō* system of agricultural cooperatives are both discredited. After a hundred and more years of modernization predicated on the superiority of Western ways, the tide may be beginning to turn and traditional, organic farming practices reassessed. The effort to create a natural, ecological balance through the reconstitution of a sustainable cycle of production, in which wastes are eliminated, may still look to be quixotic, even reactionary, but the struggle to resuscitate the Japanese paddies, dry fields, valleys, and mountains, and to reconnect the circuits that united the country's lands and waters is underway. The reconstitution of food and cultural self-sufficiency could function as part of the quest for an identity and as a precondition for a confident, cooperative Japanese involvement in creating the future international system.

When a Japanese politician can be heard declaring from the back of his hustings truck that he stands for reducing GNP growth to zero, when economists begin to distinguish between market prices for commodities such as food and the real ecological or social price, and when restaurants and hotels can offer menus that do not rely on the exploitation of distant ecosystems or peoples, we will know that the issues have begun to be faced and that the prospects for a new world order have brightened.

Notes

1. Funabashi Yōichi, "Nihon no seiki wa kuru ka," *Asahi jānaru*, September 29, 1989, pp. 52–57.

2. "Globalize Asia," *New Perspectives Quarterly*, Vol. 9, No. 1, Winter 1992, pp. 23–27, at p. 26.

3. Hayami Yūjirō et al., "Toward the Success of the GATT Uruguay Round," Seisaku Kohsoh Forum (Forum for Policy Innovation), Policy Proposal No. 29, January 1992 (Mimeograph).

4. Wolfgang Lutz, "The Future of World Population," *Population Bulletin* [Population Reference Bureau], Vol. 49, No. 1, June 1994, p. 26.

5. Gaston Fischer, "The Population Explosion: Where Is It Leading?" *Population and Environment: A Journal of Interdisciplinary Studies*, Vol. 15, No. 2, November 1993, p. 139.

6. René Dumont, "Graves menaces sur la sécurité alimentaire mondiale," *Le Monde Diplomatique*, August 1994, pp. 14–15.

7. Noel Brown of UNEP, quoted in Natasha Bita, "No Place on Earth for More Consumers," *The Australian*, March 8, 1993.

8. According to the U.N.'s Food and Agriculture Organization (FAO). See Lester R. Brown, "Facing Food Insecurity," in Lester R. Brown et al., eds., *State of the World 1994*, Worldwatch Institute, London, 1994, pp. 177–97, at p. 178.

9. Sandra Postel, "Carrying Capacity: Earth's Bottom Line," in Lester R. Brown, *State of the World 1994*, 1994, pp. 3–21, at p. 5.

10. Lutz, "The Future of World Population," p. 28.

11. Edward O. Wilson, *The Diversity of Life*, Cambridge, The Belknap Press of Harvard University Press, 1992, p. 272.

12. W. M. Hern, "Why Are There So Many of Us? Description and diagnosis of a planetary ecopathological process," *Population and Environment*, Vol. 12, No. 1, 1991, pp. 9–39. See also P. R. and A. H. Ehrlich, *The Population Explosion*, New York, Simon and Schuster, 1990.

13. Fischer, "The Population Explosion," p. 151.

14. World Bank estimates, quoted in "The Good Earth," editorial, *Far Eastern Economic Review*, September 8, 1994.

15. "Asia, a billion consumers," *The Economist*, October 30, 1993.

16. *Far Eastern Economic Review*, September 1994.

17. Quoted in Lester R. Brown, "What on Earth Is the World Coming To?" from *Vital Signs 1993: The Trends That Are Shaping Our Future*, co-edited with Hal Kane and Ed Ayres, New York, W.W. Norton and the Worldwatch Institute, 1993.

18. Ibid.

19. Lester R. Brown, Christopher Flavin, and Hal Kane, *Vital Signs: The Trends That Are Shaping Our Future, 1992–93*, London Worldwatch Institute, 1992, p. 17.

20. Norman Myers in Norman Myers and Julian L. Simon, *Scarcity or Abundance: A Debate on the Environment*, New York, W.W. Norton, 1994, p. 87.

21. Postel, "Carrying Capacity," p. 11.

22. Brown, *State of the World 1994*, p. 177.

23. Julian Cribb, "Oceans in Peril," *The Australian*, June 5–6, 1993.

24. Watabe Tadayo, *Nihon kara suiden ga kieru hi*, Iwanami bukkuretto, No. 314, Tokyo, Iwanami, 1993, p. 15.

25. Brown, *State of the World 1994*, p. 36.

26. "Grain Deficit Could Affect World Supply," *The Age*, August 26, 1994.

27. Lester R. Brown, "Overview—Entering a New Era," in Brown, Flavin, and Kane, *Vital Signs*, p. 17.

28. One estimate is that already 40 percent of the world crop, and over half the harvested acreage in the United States, goes to feed livestock (Francis Moore Lappé, "Saving a Small Planet," *Kyoto Review*, Fall 1989, pp. 20–21).

29. Tsuchida Takashi, "Nō no suitai to 21 seiki no shoku kankyō," *Kyōto Seika Daigaku Kiyō*, No. 4, January 20, 1993, pp. 2–15, at p. 9.

30. Nishida Yoshiaki, "From a Train Window: Why Is Japanese Farmland So Different from That in Europe?" *Social Science Japan*, No. 3, April 1995, pp. 10–11.

31. Tsuchida, "Nō no suitai," p. 14.

32. Philip McMichael, "Agro-Food Restructuring in the Pacific Rim," in Ravi Arvind Palat, ed., *Pacific-Asia and the Future of the World-System*, Westport, Conn., and London, Greenwood Press, 1993, pp. 103–16, at p. 105.

33. Tsūshōsangyōshō (MITI), ed., *Tsūshō hakusho*, 1992, (*Kakuron*), p. 135.

34. Hayami Yūjirō, "Tariffs Are the Less Painful Way to Go," *The Nikkei Weekly*, December 27, 1993, to January 3, 1994.

35. For a recent resume of these processes, see McMichael, "Agro-Food."

36. "Rice and GATT: Implications for Japan and Australia," *Economic Bulletin*, Australia-Japan Economic Institute, Vol. 1, No. 1, January 1993.

37. David P. Rapkin and Aurelia George, "Rice Liberalization and Japan's Role in the Uruguay Round," William P. Avery, ed., *World Agriculture and the GATT*, Boulder and London, Boulder, Colorado, Lynne Rienner, 1993, pp. 55–94, at p. 57.

38. Ono Kazuoki, " 'Nōgyō kaitai' to 'kō' no ronri," *Ritsumeikan hyōron*, No. 95, November 1992, pp. 36–44, at p. 42. However, the Maekawa Report included a vague phrase "excepting core agricultural produce."

39. For a discussion of this phenomenon, see Ono Kazuoki, *Nō to shoku no seiji keizaigaku*, Ryokufū shobō, 1994, Chapter Two.

40. Ibid., p. 25.

41. Sakamoto Shin'ichirō, "Nōgyō fukken e no michi—mō hitotsu no Nihon o saguru," *Shūkan kinyōbi*, November 19, 1993, pp. 30–45, at p. 42.

42. Ono, " 'Nōgyō kaitai,' " p. 36.

43. Seminar, Australian National University, February 14, 1994.

44. Hayami, "Tariffs Are the Less Painful Way," p. 19.

45. Up to a third of 1993 rice sales, according to Charles Smith, "Black Rice," *Far Eastern Economic Review*, January 20, 1994.

46. Udagawa gives a figure of 15,000 "nature farmers" in Japan. Taketoshi Udagawa, "Development and Transfer of Environment-Friendly Agriculture," in Asian Productivity Organization, ed., *Sustainable Agricultural Development in Asia*, Tokyo, APO, 1994, p. 111.

47. Watabe, *Nihon kara*, p. 10.

48. Geoffrey Lawrence, "Agricultural Restructuring and Rural Social Change in Australia," in Terry Marsden, Philip Lowe, and Sarah Whatmore, eds., *Rural Restructuring*, London, David Fulton, 1990, pp. 101–28, at p. 107.

49. ". . . up to $50 billion in annual assistance payments—including loans, grants, loan guarantees, direct subsidies and cash payments." Dean Baquet and Diana B. Henriques, "Agriculture Companies Still Get Federal Business Despite Abuses," *The New York Times*, October 12, 1993. (See also Claude Julien, "Complices ou insurgés," *Le Monde Diplomatique*, December 1993.)

50. Vandana Shiva (quoting a 1987 study by Mark Ritchie and Kevin Ristau), "Kazoku nōgyō to idenshi ga nottorareru," in Iba Mikako and Furusawa Kōyū, eds., *Gatto-jiyū bōeki e no gimon*, Gakuyō shobo, 1993, pp. 135–55, at pp. 138–39.

51. Ibid.

52. Murai Yoshinori, *Hōshoku Nihon to Ajia*, Ienohikari kyōkai, 1993, p. 30.

53. Bernard Cassen, "Vivre sans le GATT," *Le Monde Diplomatique*, May 1993, pp. 6–7. See also Christian De Brie, "Paysans sans frontières: pour une agriculture écologique," ibid., July 1995.

54. Evidence to U.S. Senate's Commerce, Science, and Technology Committee, October 19, 1994, quoted in Michael Stutchbury, "Nader Fires Broadside against World Trade Pact," *Australian Financial Review*, October 20, 1994.

55. Ibid.

56. Rodney E. Leonard, "Kōsei bōeki no rūruzukuri," in Iba and Furusawa, 1993, pp. 208–19, at pp. 217–19.

57. Jacques Bertelot, "Contre les aberrations du productionisme en agriculture," *Le Monde Diplomatique*, December 1993, p. 20.

58. Sakamoto Shin'ichirō, "Ah, tsui ni nōmin yaburetari," *Shūkan kinyōbi*, February 11, 1994, pp. 40–44.

59. Ibid., p. 172.

60. Susan Strange, *How the Other Half Dies: The Real Reasons for World Hunger*, London, Penguin, 1976, p. 173.

61. Murai, *Hōshoku Nihon*, p. 35.

62. Details in ibid., pp. 21–22.

63. Ibid.

64. Ui Jun, "Ajia to Nihon ni kansuru kankyō mondai," *Kankyō to kōgai*, Vol. 24, No. 2, 1994, pp. 8–17, at p. 9.

65. Wakizaka Noriyuki, "Chūgoku danomi susumu Nihon no 'shoku'," *Asahi shimbun*, January 1, 1995.

66. Vaclav Smil, "China's Environmental Crisis," *Asia-Pacific Observer* (Honolulu), Vol. 1, No. 3, October–December 1994, p. 4.

67. "Meat-Processing Sector Fact File," *Australian Farm Journal*, May 1994, p. 26.

68. Kathryn Bice, "Why Feedlots Are Turning into a Growth Industry," *Australian Financial Review*, June 21, 1993.

69. Ono, " 'Nōgyō kaitai,' " pp. 130–33.

70. Tim Stevens, "Supply of Feed Grain Nears End," *The Australian*, October 15–16, 1994.

71. "Meat-Processing Sector Fact File," 1994.

72. Geoffrey Lawrence (University of Central Queensland), talking to Phillip Adams, ABC Radio, "Late Night Live," April 1994. (Also personal communication, October 26, 1994.)

73. Geoffrey Lawrence, "Agricultural production and environmental degradation in the Murray-Darling Basin," in Geoffrey Lawrence, Frank Vanclay, and Brian Furze, eds., *Agriculture Environment and Society; Contemporary Issues for Australia*, South Melbourne, Macmillan, 1992, pp. 33–59, at pp. 34, 37.

74. Ibid., p. 39.

75. Ibid., p. 40.

76. Ibid., p. 40. See also Bill Norman, "Ruined Rivers," *The Canberra Times*, October 29–30, 1994.

77. Inoue Hisashi, *Zoku—Inoue Hisashi no kome kōza*, Iwanami Bukkuretto, No. 227, 1991, p. 22.

78. Ibid. See also Mark Ritchie, "Gatto ga Amerika no nōgyō o odokasu," in Iba and Furusawa, 1993, p. 157.

79. On levels of debt, and on low farmer income, see Lawrence, "Agricultural Production," p. 38, or Geoffrey Lawrence, "The rural crisis downunder," in David Goodman and Michael Redclift, eds., *The International Farm Crisis*, London, Macmillan, 1989, pp. 234–74, at p. 241.

80. Andrew Campbell, *Landcare*, St. Leonards, Allen and Unwin, 1994.

81. H. C. Coombs, *The Return of Scarcity: Strategies for an Economic Future*, Cambridge, Cambridge University Press, 1990, p. 15.

82. Julian Cribb, "Soil nutrient loss threatens farming," *The Australian*, October 26, 1994. A soil specialist estimated in 1994 that the value of native wildflower, essentials, and other oils for pharmaceutical or industrial chemicals could, by the year 2020, exceed $12 billion and equal the value of the country's wheat exports (John Williams, CSIRO Division of Soils, "Farming without Harming," ANZAS Congress 1994, "Environmental and Natural Resources, 2020 Vision Statements").

83. Author's visit to Leeton district of New South Wales and discussions with members of the Leeton Rice-Growers Cooperative, March 1995.

84. Itō Mitsuharu, Takeuchi Kei, Hara Takeshi, and Yuize Yasuhiko, "Kono mama de nōson wa hōkai suru," *Sekai*, July 1994, pp. 122–40, at p. 125 (Itō).

85. Rapkin and George, "Rice Liberalization," p. 78.

86. Sunaga Yoshiaki, "Kome de kokusai jukyū," *Sekai*, July 1994, pp. 152–53.

87. Inoue, *Zoku*, p. 34.

88. Tashiro Yōichi, "An Environmental Mandate for Rice Self-sufficiency," *Japan Quarterly*, January–March 1992, pp. 34–44, at p. 35.

89. Atsushi Tsuchida and Takeshi Murota, "The Scarred Face of Japan," *The Ecologist*, Vol. 9, No. 7, November 1979, pp. 221–26, at p. 222.

90. Inoue, *Zoku*, p. 34.

91. David Goodman, Bernardo Sorj, and John Wilkinson, *From Farming to Biotechnology*, Oxford, Basil Blackwell, 1987, p. 101.

92. Tashiro, "An Environmental Mandate," p. 43.

93. Watabe, *Nihon kara,* p. 48.

94. Udagawa, "Development and Transfer," p. 92.

95. Tashiro, "An Environmental Mandate," p. 43.

96. Rapkin and George, "Rice Liberalization," pp. 77, 79.

97. It is estimated that almost as much rice is thrown away in the course of a year by homes, hotels, and restaurants throughout the country as is consumed— around 10 million tons (Murai, *Hōshoku Nihon,* p. 17).

98. J. Martinez-Alier, "Political Ecology, Distributional Conflicts, and Economic Incommensurability," *New Left Review,* No. 211, May–June 1995, pp. 70–88, at p. 78 (and references there).

99. See Agriculture Ministry's table of world grain production and consumption for 1988 with estimates for 2000 in Shiba Hiroshi, "Nō no ikikata," Part 6, *Asahi shimbun*, March 31, 1993. Per capita consumption in kilograms in the advanced countries is expected to rise from 627 to 701 and that in the developing countries from 233 to 260.

100. Bruce Rich, *Mortgaging the Earth: The World Bank, Environmental Impoverishment, and the Crisis of Development*, Boston, Beacon Press, 1994, p. 317.

101. For one example in Akita Prefecture, Ogatamura Akita-komachi seisansha kyōkai, *Daichi kara no teigen*, Ogatamura, October 1991.

102. Ono, " 'Nōgyō kaitai,' " p. 303.

Part Two
Identity

4

The Regional State: Asia and the Dilemmas of National Identity

Introduction

As the millennium approaches its end, the Cold War already shrinks into perspective as a relatively brief episode, and the deeper structural transformations long obscured by its drama are likely to prove of much greater long-term significance. The combination of the political circumstance of its dissolution with the economic circumstance of the rise of the whole East Asian region lends further force to the process of historical reconsideration. From the ideological confrontation of the Cold War, some commentators see the world entering a new and no-less fraught era, in which the fault lines of rival civilizations replace those of hostile ideologies.[1]

In Japan, the quest for wealth and power, and for equality of status with the West, launched in the late nineteenth century, has clearly been accomplished. But what has the century of striving meant? And what is there now to take its place as a focus for national endeavor? Both the historical and the political questions are bound to exercise many minds in the years ahead. The relativization of the centuries of Western hegemony opens the path to consideration from a fresh perspective of many questions about what is universal and what is particular, what are the cultural underpinnings of modernization, and what might or should be the structures, values, and direction of twenty-first-century societies.

The millennium that is ending is the second of the Christian era, and its end prompts the question of why a Christian notion of time and history should have been universalized. The year that will be known as 2000 might have been universally recognized in many other ways: as 5761 (by the Judaic calendar, which counts from the time of creation); 2551 (by a Confucian calendar, which counts time from the birth of the master); either 2660 (by a Japanese calendar such as was in use for a time before and during the war, which counts from the putative birth of the emperor Jimmu), or a more modest 12, in terms of the reign year of the Japanese Heisei emperor who acceded in 1989; 4333 (by a Korean calendar, still actually used by newspapers in South Korea, which dates from the birth year of the mythical founder, Tangun); or 1378 (by an Islamic calendar, which counts from the Hejira, when the prophet moved from Mecca to Medina). This list is not exhaustive. What is important is the fact that the universalization of the Western (Julian) calendar was the product of specific historical circumstances, a series of world events that began around 500 years ago.

Early in the 1990s, the five-hundredth anniversary of the voyages of Columbus and the discovery of the New World was celebrated, marking the beginning of European hegemony in Asia, a period that now, quite clearly, is over. What began with the voyage of the Santa Maria in 1492 ended—or is about to end—somewhere between the flight of the last U.S. helicopter from Saigon in 1975 and the lowering of the Union Jack over Hong Kong in 1998. In the late 1990s, what historians, economists, and indeed even philosophers struggle to interpret is the evidence pointing to the end of a phenomenon that is 500 years old. The fulcrum of world power, once centered in the Mediterranean, then in the Atlantic, has gradually shifted across the Pacific. While the Japanese weight is at present overwhelming, the prospect that early in the next millennium it would shift further west, with Japan eclipsed by China, is already strengthening.[2]

Japan's rise is the most spectacular expression of the emerging post-Columbian world order, of which it is both cause and effect. It is nearly 100 years since the first military victory of an Asian over a European country (in the Russo-Japanese War of 1904–1905), and 1995 marks the fiftieth anniversary of the collapse of the Japanese attempt to establish its hegemony over Asia, an attempt that was plainly premature and ill conceived, but can nevertheless be seen as a pointer toward the post-European hegemony that was to emerge two generations later. It was Japan that struck the first and the second successful blows against the Columbian world order, its power first asserted against the Russians, then against the Chinese, and eventually against the Europeans and Americans. In 1945, the process ended in defeat and occupation, but in circumstances that assured that apparent defeat would be short lived.

It would be wrong to conceive of modernization as having been entered upon a slate that was blank until the impact of the West on Japan in the mid-nineteenth century, since the roots of the Japanese phenomenon may be traced back deep into the premodern, as may the complexities and ambiguities in its relationship with Asia. Indeed, one provocative recent text argues that the roots of modern Europe and modern Japan are both to be found in the "long sixteenth century" (ca. 1450–1640). At both extremes of the same Eurasian continent, when the process of distancing from continental (Eurasian) civilization (Islamic in the one case and Confucian in the other) began, both developing economies were able to overcome import dependence and prevent outflow of wealth to pay for products made necessary by the lifestyle revolution that accompanied the introduction of cotton, sugar, dyes, pottery, and tea or coffee.[3] Although Japan's closed country policies have been interpreted superficially as opposite to those accompanying European expansion, at least one Japanese scholar now believes that they are actually parallel and roughly equivalent.[4] Though often regarded as a country lacking in all mineral resources, Japan's self-sufficiency extended to possession of the raw materials for all forms of monetary wealth—gold, silver, and copper.[5] The technology development during its period of enforced import substitution was also considerable. By the time it was forceably opened to the West in the nineteenth century, Japan was, in a sense, the heir to the cultural and technological accomplishments of Asia but had already made a significant turn away from it and developed a strong sense of itself as different and distinct. The process of distancing from Asia was thus also very deep-rooted. The contemporary debate seeks a resolution to a separation from Asia that, in this view, is as ingrained as is the phenomenon of European world hegemony. Such a civilizational perspective helps to provide context for recent and contemporary phenomena that are superficially economic by locating them in the context of long-term shifts in identity.

Asia: Autonomy and Wealth

The economic phenomena of recent decades provide unambiguous evidence of change. In 1946–47 the United States accounted for 60 percent of world mining and industrial production and one-third of world exports, and Japan for almost none of either category.[6] Fourteen years later, in 1960, the U.S. economy was still preeminent, and just over eleven times the size of the Japanese, but by 1986, an enormous change had occurred: That ratio had been reduced to approximately 2 to 1. Between 1950 and 1990, Japan's economy multiplied by no less than 152 times (as against 39 times in the case of West Germany). From 1987, its per capita GNP surpassed that of the United States, in 1991 reaching $27,005 to $22,468.[7] Early in the 1990s, it was adding "a volume roughly equivalent to the GNP of France to its economy every four and a half years,"[8] and commentators were speculating as to the year in which Japan's economy would surpass that of the United States outright.[9]

Between them, the United States and Japan account for about 5 percent and 3 percent of world population respectively, but together, nearly 40 percent of world economic activity. Japanese estimates project a joint United States–Japan share of world GNP that would even continue to expand (however slightly) thereafter, although anticipating that the relative United States–Japan proportions would move slowly in Japan's favor.[10]

From the 1970s, the pattern of economic growth and prosperity long evident in Japan spread throughout the constellation of east and southeast Asian countries, making the character of the historic shift more pronounced. The so-called "four little tigers"—the Asian Newly Industrialized Economies (ANIEs) of South Korea, Taiwan, Singapore, and Hong Kong—led the world in economic growth for two dramatic decades, doubling their economies in each of them, and coming to account for 8.9 percent of world exports. The economic growth rate of these ANIEs, averaged for the decade, was 8.9 percent in the 1970s and 8.2 percent in the 1980s, almost double that of Japan and about three times that of the United States.[11] To put this in perspective, it needs to be remembered that the Japanese achievement during its miracle years was an average 9.7 percent growth rate of GDP between 1960 and 1972, followed by a 3.76 percent rate between 1973 and 1986.[12] Although the rate of growth in the East Asian tigers, and in China, has been far greater then Japan's for these years, Japan's economy still dwarfs those of the rest of the region put together, and the gap shows little sign of closing. The more poetic attempt to represent the phenomenon uses the analogy of a flock of geese spread out and following in the wake of Japan.

Table 4.1

Ratio of U.S. and Japanese GNP (as proportion of world GNP), 1970—2005

	1970	1980	1990	1995	2000	2005
U.S.	30.2	23.0	23.6	22.7	21.9	21.3
Japan	6.0	8.9	12.8	15.8	16.7	17.3

Note: Figures for 1970 and 1980 are from Endō Masatake, "Nihon tataki wa naku sameta hodo," *Aera*, January 21, 1992, pp. 14–15; 1990 figures and subsequent estimates from 1992 report from Japan Economic Research Center, "Ou, Bei, Ajia de san kyoku kōsō," *Nihon keizai shimbun*, February 25, 1992. It is interesting that this report saw no reason to doubt the long-term world dominance of the U.S.-Japan economies, or the continuing ability of the Japanese economy to strengthen its position vis-à-vis both the United States and the world.

By 1985, Singapore and Hong Kong were already at 1970 Japanese levels of per capita GNP, Taiwan and South Korea at about 1960 levels, Thailand and the Philippines at pre-1950 levels. Even if these rates of growth were to slacken somewhat, the ANIEs could expect to reach Japanese real per capita GDP for 1980 figures either just before the end of the century (for Singapore and Hong Kong) or just after (for South Korea and Taiwan).[13] In short, there would be four more "Japans" in the western Pacific region by around the year 2000.[14] The ASEAN countries—Thailand, Malaysia, and Indonesia—also entered upon dramatic growth trajectories in the 1970s, followed, most startling of all, by China (whose economy grew at a sustained average rate of 9 percent for fourteen consecutive years from 1979 to 1993).[15] Most predictions agree that growth rates throughout this region will continue at about double the world average to the end of the millennium and beyond, that is to say an average of around 6.6 percent for the ASEAN countries as against around 3 percent for the United States, European Economic Community, and Japan.[16] Poverty throughout the Asian region is expected to be more than halved during the 1990s.[17]

Although in absolute terms a very rough balance of scale had come to exist between the economies of Europe (EEC), North America (NAFTA), and East Asia, the latter had become the undisputed center of growth, with its greatest energy concentrated in Japan as the vital core radiating energy throughout the region. Japan's economic scale is such that it accounts for 66 percent of all Asian GNP (with Asia here

Table 4.2

Real GNP Trends for Twelve Countries or Regions in Asia, 1970–2001

	1970 ($US)	1980 ($US)	1990 ($US)	2001 ($US)
South Korea	1,400	2,600	5,700	10,800
Taiwan	2,000	4,200	7,600	13,200
Hong Kong	3,900	7,400	12,100	19,600
Singapore	3,600	7,400	11,700	20,500
Asian NIES (average)	1,800	3,600	7,000	12,600
Thailand	540	810	1,400	2,800
Malaysia	1,100	1,700	2,400	4,100
Philippines	570	780	720	800
Indonesia	240	430	600	1,100
Asean (average)	400	630	870	1,500
China	110	160	320	650
India	230	260	370	480
Vietnam	160	140	210	370
Japan	12,100	16,800	23,800	33,700
Average of 12 Countries	940	1,200	1,700	2,400

Note: 1990 base, 2001 estimates. Compiled by Sakura Bank, Pacific Basin Research Centre (Sakura sōgō kenkyūjō, Kan Taiheiyō kenkyū sentā [Sakura Institute of Research, Center for Pacific Business Studies], ed. *Shin seiki e no Ajia hatten no shinario*, Tokyo, Daiyamondo-sha, 1994, p. 240).

including China, India, Australia, and New Zealand, as well as the ANIEs and the ASEAN countries). This figure is based on conventional measures of GDP at prevailing exchange rates, which undoubtedly exaggerates the degree of Japanese preeminence, but however it might be adjusted—and the most radical revisionists argue that even now China, with ten times Japan's population, might constitute a slightly larger component of the regional economy—Japan stands alone in the region as industrial and financial superpower. One other indicative statistic is that, even before the huge 1995 increase in the value of the yen, the world's eight largest banks and five of the ten top global firms were Japanese.[18] The colossal imbalance between Japan and other regional countries is likely to be only slowly eroded.

In historic terms, the span of two generations saw the collapse of a 400-year-old system of European colonial dominance in Asia and the

Pacific, followed by a brief period of exclusive U.S. hegemony, which in turn is now visibly eroded and no longer exclusive. U.S. world influence undoubtedly remains complex and many faceted, and it retains a preeminent position in cultural, not to mention military terms, while its huge market continues to serve as a major engine of growth throughout the Asia-Pacific region. Nevertheless, the fact that its debt is written with thirteen digits certainly casts a shadow of doubt over its claims to superpower status. The role of Japan in transforming Asia and the Pacific Region has been central: first in overthrowing and destroying by force of arms the European colonial empires, then in subverting U.S. hegemony by economic means.

The development process that was accomplished by Europe over centuries and by the United States and Japan over about one hundred years seems to be continually contracting, so that it was accomplished in a matter of decades by the ANIEs (half a century at most, if the beginning of the process is dated to the time of Japanese imperial control in the 1930s over Korea and Taiwan), and has since proceeded rapidly in the ASEAN countries and even more recently in China.

One does not have to be a Marxist to understand that these momentous economic changes will reverberate in all spheres of life, and already the political, cultural, and military implications are beginning to be appreciated. The Confucianism that a generation ago was confidently stated to be the cause of economic stagnation is now given high marks for apparently disposing societies for growth and dynamism. Identity politics gains strength throughout the region, with the result that culture becomes contested and the notion of Asia is fundamentally reassessed.

Identity and Schizophrenia

From its encounter with the modern West in the 1860s, until today, the problem of identity has vexed Japan. The central question of Japanese identity remains: Asian or Western? Given that the world it faced in the nineteenth century was one in which modernity, and the wealth and power that went with it, was European, while Asia was synonymous with backwardness, the dilemma was understandable. Unable to respond unequivocally, Japan vacillated between insisting on being not Asian at all, and declaring itself the epitome of Asianness.

The fact is that all late-industrializing societies experience a similar phenomenon. Self-esteem is lost and the national/social identity torn as the forces of externally induced change overcome the desire to resist and assert one's autonomy. Some Japanese scholars go so far as to use the term "rape syndrome" to refer to the forceful process by which Japan was initially opened, and to suggest that the shock and resentment occasioned by it, however subsequently sublimated, have still not been fully purged.[19] If they are right, then a similar process must have occurred in all the countries of the region, obviously with more force in those that were subjected to direct colonial rule, and the rape syndrome will only be fully purged when the divided elements of the national identity are able to cohere again in a new synthesis. National independence and economic growth help create the conditions to achieve this, but the realization of a capacity to face the past objectively might also be necessary and would seem to be as difficult to achieve.

The confusion and identity crisis is compounded in the case of Japan by the ambiguity of the relationship with the adjacent Asian region. Fukuzawa Yukichi, the most influential educator and intellectual of the nineteenth century, in his famous text of 1881 entitled *DatsuA-ron,* articulated the widely felt sentiment that Japan should cast itself off from Asia, and it could be argued that the long voyage thus symbolically launched by that generation, in quest of industrial development and equality of status with the leading nations of the world, was only accomplished 100 years later. If the hypothesis of the Waseda University economic historian Kawakatsu Heita is correct, that this conscious shift of the nineteenth century was preceded by an implicit act of detachment in the seventeenth, the point of Japan's distance from Asia is reinforced. The ambiguity at the heart of Japan's present relationship with Asia can be better understood against the knowledge that Japan has twice cast off from it and for most of its modern history continued to see it as a backward region to be either avoided or led. Seen from this perspective, the process of distancing from Asia is as old for Japan as it is for Europe. In other words, it is not just that Japan is being torn between East and West, but that it has itself been a kind of "Asian West" for about as long as has Europe. The contemporary Japanese debate on identity must therefore in a sense return to the question of Asia.

Beyond this, there is the question of whether Asia exists at all. True, there is such a geographic term. It refers to that vast and amorphous

region lying between the Bosphorus straits and the Pacific and from
Siberia to Java. Asia, in other words, is a term that refers to the
region that lay beyond the pale of European comprehension, where
the European writ did not run. It was essentially an imposed identity: a fantastic ideological construct without racial or cultural
meaning, imagined by those outside a vast region to try to cope with
its almost infinite diversity by declaring those othernesses integral.
Paradoxically, the notion of Asia strengthened the farther one
moved away from it and receded as one entered into it. Few residents of Bangkok, Pusan, or Nagoya think of themselves as Asian.
There is no such thing as Asian values, Asian psychology, or even
Asian cuisine. While terms such as northeast, east, southeast, south,
and west Asia make sense for regions that share certain common
cultural, religious, or linguistic influences and therefore might be
thought of meaningfully by a single collective regional term, the
five separate entities do not add up to a whole.

Japan's detachment from Asia in the 1880s, however, was a matter
of intellectual renunciation more than political withdrawal, for it was
followed soon afterward by the first stages of the construction of Japanese imperial control over parts of China (in 1895) and Korea (in
1905). Renunciation was accompanied by misty sentimental rhetoric
about the ideals of the East, the awakening of the East, and so on,
which served to reinforce the idea that Asia was indeed backward but
that Japan was destined to revive and lead it to salvation. During the
third and fourth decades of this century, Japan articulated its distinctive
message to Asia: the repudiation of Western imperialism and white
dominance, combined with the vision of an alternative multiracial
commonwealth—a Greater East Asian Coprosperity Sphere. In other
words, Japan insisted on its own distinctiveness as leader, claiming at
the same time to be part of, but essentially superior to, Asia. Despite
the violence of its assault on the Columbian order in Asia, the alternative vision it presented in this period was thus contradictory and hollow. Its failure was, in a very real sense, the failure to project the
image of a community with which the peoples of neighboring countries could identify or that they might wish to join. In due course, the
order it created collapsed in 1945. It is notable that, outside Japan
itself, not a voice was ever raised thereafter to lament the passing of
the peculiar Japanese order of these years, or to call for its recreation,
and that even in Japan it came to be remembered not as the hegemonic

imperial system it actually constituted at the time, but for its incidental effect of having shattered Western colonial empires and hastened the course of national independence.

During the decades of its postwar rise, a reconciliation between Japan and the Asia it had invaded was blocked by the Cold War, during which Japan adopted the role of bastion of the free world *against* Asia. While other states were more or less ideological, Japan was largely a passive part of the system, concentrating on its economy and reticent about any ideological message. An anomalous state, formally dependent on the United States and its territory crisscrossed by a chain of U.S. bases, it nevertheless grew until the reality of its sovereign economic power became obvious and its scale too great for such self-abnegation. With the end of the Cold War and the collapse of the pretense of a monolithic, free, capitalist world, the search for meaning gathered force, even as the flow of Japanese money, technology, organizational skills, and energy gained momentum. The meaning of both Japan and Asia was reopened to question. Underlying the renewed attention to the question of identity was the quest for the wholeness of a new synthesis in which reconciliation could be achieved between tradition and modernity, the West and Japan, Japan and Asia.

The New Asia and the New Asianism

The past decade has seen the emergence of a new and radically different sense of Asia: no longer the passive subject of Western dominance but a dynamic region with a subjectively chosen and created identity to which definition is only gradually attaching. The economic rise of East Asia, the end of the Cold War, the relative decline in the economic importance of the United States (combined with what might be seen as strident Western attempts to impose human-rights standards or, in the case of Japan, wide-ranging political and economic policies), combine to feed a backlash of anti-Western resentment; from Singapore and Kuala Lumpur to Beijing and Tokyo, voices may be heard talking about the need to resist Western economic, political, or cultural interventions, and (in at least a few cases) about the desire to build upon the existing economic networks the cultural edifice that would be home to an autonomous Asian order.

Japanese interest in such thinking is still tentative, but is fed by the frustrations and resentments of the relationship with the United States.

Despite American rhetoric under the Bush Administration about building a new world order, and under the Clinton Administration about giving priority to the partnership with Japan, Japanese are very conscious that Japan figures in U.S. thinking, above all, as a problem. The *kenbei* (fed-up with America) mood seems to have gained much strength in the early 1990s: When the famous book by Ishihara Shintarō and Morita Akio—*The Japan That Can Say "No"*—was published, it was widely criticized in the media as irresponsible or extravagant, but when Prime Minister Hosokawa actually said "No" to President Clinton's demands for specific market share at the U.S.-Japan talks in Washington in February 1994, and the talks thereby collapsed, the Japanese public was generally supportive, many expressed open delight, and certainly no one complained.[20] In the 1995 dispute stemming from the U.S. demand that Japan buy more automobiles and automobile parts, the Japanese bemusement was captured by the television announcer who remarked in passing that it seemed now as if the United States was behaving like a twelve year old, the age that General MacArthur once grandly announced he thought Japan had attained.[21]

There have been many pointers to the rise of such a mood. Perhaps nothing articulated it more clearly than a 1993 essay by a senior Japanese bureaucrat, Ogura Kazuo. Ogura was at the time head of the Bureau of Economics in the Ministry of Foreign Affairs, and in 1994 was appointed Japanese ambassador to Vietnam.[22] Ogura's argument comprises three parts: a critique of Western orientalist views of Asia; a critique of Western civilization's Faustian character and excessive materialism; and the hypothesis of a superior, emerging civilization based on Asian values. He contrasted two Asias: one negative, a term constructed by Europeans to describe a region that holds no universal value but constitutes a field for their plunder or their pleasure, upon which universal Western moral, ethical, and political systems were to be imposed; the other positive, the newly emerging prosperous and self-confident subjectivity of modern or contemporary Asia. In the former image, he was following closely the critique of Western orientalism elaborated by critics such as Edward Said. In the latter, moving from critique to prescription, he declared that it was precisely this Asia, at once new and old, that offered a solution to the problems of humanity—rampant nationalism, Faustian pursuit of limitless desire, insatiable self-assertion, and lack of harmony in human relations with the environment. All such evils he saw as symptomatic of a deep malaise in Western civilization. A revival of Asia's traditional spirit was precisely what was needed, and, just as the West had once created a universal system on the basis of its absorption of the cultures and civilizations of Greece, Rome, Persia, Arabia, and Turkey, so now Asia, through its encounter with the West, might likewise come to generate a new universalism.

Ogura's critique of Western views of Asia and of Western civilization is neither controversial nor original; indeed, both are essentially restatements of the critique originally advanced and well-accepted in the West. Few would dispute the general position that the future of humanity depends on evolving into a softer, less exploitative, more sustainable civilization. Ogura's third proposition, however, is highly problematic. Many might wish to think that he is right, that traditional Oriental civilization already holds answers to the problems, but the Asian civilization that he sketches is an extremely diffuse phenomenon (mostly confined to the countries of East and Southeast Asia, which share a tradition that is Sinic, Confucian, and Buddhist), and precisely how it would meet the problems facing humanity is far from clear. The stress by Ogura, and others such as Singapore's Lee Kuan Yew, on supposed East Asian cultural traits—priority of family and collective over individual, discipline, studiousness, order, and cooperativeness—could be seen essentially as the imaginative projection of the sort of community they aspire to create rather than an account of what already exists. It suggests also their desire to contain capitalism to the role of mechanism of industrial development and capital accumulation, while warding off much that is seen as regrettable about the social transformation that accompanied those processes in the West.[23] Their proposition is plausible as an ideological statement about value, but should not be confused with a descriptive statement of scientific validity.

Furthermore, capitalism, which results in accomplishing the economic growth which Ogura appears to welcome, has been no less destructive of social order and nature in Asia than in the West. Marx's observation that "all that is solid melts into air" is borne out in contemporary China or Malaysia just as much as it was in nineteenth-century Germany or England. Likewise, the problems of accomplishing democracy are not obviously either greater or lesser in Asia than elsewhere, while the assumption that the authoritarianism that long characterized much of this region is due to the survival of Western colonial structures manipulated by local elites is at least questionable.

In struggling to express his sense of what constituted Asia, Ogura resorted to thinkers as diverse as Rabindranath Tagore, Okakura Tenshin, Nitobe Inazō, Sun Yat-sen, and to his two contemporaries, Lee Kuan Yew and Malaysia's Prime Minister Mahathir bin Mohamad. Needless to say, there is little coherence in the way all these people thought or think of Asia. Suffice it here to take only the sole Chinese figure who is commonly claimed as a spiritual antecedent of contemporary Asianism: Sun Yat-sen. For Sun, Asianness meant following something that he called the kingly way, the way of virtue and honor, in contrast to the "hegemonic way" of the West. His Asia comprised countries such as Arabia, Persia, Egypt, Afghanistan, and India (as well as China and Japan), but in the famous lecture on Greater Asianism that he delivered in Kobe in November 1924, he noted that European countries were also capable of committing themselves to the kingly way, and commended the case of Lenin's Russia as a model.[24] His speech is a nice example of the flexible, voluntaristic, and essentially ideological way in which the term may be interpreted. However, it seems that the authority of his name—and "Greater Asianism," the title of his lecture—is more important to the contemporary Asianist cause than the details of his thought.

Not only is Sun Yat-sen the single name acclaimed in both Beijing and Taipei, it also happens to be popular among contemporary (and earlier) Asianists in Tokyo. For them, however, the attraction of Sun Yat-sen is not only the vague general aura of his ideas but the specific way he interpreted the Japan-China relationship. In the confusion following the 1911 Republican revolution in China, the "father" of the Chinese republic, in desperation, offered Japan a free hand in Northeast China (Manchuria), which was far from his own southern base and where he exercised no power at all, if only Japan would grant him a ten-million-yen "loan" to help establish his power nationally.[25] Such a combination of Asianism and nationalism holds considerable attractions for contemporary Japanese Asianists, some of whom actually even now look to the realization of this promise—the confirmation of a special Japanese position in Manchuria—as a token of the Tokyo-Beijing axis of the neo-Asianist future.[26] The Asia to which they refer is in some ways as fanciful a construct as was Sun Yat-sen's.

Nor is the thrust of Ogura's 1993 essay obviously consistent with other of his writings. In 1992, for example, noting that Japan, alone among the industrial powers, was not part of any regional integration scheme and, sandwiched between Europe-America and Asia, ran the risk of geopolitical isolation, he argued that the only country with which it might form a long-term partnership was Australia, with which it shared the common values of democracy and freedom, as well as a commitment to the principle of the market and free trade, and common security, political, and economic interests.[27] The neo-Asianism that was to become the fulcrum of his thinking in 1993 was nowhere in evidence in 1992. Although he does not discuss them, there are indeed interesting parallels, discussed later in this chapter, between the modern history of these two countries in terms of their relationship to Asia, but the alternately Asianist and Australia-focused versions of Japan's future identity that Ogura projected were not obviously reconcilable. However, Ogura's words were enough to excite business and political leaders in Australia at the prospect of a Tokyo-Sydney axis.

There is much else that Ogura does not discuss. He is notably amnesiac. Though ranging widely through time and space, he ignores the catastrophic Japanese attempts to forge an Asian identity during the 1930s and 1940s, although that precedent must surely make for skeptical responses on the part of neighbor countries to Japanese expressions of Asianism in the 1990s. The values and orientation of original Asianism were articulated most vigorously by imperial Japan, and by political and intellectual leaders from other countries turning to Japan in the hope of securing aid or support for anticolonial struggles. The original ideals of equality and mutual support against imperialism altered greatly as they began to be put into practice, and the eventual Greater East Asian Coprosperity Sphere was little more than a grotesque parody, the order constructed by Japan being just as imperialist as the European. Without a critical reflection on the process by which this happened, including the subversion and degradation of the Asianist ideals of that generation, it is hard not to be skeptical about the prospects for the new brand of Asianism in the 1990s. Yet it is the absence of a self-critical, historical perspective that is most characteristic of the recent Japanese literature on Asianism, despite the superficial indulgence in large-scale historical allusion.

Another recent Japanese essay on the spiritual history of East Asia argues, like Ogura's, that the premodern region of Asia was characterized by differences in religion, culture, and technology as great as in climate and nature, and only became Asia through coming to realize its identity of humiliation and plunder by Europe. Asia, according to Matsumoto Ken-ichi, is therefore not a geographical term but a representation of the idea of resistance.[28] Only with the successful conclusion of the long resistance struggle, however, has Asia at last emerged as a subjectivity in the game of world history.[29] While he agrees with Ogura in this respect, Matsumoto's analysis places great stress on the difference in the way that Japan and China responded to nineteenth-century Western imperialism: both stressed their own way, their policy (*kokutai/guoti*), but Japan alone was able to construct a distinctive and revolutionary sense of its own polity as unique and superior. It did so by stressing the sacredness and prior existence of the emperor.[30] The problem of how this sense of an identity that is unique and predicated a negation of the rest of Asia could be reconciled with his support of neo-Asianism is a crucial issue, but is not addressed in Matsumoto's book. Indeed the problem is so deep seated that virtually none of the recent Asianist literature attempts even to engage with it.

Similar sentiments were expressed in the book by Ozawa Ichirō that became a best-seller, of sorts, in 1993. There was some irony in the spectacle of Ozawa, perhaps the most Machiavellian figure in late-twentieth-century Japanese politics, contrasting Oriental values, in which human beings constitute part of nature, with Western values, in which humankind is seen as conqueror and controller of nature, and in his prescription that the answer to current environmental problems lay in the move away from Western toward Eastern values. For Ozawa, however, such Asian values were represented in their purest form—not in Confucianism, but in the ancient forest dwelling society of prehistoric *Jōmon* Japan.[31] Ozawa thus epitomizes the ancient tension between Japan as Asian and Japan as distinctive and unique, and suggests that such tension remains unresolved in contemporary discourse. His discussion of this key matter was deleted in the English translation of his book that appeared in 1994.[32]

However eclectic, if not incoherent, their message might be, commentators in Japan agree that Ogura, Ozawa, and Matsumoto are giving voice to sentiments widely shared among Japanese intellectuals and bureaucrats, including officials in ministries such as Finance and Foreign Affairs, hitherto regarded as bastions of pro-U.S. sentiment.[33] At a government level, however, there is far from being any consensus on these questions. Malaysian proposals for the formation of a distinctive Asian political-economic group, with Japan playing a leading role, gain some support from business leaders, but the political doubts and difficulties associated with such a course remain large. It was notable at the Bogor APEC Summit in 1994 that there was virtually no Japanese voice to be heard at all, to the immense irritation of Asianists such as Malaysia's Mahathir ben Mohamad.

There is, at least so far, no coherent Asianist politics, nor alternative economic strategy to address the relationships between the countries of the region or between them and the United States. This is not to say, of course, that under exceptional circumstances, such as a collapse of the world trading system, the economic agenda for an Asian bloc could not be constructed, although in that event it is hard to see how Asianist sentiment would create an order reflecting distinctively Asian values or in which Japan's overwhelming economic power would not give it as predominant a political and economic role as it enjoyed in the Greater East Asian Coprosperity Sphere of the 1940s.

It is, however, problematic whether Asia would welcome the sort of shift on Japan's part that such advocates favor. The neo-Asianist prospect of a dual Sino-Japanese hegemony over Asia in the early twenty-first century is not one that stirs much enthusiasm in the region. Even among the Japanese, it is as likely to be seen with apprehension as opening the way for Japan to play a subordinate role in a Chinese World Order of the twenty-first century, as it is to be uncritically acclaimed.[34] Furthermore, the U.S. market remains of huge importance, not only to Japan but to the region as a whole, and there is no indication of any desire to liquidate the U.S. security presence in the region. And, although a distinctive East Asian popular culture is gradually becoming manifest, there is little sign of any weakening of the fascination with American cultural artifacts, the instruments of what Harvard's Joseph Nye (who in 1994 became the Clinton Administration's Assistant Secretary for Defense, International Security Affairs) calls America's soft power. Despite being anxious to preserve good relations with Japan, many would view with apprehension the prospect of an internationally isolated Japan seeking resolution of its problems through the creation of a new order in Asia.[35] Characteristic of the skepticism about Japan's motives on the part of neighbor countries is the comment by one Korean economist that whenever Japan experiences problems in its relations with Europe and America, it inclines toward Asianism while continuing to be blind to the nature of its past and present impact on its neighbor states and treating them as peripheral.[36]

In the contemporary world, whether in Japan or elsewhere in the region, Asianism (with or without the neo-) constitutes tactics rather than strategy, and rhetoric rather than substance.[37] The combination of debt, disdain, and detachment[38] that has marked the Japanese attitude toward Asia for one hundred years is rarely criticized by those who advocate a new closeness. Statements about the birth of Asian subjectivity or Asian unity are no less ideological and rhetorical today than they were in the early twentieth century. The idea that East Asian governments are somehow less intrusive or prescriptive than Western governments is ridiculed by the veteran Korean political leader Kim Dae Jung as flying in the face of the fact that "Asian governments intrude much more than Western governments into the daily life of individuals and families," reaching at times to "an Orwellian extreme of social engineering."[39] The spectacle of aging dictators mouthing neo-Confucian platitudes "as a rationale for preserving their power" is described by Derek Davies, the veteran ex-editor of the *Far Eastern Economic Review*, as "an abomination and an insult to Confucius."[40] Asianism, like all identities, is not a descriptive character but an ideological construct and a prescription for the sort of society that conservative modernizers would like to construct, in which collectivism, discipline, diligence, and filiality would be core values. In its rhetorical windiness and woolliness, it is akin to the Cold War rhetoric about Western civilization, of which the United States was standard-bearer.[41]

Asianism and Civilization Theory

Despite its vogue as intellectual trend, neo-Asianism is as problematic as was the Asianism of prewar Japan. It is interesting to note that the most ambitious recent (Western) attempt to characterize the present moment in world history was implicitly dismissive of Japanese (neo-) Asianism. According to Samuel Huntington, in his scenario of a world split along civilization lines, Asia was home to no fewer than four distinct civilizations—Confucian, Japanese, Islamic, and Hindu—with Japan the sole case of a country that is "a society and civilization unique to itself."[42] Lecturing in Japan in 1994, Huntington told his Japanese audience that they should regard this distinctiveness as a matter for pride.[43] Quite why this should be the case he did not say, and ironically, although he might have appeared to be flattering his Japanese hosts, his views highlighted the historic dilemma confronting Japan: how to be both fully Japanese and Asian.

Huntington's essay excited considerable comment, critical as well as supportive, with the sharpest, and in many ways the most insightful, critique being contained in an essay published (thus far) only in Japanese.[44]

Where Japan seemed to Huntington to be a distinct civilization in a frozen, reified cultural sense, to his critic, the Kobe University political scientist Iokibe Mokoto, it was distinctive for the entirely different reason that no country had a longer (and more bitter) experience of confronting and grappling with different cultures (or civilizations). Out of that experience at the interface, he argued, Japan had exhausted the polarities, melting them, piecemeal, into a hybrid civilization. Huntington's polemical, even apocalyptic tone reminded Iokibe of nothing so much as the interwar Japanese discourse, in which political and intellectual figures railed against a post–World War One world order, supposed to be new, in which Western hegemony was unshaken. Where the Japanese then were articulating a sense of inferiority and vulnerability, Huntington's subtext was likewise one of U.S. decline, frustration, and the search for external scapegoats. Iokibe was reminded in particular of the clashing-civilizations theories of figures such as Konoye Fumimarō, the diplomat, later prime minister, and architect of Japan's ill-fated new order, known as the Greater East Asia Coprosperity Scheme, whose 1918 essay was entitled "Rejecting Anglo-American–Style Pacifism," and Ishihara Kanji, the military genius, firm believer in the inevitability of intercivilizational, apocalyptic war, and planner of the Manchurian Incident of 1931 (which was supposed to be a first step in clearing the ground for such conflict). According to Iokibe, it was precisely because of the Japanese experience of those years, the traumas born of a long failure to cope with the sterile confrontation with Western culture (or civilization), and the eventual reconciliation of competing values that in the long run grew from it, that Japan might be capable of performing a healing and reconciling role in the contemporary arena of West versus non-West relations.

Because the process of evolution of a new, hybrid, and eclectic civilization has gone so far in Japan, Huntington's ideas did not excite much interest, much less support, but Iokibe feared that talk of a clash of civilizations might prove a self-fulfilling prophecy. While never before in history had there been such universal support for democracy and human rights (and such little ground for fearing degeneration into civilizational conflict), the radical U.S. insistence on the equivalence of

Western and universal values could only set back the process of such acceptance. What is often rejected, he argued, was not the values themselves, but the shrillness and self-righteous impetuosity of Western advocates such as Huntington.

In other words, while perhaps right in seeing Japan as different, Huntington may have missed the fact that Japan's difference might lie not in the surface manifestations of distinctness, but at a deeper level, where it might actually have achieved the reconciliation of civilizations. Hybrid was much more beautiful than pure. Japan might be seen as evidence that the confrontation and contradiction between civilizations, far from being absolute, was becoming a thing of the past.

Japan Versus Asia

To enter upon this process of reflection on the causes of failure of the Asian project in the prewar period would entail tackling the contradiction that lies at the heart of the Japanese proposition of Asianism: between shared identity with others within the region on the one hand, and the sense of Japaneseness as meaning heir to a distinct, superior, and unique quality on the other. The latter was constructed in the late nineteenth century and was the necessary counterpart to the process of sloughing off Asia that was signaled by Fukuzawa's famous text of 1881. The two identities have never been integrated, and the tension between them has varied over time. Undoubtedly, the mythology and ideology of being a chosen people helped Japan unite and resist Western nineteenth-century aggression, but the price was alienation from neighboring Asia, and the implanting in Japanese society of a deep-seated attitude of superiority that would brook no cooperation with those countries other than in terms of leadership by Japan. The sense of identity thus oscillated between the atavistic notion of being a chosen people, sharing a destiny defined by race, purity of blood, and shared cult on the one hand, and universal, confessional, voluntary notions of modernity, citizenship, science, democracy, and internationalism on the other.

The Japanese stream of chauvinism and superiority, built on the basis of the late-nineteenth-century rejection of Asia, was tied to the imperial institution as the pure and unassailable core to all orthodox constructions of Japaneseness, the embodiment of quintessential Japaneseness. Eventually, it was codified in the 1930s as *kokutai* (national polity).[45] Although that term was not used in the postwar period,

the assumptions and values it encapsulated were never thoroughly analyzed and criticized (partly because of the decision by the Allied authorities to preserve the imperial institution). The complex of cultural
nationalist ideas is described as follows by Inoguchi Takashi:

> From Meiji, the "insularity" theory, the "rice exclusivity" theory, and
> the "single race" theory came to constitute fixed parts within the dy-
> namic fusion of the emperor system. Not only did they serve to rein-
> force the legitimacy of emperor system control, but they also
> contributed toward the political stability and social durability that con-
> stituted the base for economic development. In the process of modern
> state formation, many myths were developed to reinforce control. Al-
> though they served to implant a spirit of ethnic identity, of which peo-
> ple had not until that time been very conscious, yet at the same time
> they were accompanied by the evils of war, oppression, and discrimina-
> tion. It is precisely this spirit that, according to [former Prime Minister]
> Nakasone Yasuhiro, constitutes the indispensable foundation for the
> preservation of stability and prosperity in a world filled with confusion
> and scheming.[46]

The kernel of ethnic identity and cultural nationalism in Japan, unlike other countries active in proclaiming the new Asianist cause, is
actually hostile to Asia. The enthusiasm of Southeast Asian leaders for
Confucianism can scarcely be shared for the reason that Confucianism,
which in one way or another is central to the Southeast Asian construction of the new Asian identity, is commonly perceived as an unassimi-
lated foreign ideology in Japan. The critique of it that was made in the
eighteenth century as a demeaning, foreign incubus on the pure essence of Japanese culture is still widely maintained. The thorny nettle
of how Asianness and Japaneseness might be represented in the new
order has been no more resolved in the 1990s than it was in the 1930s
and 1940s.[47]

When Nakasone Yasuhiro, prime minister in the mid-1980s, proclaimed the importance of clarifying the myths that bound the nation
together and linked it to its past, and of proclaiming to the world a
distinctive Japanese identity, he was thinking in purely national, not
regional, terms.[48] The group of Kyoto-based scholars who responded
to his call looked back to the preagricultural, forest-dwelling, hunting-
and-gathering Jōmon society, in which they found a harmonious, ecologically sound, animistic community that impressed a distinctive and

apparently permanent mold on the deep or subconscious mind of the subsequent peoples of the archipelago. That pattern was unique and was supposed to owe little or nothing to influences from the neighboring Asian continent. It was most purely transmitted through the imperial institution as it was crystalized in the time of Prince Shōtoku (574–622), although the deep consciousness of all Japanese was shaped by it, and concepts such as *wa* (harmony), *ie* (household, as distinct from individual), *aida* or *aidagara* (space or in-betweenness, as distinct from thatness or thereness), and concave-patterned (i.e., receptive) rather than convex-patterned (i.e., outward-thrusting) were characteristic of it.[49] The 1980s thus present the curious spectacle of "a culture vigorously determined to Orientalize itself,"[50] although attempting to reverse the conventional value judgment of the Oriental as merely exotic.

This Japaneseness discourse had little to say about how to square the circle of the imagined community of uniqueness by finding in it something that is also recognizably Asian, let alone universal. The organic, essentially mystical, formulaic slogans, imposed from above in an attempt to preempt popular aspiration and mobilize and coopt— from interracial harmony and coprosperity in the 1930s and 1940s to the most contemporary symbiosis (kyōsei)[51]—work internally to organize and mobilize, but are markedly less successful at articulating any sense of regional identity.

As the repertory of imperial and kokutai myths of uniqueness, exclusiveness, and superiority was revived, regained respectability, and was articulated at the highest levels, the legal principle that the years should be known by the name of the reigning emperor was established (by the Gengōhō in 1979); Japan was declared a monoracial society and a natural community (*shizen kyōdōtai*), not a nation formed by contract, in contrast to the polyglot America, whose problems were put down to its "many Blacks, Puerto Ricans and Mexicans."[52] The Yamato race that Prime Minister Nakasone insisted had been living "for at least two thousand years . . . hand in hand with no other, different ethnic groups present [in these islands],"[53] and was therefore pure and homogeneous, had had an easier time becoming an "intelligent society."[54] Nakasone was far from unique, but he was the most powerful and articulate advocate of the cause of clarifying the national identity, liquidating the postwar, and reasserting internationally the unique virtues of Japaneseness.

Between the atavism of Nakasone's cultural uniqueness and the opportunism of Ogura and Ozawa's Asianism, there is, as yet, no sign of a bridge. But while that problem remains, the frustration with the U.S. relationship deepens and, with or without any deep thinking about the nature of civilization, it has the capacity to influence events in uncertain ways. As a one-line jingle put it: "If things don't work out with the Americans, we can always try Asia" (*Amerika wa dame nara, Ajia ga aru sa*).

Alternatives

Although there are plenty of pretenders to the role of conductor of a neo-Asianist symphony in contemporary Japan, there is little agreement on the score, and continuing dispute on tone and key. While none would dispute the importance of good (and better) relations with the countries of the region, many would resist the notion that Asianism is the way to go.

The most thoughtful (and profoundly humanist) reflections within Japan on the question of identity are those that eschew simple formulas and critically dissect or deconstruct not only notions of Asia but also those of what is Western, Japanese, and universal. The context of the search for value is the global crisis of the post–Cold War era, polarized (as Mushakoji Kinhide, former vice-rector of the United Nations University and distinguished peace researcher, puts it) between two trends:

> a centralizing trend justifying itself through global universal values, and a more diversified trend toward decentralization, where democratic and autocratic orientations operate side by side.[55]

The critique of the pretense to universalism enveloped within the former should not be allowed to conceal the autocratic elements in the decentralized alternative prescriptions, of which Asia is a prominent one, in the latter. Mushakoji points out that Asia is a very amorphous notion, containing within it anything from Confucian, rational, bureaucratic hierarchy on the one hand to the (often forgotten) self-organizing, Daoist (Taoist) counterculture on the other, where the local communities develop, more or less independently from the local authority of the emperor, their own communal life based on popular values and traditions relatively free from the central and centralizing authorities.[56] In this Daoist stream he finds the possibility of "a postmodern alternative ideology stressing self-organization and ecological symbiosis," that would be an alternative to the Confucian bureaucratic rationality of the traditional Pax Sinica.[57] Mushakoji is almost unique among contemporary Japanese intellectuals in his cheerful embrace of the anarchic, destabilizing, and decentralizing creative chaos that flows from the Daoist tradition.[58] Mainstream Japanese intellectuals would be uncomfortable with his stress on the individual, liberty, and social protest. Although his efforts at deconstructing Asia, and focusing attention on the anti-Confucian elements within it, make his a lonely voice, it is a profound and possibly a prophetic one in the contemporary Japanese debate on identity.

However, the discourse in which Mushakoji constitutes a sort of basso profundo is, even in the middle ranges, quite broad. Alternative prescriptions for Japan to renegotiate its relationships with its neighbor countries abound, and are likely to be further refined as the debate evolves. Most would start from the need to recognize fully the consequences of Japanese aggression in the 1930s and 1940s, and, where appropriate, offer compensation to the victims. Doi Takako, speaker in the Lower House of the National Diet, has proposed formal legislation to this effect. A prominent former diplomat, Sunobe Ryōzō, expands upon this by arguing that Japan has no alternative but to join both Europe and Asia simultaneously (*nyū-A nyū-O*), striving for the closest partnership with Korea, while declaring commitment to the universal values of human rights and democracy.[59] Ogura's own immediate successor in the Ministry of Foreign Affairs argued that, while a recognition of some of the common factors underlying nation building and economic growth in the region—such as diligence, a work ethic, sense of duty—was appropriate and unobjectionable, the jump from this recognition to the declaration that "Asia Is One" carried two serious risks: a blindness to the immense diversity of Asia, and a tendency to see things in terms of a dichotomy of Asia versus non-Asia.[60] He, too, stressed the need to define Japan's regional and world orientation in universalist terms of human rights and democracy, thus implicitly rebutting the argument of those who would say that these were European values, inappropriate for Asia.[61]

These critical or alternative responses to the Asianist debate are neatly summed up in another comment by Inoguchi, who argues that Japan should desist from the obvious either-or polarities and join together with the people of Asia in sloughing off Asia (*datsu-Ajia*). However paradoxical sounding, what he meant was that it was time not to embrace or reject, but to transcend Asia. His prescription recognized the emptiness of the slogans about entering Asia and the importance of constructing inter- and intraregional relationships simultaneously.[62] The historian Iriye Akira makes a similar point, that to achieve a truly postmodern sense of regional community, one not centered on Japan, it would be necessary to move toward the transcendence of the limits of the modern (Westphalian) state and to expand the notion of Asia to include the Pacific (embracing Central and South America), creating a universal and inclusive, rather than exclusive, notion of humanity.[63]

To do this, however, may entail a step that sounds even more para-doxical: actually to slough off Japaneseness (*datsu-Nichi*), referring to the contrived identity imposed on the people of the Japanese islands as a unique, blood-ordained, and racial essence, concentrated in its purest form in the imperial family, which sets the Japanese people apart from and superior to other peoples.[64] In ancient times, the Japanese archipel-ago was the home to many different peoples and the center of complex networks of regional trade and cultural communication. The myth of being a special and superior people was created precisely to compensate for the sense of vulnerability against the powerful kingdoms that emerged in the seventh century on the Korean peninsula and to conceal the origins of the Japanese imperial family among the defeated clans of peninsular wars. The myths associated with legitimizing imperial rule were consolidated as a coherent doctrine by the scholars of the National Learning (*Kokugaku*) school during the Edo period and then adopted as ramified ideology-cult-religion by the modernizing Meiji state in the late nineteenth century. The identity thus imposed on Japan was im-plicitly chauvinist, combining an exaggerated assertion of Japan with denigration of the non-Japanese. While it undoubtedly facilitated mod-ern nation building and made possible Japan's successful resistance to Western imperialism, the cost it exacted was great.

Because the emperor, or rather the imperial institution, lies at the center of this historically constructed Japaneseness, and anything asso-ciated with the emperor is still protected by a combination of supersti-tion and terror, the process of rethinking and renegotiating the national identity in such a way as to enable Japan to become an equal of its neighbors and Asia to be transcended—or dissolved, as Inoguchi pro-poses—will be far from easy.

Asia as Seen from the South

The questions of identity and Asia are far from being unique to Japan. A country with which it merits comparison is one with which Japan is rarely compared: Australia. Like Japan, Australia in the nineteenth century adopted policies of monoethnic, racial superiority, denigration of its aboriginal inhabitants, chauvinism, and rejection of Asia. While Japan declared its sloughing off of Asia, Australia declared itself white, and both insisted on their superior racial qualities. Both in recent decades debate how best to enter, or, at least associate more closely with, Asia.

In Australia, a profound national reorientation has been underway during the past three decades that has affected the sense of national identity at the deepest levels. Partly, the process has been occasioned by the huge shifts in economic orientation as the importance of the onetime mother country, Britain, faded, and that of regional neighbor countries grew, until at present about 60 percent of Australian exports are going to Western Pacific countries. But noneconomic considerations have also been important. The crimes committed against the aboriginal peoples in the name of nation building were recognized and redress attempted—through a combination of land rights, compensation, and welfare and education measures. In place of the "White Australia Policy," a nondiscriminatory immigration policy and a comprehensive set of policies generally known as multiculturalism was adopted. While there are undoubtedly problems in the implementation of such measures—continuing aboriginal poverty and discrimination, occasional racist expressions in public life, etc.—nevertheless, the national identity is in the process of a fundamental restructuring and reorientation. The symbols of nationhood—flag and anthem—have been opened to debate, with a new anthem adopted some years ago and further changes quite possible in the future, and a new flag under discussion. The process is expected to culminate, by the year 2000 or thereabouts, in Australia becoming a multiracial and multicultural republic.

From the late 1980s, paralleling the trend in Japan, the debate in Australia over identity came to include the issue of how to relate to Asia: Was Australia already, could it, or should it try to become part of Asia? Though the issues are complex, the simplest way to resume this debate would be to say that it is moving in the direction pointed to by Inoguchi, Iriye, and others for Japan: forging close, friendly, and cooperative relations with the countries of the region and striving toward the articulation of an open, inclusive, regional Asia-Pacific identity. Without actually becoming Asian, Australia is struggling to articulate a regional universalism and to become simultaneously post-European and post-Asian, transcending both its own European racial and cultural heritage and any racially or culturally specific Asia.

Prospect

In the long term, the historic phase of European world hegemony that began some 500 years ago has ended. While there is obviously an economic sense in which it could be said that an Asian era is dawning, little is clear about what such an era would stand for in terms of values, identity, or civilization. For Japan, the debate about the 1881 system (by which an Asian identity was repudiated) is at least as important as debate about the 1955 system (of conservative political hegemony during the Cold War). Until the innate contradiction upon which the prewar Japanese Asianist dream was constructed is openly and critically addressed, the idea of Japanese participation in a new Asianist era deserves to be viewed with skepticism. Too easily could the kyōsei (symbiotic) relationship of which contemporary Japan speaks slide, as did the Asianist ideals of a previous generation, into the sort of coprosperity that existed under the old Greater East Asia Coprosperity Sphere.[65]

The best guard against this happening will be the extent to which the problems of Asia-in-Japan are addressed simultaneously with those of Japan-in-Asia. Commonly, the ideology of the latter is confined to intellectual posture, and the role of Japan-in-Asia thought of in terms of a narrow focus on what is regarded as the Japanese national interest. Yet Japan's regional presence and role is likely to mirror the sort of relationships and the sort of Asian identity that is constructed within Japan itself, and just as the Greater East Asian Coprosperity Sphere combined chauvinism and aggression abroad with discrimination at home, so any rhetoric about a new Asian order has to be matched against the reality of that order as constructed within Japan. Incidents suggestive of continuing discrimination against Asian people are, however, common in Japan. The treatment of these three categories of Asian women in Japan may be taken as illustrative of the problem.

If the abuse of women from throughout Japanese-occupied Asia under the so-called "comfort women" system (see Chapter 6) was symptomatic of the racism, chauvinism, and sexism of the prewar and wartime order, then contemporary Japan has constructed a system for the exploitation of Asian women that is in some ways analogous. Just as estimates of the numbers of wartime comfort women range from 100,000 to 200,000, so today a figure of at least 100,000 is put on the number of women from neighboring Asian countries who are employed in the "water trades" as entertainers in nightclubs, snack bars, or karaoke lounges. Many of them enter Japan illegally, drawn by false promises of employment, but they quickly fall into the clutches of a violent, organized human trafficking in which rape, forced prostitution, and sexual slavery are common. Matsui Yayori, the Japanese journalist and long-term Southeast Asian correspondent for the major national daily paper, the *Asahi*, estimates that there are probably 40,000 such contemporary comfort women in Japan. Many are from Thailand and the Philippines, with somewhat smaller groups from other countries such as Taiwan, China, and Korea.[66] Japan, in Matsui's view, ranks as the world's largest trafficker in human beings. Japan is a party to both the United Nations Convention for the Suppression of Traffic in Persons and the Exploitation of Prostitution of Others (1949) and the Convention of the Elimination of All Forms of Discrimination Against Women, or CEDAW (1979), but its courts and police have turned a blind eye to evidence about the structure of systematic exploitation and abuse, just as the Japanese government until 1993 treated all the wartime comfort women as simply prostitutes.[67]

A second group of Asian women has been brought to Japan in the past decade as marriage partners for young men of Japan's isolated rural communities. There are 1,000 Japanese small businesses involved in matching the demand of the depopulated Japanese countryside with a supply of brides from Southeast Asia, Korea, and China, and this in effect has become another commodity market, highly lucrative at about four million yen per head, more or less equal to what the family of a Japanese male would normally expect to pay toward a wedding.[68] Though some of these relationships succeed in bridging the gap of language and culture, and they carry a potential for opening Japanese rural and mountain communities to a fresh and direct sense of Asia through the creation of cross-border family networks of cooperation and understanding, in fact the common assumption is that the women will submerge and negate their Asian identity as a condition for entry into Japanese society, and that their children will be nothing but Japanese.

The experience of many of these women is isolation and discrimination.

Korean schoolgirls constitute a third group. Dressed in the Korean national dress of *chima* and *chogori,* they are easily recognizable, even though they are mostly third-generation Japanese residents with little or no direct connection to Korea. Their conspicuous difference, however, is an affront to the pretension of Japanese racial and ethnic homogeneity, and they are periodically subjected to racial abuse and even attacked by knife-wielding men who slash their dress while they are traveling to or from school.[69] In 1994 alone, there were 156 reported cases of such attacks from January to July.[70]

Japanese Asianists tend to have little, if anything, to say about such incidents, which probably in truth have nothing to do with the agenda they are intent upon, but the persistence of the problems of all three groups of Asian women in Japan suggests the need to consider the internal Asianization of Japanese society, and make progress in securing the human rights of such Asians-in-Japan at the same time as scrutinizing the agenda for new Japan-in-Asia roles.

However, beneath the shrill and in some cases reactionary romanticism of some contemporary expressions of Asianism in Japan may be heard voices calling for a different sort of adjustment of the Japanese identity. Such an adjustment would involve the opening of Japanese society through the creation of a sense of Japaneseness that is tied to simple humanity and citizenship rather than to racial or genetic qualities, and the pursuit of reconciliation in the region in the context of a global orientation and in a matrix of global commitments, as "a global civilian power" (in Funabashi Yōichi's phrase).[71] Pursuing such a path, Japan might play a role as mediator, assisting at the birth of a truly global civilization rather than participating in sterile (if not apocalyptic) confrontation between civilizations. If the rifts that have divided the Eurasian continent for some 500 years can be healed and a wholeness restored there, that could be a big step in the right direction.

Notes

1. Samuel P. Huntington, "The Clash of Civilizations," *Foreign Affairs*, Vol. 72, No. 3, Summer 1993, pp. 22–49.

2. David Shambaugh, "Introduction: The Emergence of Greater China," *The China Quarterly*, No. 136, December 1993, p. 653.

3. Kawakatsu Heita, Ed., *Atarashii Ajia no dorama*, Tokyo, Chikuma shobō, 1994.

4. Ohashi Ryōsuke, in ibid., p. 171.

5. Ibid., p. 160.

6. Shibagaki Kazuo, "The Development of Japan and its External Relations from 1945 to the Present," *Annals of the Institute of Social Science* (Tokyo University), No. 35, 1993, pp. 123–56, at p. 125.

7. Keizai Koho Center, *Japan 1994: An International Comparison*, Tokyo, 1993, p. 11.

8. Karel van Wolferen, "No Brakes, No Compass," *The National Interest*, Fall 1991, pp. 26–35, at p. 31.

9. Around the turn of the century, according to van Wolferen, or "in ten or twelve years," according to Kenneth Courtis of Deutschebank Capital Markets in Tokyo. (See discussion of March 26–27, 1992 in Armand Clesse, E. B. Keehn, Inoguchi Takashi, and J. A. A. Stockwin, eds., *The Vitality of Japan: Sources of National Strength and Weakness*, London, Macmillan Press, forthcoming, 1995).

10. Other estimates differ. A generally accepted figure for 1991 gives the United States 26.4 and Japan 15.5 percent of world GNP. See Sakura sōgō kenkyūjō, Kan Taiheiyō kenkyū sentā (Sakura Institute of Research, Center for Pacific Business Studies), ed., *Shin seiki e no Ajia hatten no shinario*, Tokyo, Daiyamondo-sha, 1994, p. 65.

11. It was 4.5 and 4.2 percent respectively for Japan, and 2.8 and 2.6 percent in the case of the United States. See table in Sakura sōgō kenkyūjō, *Shin seiki*, p. 65.

12. N.a., "Hi wa mata noboru," *Tōyō keizai*, March 5, 1994, pp. 6–10, at p. 8.

13. Sakura sōgō kenkyūjō, pp. 151–52.

14. Isomura Naotoku, *Ajia kara no chōsen*, Tokyo, NHK, 1988, pp. 151–52.

15. Sakura sōgō kenkyūjō, *Shin seiki*, p. 197.

16. Fukada Yūsuke, "Nihon yo, Ajia o miyo," *Bungei shunju*, March 1992, pp. 144–53, at p. 152.

17. N.a., " 'No 1 wa Ajia' majika ni," *Asahi shimbun*, May 23, 1994, p. 14.

18. Mark Selden, "China, Japan, and the Regional Political Economy of East Asia, 1945–1995," forthcoming in Pater Katzenstein and Takashi Shiraishi, eds., *Japan in Asia*, Ithaca, New York, Cornell University Press. (My thanks to Mark Selden for access to this unpublished text.)

19. Kishida Shū and K. D. Butler, *Kurobune gensō*, Tokyo, Seidosha, 1992, pp. 30 ff.

20. Suzuki Kenji, "Arata na Ajiashugi no ayausa," *Ekonomisuto*, March 15, 1994, pp. 44–47.

21. Kume Hiroshi, "News Station," Asahi TV, May 24, 1995.

22. Ogura Kazuo, " 'Ajia no fukken' no tame ni," *Chūō Kōron*, July 1993, pp. 60–71.

23. See, for one example of his thinking, Fareed Zakaria, "Culture Is Destiny—A conversation with Lee Kuan Yew," *Foreign Affairs*, Vol. 73, No. 2, March-April 1994, pp. 109–26.

24. Sun Yat-sen (Son Bun), "Dai-Ajiashugi," lecture delivered at Kōbe kōtō jogakkō, November 28, 1924, translated by Imazato Tadashi, in Ichiji Yoshitsugu and Yamaguchi Ichirō, eds., *Sonbun zenshū*, Tokyo, Shakai Shisōsha, 3 vol., Vol. 3, pp. 361–75.

25. On the recent discovery of documentation of this commitment, see Kyōdō, "Sonbun ga Manshū soshaku o mitsuyaku?" *Yomiuri shimbun*, May 22, 1995.

26. Uno Masami, *1994 nen—Nihon wa Chūgoku e iku*, Tokyo, Gakken kenkyūsha, 1993, pp. 267–68.

27. Ogura Kazuo, "Chiiki tōgō to Nihon no sentaku," *Gaikō Forum*, December 1992, pp. 4–11.

28. Matsumoto Ken-ichi, *Kindai Ajia seishinshi no kokoromi*, Chūō Kōronsha, 1993, pp. 192, 199.

29. Ibid., 249.

30. Ibid., pp. 76 ff.

31. Ozawa Ichirō, *Nihon kaizō keikaku*, Kōdansha, 1993, p. 175.

32. *Building for a New Japan*, New York, Kōdansha International, 1994.

33. Suzuki, "Aratana Ajiashugi," p. 22.

34. Nakajima Mineo, in Inoguchi Takashi, Nakajima Mineo, and Okonogi Masao, "Zadankai: Ajia ni wa fukusō suru ampo nettowāku ga yoku niau," *Ekonomisuto*, March 15, 1994, p. 36.

35. Okonogi Masao, ibid., at p. 36.

36. Kim Yong-ho, "Ajia shimin shakai mezashi," *Asahi shimbun*, May 6, 1994.

37. For a thoughtful analysis of the phenomenon, see Eric Jones, "Asia's Fate: A Response to the Singapore School, *The National Interest*, Spring 1994, pp. 18–28.

38. Inoguchi Takashi, "Japan and Pacific Asia: Reflections on the Fiftieth Anniversary of the End of World War Two, *The Japan Foundation Newsletter*, Vol. 22, No. 5, February 1995, pp. 1–5.

39. Kim Dae Jung, "Is Culture Destiny?" *Foreign Affairs*, Vol. 73, No. 6, November–December, 1994.

40. Derek Davies, "Neo-Confucian Ploys Just a Cynical Abuse of Power," *The Weekend Australian*, December 31, 1994–January 1, 1995.

41. Ivan Hall, "Japan's Asia Card," *The National Interest*, Winter 1994–95, pp. 19–27, at p. 20.

42. Huntington, "The Clash of Civilizations," at p. 28.

43. "Minshuka no 'ashiba katame' o kataku," *Asahi shimbun*, April 11, 1994.

44. Iokibe Makoto, "Shin sekai chitsujo ron o koete," *Asution*, No. 31, Winter 1994, pp. 16–33.

45. See my essay "Kokusaika: Problems in Japan's Deep Structure," published in Japanese in *Kokusai kyōroku kenkyū*, Vol. 2, No. 1, June 1994, pp. 71–90, and in Korean in *Changjak kwa pip'yong*, Vol. 22, No. 2, 1994, pp. 122–49. English publication in Donald Denoon, Mark Hudson, Gavan McCormack, and Tessa Morris-Suzuki, eds., *Multicultural Japan: Palaeolithic to Postmodern*, Cambridge, Cambridge University Press, forthcoming, 1996.

46. Inoguchi Takashi, *Nihon—keizai taikoku no seiji unei*, Vol. 6 of Higashi Ajia no kokka to shakai, Tokyo Daigaku shuppankai, 1993, p. 164.

47. See my paper cited in footnote 45. For a good introduction to this problem: Ian Buruma, "A New Japanese Nationalism," *New York Times Magazine*, April 12, 1987, and the subsequent exchange between Buruma and Umehara Takeshi (head of Nichibunken) in Japanese in *Chūō Kōron* in August and October 1987. Also the paper by Peter Dale, "Tendenzen der Japanischen Kulturpolitik," Conference of German Social Scientists on Japan, Loccum, Germany, November 7, 1992. On the controversy surrounding

Nichibunken participation in a conference on Japanese identity held at Australian National University in September 1993, see my "Kokusaika, Nichibunken, and Australia-Bashing" in *Asian Studies Association of Australia Review*, April 1994, and Richard McGregor, "Academics embroiled in Japan studies row," *The Australian*, April 24, 1994.

48. For succinct treatment of this question, see Yamamoto Haruyoshi, "'Nihongaku' saikō" (Revival of "Japan Studies"), in Yamamoto, ed., *Gendai shisō no shōten*, Keisō shobō, 1987, pp. 98–124, and Ajisaka Makoto, " 'Shin Kyōto gakuha' no Nihon bunkaron" (The Japan culture theory of the "New Kyoto School"), *Bunka Hyōron*, May 1986, pp. 97–114.

49. If one was to single out one work of the considerable literature written in this spirit, it might be Umehara Takeshi, *Mori no shisō ga jinrui o sukuu* (Forest thinking to the aid of humanity), Shōgakukan, 1991.

50. Roy Andrew Miller, *Japan's Modern Myth: The Language and Beyond*, New York, Weatherhill, 1982, p. 209.

51. For fuller discussion of this matter, see my "The Emptiness of Affluence: Vitality, Embolism and Symbiosis in the Japanese Body Politic," in Clesse, Keehn, Inoguchi, and Stockwin, *The Vitality of Japan*.

52. Quoted in Yamamoto Haruyoshi, 1987, p. 100.

53. Yasuhiro Nakasone, speech of July 1985, quoted in Higuchi Yōichi, "When Society Itself Is the Tyrant," *Japan Quarterly*, Vol. 35, No. 4, October–December 1988, pp. 350–56, at p. 351.

54. Nakasone speeches, quoted in William Wetherall, "Nakasone Promotes Pride and Prejudice," *Far Eastern Economic Review*, February 19, 1987, pp. 86–87.

55. Mushakoji Kinhide, "Japan, the JapaNIES, and the Japanese in the Post-Cold War Asia-Pacific Region," *PRIME* (International Peace Research Institute, Meiji Gakuin University), No. 1, April 1994, pp. 13–31, at p. 23.

56. Kinhide Mushakoji, "Post-modern Cultural Development in East Asia: Beyond the Japanese Version of Confucianism," in Eleonora Barbieri Masini and Yogesh Atal, eds., *The Futures of Asian Cultures*, Bangkok, UNESCO, 1993, pp. 57–80, at p. 68.

57. Mushakoji, "Japan, the JapaNIES," p. 26.

58. Ibid., p. 25.

59. Sunobe Ryōzō, " 'Kokutoku' o motte nyū-A nyū-O o," *Gaikō Forum*, 1992, No. 2, pp. 2–3.

60. Ikeda Tadashi, " 'Ajiashugi' de nai Ajia gaikō o," *Gaikō Forum*, February 1994, pp. 52–60, at pp. 52–53.

61. Ibid., p. 58.

62. Inoguchi Takashi, in "Zadankai," 1994, p. 39.

63. Iriye Akira, "Nihon to Ajia—hyakunen no omomi," *Sekai*, February 1995, pp. 45–53.

64. For a fuller enunciation of this theme, see my "Kokusaika: Impediments in Japan's Deep Structure," in Denoon, Hudson, McCormack, and Morris-Suzuki, *Multicultural Japan*.

65. Aoki Tamotsu, "Ajia jiremma," *Asution*, No. 27, winter 1993, pp. 16–40, at p. 21.

66. Matsui Yayori, "Kokusai jinshin baibai to Ajia josei no jinken," *Sekai*,

February 1995, pp. 113–20. Matsui includes a list of 27 cases of murder, suicide, and violence against Asian women for the years 1991–93.

67. Takahashi Hiromichi, "The Shimodate Incident," *Ampo—Japan-Asia Quarterly Review*, Vol. 25, No. 2, 1994, pp. 2–6.

68. Nakamura Hisashi, *Hitobito to Ajia*, Iwanami shinsho, 1994, pp. 21–47.

69. Henshūbu, "Muchi to sabetsu—chima to chogori jiken," *Ryu*, No. 14, October 26, 1994, pp. 2–4. Also Ben Hills, "The Ugly Secret of the Treatment Japan Metes Out to a Minority," *Sydney Morning Herald*, July 5, 1994.

70. Shimojima Tetsurō, " 'Chima chogori kirisaki jiken' o ou," *Sekai*, November 1994, pp. 185–96, at p. 185.

71. Funahashi Yōichi, *Nihon no taigai kōsō*, Tokyo, Iwanami, 1993.

Agricultural scene in Iwate Prefecture. (Local "Kōjinsama" shrine set amid rice fields at Tōnoshi.) (Tomita Fumio, Sekai Bunka Foto, © Jiji Gahōsha)

Agricultural scene in Nagano Prefecture (at Iiyama-shi) (Maeda Shinzō, Tankei Photo Library, © Jiji Gahōsha)

❶乱開発されたままの「一条山」現況

❷再開発案　山はなくなり宅地となる

❸当時開発許可案　この姿にまで是正を

Ichijōzan, Kyoto ("Mohican Hill"). Shows current (1993) state, with computer simulation of prospects if development, commenced in 1982 and now-frozen, were to resume, and of what a restored mountain might look like (Nara Iwao and Tsuchida Takashi, *Kino* [Kyoto Seika University] *Review*, no. 23, 20 March 1992)

"Garbage Palace," Karin-dōbata, Kashiwara-shi, Osaka Prefecture. From 1976 to 1991 the non-combustible waste of the neighboring villages and towns—refrigerators, washing machines, plastic materials, etc.— was crushed, mixed with concrete, and then dumped, for ever, in the 27,000 blocks which now line this rural valley (*Asahi shimbun*, 30 April 1992)

Sluice gates for the Nagaragawa Dam, which began operation in May 1995 (*Asahi Graph*, 9 June 1995, © Asahi shimbun)

"Ocean Dome," Miyazaki Prefecture (Kyushu.) ("The world's largest indoor water park" with "the world's largest artificial wave-making equipment.") (Akiyama Tadasuke, Jiji Gahosha, *Pacific Friend*, October 1993)

"Paradise Within a Paradise" (© Sea Gaia Phoenix Resort, Miyazaki, Japan)

Huis Ten Bosch, Nagasaki Prefecture ("17th century Holland" resort village) (Author, November 1994)

Huis Ten Bosch, Nagasaki Prefecture (Author, November 1994)

Huis Ten Bosch, Nagasaki Prefecture (Author, November 1994)

Tokyo Trans-Bay Highway (during construction) (*Asahi Graph*, 9 June 1995, © Asahi shimbun)

Tunnel under Tokyo Bay (excavated and constructed at depths up to 60 meters by giant "shield" machines capable of advancing at 150 meters per month.) (*Asahi Graph*, 9 June 1995, © Asahi shimbun)

Tokyo "Waterfront Subcenter," site of projected "Teleport Town" and of the ill-fated "World City Expo Tokyo '96," resort hotel in foreground and heliport at top right (*Aera*, 17 April 1995, © Asahi shimbun)

Kobe Earthquake: The city of Kobe seen from offshore on 17 January, the day of the quake, facing "Harborland" and the still incomplete Oriental Hotel, with Mt. Rokko in background (*Asahi Graph*, 1 February 1995, © Asahi shimbun)

Collapsed segment (at Higashi Nada) of brand-new Hanshin Expressway. On day of Kobe Earthquake, 17 January 1995 (*Asahi Graph*, 1 February 1995, © Asahi shimbun)

Collapsed bridge of Hanshin Expressway near Kobe (Nada), 17 January 1995 (*Asahi Graph*, 1 February 1995, © Asahi shimbun)

Hanshin Railway between Oishi and Shinzaike, Nada, Kobe, 17 January 1995 (*Asahi Graph*, 1 February 1995, © Asahi shimbun)

Day Two of Greater East Asian Conference, National Diet, Tokyo, 5 November 1943. Delegates from Japan, Manchukuo, Thailand, Philippines, Burma, and China (Wang Jing-wei government) (© Asahi shimbun)

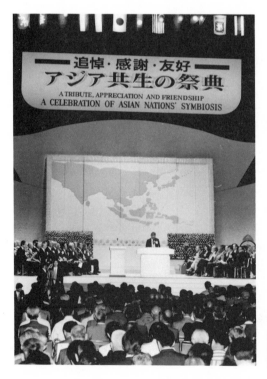

"Celebration of Asian Togetherness" Festival, Budōkan Hall, Tokyo, 29 May 1995 (© Asahi shimbun)

5

The Peace State: Dilemmas of Power

The 1946 and 1955 Systems

As the end of the century approaches, Japan faces a series of commemorations and choices, occasions to reflect on the past, take stock of the present, and anticipate the future. The end of the Cold War was followed by the first overseas dispatch of Japanese military forces (1992), the fiftieth anniversary of the defeat in World War Two (1995), the promulgation of the 1946 Constitution (1996), and the increasing possibility of elevation to "Great Power" status on the U.N. Security Council. In the wake of the Cold War, suddenly freed of its role as a frontline state between two worlds, Japan might have been expected to articulate a distinctive vision of the sort of world order its people aspired to create. Instead, denying any such intent, Japan suffered a failure of will and imagination, leaving the construction of a new world order in the hands of the Western powers. Ironically, the long crusade to revise the Constitution, pursued during the Cold War by the conservative Liberal-Democratic Party, but blocked by the socialist opposition, advanced much closer to fruition with the collapse of LDP rule and under a socialist prime minister.

Japan is extremely sensitive to external criticism of the structural underpinnings of its economy, at times denouncing it as "bashing," but at the same time it is very tolerant of interventions aimed at subverting or drastically changing the constitutional commitment to pacifism. At various times in recent decades, the U.S. Secretary of Defense has suggested that an appropriate level of military expenditure for Japan might be around 2 to 3 percent (1976); that Japan faced a simple choice between guns and caviar (1980); and in 1994 (following similar statements by the U.N. Secretary-General) that Japan should revise its constitution to allow greatly expanded participation in U.N. peacekeeping activities.[1] The intervention in Japanese affairs was, in each case, evident. The uproar that might be expected if a Japanese politician (or U.N. official) were to suggest that the United States drastically revise its defense policy or amend its Constitution may well be imagined. While governments, media, and defense bureaucrats throughout the region lend their best efforts to persuade Japan to come off the wagon of pacifism, voices urging retention and even extension of the principle as a basis for the new world order are rare. This chapter argues that the greatest contribution that Japan could make to its region and the world would be to insist on its "difference" as a peace state, pointing the way toward a twenty-first century "peace world."

Though political attention in Japan after the end of the Cold War tended to focus on relatively mundane matters—continuing economic stagnation and negotiations with Washington over market share, electoral reform, political-party restructuring—there were deeper issues and forces involved. Approaching the end of the twentieth century, Japan was simultaneously facing the constitutional choices of the eighteenth and the twenty-first century centuries: establishing the priority of civil society over the state on the one hand, and on the other, the primacy of pacifism and globalism over the notions of armed state power and absolute sovereignty rooted in the nineteenth century. It has become commonplace to say that the "1955 system"—the term sometimes used to describe the Cold War political arrangements that for long ensured conservative hegemony—is at an end. The conservative party dominance that began with the formation of the Liberal-Democratic Party in that year ended thirty-eight years later in 1993, and the main opposition party formed in 1955, the Japan Socialist Party (which later became the Social-Democratic Party of Japan, or SDPJ) ended its long years in the political wilderness and finally entered into a coalition reform government in 1993, and in 1994 its leader became prime minister. The demise of the 1955 system was evident. But a deeper crisis is only slowly becoming apparent: the crisis of the "1946 system."

In 1946, while parts of the wartime system were dismantled and trials were being prepared for some military leaders, the key structures of the postwar Japanese state were put in place. The Constitution was drawn up and adopted. The emperor, having been granted immunity from prosecution as a war criminal, was confirmed as center of the constitutional system (Chapter One of the Constitution, Articles One–Eight), while the state adopted pacifism as a central principle (Chapter Two, Article Nine). A shift on the part of the Japan Communist Party, then center of opposition to the disgraced "old order," helped make possible the cobbling together of the constitutional package. The disavowal of republicanism by the Communist Party, which shifted from republicanism to acceptance of a emperor-centered state and cooperation with the American GHQ, may be seen as a precondition for the 1946 system (the package of American-sponsored symbolic emperorship and state pacifism).[2] The issue, thus closed, has never been reopened.

Although the 1946 Constitution declared the sovereignty of the people, it did not reject the 1889 Imperial Constitution. Indeed, its first eight articles concerned the position of the emperor, who also managed to convey the continuity of the regime by ensuring that he formally presented the new Constitution (introduced by his own unique personal pronoun, *Chin*) to the Diet as a revision of the 1889 Constitution (which had been presented to it by his grandfather). Furthermore, the date of promulgation was November 3, 1946, the birthday of the Meiji emperor. The procedure was the more remarkable in view of the fact that the Japanese imperial house was undoubtedly lucky to survive 1945.

The decision to foreclose the question of war responsibility by granting immunity to Japan's wartime supreme commander, the emperor, was the first step in the construction of a system of cover-up and devolution of responsibility downward onto lower ranks (who were commonly seen as scapegoats), which led, in due course, to denial of responsibility altogether. The outcome of the trials, the execution in December 1948 of the first group to be tried, followed the next day by the release of the others and their rapid elevation to the highest offices in the land, was the second. The failure of the Japanese state, once independence was restored to it in 1952, to consider the question of war crimes at all, in stark contrast with its German counterpart, was the third, which followed inevitably from the other two. The Japanese inability to settle questions of war responsibility to the satisfaction of people in the countries that once suffered under the imperial yoke, let alone to the satisfaction of its own people, can thus be traced back ultimately to the 1946 settlement, the trade-off between immunity of the emperor and his installation as (symbolic) center of the new constitutional order in Chapter One of the Constitution, and the declaration of state pacifism in Chapter Two. According to Urata Ichirō, professor of law at Hitotsubashi University, had Japan been allowed or encouraged to deal with the issue of war responsibility, the process might well have led to the abolition of the emperor system and to Japan thereby becoming a truly "normal" state for which an Article Nine would not have been deemed necessary; the retention of the imperial institution made Article Nine necessary as a guarantee of American interests.[3]

The constitutional role of "symbol" assigned to the emperor, however, was unprecedented and unclear. It was complicated by his continued performance of the quasi-religious role of Shinto high priest and by the persistence of national myths and superstitions about the purity and superiority of the Japanese identity built around the historically constructed imperial institution that remained central to nationalist discourse. The myths that celebrated the divine origins of Japan were revived through the reinstating in 1966 of the prewar *Kigensetsu* (commemorating the founding of Japan by the gods) in only slightly modified name as National Foundation Day, and in 1979, the rule that years should be known formally in accordance with the chronology of the reigning emperor (Gengōhō) was adopted. Thus the year 1995 would be known officially as Heisei Seven, or the seventh year of the emperor who acceded to the throne in 1989.

The constitutional ban on religious activity by the state was evaded by the adoption of logic-chopping formulas to separate the religious from the political moments of imperial funeral, accession, wedding, and commemorative rituals. Prime ministers and cabinet members participating in the rituals at Yasukuni honoring the war dead, especially since the mid-1980s, claimed that they did so as private individuals.

The universal aspiration of the existing Constitution was thus watered down by a liberal infusion of Japanese spirit. Although the texts belong to different traditions, the ethos underlying them was continuous, and the parentage of the Meiji Constitution (1889–1946), which specified the subordination of human rights to state interest, clear. Rights were located within a relativistic framework of social mores and conventions, flanked, on the one hand, by the still sublime and unchallengeable imperial authority, and, on the other, by the precise and detailed regulations of policemen and bureaucrats.

As the liquidation of the 1955 system proceeds, attention may be expected to shift gradually to the 1946 system. When that happens, it will become apparent that there were two central components to the settlement of that year: the symbolic emperor system and the peace state. Debate about that settlement will be much more sensitive and difficult than debate over liquidation of the 1955 system.

Approaching the fiftieth anniversary of the war's end, the problem of war responsibility and compensation (discussed in detail in Chapter 6) assumes greater rather than lesser prominence as a political issue. Although the imperial system seems secure, protected by a combination of taboo and terror not wholly different from those that had been erected around the institution one hundred and more years ago, the other plank of the 1946 system, state pacifism, having eroded gradually over the intervening decades, was brought to the brink of collapse by the waves of receding Cold War. It is time, as one of the most influential voices of the age (Ozawa Ichirō) puts it, for Japan to become a normal country.

Nothing could have more dramatically highlighted the effort across the political spectrum to redefine and rethink the issue of Japan's place in the world than the decision at an extraordinary national convention of the Social-Democratic Party of Japan in September 1994 that the country's Self-Defense Forces (SDF) would no longer be regarded as unconstitutional. If one of the fundamental certainties of political life could be so suddenly and rudely transformed, then others too must be seen as negotiable. The constitutional debate began to open on a wide front. Where previous generations had concentrated in tortured debate on the question of the constitutional legitimacy of the SDF and on the need for revision of the Constitution in order to resolve its status, in the early 1990s, that question was generally set aside. Instead, the focus shifted to the question of whether Japan could perform a characteristically great power role as permanent member of the U.N. Security Council without revising the Constitution. As the political contours of the 1955 system are redrawn, and political parties with little discernible ideological difference emerge, attention may be expected to turn to the deeper questions involved in the 1946 system.

Constitutional Pacifism

Constitutions are instruments defining the powers of government. Written or unwritten, they spell out the balance of powers and duties between states, their bureaucracies, armies, and governments on the one hand, and their subjects, citizens, peoples, or civil societies on the other. Inevitably, they reflect the time of their conception. There is no absolute statement of the ideal mode of government, no answer to the question that is not temporary and provisional; yet the matters involved are of such moment that any proposal to change a constitution stirs the fear that liberties gained in the struggle for an existing constitution might be lost or constrained rather than expanded as a result. The Japanese constitutional debate involves the three issues that may be described as classic in constitutional theory—location of sovereignty, division of powers, and definition of the rights and duties of citizens and state—but it also involves a fourth issue, the declaration of state orientation (as pacifist), which is unusual, and it is around this that debate has centered, between those who would delete all or part of this clause and those who insist on its strict and literal interpretation.

Modern Japan has had two constitutions: the imperial one of 1889, which stressed the august and absolute authority of the emperor, the unique and superior qualities of the Japanese people, and the duties of the latter to the former; and the postwar Constitution of 1946, which proclaimed the sovereignty of the people, proclaimed unequivocally their rights as citizens, established formal separation of powers, and declared the already-mentioned commitment to state pacifism. It retained the emperor, not as sovereign but as "symbol of the state and of the unity of the people, deriving his position from the will of the people" [Article One].

This postwar Constitution was drawn up in 1946 in the distinctive historical moment of idealism and revulsion against war, before the Cold War with its very different priorities intervened. The pacifism of the time was expressed in Article Nine:

> Aspiring sincerely to an international peace based on justice and order, the Japanese people forever renounce war as a sovereign right of the nation and the threat or use of force as a means of settling international disputes.
>
> In order to accomplish the aim of the preceding paragraph, land, sea, and air forces, as well as other war potential, will never be maintained. The right of belligerency of the state will not be recognized.

Other constitutions, from that adopted by the French Republic in 1791, have outlawed aggressive war, but this one went much further by outlawing war itself and the possession of armed forces capable of waging it. Article Nine, which has been subject of continuing controversy, public debate, and legal challenge, was paralleled only in the Costa Rica Constitution of 1948 (Article Twelve), although there it was coupled with its natural corollary, the commitment to state neutrality. No sooner had the ink dried and the Constitution come into force (in May 1947), than its contents were regretted by the occupying U.S. forces, and successive U.S. administrations thereafter concentrated on circumventing, if not subverting it.

Already in the third year of the Constitution, Japan was being called upon to mobilize a 300,000 man army to support the U.S. effort in Korea; Richard Nixon, visiting Tokyo as vice president in 1953, referred to the peace clause in the Japanese constitution as a U.S. mistake,[4] and efforts to get Japan to establish, upgrade, and expand its military were constant thereafter. Significant elements of the Japanese political leadership also opposed the Constitution, singling out the prescriptions of Article Nine as an intolerable restraint on Japanese sovereignty. Commonly, it was referred to as something imposed on Japan from outside (*oshitsuke*), and therefore non-Japanese. In the context of the Cold War and the Korean War (1950–53), the literal clauses of the Constitution were gradually reinterpreted, and a "national police reserve" was established in 1950. (In 1954 this became the Self-Defense Force.) In the 1990s, the SDF was one of the world's greatest military forces, and it was the beneficiary of the second-largest budgetary allocation of any military in the world.

In other words, despite the plain terms of Article Nine, land, sea, and air forces were established. The constitutional propriety of doing so was contested from the start, and indeed, has never ceased to be contested. Although the existence of the SDF was gradually accepted, each stage of its expansion was undertaken by governments in the teeth of overwhelmingly negative public opinion.[5] Though the public gradually resigned itself to the existence of the SDF, at the same time the Japanese people continued to embrace Article Nine with fervor and recorded immense support for it in successive opinion polls. Opponents of constitutional revision were in a majority throughout the Cold War decades from 1955, by as much as 80 percent in the 1980s.[6]

While support for the Constitution characterized grass-roots Japanese politics, opposition to it, including but not confined to Article Nine, was a cornerstone of conservative politics throughout the Cold War period (and a plank in the LDP party platform since 1955). While the so-called "conservative" forces were committed to radical reform, the so-called "radical" or "progressive" forces were committed to preservation of the Constitution. In reality, the labels in Japan were themselves products of the Cold War: conservative meaning pro–radical reform of the Constitution (though this camp includes both those who wished better to serve the United States in the Cold War and those who marched to a different, nationalist, drum), and radical or progressive, meaning neutralist, pro-China or pro-"socialist," but above all constitutionalist.

Japanese governments took the view that the Constitution could not be interpreted as denying the right of self-defense, which was inherent in all states, and that the forces necessary to exercise such a right could not be described as "war potential." War potential was defined as meaning only military capacity beyond the necessary minimum requirement for self-defense,[7] and self-defense itself remained flexible and undefined. Similarly, the operation of the Japan-U.S. Security Treaty of 1951, which authorized the continued presence of substantial U.S. forces in Japan, was regarded as quite unproblematic under the Constitution. This thinking was predicated on the existence of a state right that was superior and anterior to the Constitution, so that the Constitution did not embody the whole fundamental charter of the country. It was a subtle, if not casuistical doctrine, whose justification in constitutional theory was dubious.

In a famous judgment, the Chief Justice of the Tokyo District Court, Date Akio, held in March 1959 that the U.S.-Japan Mutual Security Treaty was unconstitutional, and therefore the presence of U.S. troops in Japan under that treaty was also unconstitutional. It seemed that Japan would have to desist from any military pact and disband its own then-fledging forces. It was a momentous judgment, challenging the international Cold War order, as well as the domestic one. However, on review, the Supreme Court held that the constitutionality of acts of government would not be questioned unless there was "clearly obvious unconstitutionality or invalidity," and that, although Article Nine banned the possession or use of "war potential," U.S. forces in Japan were not *Japanese* war potential and were, therefore, not banned.[8] In a subsequent case in 1976 (the Naganuma case), the court went further, holding that the question of constitutionality of the SDF was a political matter, involving legislative judgment, in which it would therefore not intervene. In other words, judicial challenges failed to block the SDF or force it to be dismantled. Despite that, however, lawyers specializing in constitutional matters have persisted in the view that it is not constitutional.[9] Subtleties worthy of medieval theology characterize the discourse.

The gap between the pacifist principle of the Constitution and the reality, once established, grew and widened. The judiciary, when invited to pronounce upon it, took the view that the Japanese division of powers was one in which the will of the legislature took precedence, despite the powers granted it under Article Eighty-One to determine the constitutionality of any law, order, regulation, or official act.

Later, insofar as any further constitutional question was posed by the presence of nuclear weapons in Japan (under the treaty arrangements with the United States), the Japanese government adopted the device of saying it would not ask (and the United States would not specify) what weapons were carried on U.S. warships or stored in U.S. bases. Thus, Japan has long been host to the ultimate "war potential," and may well continue to be, despite the end of the Cold War, a matter that its government contrived to conceal, and on whose constitutional propriety its courts have never been called to comment.[10]

The strictly self-defensive role defined for the SDF in 1954 was also gradually modified. From 1981, they began to participate in collective security maneuvers and to adopt an extended defense line stretching from territorial waters to a 1,000-mile sealane perimeter. While the integration of Japanese troops within a "free world" force under U.S. command made the process acceptable to the United States, the very notion that Japan had entered into a military alliance was enough to bring down the Suzuki government in 1982. In 1983, Prime Minister Nakasone declared Japan an unsinkable aircraft carrier for the free world. In 1987, the ceiling of 1 percent GNP on military expenditure (declared by the Cabinet in 1976) was lifted, also by Prime Minister Nakasone. From the late 1980s, Japan was the preeminent military power in the region, and its forces were supported by a financial commitment larger than that of nuclear powers such as Britain or France.[11] Between 1988 and 1992, Japan was also the world's second-largest arms importer; being a good customer (for U.S. weapons) was evidently more important to its powerful allies than abstract questions of constitutional principle.[12]

Peacekeeping and the United Nations

Throughout the Cold War decades, the constitutional fabric was stretched to the breaking point by such formulas, and its spirit came to be honored more in the breach than the observance. One commentator drew the analogy with a former alcoholic who, having once renounced alcohol completely, declares that his prohibition will apply only to excess alcohol, and then, having begun with beer, begins to turn to the whiskey bottle.[13] The Persian Gulf crisis and war of 1990–91 confronted Japan with a peculiar conjuncture: For the first time, it was called upon to respond to a conflict without a Cold War dimension. Under immense pressures to join the U.S.-led Western alliance in the gulf, Japan responded with support that was exclusively financial. Its contribution of $13 billion toward the Western war chest, however huge, not only did not silence the "free rider" criticisms of its defense policy, but it stirred further calls to go beyond the commitment of mere money and commit men (and blood). Such demands won little public support, but they were welcomed by those elements within Japan that had long sought to convert the SDF into a regular military force capable of the overseas projection of Japanese national interests, i.e., moving from self-defense to defense. When the matter of sending SDF units abroad became an issue in 1991, only 5 percent of constitutional lawyers thought it permissible. Among ordinary people, 59 percent thought such dispatch problematic under the Constitution.[14] Even the hawkish Kishi Nobusuke (prime minister from 1957 to 60) had stated in April 1960 that the Constitution forbade the overseas dispatch of forces.[15] When a Peacekeeping Bill was eventually passed in June 1992, polls recorded a mere 15 percent support (39 percent opposition and 40 percent in the curious category of seeing it as "inevitable," i.e., a matter on which U.S. pressure was so strong as to be irresistible).[16] The bill was adopted in a mood of fatalistic acceptance. Just as every stage, from the initial formation of the SDF in 1954 through its many expansions, had been undertaken, it was seen as undesirable but unavoidable. Once it was done, however, as with all previous encroachments on constitutional principle, public opinion gradually adjusted to the fait accompli and support slowly rose.[17] By May 1994, 48.4 percent support for SDF participation in U.N. peacekeeping operations was reported, with only 30.6 percent opposed.[18]

The 1992 Cambodian peacekeeping commitment was a token,

hedged with qualifications and conditions, and essentially symbolic, but the symbolic weight was heavy. On the one hand, the absolute ban on the overseas dispatch of the SDF, having lasted forty years, once breached would never be reinstated, and the conditions attached to such dispatch could only be relaxed thereafter. Perhaps more importantly, the forty-year justification of the existence of the SDF on grounds of "inherent right of self-defense" was effectively abandoned, since no one argued that Japan's defense was threatened in Cambodia or, after a further (small) force was sent to Mozambique in mid-1993, in Africa. These questions of principle were submerged in the popular desire to support what was seen as the worthy cause of the United Nations and to contribute to the construction of a new world order.

The overseas dispatch of the SDF to various U.N. theaters in the early 1990s therefore opened the constitutional legitimacy of Japan's military forces to renewed and serious doubt. These were limited operations in support of a U.N. cause, and Japan's role was restricted to nonmilitary activities, which prevented it from being involved in the 1994 Somalian operations of the United Nations.[19] Still, the worthy goal of U.N. cooperation became the instrument to defeat the constitutional inhibition on the overseas dispatch of the SDF, and it amounted to a subversion of constitutional principle. Of the many forms of cooperation possible, the Japanese government insisted that its responsibility to the world community had to be met by the dispatch of that force whose existence had for forty years been justified exclusively in terms of the defense of home territories. The tasks performed in Cambodia—such as road building—could as well have been performed by civilian contractors, and the tasks that most needed to be performed—such as the clearing of mines from the countryside—presented technical challenges beyond the capacity of the SDF and positively called for the application of the technical resources of the Japanese corporate sector. A commitment by a company like Sony or Matsushita to develop and deploy the technology needed to clear the Cambodian countryside of mines would have been a real contribution.

Outside Japan, however, the post–Gulf War Japanese readiness to cooperate in multilateral peacekeeping efforts was commonly acclaimed by pundits and politicians as a sign of a new maturity and openness.[20] International support for the principles entrenched in the 1946 Japanese peace constitution was, by the 1990s, almost nonexistent. Pragmatism or realism was preferred to idealism or pacifism. In its insistence that a more positive Japanese engagement with the world should be measured by military standards, it meant that the emerging world order was still not so new. The so-called "flexible" interpretation of its Constitution that was being urged on Japan, applied first to military matters, could be seen as establishing a dangerous precedent. The abandonment (or erosion) of constitutional principle in any country is ominous; it was especially so in Japan, which once in the past slid into militarism and war because there were no constitutional restraints. The most flexible of constitutions have been those subject to the whim of dictators.

The question of Japanese membership in an expanded U.N. Security Council (UNSC) also has considerable relevance. The Japanese claim to membership is based on economic weight and contribution to U.N. budgets (second only to the United States) and on the need to rethink the postwar settlement under which the world's then-victorious allied powers (United States, Britain, France, Russia [Soviet Union], and China) were rewarded with permanent seats on the Council. The fiftieth anniversary of the U.N.'s foundation would seem an obvious time to undertake structural reform, and the Japanese government began making its claim during 1992, at first in terms of a thorough reform of the United Nations, but then unconditionally.[21] The formal claim was submitted to the United Nations by Japanese Foreign Minister Kōno Yōhei in September 1994.[22] However, membership by Japan in such a group of nuclear-power states raises obvious problems. Japan's Constitution is radically different from the U.N. charter in that it specifically rules out something that the Charter (Article Two, Clause Four) accepts: the *enforced* settlement of disputes. Membership in the UNSC of a state that championed and vigorously promoted nonmilitary solutions to conflict (and sought the long-term resolution of the structural causes of violence), while abstaining from any role in imposed military settlements, might seem desirable, but both the existing permanent members and the Japanese government itself have operated on the assumption that if Japan became a permanent Security Council member, it would make every effort to behave like an "ordinary" superpower. It seems much more likely that a seat on the UNSC would propel Japan in the direction of being a conventional "great power" than propel the United Nations or the other powers in the direction of general disarmament. A cartoon in the Asahi's weekly journal *Aera* expressed it succinctly: Japan's Prime Minister

(Murayama) is shown confronted by a choice between two seats, a comfortable armchair proffered by Bill Clinton, but on the condition that he bring Japan's commitment to participation in U.N. peacekeeping operations with him; otherwise, U.N. Secretary-General Boutros-Ghali had a baby chair for him.[23]

It would be easier to understand Japan's enthusiasm for an expanded role in the United Nations if its record in the ratification and implementation of U.N. human rights conventions and ILO conventions were better. Instead, Japan has ratified only seven of the twenty-five major instruments in the former category, a similar proportion of the latter.[24] Even in U.N. debates on nuclear matters, Japan shows no evidence of seeing any special role as a nuclear victim country. The pacifist philosopher and critic Hidaka Rokurō expressed astonishment that in the early 1980s, Japan, the world's sole victim of a nuclear weapon, took a position of opposition to a resolution on the nonuse of nuclear weapons. Even in the post–Cold War 1990s, it consistently abstained on nuclear-free zone proposals and in general supported the nuclear privilege of the superpowers.[25] This suggests that the Japanese government is not so much driven by commitment to the principles of the U.N. charter as by desire for the power and status of a seat on the Security Council.

Dilemmas of Revision

While the German and Italian postwar constitutions have undergone many revisions (forty in the case of the German Basic Law and seven of the Italian Constitution), the Japanese Constitution has remained intact, despite decades of government efforts to revise it. Although Article Ninety-Nine spells out that all public officials must respect and uphold the Constitution, LDP and government members, supported by the United States, led the movement to revise it. Kishi Nobusuke was for long head of the Dietmen's Association for Establishment of an Autonomous Constitution (established 1955), and of the Assembly for the Establishment of a Sovereign Constitution (established 1970). Nakasone Yasuhiro, prime minister in the mid-1980s, was critical of the Constitution as not reflecting "the history, tradition, and culture of the Japanese people," that is, as not being "Japanese." As a young politician, in 1955, he had first authored a draft revised constitution, and in the 1980s, he even composed a song of constitutional revision.[26]

Inaba Osamu, when justice minister in 1975, declared in the Diet that the Constitution was flawed and should be revised. He too participated openly in the revision movement, as did his successor as justice minister in 1980.[27]

It is true that the so-called mainstream of Japanese conservatism had little interest in this plank in their party platform and was therefore quite cool to the idea of constitutional change. Although Prime Ministers Kishi and Nakasone were constitutional hawks, others were doves. Prime ministers from Yoshida Shigeru (prime minister five times between 1946 and 1954) to Miyazawa Kiichi (prime minister 1991–93) believed in sticking fast to the Constitution and withstanding U.S. defense and military pressures by gradual and minimum concessions. As the post–Cold War debate gathered force, Miyazawa issued a book opposing the idea of constitutional reform and calling for steps to give more practical implementation to the peace clauses that existed.[28] Still, the persistence of the gap between government and people on the issue of the Constitution was a highly unusual feature of Japanese constitutional arrangements throughout the Cold War.

Whoever wrote it, however, the Japanese people evidently embraced the Constitution and its pacifist sentiments, and the socialists were passionately conservative on constitutional matters.[29] Though later attacked as an imposition on Japan, surveys in 1946 found extraordinary public support for Article Nine, running at around 70 percent.[30] Formal revision, which under Article Ninety-Six requires a two-thirds majority in both houses, followed by a majority of those voting in a referendum, gradually came to be seen as impossible. Instead, a process of informal revision—revision by interpretation—assumed central importance. Behind the constitutional screen of pacifism, a different set of priorities flowed from the deeper substance of the Cold War and the U.S.-Japan relationship. As the idealism of 1945 faded in the Cold War passions of East-West confrontation, the Security Treaty articulated the second thoughts of the United States, and to a lesser extent, Japanese elites. From 1951, Japan was subject to two constitutions: the nominal pacifist one of 1946, and the actual (unwritten and militarist) one that stemmed from the U.S.-Japan Security Treaty of 1951 (the base of the political system that was consolidated in 1955). The challenge for the post–Cold War debate is to find some path to resolve this contradiction.

In relation to Article Nine, in short, abstract constitutional principle yielded from a very early period to political expediency. The record in other areas is similar. A process of gradual attrition is clear in the two central areas of the emperor and Shinto religious rites on the one hand, and civil rights on the other. Theoretically, one might have expected that, under the constitutional framework of division of powers, the Supreme Court would constitute a significant countervailing force, but under the long one-party conservative dominance, all of its members were appointed by the same ruling political party, and (as noted above) the Supreme Court played a deliberately noninterventionist role in matters to do with the Constitution. Lawyers despair of appeal to abstract constitutional rights, and some observers go so far as to query whether Japan should be regarded as a state ruled by law. To turn Japan into a modern constitutionalist state, according to revisionist scholar Karel van Wolferen, would require "realignments of power akin to those of a genuine revolution."[31]

Rights

Although the issues concerning peace and defense have focused most attention, constitutional problems are by no means confined to them. The failure of the Allied occupation and the postwar reform to puncture thoroughly the cloud of imperial absolutism bequeathed to postwar Japan a problem of sovereignty or imperial status and of civil or popular rights, opposite sides of the same coin. Basic civil and human rights, apparently guaranteed by the Constitution, in practice have been seen as abstractions subordinate to a surviving, premodern notion of Japaneseness. Despite the 1946 declaration by Emperor Hirohito that he was man, not god, and contrary to the constitutional idea of fundamental human rights as the "fruits of the age-old struggle of man to be free" (Article Ninety-Seven), the Constitution still begins with a series of clauses about the emperor, whose succession is still determined by "household" rules beyond political scrutiny and in accord with patriarchal lines of descent in breach of Japan's commitment to international treaties on sexual equality. In practice, the Constitution failed to open the space within which criticism or opposition to the emperor system ("symbolic" as it is defined) might be conducted.

Though not subject to any legal constraint, therefore, the republican cause in Japan is still proscribed with no less force than were "dangerous thoughts" in prewar Japan, and it would be a bold or foolhardy citizen indeed who would take the right to freedom of expression to the point of uttering the view that republicanism might be a more appropriate form of state organization for a mature democratic polity than (symbolic) emperorship. In this sense, the 1946 system has clearly gained strength, neutralized opposition, and proved enormously successful. However vigorous the current constitutional debate, it has not begun to address this issue.

The fascination with imperial absolutism and the associated feudal notions of loyalty and service, defined as quintessentially Japanese in contrast with the imposed postwar system, has remained strong. The three most important postwar prime ministers, Kishi, Tanaka, and Nakasone, all at one time or another declared their belief that education would be better if the values of the 1889 Imperial Rescript on Education were restored to a central place; that is, if education served to clarify Japanese notions of polity, sovereignty, and head of state rather than imbue students with a sense of their constitutional rights.[32] Furthermore, censorship of school texts continues. The long crusade (beginning in 1965) by prominent historian Ienaga Saburō in the courts to defeat censorship of his school texts in Japanese history by the Ministry of Education has been unsuccessful. The Supreme Court ruled in March 1993 that the screening of school texts did not violate constitutional guarantees of freedom of expression.[33] The constitutional rights to freedom of conscience, opinion, religion, and to freedom from censorship and academic freedom (Articles Nineteen, Twenty, Twenty-One, Twenty-Three), though central to the democratic system, are all in some measure problematic. No regulation on the freedom of expression has ever been held unconstitutional.[34] The constitutional right to freedom of speech is in practice of little avail to protect the rights of those expressing unpopular views. Thus, the mayor of Nagasaki could be hounded mercilessly by rightists and then subjected to an assassination attempt for having expressed a simple and unexceptionable view (in December 1988) that some responsibility for the war should attach to the emperor.[35] Likewise, Nakaya Yasuko, a Christian and the widow of a member of the Self-Defense Forces, failed in her judicial attempts to prevent her husband being enshrined by the state as a Shinto deity.[36] And organizations such as the Japan Teachers' Union, a powerful, socialist-leaning, and therefore constitutionally conservative organization, regularly faces right-wing harassment of such intensity that it is hard put to find a town ready to allow it the use of facilities necessary to hold its annual meeting.

Articles Fourteen and Fifteen proscribe discrimination in political, economic, or social relations "because of race, creed, sex, social status, or family origin." In keeping with the universal spirit of the Constitution as a whole, these rights attach, according to the English text of the Constitution, to "all people." However, that provision was drastically diluted in the Japanese text, where "all people" was translated as "all Japanese citizens."[37] The experience of Japan's aboriginal inhabitants (the Ainu), or of women, foreign residents in Japan (especially Koreans), outcast residents (burakumin), etc., is that such guarantees have been worth little in practice. The aboriginal peoples, for example, struggle in vain to assert their claim to relatively minor things, such as the right to fish the rivers of their homelands, let alone even begin to assert any rights to land. The government of their country does not recognize the Ainu as negotiating partners. The negotiations in Australia leading to the recognition of aboriginal land rights (the Mabo legislation) in December 1993, and the apology by the New Zealand prime minister in May 1995 for nineteenth-century aggression and deprivation of land of the indigenous Maori inhabitants, were therefore of great interest to the Ainu people, although these events were only minimally covered in the Japanese media. The prospect of any apology by the Japanese government, or moves to make reparation to the Ainu and other indigenous peoples for their long history of displacement, oppression, and discrimination, seems in the mid-1990s impossibly remote. It was only in 1994 that an Ainu representative, for the first time, formally took up an SDPJ seat in the upper house of the national Diet.

Article Twenty-Eight guarantees to workers the right to organize, bargain, and act collectively, yet the militant union movement of the early postwar decades was unable to call on any constitutional protection as its rights were sacrificed to the goal of untrammeled corporate growth, and in 1973, the Supreme Court declared valid the absolute prohibition of strikes by public-sector workers.[38] Despite the provisions of Articles Thirty-One to Thirty-Eight on civil rights in relation to the criminal law, including the unequivocal Article Thirty-Eight banning criminal conviction on the basis of confession, constitutional rights have been consistently ignored in criminal cases and many convictions (and death sentences) passed, some of them only reversed during the 1980s, after thirty or more years.[39] Despite Articles Ninety-Two to Ninety-Five on local autonomy, the nineteenth-century traditions of centralism were reestablished and strengthened in the late-twentieth-century Japanese state to such an extent that much of the popularity of Hosokawa Morihiro, when he became prime minister in 1993, derived from his pledge to revitalize the regions by a politics of decentralization. It was to prove a vain hope.

In one matter, it is true, the Supreme Court has ruled the actions of the government unconstitutional. After 1976, it consistently held the electoral system unconstitutional in its discrimination against urban voters. However, it has declined to do anything to enforce that judgment, taking the view that in the constitutional division of powers, the legislature was "the highest organ of state power" (Article Forty-One), and that it would cause "unthinkable" confusion to cancel the outcome of elections.

Revision Proposals

Cold War

During the Cold War, the position was relatively straightforward: the ruling Liberal-Democratic Party opposed the existing Constitution as imposed (*oshitsuke*) and was committed to its revision, though taking that commitment gradually less-and-less seriously as the political realities indicated it was impossible. It also was the defender of both the Security Treaty with the United States and the existence of the Self-Defense Forces. The Socialist and Communist parties, on the other hand, supported the Constitution and argued that Article Nine required a posture of unarmed neutrality.

Various detailed proposals for constitutional reform were published, although none was ever specifically endorsed by the LDP. They shared a tendency to return to the values of the Constitution of 1889 and were essentially reactionary. Typical is the influential draft published by Nakagawa Yatsuhiro in 1984.[40] It deleted reference to popular sovereignty, restored the crime of lèse-majesté for any assault on the dignity of the emperor, deleted the war-renouncing clauses of Article Nine and established the emperor as commander-in-chief of the National Defense Army, made human rights clauses conditional on requirements of public order or state security, and restored the prewar idea of kokutai (national polity) by denying the right to exist to political groups that opposed the basic order and principles of the state. It also established a duty for citizens to serve, as required, in the defense of the country (opening the way to conscription). These were themes common to the revisionist camp throughout the postwar decades. Revisionism was characterized by resentment of the 1946 Constitution and the desire to restore key elements of the system that had preceded it.

Post–Cold War

In the 1990s, however, the constitutional debate underwent a fundamental change. The sudden end to the Cold War, the diminished role of the U.S. alliance, intensified world pressures on Japan to play a more active role in the world, general disgust with the institutionalized corruption of the political system, and the approaching fiftieth anniversary of the 1946 Constitution combined to reopen, while also changing the terms of, the debate. Just as significant was the fact that memories of war—the defeat, destitution, and hunger—had faded with the decades and in the light of the glitter and prosperity that followed. The generation that had experienced the war slowly passed away. The passions of the decades that divided over constitutional revision (*kaiken*), with its shadow of rearmament and war, and defense of the Constitution (*goken*) with its proud posture of unarmed neutrality, became muted in the post–Cold War world. Major business groups came out for the first time in open support of constitutional revision.[41] Newspaper and electronic media surveys in March–April 1993 showed for the first time that more people, even an overall (though tiny) majority in one survey, stood for revision than for defense of the Constitution.[42] Of the political parties, only the Japan Communist Party (which, ironically, had opposed Article Nine in the debates of 1946) gave it unqualified support in the 1990s. Elsewhere, all agreed that it should either be interpreted to mean something quite different from its literal terms, supplemented by legislation in the form of a "basic law" on peace or security that would clear up any uncertainties, or revised outright.

The change by the right was particularly dramatic. No longer was constitutional revision a rallying cry for those who would turn back the clock to what they imagined had been the secure order of imperial Japan, in which behavior had been regulated in fine detail by moral precepts and traditions. Henceforth, the constitutional revisionists began to look *forward,* offering their prescriptions for coping with

Japan's role in a world only slowly coming into existence. The taboos that had surrounded the constitutional issue slowly dissolved. The old left-right axis was transcended and the discourse redefined between sides who agreed on the unsatisfactory nature of the status quo, the sterility of the old pro– and anti–Article Nine debate, and the desirability of finding positive ways to contribute to world society.

The spectrum of positions on the Constitution is complex. It may in very schematic terms be represented on right-left lines, but the divisions have been blurred as a result of divisions in the ranks of both revisionists and constitutionalists alike in the post–Cold War period. To consider first the right, it is divided in terms of tactics into two groups: those who want to delete or amend Article Nine so that Japan can become a "normal" country with "normal" armed forces able to protect and project the national interest, and those who believe in similar ends but see revision as not necessary to achieve them. To revise or not to revise is a question that no longer divides right from left, but divides both right and left from within.

The Right

Constitutionalism (or "Revision by Interpretation"). This group includes those who share the same distaste for the 1946 Constitution as something imposed (by the U.S. occupation), but have concluded that revision is not necessary. Japan can become a normal country with normal armed forces by the simple device of choosing to interpret the existing Constitution as permitting it. They favor retention of the pacifist commitment of Article Nine, but essentially as a facade behind which an ordinary country, unencumbered by expressions of pacifism, might be constructed. Most closely associated with this position is the politician Ozawa Ichirō.

Ozawa, formerly secretary-general of the LDP and close aide to Kanemaru Shin, who defected from the LDP in 1993 to play the key role in the formation of the Japan Renewal Party (which subsequently merged with other groups to form the New Frontier Party), has become the central figure in these developments. In the context of postwar conservatism, he was the pioneer who was able to articulate a forward and future-oriented interpretation of the Constitution, borrowing wholesale from traditionally leftist internationalist idealism but tied to a vision of Japan as a great power, thereby appealing to nationalist

Table 5.1

Constitutional Perspectives

1. Cold War

Right	**Left**
Anti-constitution	*Pro-constitution*
LDP	JSP, JCP
SDF + U.S. Security Treaty	Unarmed neutrality

2. Post–Cold War

Right	**Left**
(i) Revisionist	*(i) Constitutionalist*
Yomiuri Group	JCP, Some socialists and intellectuals
SDF + U.S. Security Treaty	Unarmed neutrality
(ii) Creative Reinterpretation	*(ii) Creative Reinterpretation (a)*
Ozawa Ichirō	SDPJ
SDF + U.S. Security Treaty	SDF +U.S. Security Treaty
	(iii) Creative Reinterpretation (b)
	Iwanami Group (Peace Basic Law)/Asahi Group (International Cooperation Law)
	Minimum defensive force

sentiment. It is ironic that Ozawa should have emerged at the center of post-LDP reformist politics, since as a protégé of Tanaka Kakuei in the 1970s he had learned the basic lesson of unreformed Japanese politics: "Politics is strength; strength is numbers; numbers is money."[43] Despite the fact that he emerged to power and influence in the late 1980s and early 1990s at the height of the money politics and interest politics of Japan, Ozawa proved he was not just a machine politician. His vision entailed wholesale reform of political structures and developed a uniquely active, interventionist style of advancing it, while carefully avoiding exposure in such vulnerable (but relatively insignificant) positions of merely nominal power as prime minister. His orchestration could be detected behind the lurches from single-party LDP rule toward a two-party conservative system in which the old Socialist Party would be neutralized and incorporated, and from a multimember constituency electoral system to a single member, small constituency system. His skill at responding to and channeling the popular resentment of endemic political corruption, international isolation, and the political weakness approaching impotence of the Japanese government had to be admired. Still, it was far from clear that the reforms would in the end either dent the entrenched powers of the bureaucracy or advance the cause of devolution of power from Tokyo to the regions, let alone resolve the endemic corruption.

For Ozawa, Japan's pursuit of exclusively economic might had turned it, in his telling phrase, into a grotesque "one-lung state,"[44] and it was time to become a normal state and to claim a seat on the U.N. Security Council. During the debates on U.N. Peacekeeping, the LDP's Special Study Group on Japan's Role in the International Community, which he headed, offered the justification that the words of the preamble to the Constitution about Japan being "desirous of contributing honorably to international society" should take precedence over the literal expression of Article Nine.[45] Subsequently, Ozawa argued that even participation in a U.N. standing army presented no constitutional difficulty.[46] In other words, Article Nine forbade only overseas military operations without U.N. sanction, not the possession of forces or their deployment on U.N. missions. The frontiers of revision by interpretation (kaishaku kaiken) had been continually stretched over the years, but never in such a bold and radical way, an approach that is sometimes referred to in Japan using this term.

By tying the constitutional issue to the question of a Japanese contribution to building a better world, if not exactly a new world order, Ozawa succeeded in touching a deep nerve. The criticism that adherence to Article Nine amounted to a selfish and unprincipled "pacifism in one country," that Japan's wealth and stability was owed, to some extent, to its free ride on U.S. defense through the Cold War years, and that its extraordinary economic engagement with the world obliged it to take a greater responsibility for peace and order was persuasive. For forty years, the call for revision of Article Nine had been part of an explicitly nationalist agenda but, by proposing a revision by interpretation that would allow Japan to perform in the role of world citizen, Ozawa managed to present substantially the same agenda in a quite different light, as part of an idealistic, forward-looking, and internationalist contribution to a new world order. The reactionary political agenda of the 1950s and 1960s, gradually abandoned as practical politics in the 1970s and 1980s, thus became part of reformist politics in the 1990s.

However, Ozawa's belief that the gulf between the reality and the literal terms of the Constitution could be ignored and revision by interpretation continued, was problematic. His agenda was a reformulated and more open and internationally oriented nationalism, but it was distinctly within the nationalist tradition, and it continued to treat the plain words of the Constitution as a problem to be overcome rather than a charter to be fulfilled.

Revision: The Yomiuri *Group.* The proponents of overt revision inherit the distaste for the existing Constitution and appeal for the drafting of a *Japanese* constitution to replace the one imposed in the circumstances of defeat and occupation fifty years ago. They stand for changes designed to achieve the normalcy of Japan as a state legitimately and constitutionally possessing and deploying armed forces.

The post–Cold War transformation of constitutional thinking on the right or conservative front has been remarkable. The idea of restoring the essential features of the 1889 (Meiji) Constitution that was present throughout the Cold War decades seems to have been abandoned. The vision of Japan as a great power, with its permanent seat on the Security Council, is a powerful attraction for nationalists, but it is combined with a very dovish, internationalist, and peace-oriented stance in which much is borrowed from the traditionally leftist camp. A major and detailed set of proposals was published in the media of the *Yomiuri* newspaper, and may be known as the *Yomiuri* proposals.[47]

On November 3, 1994, the *Yomiuri,* which, with a circulation of around ten million is the largest newspaper in the world, took the extraordinary step of including in its regular daily edition an eight-page supplement containing the full text of its proposed constitutional revision, with detailed arguments and the text of the Constitution to be replaced.[48] It was proposed that Article Nine should be amended (at latest by the end of the century), that Japan should be able to possess armed forces (the SDF being converted into a conventional national force), and that a Basic Law on Security should be enacted. However, it treated the issue of Article Nine in a very circumspect manner: the first paragraph of the existing Article Nine—renouncing "war and the threat or use of force as a means of settling international disputes"— would be retained but the second—that "land, sea, and air forces will never be maintained"—deleted and replaced with clauses renouncing "indiscriminate weapons of mass destruction," outlawing conscription, and authorizing the establishment of "an organization for self-defense." A new chapter on international cooperation would set out the aspiration to eliminate from the earth "human calamities caused by military conflicts, natural disasters, environmental destruction, economic deprivation in particular areas and regional disorder," and would commit Japan to dispatch its Self-Defense Forces "for the maintenance and promotion of peace and for humanitarian support activities." Other clauses would elaborate on existing human-rights provisions, adding clauses on privacy and on environmental rights, and provide for strengthening the Diet and the role of the prime minister. The position of emperor would remain virtually unchanged, but the clauses defining it would be relegated to second place after those declaring the sovereignty of the people.

The prefatory statement attached to the draft declared that the objective was "not so much to maintain the principles of the existing Constitution (such as pacifism) as to *reinforce them,*"[49] (emphasis added). This was a remarkable admission that the agenda for post–Cold War politics in Japan had been set by the pacifist and idealist left. Although the subsequent editorial in the paper on the first day of 1995, referring to the need to devise and pass on to future generations a constitution that it would not be ashamed of, showed the continuing resentment over American influence, the commitment to pacifism by a major right-wing media group was the clearest possible testimony to the strength of popular pacifism and internationalism.[50]

The very moderation, and the adherence to the main features of the 1946 Constitution in this proposed revision, surprised many, satisfied few, and angered those who believed that only a radical revision would suffice. Some noted that the call for revision of Article Nine in order to legitimize the possession of the SDF forces implied the recognition that the existing arrangement, and the Japanese defense structures of 1954–95, were at best problematic under the Constitution. At the same time in Britain, critics caustically noted that drastic revision of constitutional arrangements, including a possible end to the monarchy and the dissolution of the United Kingdom into its component parts, was being contemplated.[51] By contrast, the *Yomiuri* draft seemed to lack philosophical coherence; it was silent on questions such as the devolution of political power from Tokyo to the regions and appeared generally conservative and lacking in vision. To some on the right, it even appeared as a prescription for making the Japanese people "spineless."[52] Others were astonished that the *Yomiuri* should have thrown its very considerable weight behind such a campaign so soon after the socialist shift under Prime Minister Murayama had apparently ended political differences over the constitutionality of the Self-Defense Forces. In 1994, the fact that a voice of the right should advocate popular sovereignty, peace, human rights, and environmental protection was a mark of how far the debate on constitutional revision had proceeded since Kishi and other wartime figures had launched it in the 1950s when they entrenched in the party platform of the LDP the commitment to "establishment of a sovereign constitution."

Whatever the merits of the proposal, however, it served to remove taboos on a delicate subject. The insistence on popular sovereignty and the relegation of the clauses on the symbolic emperorship to Section Two showed the attempt to make a clean break with the camp of traditionalist, or (ultra-) nationalists, who in the early postwar decades had looked to reform of the Constitution as the way to reconstitute the state on Japanese lines around a restored emperor. In the 1990s, there was little to be heard from proponents of such a view.

The *Yomiuri* group proceeded in 1995 to publish a further elaboration of its views, this time concentrating on measures to reinforce the powers of the prime minister and Cabinet to cope with emergency situations (with the January 1995 Kobe Earthquake and the March 1995 sarin attack in the Tokyo subway in mind), involving the passage of a Comprehensive Security Basic Law and the establishment of a Comprehensive Security Council (under the prime minister) designed to be able to act quickly in response to any emergency in the areas of national defense, terrorism, or natural disaster.[53] The proposal also declared the legitimacy of Japanese participation in collective security arrangements, and urged the extension of the U.S.-Japan Security Treaty into a full-fledged bilateral security treaty under which Japanese forces could as much be dispatched to the defense of the United States as vice versa.

Outside Japan, little attention was being paid to the evolution of the debate on the Constitution. The prominent revisionist scholar Karel van Wolferen, however, writing in the Japanese media, gave unequivocal support to the 1994 *Yomiuri* proposals. He acclaimed them as opening the sort of urgent debate on key questions of the distribution of power that was necessary to begin reclaiming power from the bureaucracy and placing it in the hands of elected democratic officials. He declared the existing Constitution "utopian and unrealistic" and a new constitution "indispensable" to solving Japan's crisis of drift and irresponsibility.[54]

The Left

The left (however inappropriate such a term is to describe those who are essentially conservative in constitutional matters), once united after the Cold War, came to comprise two different groups: the traditionalist, or literalist, constitutional defense (or goken) diehards and the *zōken* (creative constitutionalist) revisionists. Both advance positive prescriptions for how to cope with the new world circumstances and agree on the importance of preserving the peace commitment of Article Nine, but they disagree on how to go about it and how to handle the Self-Defense Forces and the Security Treaty. The "literalist" group insist on unilateral Japanese disarmament and strict observance of the no-war potential rule, while the creative constitutionalists have come to believe that observance of the spirit of that clause demands significant accompanying political and institutional reform, in particular the passage of a Peace Basic Law.

Diehard Constitutional Defense (Goken). So far as political parties are concerned, the literalist diehard position is now held exclusively by the Japan Communist Party. Apart from the Communist Party, however, there are many individuals and groups loosely affiliated with the Socialist (subsequently Social-Democratic) Party, who have been striving to combine a strict and literal interpretation of Article Nine on the unconstitutionality of the Self-Defense Forces with a positive and outward-looking agenda for Japan to articulate an active foreign policy appropriate to the world's first peace state. Unilateral disarmament and the entrusting of national security to the United Nations and the international community remains the central plank on their platform. But to adapt the requirements of unarmed neutrality to changed circumstances, for example, they propose the internationalizing of Article Nine, urging its inclusion in the constitutions of all countries in the region.[55]

This group argues, in effect, for Japan to insist on its distinctiveness as a peace state, flesh it out with an appropriate economic, political, and diplomatic role on the world stage, and work vigorously to expand its "pacifism in one state" into a "pacifism for one world." One proposal for the implementation of this view was to say that the constitutional requirement of nonmaintenance of war potential could be accomplished over a five-year transition period of disarmament and dissolution of the SDF in gradual stages, involving successive cuts of 20 percent in military expenditure, with the monies being transferred into equivalent increases in refugee and humanitarian aid, support for U.N. medical and electoral teams, and general relief and development programs for the South.[56] The military alliance with the United States would have to be renegotiated. Implementation of such a vision would not be cheap. Prominent political analyst Takabatake Michitoshi envisages Japan becoming the center for basic research on AIDS, renewable energy, and a multiplicity of international contribution measures that might cost an amount equal to about 3 percent of GNP.[57] However, while the "constitutional defense" position still enjoys strong public support, it was clearly shaken by the desertion of the SDPJ in 1994.

So far as the Socialist Party (or SDPJ) is concerned, defense of the Constitution and resistance to the LDP desire for its revision long constituted a central plank of its identity. But this sense of identity steadily eroded, and the party itself was torn as public-opinion surveys showed an overwhelming majority of people committed to the logically difficult position of wanting to retain Article Nine while at the same time accepting the constitutionality of the Self-Defense Forces. Wrestling with the contradictions of public thinking on defense issues and the ongoing exigencies of the Security Treaty with the United States, the Socialists slowly changed their ground. In 1984, the party chairman, Ishibashi Masashi, proposed a tortured and casuistical formula according to which the SDF would be seen as "unconstitutional, but legal."[58] Thereafter, the consensus within the party around the constitutional issue further eroded. After joining Ozawa Ichirō and other former Liberal-Democratic Party stalwarts in government in 1993, the SDPJ showed an increasing readiness to compromise on constitutional matters. By mid-1993, its leader, Yamahana Sadao, was an advocate of the sort of creative constitutionalism (zōken), which would call for the passage of a Security Law to supplement the Constitution and clarify the legitimacy of the Self-Defense Forces.[59] The desire to adapt to the status quo that had been created by forty years of conservative (and Cold War) hegemony seemed to have overwhelmed the original pacifism that had sustained the party for so long. Though many ordinary members stood firm, the party itself was thereafter divided.

In September 1994 came the most dramatic moment in the history of the Socialist Party: the decision by vote at its annual congress to reverse course on basic principle, recognize the SDF as constitutional, the minimum necessary for self-defense (and set aside any objections to its overseas dispatch on U.N. missions), support the *Ampo* security alliance with the United States, abandon reservations about the development of nuclear power, and accept (and enforce in schools and public institutions) the long-contested *Kimigayo* as national anthem and *Hinomaru* as national flag.[60] Since its foundation, its identity as a political party had been founded on fierce opposition to all of these positions. Although the party platform included vague statements about the adoption of a Basic Security Law, under which the size of the SDF would be cut down and possession of weapons for offensive purposes forbidden, the endorsement of the status quo bequeathed by the Cold War was bound to outweigh any such pledges about the future.[61] The sense of shock at the change was palpable. Nothing could have more sharply demonstrated the transformation of the political landscape.

In historic terms, such a political volte-face is known in Japan as *tenkō*, the term applied most famously to the renunciation of their proletarian faith and conversion to the cause of Japan as a nation by communists after 1931, followed in 1939–40 by the abandonment of opposition to Japanese militarism on the part of intellectuals and political parties and their incorporation in the new order of Prime Minister Konoye Fumimarō. Those who drew such analogies advanced gloomy prognoses.[62] A seasoned political commentator, Takabatake Michitoshi, noted ominously in 1993 that the political reforms underway offered neither diagnosis nor cure for the collusive system of Japanese politics, but that their language—"political purification," "clean politics," the "structural fatigue" of the old system, and the need for restoration of "strong leadership"—matched closely the language heard on the eve of fascism as the political parties collapsed into the embrace of the new order in the 1930s.[63] Other commentators referred bleakly to the beginning of a new phase of "Japanese-style fascism."[64]

Shortly afterward, in May 1995, when the party decided to dissolve itself as part of the search for a new political order, the shock was cushioned by the sense of its inevitability: A party that had abandoned its key positions without articulating any new vision was already politically dead anyway. And although there was talk of a new political alignment along conservative and liberal lines, the traditional, "par-ish-pump" politics of interest continued to hold sway over that of political principle, and there was little sign of an alternative vision being embraced by the socialists to substitute for that which they had abandoned.

Creative Constitutionalism (Zōken). If the Socialist Party itself thus seemed paralyzed before the problem of how to square the circle of constitutional idealism and pragmatic acceptance of the need for some kind of self-defense, a group of intellectuals closely connected to it did make a concerted effort to find a solution. They may be known, from the Iwanami publishing house that published their proposals in the monthly journal *Sekai*, as the Iwanami group. Their proposal centered on enactment of a Basic Peace Law, akin to the existing Basic Law on Education (1947) and Basic Law on Agriculture (1961), which would prescribe a detailed path for the implementation of the constitutional principle, complementing Article Nine by breathing life into its special qualities as a charter of peace.[65] In imaginatively recasting the argument over the Constitution, it could be said that they performed a similar role on the left to that of the *Yomiuri* group and Ozawa on the right.

For this group, the Constitution should be retained unamended, but supplemented by such a Basic Law that would clarify the status of the SDF and legitimize it by dividing its functions into two: a Territorial Guard with defensive capacities restricted to Japanese soil (abandoning claims to the defense of 1000-mile sea lanes and stripped of the sort of power to intervene in domestic political matters that it now has under Article 3.78 of the SDF Law), and a distinct International Relief Force for U.N. service. Article Nine would be further fleshed out by the adoption of policies appropriate to Japan as a peace state, including contribution to the promotion of regional and world disarmament; and reconciliation, first with Japan's own neighbors through apology and compensation for the wounds of the last war, and thereafter by build-ing networks of peace and cooperation (involving the gradual dissolu-tion of the existing military treaty with the United States and the replacement of all such military treaties by regional collective security agreements). While the *Yomiuri* group would transform the SDF into a conventional National Army, the Iwanami group would legitimize but at the same time drastically change it. It would also attach high priority to the establishment of a Ministry for Peace and Disarmament, and would strive for the creation of an international police force to which Japan's security would, in due course, be entrusted. The combination of principle and pragmatism underlying the Iwanami position is also evident in the group's historical critique of postwar Japanese pacifism's utopian and unrealistic tendencies, its uncritical leaning toward the socialist bloc, and its failure to address seriously the question of defense during the long years of the Cold War.[66] These claims aroused heated debate.

At the end of 1994, the nine scholars of the Iwanami group issued a second statement, which addressed the large questions of Asia-Pacific security and proposed a bold, imaginative, and radical series of ideas about how to plan for the twenty-first century.[67] Where *Yomiuri* would simply confer unambiguous constitutional legitimacy on the existing Self-Defense Forces, Iwanami would insist that the minimum defensive force (*saishōgen bōgyoryoku*), which it saw as constitutionally legitimate, was fundamentally different from the notion of "necessary minimum force for self-defense" (*jiei no tame no saishōgen no jitsuryoku*), in which terms LDP governments had long justified the existence of the SDF. It could legitimize only special units akin to the coast guard and police (armed units whose constitutionality had never been contested), not the formidable army into which, in fact, the Self-Defense Forces had evolved. The force the Iwanami group envisioned would be similar to a citizen militia rather than an army. It would be based on the principles of democracy and openness, and serve the mission of protecting people's lives and property rather than the state as such. The gradual transformation of the existing Self-Defense Forces, which had constituted a subsidiary part of the U.S.-led regional military forces during the long Cold War, would require the negotiation of a completely new framework of regional security. As for Japan's international responsibilities, in the context of post–Cold War disputes, commonly arising from issues of race, culture, religion, or economy, traditional military units were of diminishing relevance, and the use of armies for a combination of military and nonmilitary purposes carried a real possibility of exacerbating rather than resolving conflict. Consequently, Japan should commit itself to establishing something that would be organizationally quite distinct from any national defensive force.

The central perspective of the Iwanami prescription was adopted and spelled out in some respects in more detail in the country's second largest newspaper, the *Asahi shimbun*, on Constitution Day (May 3) in 1995. The country's largest media groups thus were entered on opposite sides of the burgeoning national debate on the Constitution.[68] The *Asahi* proposed that Japan claim a sort of conscientious objector status among nations, by reason of its insistence on exclusively nonmilitary contribution to the world community. It advanced a program for radical overhaul of the country's defense and international-relations policies to be carried out by the year 2010. The Constitution should be left intact, but supplemented by an International Cooperation Law (paralleling the Iwanami's Basic Peace Law) and the assumptions and policies of the country's aid program subjected to a process of thorough reconsideration, with the prime minister assuming direct control, all information being opened, and the performance of the program regularly debated in the Diet. Japan should adopt a particular orientation toward helping the poorest countries and addressing the global problems of militarization, population explosion, and global environmental deterioration. The Cold War defense alliance relationships should be revised, the U.S. military presence in Japan reduced and eventually eliminated, and the Self-Defense Forces drastically scaled down (by 50 percent in the case of the Ground Self-Defense Forces) and turned into a garrison force with the exclusive mission of defense of the Japanese islands from local aggression. A separate Peace Support Corps should be established, made up of engineering, medical, rescue, communication, and civilian police units, to engage in international relief tasks, but no Japanese armed personnel should ever be sent abroad. In its essentials, this was very close to the Iwanami plan, and the commitment of the massive resources of the *Asahi* to the promotion of this case over the coming years will ensure that the issues are well canvased.

The quest for a new and creative way of engaging Japan in the construction of a post–Cold War order is strong in these proposals. They are rooted in the perspective that it is time to seek reconciliation and permanent peace with Japan's Asian neighbors, first by an honest and sympathetic confrontation with the issues of war responsibility and compensation, then by rethinking the bases of the security system of the Cold War that was put in place in 1952 following the end of the American occupation. They raise the long-unspoken question of the U.S. alliance with Japan, the bases and associated exercises and maneuvers that formed such a key part of the Cold War framework, all of which they urge be renegotiated, gradually emptied of military content, and subsumed by a new, regional security system based on equality. Their orientation to a world in which the significance of the military is progressively shrunk and the peaceful resolution of conflict given greatly increased attention, their priority to regional, Asian considerations, and especially their readiness to radically rethink the relationship with the United States, combine to make these proposals the most interesting and forward-looking to emerge from Japan since the end of the Cold War.

Two qualifications have to be entered. The debate focuses almost exclusively on defense and security considerations and on Article Nine. The issues of human rights, privacy, and the environment remain secondary considerations, and the underlying assumptions of what is referred to earlier in this chapter as the 1946 system remain to be fixed. Until the assumptions underlying the constitutional package imposed on Japan in the early days of the U.S. occupation, including the role of the emperor, can be freely faced and discussed, the debate remains incomplete.

Outlook

The new configuration of Japanese politics makes it impossible to predict the outcome to this contest. As the intellectual and moral contours of the debate to be fought out in the Japanese political arena of post-LDP hegemony emerge, the combined weight of the pragmatic realism of the Ozawa-*Yomiuri* forces might seem bound to outweigh the idealism of the now-divided constitutionalists. Moreover, as the governments of the region instinctively understand realism, and are commonly attuned to hear only official voices (which has meant those of one or other LDP faction), they would be profoundly worried at any signs of a serious outbreak of pacifism in Tokyo. Beyond Japan, the absence of any concerted voice of support for Japanese pacifism, or constitutionalism, is notable. True, powerful voices from outside are raised, but they are heavily revisionist and out of sympathy with the desire of many Japanese to be different.

Facing the emerging twenty-first-century world order, Japan has somehow to address the problem of the evisceration of Article Nine through four decades of revision by interpretation, which has forced a wide gap between facade and reality. It is true that popular Japanese pacifism has exercised a unique restraint on successive Japanese governments and transformed the terms of the constitutional debate so that the conservative nationalist and rearmament perspective of the 1950s and 1960s has been drastically revised in the 1990s. Yet implementation of the purist constitutional stance—unarmed neutrality, dissolution of the SDF, and termination of the Security Treaty with the United States—however constitutionally proper, would cause social and political upheaval simply by reason of having to undo the work of those decades. Many who would agree with the purists in the abstract might recoil from these practical implications of what would be necessary. The Iwanami group calls for a Basic Law on Peace and the subsequent *Asahi* call for a drastically scaled-down Self-Defense Force and the enactment of an International Cooperation Law constitute attempts to seize the initiative by reformulating the peace-state case, but it is hard for them to deny that, like Ozawa, they are in fact calling for a kind of revision by interpretation. The four decades of constructing this status quo have bequeathed a huge problem to the present generation.

The outlook is opaque. The Article Nine purists have been forced into the position of appearing to be radical, since their essentially conservative program would require the largest adjustments to the existing Japanese state. The Iwanami and *Asahi* groups, while rearticulating the popular commitment to the ideal of a better world based on regional and global security (rather than national sovereignty) and having no place for national armies, have tempered that idealism with the recognition that, while determined to resist change to the Constitution, more and more people now accept the existence of some defense force. While the nationalist orientation of the Ozawa-*Yomiuri* perspective toward an end-of-century Japan that is in every sense (save, perhaps, the nuclear) a great power has undoubted appeal, it remains to be seen whether its advocates will be able to harness the forces of postwar Japanese idealist pacifism to their cause.

The constitutional debate is an important window on the way that the Japanese people think of themselves and how they would like to be seen by the world; in a profound sense, it is about identity. The steady weakening of interest in articulating a sense of being different, a unique constitutional peace state committed to the resolution of conflict by means other than the use of force, and striving to create a new world order based on such a distinctive value, is depressing testimony to the loss of idealism. Ordinariness in itself, with its associations of modesty, decency, simplicity, is no bad thing, but the ordinariness that

Ozawa (and others) aspires to achieve for Japan sounds depressingly like the ordinariness of a great power, hardly, if at all, different from other great powers, shorn of the inhibitions that long attached under the post-1945 settlement, no longer a "one-lung" peace state but possessing the full complement of military enforcement powers and a seat on the U.N. Security Council.

It is up to the Japanese people to decide whether this is what they want and whether they are prepared to revise or reinterpret their Constitution to accomplish it. It is up to them, in short, to decide what they wish to offer to the new millennium. The issues are, however, of broad concern throughout (and beyond) the region. It is time that they were better understood outside the country and that the Japanese peace movement was given even a modicum of the support that is given to those who favor Japan becoming a normal power.

Notes

1. Secretaries Schlesinger (1976), Brown (1980), and Perry (May 6, 1994) respectively, and Boutros-Ghali in 1992. See, in relation to Perry and Boutros-Ghali, Asai Motofumi, "Kaiken shikō no naka no Nagano hatsugen," *Sekai*, July 1994, pp. 84–87, at p. 86.

2. See the provocative text by Wada Haruki, "55-nen taisei to heiwa no mondai," presented to the 1993 meeting of the Japan Peace Studies Association (Nihon Heiwa Gakkai), Chūō University, November 13, 1993, and reproduced in revised version in "Sengo kakushin sōkatsu to tenbō," Rinji zōkan *Sekai* ("Kiiwado sengo Nihon seiji 50-nen"), No. 594, April 1994, pp. 225–30.

3. Urata Ichirō, "Heiwashugi no rikai no shikata," Watanabe Osamu et al., eds, *"Kempō kaisei" hihan*, Tokyo, Rōdō jumpōsha, 1994, pp. 187–241, at p. 190.

4. Watanabe Osamu, "Kempō wa dō ikite kita ka," *Iwanami bukkuretto*, No. 85, 1987, p. 15.

5. See, for example, tables in *Asahi shimbun*, May 3, 1992, p. 8.

6. *Mainichi shimbun*, April 29, 1987.

7. According to a unified view of the government, dated November 13, 1972. See Urata, "Heiwashugi," p. 194.

8. For a summary of the case, see Alfred C. Oppler's entry in the Kodansha *Encyclopedia of Japan*, Tokyo, 1983, Vol. 7, pp. 274–75.

9. Seventy-eight percent of such specialists, according to a survey of October 1991. See *Asahi shimbun*, May 3, 1992, p. 8. See also Yamauchi Toshihiro, *Heiwa kempō no riron*, Tokyo, 1992, and also his "Kempōgaku no shōten," *Asahi shimbun,* April 15, 1994.

10. Former ambassador (Edwin) Reischauer caused a furor in 1981 by revealing publicly what had long been assumed, that U.S. nuclear weapons were commonly carried into and stored at Japanese port bases. Former Pentagon staffer Daniel Ellsberg confirmed his account.

11. Number six in the world in 1993 by Japanese government figures, but number two if calculated by NATO standards, way above either Britain or France (Kōketsu Atsushi, "Kokugunka suru jieitai," *Shūkan kinyōbi*, September 30, 1994, pp. 5–9).

12. Ibid.

13. Urata, "Heiwashugi," p. 195.

14. *Asahi shimbun*, November 10, 1991.

15. Urata, "Heiwashugi," p. 205.

16. *Nihon keizai shimbun*, June 1992.

17. See table of opinion poll surveys from the *Asahi* in Watanabe Osamu, Ed., "90 nendai kaiken ron no nerai to sono tokuchō," 1994, p. 169.

18. Ako Washio, "Peacekeeping Debate Falls by the Wayside," *Japan Times*, May 24, 1994.

19. "Bid for UN Seat to Carry 'No Fighting' Caveat," *The Nikkei Weekly*, September 12, 1994.

20. When an Australian Senate committee looked into the question of Japan's defense policies in 1993, mine was the only voice to raise constitutional problems or to oppose the steady rise of Japan as a military power. See Senate Standing Committee on Foreign Affairs, Defense and Trade, *Japan's Defence and Security in the 1990s*, Canberra, Senate Printing Unit, 1993.

21. Sasaki Yoshitaka, "Gunji kōken naki jōnin rijikoku wa aru ka," *Aera*, September 19, 1994, pp. 23–27.

22. *The Nikkei Weekly*, October 3, 1994.

23. No-río, in *Aera*, September 19, 1994, p. 25.

24. United Nations, *Human Rights International Instruments*, Chart of Ratifications as as December 31, 1993, New York and Geneva, 1994. On the ILO conventions, see Nishikawa Jun, "Zadankai" (with Teruoka Itsuko and Nakamura Tatsuya), "Kakudai keizai kara seijuku keizai e," in Rinji zōkan *Sekai*, No. 594, April 1994, p. 276.

25. Hidaka Rokurō, " 'Hankaku' to iu koto," *Asahi shimbun*, June 7, 1982, and "Heiwa ishiki to 'heiwa seisaku'," *Sekai*, February 1994, pp. 54–66.

26. See Gavan McCormack, "Beyond Economism: Japan in a State of Transition," in Gavan McCormack and Yoshio Sugimoto, eds., *Democracy in Contemporary Japan*, Armonk, New York, M.E. Sharpe, 1986, pp. 56–59. (For some lines from Nakasone's song, see Okudaira Yasuhiro, *Kaiken ronsha no shuchō*, Iwanami bukkuretto, No. 19, 1983, p. 17.)

27. Odawara Atsushi, "Kempō 9-jō wa songoku no 'kanawa' buryoku fu kōshi ga gensoku," *Aera*, May 4–11, 1993, pp. 66–67.

28. Odawara Atsushi, *Shin gokenron sengen—21 seiki no Nihon to sekai*, Asahi shuppan, 1995.

29. For a detailed study of the process, see Koseki Shōichi, *Shin kempō no tanjō*, Chūkō shinsho, 1989, or (in English), "Japanizing the Constitution," *Japan Quarterly*, Vol. XXXV, No. 3, July–September 1989, pp. 234–40. See also Itō Naruhiko, "Kyūjō yōgo, ishō kaisei no ronri," *Sansara*, May 1993, pp. 56–63.

30. *Mainichi shimbun*, May 27, 1946, quoted in Tsuneoka Setsuko, "Pacifism and some misconceptions about the constitution of Japan," in Tsuneoka Setsuko et al., eds., *The Constitution of Japan*, Kawade shobō, 1993, pp. 120–53, at p. 126.

31. Karel van Wolferen, *The Enigma of Japanese Power*, London, Macmillan, 1989, p. 433.

32. Okudaira Yasuhiro, "Some Consideration on the Constitution of Japan," *Occasional Papers in Law and Society*, No. 3, Institute of Social Science, University of Tokyo, December 1987, pp. 32–34. See also Yamazumi Masami, "Educational Democracy versus State Control," in McCormack and Sugimoto, *Democracy in Contemporary Japan*, pp. 90–113.

33. Irene Kunii, "Japanese Judiciary Backs School Books Censorship," *The Age*, March 17, 1993.

34. Okudaira, "Some Consideration on the Constitution," p. 19.

35. Norma Field, *In the Realm of a Dying Emperor*, New York, Vintage, 1993, pp. 177–266.

36. Ibid., pp. 107–74.

37. "*Issai no shizenjin*," the literal Japanese translation used in the early versions, eventually becoming "*subete kokumin*." See Koseki, *Shin kempō*,

38. Ibid., p. 16.

39. Gavan McCormack, "Crime, Confession and Control in Contemporary Japan," in McCormack and Sugimoto, *Democracy in Contemporary Japan*, pp. 186–94.

40. Nakagawa Yatsuhiro, *Shin Nihonkoku kempō sōan*, Yamate shobō, 1984.

41. Watanabe Osamu, "90 nendai kaikenron no nerai to sono tokuchō," in Watanabe Osamu et al., eds., *'Kempō kaisei' hihan*, Tokyo, Rōdō jumpōsha, 1994, pp. 18–73, at pp. 41, 55–56. Also Mori Hideki, "Kokusai kōken-ron to kokuren," in ibid., pp. 244–98.

42. Opinion survey conducted by *Yomiuri shimbun* in March 1993 showed that, while defenders of the constitution had diminished from 51.1 to 33 percent between 1991 and 1993, those in favor of revision had increased from 33.3 to 50.4 percent. This figure then fell (to 44.2 percent) in 1994 but rose again to the same 50.4 percent in the 1995 survey. (See Nakano Hōkan, Kempō to sedai ishiki," *This Is Yomiuri*, June 1995, pp. 146–51, at p. 147.) See also Sotooka Hidetoshi, "Iwanami vs. *Yomiuri*—media ga shikakeru kempō ronsō no shin jidai," *Aera*, May 4–11, 1993, p. 21.

43. Quoted in Kunihiro Masao, "Iwayuru 'kaikakuha' no seitai o mitari," *Sekai*, August 1993, pp. 62–67.

44. Ozawa Ichirō, *Nihon kaizō kaikaku*, Kōdansha, 1993, p. 105.

45. Watanabe Osamu, " 'Kyujō' toppa e gōin na zenbun kaishaku," *Asahi shimbun*, March 19, 1992 (evening); also see excerpts of the Ozawa committee document in *Liberal Star*, March 15, 1993.

46. Ozawa, *Nihon kaizō*.

47. Inoki Masamichi et al., eds., " 'Kempō mondai chōsakai' no dai ichiji teigen,"(December 1992), in *Kempō mondai o kangaeru*, Yomiuri shimbunsha, 1993.

48. *Yomiuri shimbun*, November 3, 1994, also reproduced in the monthly, *This Is Yomiuri*, December 1994, and (as a translated English pamphlet) in *A Proposal for the Revision of the Text of the Constitution of Japan*, Yomiuri shimbun, 1994.

49. "Kokuminteki rongi o makiokosō," editorial, *This Is Yomiuri*, December 1994, p. 42.

50. "21 seiki e ima nani o nasubeki ka," *Yomiuri shimbun*, January 1, 1995.

51. *The Economist*, October 22, 1994.

52. *Shūkan shinchō*, November 17, 1994.

53. Yomiuri kempō mondai kenkyūkai, "Sōgō anzen hoshō—seisaku daikō o teigen suru," *This Is Yomiuri*, June 1995, pp. 104–28.

54. "A Letter to Japanese Citizens," Part 52, *Sapio*, December 8, 1994, pp. 38–39.

55. On the December 1991 formation of the "Heiwa kenpō o sekai ni hirogeru kai" (Society for extending the Peace Constitution to the World), see, for example, Itō Naruhiko, "Guntai de heiwa wa kizukeru ka," *Ekonomisuto*, April 20, 1993, pp. 48–51.

56. Itō Naruhiko, personal communication, November 1993.

57. Takabatake Michitoshi, in Rinji zōkan *Sekai*, No. 594, April 1994, p. 244.

58. Fukushima Shingo, "Jieitai 'iken gōhō' ni hashiru Ishibashi shakaitō no shingi," *Asahi jānaru*, February 10, 1984, pp. 14–18.

59. *Gekkan shakaitō*, June 1993, quoted in Yoshikawa Atsushi, "Kaikenron no dōkō to 'jieiken' ron no otoshiana," *Gekkan Forum*, November 1993, pp. 34–42, at p. 39.

60. Various media reports. See for example in English, "The End of Socialism," *The Economist*, July 30, 1994, or "Right Turn," *Far Eastern Economic Review*, September 15, 1994.

61. Katō Hidenaka, "New Socialist Platform Denounced as Unrealistic," *The Nikkei Weekly*, September 5, 1994.

62. See, for example, Yamakawa Akio, "Konnichi no kaiken kōgeki to sanzen-go sengen undō," Iida Momo, Hoshino Yasusaburō, Yamauchi, Toshihiro and Yamakawa Akio, *Kempō tokuhon*, Shakai hyōronsha, 1993, pp. 20–32, at p. 29.

63. Takabatake Michitoshi, "Seikai saihen wa kaikaku ni arazu," *Sekai*, August 1993, p. 23.

64. Kaneko Masaru, "Jimintō no seiken bankai ni te o kashita shakaitō," *Shūkan kinyōbi*, July 8, 1994, p. 6.

65. "Kyōdō teigen: 'Heiwa kihonhō' o tsukurō," by Koseki Shōichi et al., *Sekai*, April 1993, pp. 52–67. English translation of this and the other paper by Koseki et al. (cited in note 67) in *Peace and Regional Security in the Asia-Pacific: A Japanese Proposal*, edited and introduced by Gavan McCormack, Working Paper No. 158, Peace Research Center, Research School of Pacific Studies, Australian National University, 1995.

66. See the two Wada texts, "55-nen taisei," and "Sengo kakushin."

67. Koseki Shōichi et al., "Ajia Taiheiyō chi'iki ampo o kōsō suru," *Sekai*, December 1994, pp. 22–40.

68. "Kokusai kyōroku to kempō," *Asahi shimbun*, May 3, 1995. (See English text in *Asahi Evening News* of the same day.)

Part Three
Memory

6
Remembering and Forgetting: The War, 1945–95

Introduction

Other chapters in this book discuss ways in which the Cold War modi-fied the international framework, and thereby the domestic balance, of postwar Japan. But before the postwar and the Cold War was "The War," and when that term is used, no one is in any doubt as to which war is meant. Although its shadow is indubitably lengthening over late-twentieth-century Japan, it shows no sign of fading into the light of a new day. New horrors continue to be exposed, from mass graves or "people-reducing kilns" (*renjinro*) of atrocity victims in Thailand and China to mysterious heaps of human remains in Japan itself. War-time stockpiles of Japanese chemical weapons continue to kill and injure people in China. The children of the grandiose multicultural visions of a new Asian order, abandoned in China amid the ruins of the collapsing Japanese empire in 1945, now in middle age troop forlornly around Japan seeking their lost families and an understanding of their own identity. Countless victims of torture or ill-treatment throughout the region continue to suffer the effects of the cruelty of a half century ago. In many corners of the Japanese empire that collapsed fifty years ago, victims stir, lodge complaints, demand apologies and compensa-tion. The question of how the war should be remembered, even what it should be called, continues to trouble a generation that is increasingly removed from the events themselves.[1]

That the settlement of war issues should have become a politically urgent matter in the 1990s is itself remarkable. While the Cold War order struggles to give birth to a new world order, and Japan officially lays claim to a seat on the U.N. Security Council, disconcerting voices from the victims of the old order are raised; abused women, abandoned children, forgotten former colonial subjects, all now in their old age, call to account the heirs of the Japanese state. The collapse of military-authoritarian regimes (in Taiwan, South Korea, the Philippines) and the transformation of communist governments (in China and Vietnam) mean that the spaces characteristic of "civil society" begin to emerge and multiple voices to be expressed. Politicians continue to resign over their statements about the war, and bureaucrats split fine hairs in search of the appropriate nuance of expression to convey official Japanese sentiments about it to neighbor countries in such a way as to assuage the anger, pain, and resentment of their peoples without offering any compensation. Japanese courts face a surge of legal claims for apology and compensation, and the National Diet searches for some formula to resolve legislatively the issues of responsibility and compensation. Elsewhere, Germany's president was spending much of his time apologizing to neighbor countries over the deeds of his Nazi predecessors; the U.S. government apologized and compensated Japanese residents interned during World War Two and apologized to native Hawaiians for the U.S. role in the suppression of an 1893 rebellion; the pope apologized to the Czech people for Catholic violence in the seventeenth-century religious wars; and New Zealand's prime minister apologized (and offered compensation) to the indigenous Maori people for the violence and displacement they had suffered during British settlement in the nineteenth century. In Japan, however, the span of fifty years was both too long and too short.

Apologies and Apologias

The collapse in 1993 of the thirty-eight-year-long rule of the Liberal-Democratic Party served to lift the lid off issues long buried and half-forgotten. When the conservative monopoly on political power was broken and a coalition government of reformers came to power, hopes for a breakthrough, perhaps even a settlement, of the long-festering issues were high. In the event, however, at least in the short term, confusion deepened, and the bureaucratic insistence that all war issues were "irrevocably settled" was unshaken.

Hosokawa Morihiro, the first prime minister of the post-LDP era, held a press conference on August 10, 1993, following his accession to office, and broke with precedent by referring to Japan's "aggressive war." In his inaugural speech on August 25, he declared his feelings of deep regret over "the unbearable sufferings caused to so many by Japan's aggressive behavior and colonial control," and on his first overseas visit as prime minister, to Seoul, after referring to the period of Japanese colonial control over Korea, "reflecting deeply as an aggressor," he issued a "profound apology." Predecessors had apologized but had never conceded that Japan was an aggressor or that its role in Asia had been that of a colonial power. So attention focused immediately on what this new attitude might portend in concrete terms. However, Hosokawa was taking a position well in advance of his government, and nervous bureaucrats hastened to insist that actually no change in policy was to be expected. Even in the first statements from Hosokawa, the shift from reference to aggressive *war* to aggressive *behavior* marked a concession to bureaucratic and political pressures, and although his words encouraged a barrage of compensation claims, he held firm to their line that all matters of compensation had already been settled by treaty. Far from resolving the issues of responsibility and compensation, he merely reopened them.[2]

In the second post-LDP government, that of Hata Tsutomu in 1994, Minister of Justice Nagano Shigeto made a statement that encapsulated the major unresolved contradictions. He told a newspaper that the war waged by Japan in the 1930s and 1940s should not be seen as a war of aggression since "the intent had been to liberate colonies and establish a Greater East Asian Coprosperity Sphere," that the Nanking massacre of December 1937 was a "fabrication" (*detchiage*), the latter something he could attest from personal experience since he himself had been in Nanking immediately after the supposed events, and that the so-called comfort women were nothing but "military prostitutes" (*kōshō*).[3] The "Nagano statement" created a sensation, especially outside Japan. Actually, as later became clear from the full text of the interview, he was conceding killings, pillage, and rape by Japanese forces, but arguing that they had occurred in the context of a just and necessary war for Asian liberation and that they were in any case not of such a scale as to warrant the term "massacre"—atrocities, or crimes, perhaps, but not "massacre."[4] Nagano resigned two days after having made his statement, apologizing abjectly (if unconvincingly).

What was remarkable about the episode, however, was not so much the fact that the statement was made as that Nagano had been appointed to the position of Minister of Justice in a reform cabinet in the first place. A graduate of the 1941 class of the Japanese Imperial Military Academy, he served as a young officer in China during the war, and later had a long career in the Japanese military (Self-Defense Forces), rising to army (Ground) Self-Defense Force Chief-of-Staff before retiring in 1980 and entering the Diet in 1986 as an LDP candidate. His rise to cabinet status in 1994 nicely reflected the continuities, even after fifty years, between wartime and postwar Japan. In 1937, he was a fifteen-year-old schoolboy, so the reliance on his own memory of what had happened in Nanking immediately after the events turned out to be based on his visit to that city as a young officer in 1941, four years after the massacre. He was, at that time, a member of the very organization, the Imperial Japanese Army, that had been responsible for the atrocity in the first place.[5] His military experience in wartime and postwar Japan, and his strategic expertise, were so valued that he was included without question at the heart of the group of politicians that withdrew from the LDP and regrouped under a reform platform in the political reorganizations of the early 1990s, and he was Director of the Japan Strategic Studies Center, whose president was Ozawa Ichirō. The appointment as Minister of Justice of a man whose career had been spent in the military, who remained proud of the record of the Imperial Japanese Army and his role within it, and who was known as a public advocate of constitutional revision and conscription, had not seemed at all odd to Prime Minister Hata in the first place, and when he first heard of Nagano's statement, he did not think it serious enough to warrant either dismissal or resignation from the Cabinet; only the unexpected force of international opinion led him to change his mind.[6]

Furthermore, though Minister of Justice in 1994, Nagano had evidently turned a blind eye to the succession of materials about Nanking that had been published in recent years, including detailed dispatches by Nazi German diplomats in Nanking reporting the massacre to their government, and from former Japanese soldiers recounting their own experiences.[7] By 1994, there was no room for any reasonable doubt that a gross atrocity had occurred, although equally obviously there was not, and could not have been, any body count. The numbers given by the Tokyo Trial in 1946 and long asserted by the Chinese authorities (300,000) could not be strictly accurate. The conservative military historian, Hata Ikuhiko, puts forth a figure of 40,000 victims.[8] The neo-nationalist politician, Ishihara Shintarō, reckons 20,000 to 30,000 (although he had once denied the killings completely, using the same word, detchiage, or fabrication, in an interview with *Playboy* in 1990, as did Nagano in 1993).[9] But given that separate killings, some in the order of tens of thousands, occurred in hundreds of separate locations around the city, the figure originally cited at the war crimes tribunal may not have been very far off the mark.[10] Whatever the precise scale, the plain fact is that terrible deeds were committed by Japanese forces acting in the name of their emperor in those December days of 1937, and the representation of them by a Japanese Minister of Justice in 1994 as a fabrication was eloquent testimony to the continuing confusion in Tokyo about the nature of the war.

Despite defeat, postwar reorganization, and the wealth of evidence about its nature and deeds that had emerged over the decades, Nagano's pride in the old imperial army had remained unbroken, and the punishments meted out by the International Military Tribunal for the Far East, more commonly known as the Tokyo Trial, had no legitimacy. He was not exceptional in holding such views. By the 1990s, veterans such as he had become few, but in leading political and bureaucratic circles, they were taken more or less for granted, and among LDP Diet representatives in particular, his views were common.[11]

In August 1994, a matter of months after the Nagano statement, Sakurai Shin, the Director-General of the Environment Agency in the cabinet of Murayama Tomiichi, told a press conference that Japan had not gone to war out of any aggressive intent, and declared that it was thanks to Japan that Asia had been freed of European colonial control and most countries gained their independence. He too was promptly persuaded to resign.[12] Then in October, the Minister of International Trade and Industry, Hashimoto Ryūtarō, told the Diet that he doubted whether the Japanese war against America, Britain, and Holland should be seen as an aggressive war, and insisted that there had been no Japanese intention to fight against Asian countries, only against the United States and other Western countries.[13]

Germany and Japan

In this series of statements, denials, and retractions, the unresolved problem of historicizing, assimilating, and overcoming the war was apparent. Many commentators have noted the profound difference in this respect between Japan and Germany.[14] In Germany, opinion polls suggest that more than three-quarters of those born after 1945 see the end of the war as "liberation."[15] In Europe too there are those who deny the "final solution" and refer to Auschwitz as a fabrication, but their marginalization, and the continuance of trials arising from the criminal deeds of Europeans during the war of fifty years ago, contrasts sharply with the way such views are expressed and the perpetrators of horrors in Asia honored. While prominent European proponents of the view of the Holocaust and its concentration camps as fabrications pay little attention to Japan, they are cited with approval and understanding by neo-nationalists in Tokyo.[16] The influential *Far Eastern Economic Review* commented in August 1994 that in contrast with Germany, Japan had failed to achieve even a minimal national consensus about its behavior during World War Two.[17] In Australia, the Tokyo correspondent for *The Age* and *Sydney Morning Herald*, Ben Hills, wrote of the contrast between Germany and Japan in the following terms:

> But imagine a country equally responsible for a war in which upwards of 20 million people were killed, whose armies committed atrocities of the nature of Hitler's "final solution,"—and yet which 50 years on is still living in a fantasy world of denial and disbelief. Imagine a country where Adolf Hitler never died, but lived on to a ripe old age, stripped of his absolute powers but still worshipped by his people. Imagine a country where schoolchildren still line up each morning to salute the swastika, and sing the anthem of the Hitler Youth. Imagine a country where Government ministers regularly pronounce that Auschwitz never happened, and the invasion of Poland, Czechoslovakia, Holland and France was really aimed at "liberating" those countries.[18]

Whatever the indications of a recrudescence of neo-Nazism in German society, the public stance taken in the name of the government and state has been unequivocal, from Willy Brandt's apparently spontaneous prostration before the remains of the Warsaw ghetto in 1970 through the national mourning on the fiftieth-anniversary commemoration of Kristalnacht in 1988. Special legislation was passed in 1979 to remove any immunity under the statute of limitations for Nazi war crimes committed fifty or more years ago. Nothing demonstrated more clearly the effort to grasp and confront the responsibility for the Nazi past than the remarkable 1985 Bundestag speech by the federal president, Richard von Weizsäcker, on the fortieth anniversary of the war's end. In it, he acclaimed May 8, 1945, as "a day of liberation . . . from the inhumanity and tyranny of the National-Socialist regime," enumerated the many crimes committed not only against the general category of civilians (and including the enormous crime of the Holocaust) but also and specifically against Gypsies, homosexuals, the mentally ill, people who died for their religious or political beliefs, resistance fighters, and, in particular, "the women of all nations," who bore "perhaps the greatest burden."[19] The participation of German troops in a march down the Champs Elysées in 1994 served to demonstrate that the war wounds were slowly healing and to highlight the contrast with East Asia, where a similar event in Seoul or Peking would be unthinkable. The spirit of mourning, reconciliation, and shared memory that marked the fiftieth-anniversary commemorations in Europe was markedly absent in Asia.

Despite Japan's similarity with Germany in that both were allies and that Allied tribunals sat in judgment on war-crime responsibility for both countries, the dissimilarities were marked. There was an obvious German opposition to Hitler, not only on the left, but in the churches, on the old aristocratic right, even within the army (some of whose senior officers tried to kill him), and reforms at war's end radically transformed the German state so that the view of VE Day as the day of German liberation was widely accepted. In Japan, by contrast, it was the circumstances of the war's end, especially the firebombing of Tokyo and other major cities, followed by the nuclear bombing of Hiroshima and Nagasaki, that remained fresh in people's minds; as a result, the sense of being victim was stronger than that of having been aggressor. Opposition to the cause of the war had been minimal, and from war to postwar, the Japanese state maintained an essential continuity of sovereign, bureaucracy, and (with few exceptions) political leadership; its courts have never recognized any criminality of state or of individual war actions. As for the Supreme Commanders of the German and Japanese forces, one died ignominiously in his Berlin bunker, thereby escaping certain punishment and execution, while the other lived on, was declared immune from interrogation or prosecution (with the judges of the tribunal under instructions to prevent any material that might reflect adversely upon him), and eventually died in his bed forty-four years later, his funeral providing the occasion for an almost unprecedented gathering of world dignitaries. In the postwar era, the Americans and their Japanese protégés joined in working to reestablish a sort of secular, but no less protective, aura around the imperial institution. Those who made direct allusion to the emperor in any but the appropriately respectful terms could expect to experience harassment, violence, or even assassination, while academics fought long and dispiriting battles in the courts to try to establish the right to describe the war as aggressive, or to refer to the existence of bacteriological warfare units such as Unit 731, or to mention the Nanking Massacre.

It is symptomatic of the confused moral climate of postwar Japan that confinement to Sugamo Prison should then have come to be regarded as a matter for pride rather than shame, and that the network of contacts developed among the Class A war criminals held there should have become central to the evolution of the postwar state. There the group of Class A war criminals who had the good fortune to miss the first trials and be held over for the second round watched with relief as the atmosphere around them was transformed. Not only did they survive unscathed, but they were able to bathe in the first chill of the Cold War reversal of Allied policy. The second round of trials was canceled, and they were released from prison in December 1948, the day after the execution of their less-fortunate colleagues. Their fellow countrymen held them in no disrespect for whatever they might have done. Their prison connections were to prove thereafter invaluable: war loot accumulated on the adjacent continent was widely believed to have served as an early slush fund in the building of conservative and anti-communist political organizations and parties, and by 1957, one of the Sugamo alumni, Kishi Nobusuke, became prime minister. Kishi made clear in his memoirs that he rejected the Tokyo Trials from the start as "an utter farce," motivated completely by the desire for "political revenge."[20] He bitterly resented the Constitution established under the U.S. auspices as part of an American design to "remove the backbone from the Japanese people," and devoted his life after release from Sugamo, including his three-and-a-half-year spell as prime minister, to campaigning against it.[21] He remained committed to the cause of the "sacred" war, his only sense of responsibility being that Japan had lost it.[22]

The closest European parallel would be if Albert Speer, whose wartime role most resembled that of Kishi, had emerged unrepentant from a short prison term and soon afterward assumed the highest political office in the West German state. The continuity of wartime and postwar Japan was such that the thinking of key wartime figures like Kishi remained an unbroken thread long after the war, surfacing from time to time during the long era of LDP hegemony not only in statements and activities that marked Kishi's own long career but in statements by other ministers, such as Fujio Masayuki, then Minister of Education, in 1986, to the effect that Japan's assimilation of Korea in 1910 had been by perfectly proper joint agreement between the representatives of the then states (and therefore could not be described as "colonial"), or by Okuno Seisuke, Minister at the National Lands Agency in 1987, to the effect that Japan, being the only country with the resolve to resist the colonization of Asia by the "white races" should not be accused of aggressive intent, or the statements of Nagano, Sakurai, and Hashimoto already mentioned.[23] In the long postwar career of the Showa emperor, Hirohito, there was no hint of the slightest sense of personal moral responsibility for the war, and on the one occasion when he was confronted with a direct question as to his own responsibility, he responded with an extraordinary evasion: "Not being particularly well-versed in the area of literature to do with the matters to which you refer, I do not understand it very well and so cannot respond to the question."[24]

The Ministry of Education too has long and stubbornly insisted on the view that the war was not aggressive, that the atrocities of Nanking or of Unit 731, and the mass enslavement of the comfort women was not historically proven; that Japan, unlike the European countries, had not ever been a colonial state; and that the bombings of Hiroshima and Nagasaki turned Japan into the war's victim. Consequently, a generation of children has grown up with a minimum sense of the realities of the war, many of them even believing that, if there was a war, Japan must have won it. Trials have been dragging on in the courts for thirty years to try to secure the freedom to write about Japan's aggression in history textbooks.

In the 1980s, both Japan and Germany experienced a distinctive process of historical adjustment as the memory of the violent disruptions in their pasts that began in 1933 for Germany and 1931 (though much more equivocally) for Japan, and that ended in catastrophe for both in 1945, began to fade. In (West) Germany the *Historikerstreit* (Historians' Quarrel) raged for several years from 1985, prompted in part by the von Weizsäcker speech but more broadly by the desire to set some sort of seal upon the Nazi period by historicizing or relativizing it. Conservative, nationalist historians such as Ernst Nolte and Michael Stürmer sought to overcome the implication of a uniquely "German" crime by constructing a comparative framework in which Nazi crimes would be assessed alongside the crimes of Stalin, and (for some at least) those of the United States in Vietnam.[25] The underlying mood seems to have reflected the desire to recover a sense of Germanness or German identity appropriate to a new, prosperous, and generally guilt-free generation. To some participants in the debate, Hitler's politics, especially his anti-communism, although not his attempt to exterminate the Jews, became "understandable, and, up to a certain point, indeed, justified," and the Allied war effort embodied the long-range (anti-German) aims of rival European powers as much as any moral principle. To others, however, such as the philosopher Jürgen Habermas, the Holocaust was an absolutely unique and unprecedented state crime and the revisionists were peddling "a Nato philosophy colored with German nationalism."[26] While disagreeing profoundly on the scale and the uniqueness of the Nazi crimes, however, both sides agreed on the criminality of Nazism and on the need to historicize the Nazi phase of the German past.

In Japan, the same desire to move decisively beyond the darkness of the past and the same search for an affirmative identity to match the contemporary economic might was at work, but the form and content of the debate was very different. One commentator remarked on the comparison between the two countries, with only mild exaggeration, that Japan was full of conservative nationalists like Stürmer, but had no radical voices like Habermas at all.[27] Indeed the difference was profound: in contrast with Germany, where revisionism consisted in attempting to turn back the clock and to restate, in however qualified and limited a way, the Nazi (or at least the German) venture, in Japan, the legitimacy of the war has scarcely been dented in establishment circles (as witness the recurrent statements from high government officials), and revisionism properly refers to the effort to overcome entrenched historical views by representing the war as aggressive, imperialist, and brutal. The established forces of conservative nationalism in Japan continue to resist the revisionists, and to be sharp and unequivocal in their defense of the cause of the war, their rejection of such notions as colonialism or aggression, their negation of the verdicts of the Tokyo Trial (and the view of history associated with it), their denial of the massacre at Nanking, and their demand for the restoration of state rituals in honor of the war dead. While the Historikerstreit was raging in Germany, in Japan, Prime Minister Nakasone was declaring a commitment to "settle the postwar accounts" (*sengo sōkessan*), and the utterances by Fujio, Okuno, and Nagano were being made at the highest levels of state.[28] Apart from this attempt to declare an official caesura to the apologetic Japanese posture in world affairs by relegating war issues firmly to the past, Nakasone also lent his support to the drive to establish and officially propagate a positive national image for the future.

The struggle to relativize and historicize Japan's past is doubly complex: Conservative nationalists, while insisting on the historicity of Nanking, resist any historicist probe into the kernel of Japanese identity, for there stands the inscrutable figure of the emperor; revisionists, on the other hand, while insisting on the unique, and almost exhistorical horrors of the war, want to relativize conservative (emperor-centered) notions of essential Japaneseness. Debate about the war thus moves into debate about the Japanese identity, at which point the constraints of taboo and terror come into play to inhibit discussion of the role of the emperor.

The working of such constraints to deter debate on the core questions is dramatically illustrated by the case of the mayor of Nagasaki, Motoshima Hitoshi. In answering a question in the local assembly on December 7, 1988, Motoshima remarked that of course some responsibility for the war must attach to the emperor (who was then on his deathbed).[29] It was a mild and unremarkable statement, but a huge campaign of vilification and intimidation was launched against him because of it. Just over a week after the statement, there were twenty-five truckloads of paramilitary rightists (about seventy people) surrounding his offices and blasting him with high-decibel invective and martial music; a few days later, it was up to eighty-five trucks, with 260 people from sixty-two different ultranationalist groups, and threats were extended from Motoshima personally to his family and children.[30] On January 18, 1990, a right-wing extremist assassin shot at him from behind, puncturing his lung and very nearly ending his life. The ferocity of the response to Motoshima's mildly worded statement was related partly to the hysteria that was then building over the long illness and expected demise of the emperor, and partly to the sense of shock that such views should be expressed by a conservative local politician. It showed dramatically the continuing difficulty in opening to rational discussion basic questions of responsibility for the war.

One explanation of the Japanese phenomenon is psychoanalytical, interpreting the continuing alternation of statements such as Hosokawa's war contrition and Nagano's protestation of innocence as evidence of the deep rift between Japan's inner and outer self. In this view, the schizophrenia of modern Japan began with the forced opening of the mid-nineteenth century when the "inner self" of tradition was forced to recognize its impotence to the West. The split between a modernizing and Westernizing "outer self" and a true Japanese "inner self" thereafter widened, with the suppressed inner self tending to become more and more unrealistic and inclined to indulge in delusion, rejecting the modern Western shape of the national polity and insisting shrilly on the imperial view of history. Integration of the two parts of the sundered identity was only accomplished through the explosive liberating process of the Pacific War. After the defeat, and the resumption of an even more thoroughgoing Westernizing path, the split was reinforced. Vacillation between the two has characterized the postwar era, punctuated not only by statements but occasionally by dramatic explosions such as Mishima Yukio's botched theatrical attempt to restore the ascendancy of the "inner." In this view, the attempt by political leaders such as Hosokawa to negate the war to which the inner self still clung was an unbearable affront, and the response uttered by Nagano and others, however divorced from reality, the inevitable explosion of the repressed and denied inner self. The process of healing can only be accomplished, and an integrated whole be regained, when dialogue between the two is entered into and each becomes able to recognize the partial truth of the other.[31]

Nanking, although an enormously important incident of the war, therefore, was no more than a fleeting moment. If it could be seen as an isolated phenomenon, in which unnecessary and regrettable killings occurred in the heat of battle on or adjacent to the battlefield, and not as the result of specific strategies or orders, it would not affect one's judgment of the war as a whole. The extraordinary contest to pin back the number of victims and to avoid the term massacre (*dai gyakusatsu*) is part of a quantitative and qualitative contest over Nanking as a central symbol of the war. While Nagano and his colleagues most determinedly resist the Nanking massacre thesis, they do so because they hold to a certain interpretation of the war as whole; like Mr. Kishi in his Sugamo cell in 1946, they still see it as a sacred cause that, unfortunately, Japan lost.

Yet the plain fact, however unpalatable, is that Nanking was replicated in Singapore and on the Malay peninsula and elsewhere in count-less towns and villages in Manchukuo, China, Southeast Asia, and the Pacific between 1941 and 1945. For this reason, the "isolated and unfortunate incident" interpretation does not hold water.[32] Instead, Nanking has to be seen as a characteristic episode, in which the very fabric or tissue of the war was revealed. That quality, its DNA, if you will, was consistent throughout time and space and was rooted in the conviction that the Japanese cause was sacred and superior, and the end of Japanese victory an absolute good of such magnitude as to justify whatever means were necessary to accomplish it.

War Responsibility: Crime and Cover-up

Never directly negated, after 1945, the war merely slipped away from people's minds. Preoccupation first with day-to-day matters of sur-vival, then (in the 1960s and 1970s) with high growth and income doubling, then (in the 1980s) with affluence and consumption, served to obliterate the memory of the war. Economism and the pursuit of self-interest was the leitmotiv to the long peace that followed the bar-renness of total subordination to the wartime state. The trials were regarded as the inevitable consequence of defeat, but there was more sympathy than detestation for those who were subjected to them. The central tenet of the indictment—of a Japanese conspiracy dating from 1928 to wage war on the world—was never taken seriously (and in due course came to be dismissed by Western historians too).[33] Not only did the findings and the punishments meted out by the allied tribunal in Tokyo fail to create a sense of justice and clarify to the satisfaction of the Japanese people the reasons for the war, but they were commonly seen as an inevitable exercise of victor's justice. Similarly, the B and C Class trials held at many locations throughout the region were pro-foundly flawed, not necessarily aggressively slanted to serve the inter-ests of the victors or to pursue vengeance, but often careless of the rights of defendants and ignorant of the social and cultural context of Japanese actions.[34] In sum, the public attempts to affix responsibility lacked credibility from the start.

The proceedings in the Tokyo tribunal reflected the perspective of the leading Allied powers. They were predicated on the assumption that only the defeated powers could be guilty, and they gave promi-nence to matters such as the Pearl Harbor attack and the treatment of

Western prisoners. In none of the trials was Japan's colonial record taken into consideration. This was perhaps scarcely surprising given that Japan was being tried by a group of powers with strong colonial interests. Seventy percent of the seats on the bench of the Tokyo court were occupied by the Western powers that had accounted for around 10 percent of the war damage and suffering, while only three Asian countries were represented; Nationalist China, India, and the Philippines.[35] In sharp contrast to the Nuremberg trial, where crimes against German citizens—Jewish and others—were central to the indictment, Japanese crimes against Koreans and Taiwanese, both Japanese wartime subjects, were not considered. Not until four decades later did the idea come under consideration that crimes deserving of prosecution by Japanese tribunals might have been committed against the Japanese people as well as against others.[36]

The distinction between the China and Asian-Pacific wars has commonly been fudged by reference to *the* war, and it was not clarified or pursued by the Tokyo Trial. The war was *both* colonial—an extension and escalation of the China Incident that was rooted in the Japanese aim to establish hegemonic control over East Asia—and imperialist, driven by interimperialist rivalry for control of the resources of Southeast Asia. In 1960, Takeuchi Yoshimi was the first major historian to shift the focus of war responsibility on to the question of Japanese colonialism, while being at the same time adamant that Japan alone could not be blamed for the interimperialist phase of the war.[37] However, while Takeuchi distinguished the two in order to focus attention on the negative sense of Japanese colonial rule, Hayashi Fusao did so with positive intent, to reaffirm the legitimacy and ideology of the war more or less as it was represented at the time. His *Dai tōa sensō kōteiron*, or "Affirmation of the Greater East Asian War," published in 1963, saw the conflict of 1931–45 in the long historical context of Japan's one-hundred-year struggle to contain the expansion of Western imperialism into Asia; Japan for him emerges as the champion of Asia. There is little new in the debates between contemporary historians on these questions, but it is notable that the greater political weight still attaches to views expressed by Hayashi, in the sense that the question of Japan-in-Asia continues to be more commonly framed in terms of Japan's long crusade against the West rather than as a Japanese variant of colonialism (as argued by Takeuchi). The shock occasioned in Japanese political and bureaucratic circles when, forty-eight years after the defeat, Hosokawa became the first prime minister to refer to Japan's war as aggressive and colonial, was understandably profound, and Nagano's outburst, which followed it shortly afterward, may be seen as its inevitable rejoinder. Fifty years has not been long enough for Japan to reach any consensus on what the war was about.

In short, the ideological terms in which the war was represented at the time live on scarcely challenged in postwar popular consciousness. Like Kishi, Nagano, and Sakurai, many continue to believe in the purity of purpose of the continental and China phases of the war (particularly the Manchurian dimension of it), and like Hashimoto, many, perhaps even most people, believe that responsibility for the hostilities with the Americans and Europeans in the second phase of the war that followed Pearl Harbor should be shared. They are not persuaded that there was anything particularly brutal or outlawlike about the way in which the war was pursued. In particular the belief that both sides bore their share of responsibility for the Pacific phase of the war, and that the Allied embargoes and refusal to negotiate left no alternative to war, is common.[38] The view expressed by the eighty-three-year-old radical philosopher Kuno Osamu in 1993, that in the Pacific war Japan might have had "about three parts right" on its side, is probably widely shared.[39] The political scientist Inoguchi Takashi reckons that more than half the people in Japan would agree with the Hashimoto statement about Japan having been guilty of aggression toward Asia but not toward the West, and resentful that the world should continue insisting on a life sentence for Japan for crimes that have been forgotten and forgiven by the Europeans and Americans.[40] It is still too early to weigh these matters in the scales of history, he adds, quoting the comment of Zhou Enlai (mistakenly attributed to Mao Zedong) that even after 200 years, it was too early to pass judgment on the French Revolution.

The foreclosing of the issue of war responsibility and the early Allied decision to collude with the defeated enemy in diverting responsibility away from the imperial institution,[41] as well as deliberately to cover up the crimes now commonly regarded as the most serious (such as those of Unit 731), in return for securing the cooperation of its principals, rank among the earliest decisions of the Cold War. A cover-up at the center meant obfuscation and displacement of responsibility from higher to lower (what is known in Japanese as *katagawari*, or passing of a burden from shoulder to shoulder), and it occurred as a result of concerted and deliberate decisions by Allied (almost exclusively American) and Japanese authorities.

The confusion that still surrounds the issue of war responsibility and war compensation stems from those early decisions, and the removal of the Cold War framework after 1990 again exposed these unresolved questions, with curiously greater urgency than when they were set aside nearly fifty years ago. The important point is that the cover-up of the responsibility of those who either were, or might have been, key figures was characteristic, and responsibility for the processes of obfuscation, transfer, and scapegoating, was shared between the Allies (Americans) and the Japanese. On the legal principle of responsibility stemming from "complicity after the fact," after August 1945, responsibility for Japanese war crimes is shared by both sides. The Americans (and the West in general) *share* responsibility for these crimes such as those against the comfort women, based on this little-understood but absolutely crucial principle. As for the Japanese people themselves, they have yet to take a position publicly, that is to say through either their legislative or judicial institutions, on the locus of responsibility for the war and its crimes.

Official History Versus Public History

It became clear in the months leading up to the fiftieth-anniversary commemorations in 1995 that the problem of how and what to remember was not exclusive to the defeated: the Allies were all caught up in anguished reconsiderations of one or other aspect of the record of their country's wartime deeds, from the British bombing of German cities such as Hamburg and Dresden to the French record of collaboration with the Nazis, and, most painfully of all, the American decisions to destroy Tokyo by incendiary bombing in March 1945 and Hiroshima and Nagasaki by nuclear bombs in August. The various tribunals that had deliberated on war crimes in the postwar years all proceeded on the assumption that war crimes could only have been committed by the enemy, and the idea that leaders of the victorious Allied states might have also deserved to be arraigned in the dock along with the Nazis was not even considered. The pain of seeking to face objectively the momentous decisions taken in extremis fifty and more years ago and transforming understanding of them from the propaganda level of official history to the universal truths worthy of public history is not confined to one side.

The project to conduct an exhibition in the Smithsonian Institution's National Air and Space Museum in Washington became the occasion of a bitter contest between rival versions of the American national memory.[42] From the spring of 1993, a plan was gradually developed to mark 1995 with a special exhibit devoted to the bombing of Hiroshima and Nagasaki, under the provisional title of "The Crossroads: The End of World War II, the Atomic Bomb and the Onset of the Cold War." It would feature the restored *Enola Gay* itself, the B–29 bomber from which the "Little Boy" bomb was dropped on August 6, 1945, with a series of panels surrounding it that would raise questions about the strategic and moral nature of the bomb's use and about the nuclear age that was thereby inaugurated.[43] Materials borrowed from Hiroshima and Nagasaki that would show graphically the experience of those caught up within the mushroom cloud would be included, and they would query whether the bomb had been necessary to achieve Japanese surrender or to what extent it had to be dropped in order to justify the huge expenditure of its development, to satisfy scientific curiosity, or to intimidate the Soviet Union (thereby marking also the first act of the Cold War).

When news of preliminary plans was reported, however, a protest campaign was launched that gradually assumed massive proportions. It drew upon the support of the National Air Force Association and the American Legion (with about three million members), and in September 1994, Resolution 257, which was critical of the project, was passed unanimously on the floor of the Senate, stating that the exhibition, even as by then revised, would be "revisionist, unbalanced and offensive," declaring that the bomb had been instrumental in saving the lives of both Japanese and American people and "in helping to bring World War II to a merciful end." The idea that the U.S. Air Force might have been guilty of a war crime and that the citizens of Hiroshima and Nagasaki might actually have been innocent victims was intolerable, and the viciousness and criminality of the Japanese war machine, and the possibly prolonged fighting and large-scale casualties on both Allied and Japanese sides that might have been expected from an Allied landing and battle for the archipelago, island by island, had to be given due prominence.

The perception in Japan of the bombing of Hiroshima and Nagasaki

is complex. It is probably true to say that most people see it as a crime
of such magnitude as to warrant analogy with Auschwitz.[44] The respected mayor of Nagasaki, Motoshima Hitoshi, explicitly links these
two as the greatest crimes against humanity of the twentieth century.[45]
The distinguished historian Ohe Shinobu equates three episodes as the
centrally criminal components of World War Two: the destruction of
Hiroshima and Nagasaki, Japan's Unit 731, and Auschwitz, each of
which, he adds, also represented a new dimension in warfare in the
form of atomic, bacteriological, and chemical (ABC) warfare respectively, and two of which were reserved from punishment in the political and judicial settlements that followed.[46] At the same time,
however, the Resolution 257 view of Hiroshima and Nagasaki also has
deep roots in Japan, having been first proclaimed in the immediate
aftermath of the destruction by none other than the emperor, Hirohito,
who was therefore the very first to absolve the United States for use of
the weapon and to suggest that it was a hammer of virtuous punishment rather than a new weapon of mass terror. Ohe argues that Hirohito may well have been relieved to hear of the destruction of the two
cities, since it thereby gave him a pretext to bring the war to an end in
such a way as to retain the national polity (centering on his own imperial institution), which was then threatened much more seriously by the
Soviet Union than by nuclear devastation.[47] In return for his act of
absolution, by which he represented the destruction of Hiroshima and
Nagasaki as simply the irresistible force to which Japan had no alternative but to submit, Hirohito was himself absolved, as in due course was
the key Japanese bacteriological-warfare unit.

The outraged critics of the Smithsonian were thus aligning themselves with Emperor Hirohito, and official Japan, against the many
Japanese citizen's groups and the residents of Hiroshima and Nagasaki
who insist that the use of the bomb was criminal. The indignation
provoked in veteran and political circles in the United States by the
attempt to question the "sacred truths" within which the horrors of
Hiroshima and Nagasaki have officially been enveloped since 1945
nicely matched that expressed in Japan by men such as Nagano and
Okuno: On both sides, self-righteous, angry men, virtuous and moral
according to their own standards, were determined to allow no question to be raised against what they saw as truth. As the dispute in the
United States grew, the original plan was gradually revised, so that
photographs of the damage caused by the bomb were reduced from

sixty-two to thirty-eight, of which only six (instead of a planned twenty-one) featured victims' faces, and the items to be borrowed from Hiroshima and Nagasaki reduced from twenty-seven to eight, eliminating pitiful relics such as a blasted lunchbox, items associated with children, or (from Nagasaki) a melted rosary and a statue of the Virgin Mary. The legacy of the bomb was reduced from a detailed study of the radiation sickness and death and the nuclear era that had thereby been opened to the role of the bomb in bringing down the curtain on the last act of the war. Many scholars entered the lists, protesting that the process of revision amounted to "historical cleansing," comparable to the sanitizing of its war history by Japan's Ministry of Education by textbook "screening."[48] But in due course, the director of the museum, Martin Harwit, resigned, and the exhibition was reduced to a truncated form featuring the front half of the *Enola Gay*, with a simple plaque and a video, without any commentary on the issues.[49]

No one can now know for sure what would have happened had the bombs not been dropped on the two hapless Japanese cities. While Admiral William David Leahy confided to his diary on June 18, 1945, that he thought about 63,000 Allied casualties (dead and wounded) could be expected if an autumn invasion of Japan's main islands were to be undertaken, President Truman later put the much larger figure of 229,000 lives saved by the bomb, and in the outraged protests over the Smithsonian affair, that figure grew to nearly a million.[50] In the evolution of so-called strategic bombing, which came to mean the indiscriminate bombing of innocent civilian populations, both the fascist Europeans and the Japanese militarists played their roles, but the United States in due course surpassed all prior practitioners. The incendiary bombing of Tokyo and other cities in napalm firestorms "scorched, boiled, and baked to death"[51] about 100,000 people in Tokyo alone, more than died in Dresden and Hamburg combined, or double the number killed in the London Blitz.[52] The question that was rarely, if ever, asked in the exchanges of 1994–95 was the ancient philosophical dilemma: Could a "good" end justify a "bad" means? In other words, in order to achieve a Japanese surrender and thereby avoid the killings of however many Japanese and Allied lives that would have resulted from prolonged fighting in a mainland front of the war, was it legitimate to have deliberately targeted Japan's civilian population? Put a little more starkly, if it had seemed that the killing of, say, one hundred (or one thousand) children and one hundred (or one thousand) old folk might have persuaded the Japanese government to surrender, would it have been legitimate for the Allied command to have dispatched, like Herod, a special unit to fulfill such a mission? The numbers of those in such categories that were killed, and that could have been known to the planners of the raids would be bound to die, were much greater then this. As Nagasaki mayor Motoshima Hitoshi put it, "Does avoiding the death of servicemen justify the sacrifice of tens of thousands of guiltless noncombatants?"[53]

In the context of the war that was being fought in mid-1945, this might seem an impossibly abstruse conundrum. Perhaps it is. But the point is that an immense moral confusion had been spread over the world in the interval between the first and second World Wars, as all states came to adopt the pragmatic view that the end justifies the means. As a result, the Japanese determination to crush all resistance in China by whatever means were necessary is difficult, if not impossible, to distinguish in moral terms from the American resolve to use whatever means were at hand to crush the Japanese resistance of the summer of 1945. Furthermore, in the stifling of debate and the insistence on the monopoly of an "official" version of truth, even at the distance of fifty years, a tragic equivalence is maintained. The point that has been made previously about the Allied complicity in the Japanese crimes of Unit 731, and in the prostitution of the women of Asia, is reinforced in this. The official Japanese reluctance to concede to the criminality of its wartime behavior owes much to the conviction that guilt was not confined to one side of the war, and that is undeniably true. In the early months of 1995, a major difficulty that faced Prime Minister Murayama as he attempted to steer through the Diet a resolution expressing Japan's official regret and apology over its colonialism and aggressive war was the widespread conviction that Japan had done nothing more or less than other (Western) countries had done, and the objection to being put alongside Nazi Germany in a category of exceptional, even unique, evil.

Compensation: Germany and Japan

In the scales of the twentieth century, the misery, suffering, destruction, and dislocation caused by Japanese expansion and war in mid-century was of a magnitude comparable to the German, and the contrast between the two countries in terms of how they face their own history at century's end is striking. The contrast between Japan and Germany in respect to the payment of war compensation is stark. In reparations, compensation, and pensions, by 1991, the German government had paid out the sum of 86.4 billion marks (6.9 trillion yen), and the German Treasury estimated that payments of a further 33.6 billion marks (2.7 trillion yen) would continue until the year 2030, for a total of around 10 trillion yen (roughly one hundred billion dollars). The payments go from federal and state governments and private companies to an enormous range of public and private institutions in Israel and Europe, from the state of Israel to the 13,000 East German "heroes of the resistance."[54] In the official histories of major German companies such as Daimler-Benz and Volkswagen, the use of wartime slave labor is fully acknowledged.[55] By comparison, Japan had paid out a paltry 250 billion yen, forty times less, and less than is paid in a single year in pensions and benefits to Japanese veterans and their families.[56]

The greatest contrast is not the discrepancy in monetary compensation that has been paid, for money, however important, is secondary. It is attitude, or what in East Asia is known as sincerity, that is crucial. The carefully calibrated expressions of regret—of the kind that Zhou Enlai is once said to have described as appropriate for when one has spilled a cup of tea over a lady's dress—contrast sharply with the violence that occurred. The consistent Japanese focus on its war experience as victim (Hiroshima and Nagasaki), rather than as aggressor (Nanking, Singapore, and countless other cities), contrasts with Germany's public penitent stance. The continuing efforts to sanitize the history that is taught to the country's youth, and especially to deny the massacre at Nanking and the atrocities of Unit 731 at Harbin and elsewhere, and the countless atrocities against women, evoke distrust and suspicion on the part of Japan's neighbors. Financial compensation, it is understood, would be hollow without honest confrontation with the historical record in Tokyo and the assumption of a moral responsibility by the contemporary Japanese state for the innocent victims of the crimes of their fathers.

In insisting that all compensation claims have been irrevocably settled, the Japanese government rests on specious legal ground. The forty-eight signatory nations to the San Francisco Peace Treaty of 1951 declared in Article 14 (a) that Japan had an obligation to pay compensation for damage and suffering caused, but added in Article 14 (b) that they renounced any such entitlement in view of the weakness of the

Japanese economy.[57] Only the Philippines and (South) Vietnam reserved their rights, and in 1956 and 1960, reparations agreements were reached, for the payment of $550 million in goods and services and $250 in loans to the former and $39 million to the latter (plus various amounts of loans also). Burma (Myanmar), which was not a party to the San Francisco Peace Treaty, and Indonesia, which did not ratify it, also reached similar agreements with Japan in 1954 and 1958, and were paid $250 million with an additional $80 million in commercial credits in the former case, and $223 million in goods and services and $400 million in loans in the latter.[58] These four are the only countries that concluded formal reparations agreements with Japan.

Four separate agreements with other countries are sometimes grouped together with the others as de facto reparations. They are South Korea, Singapore, Malaysia, and Micronesia. Although reparation was not mentioned, when relations between Japan and South Korea were eventually normalized in 1965, $300 million in outright grants and $200 million in loans, plus an additional $300 million in private-sector credits, were approved as "a complete and final settlement of all property rights and claims." Likewise, various agreements were negotiated in 1967 and 1968 with Singapore and Malaysia, each of which was given $8 million (2.9 billion yen) in "blood-debt" agreements. Though tantamount to reparations payments, these monies went to the state authorities in the form of ships or shipbuilding equipment, nothing of any relevance to the actual victims.[59] And the Micronesia Agreement of April 1969 had both Japan and the United States agreeing to pay $5 million in goods and services to the islands.[60] These monies were clearly of the nature of consolation rather than compensation and, since losses are reckoned to amount to $34.3 billion, met only a small fraction of the actual demands.[61]

Characteristic of all agreements is that they were conducted between states, with little or no input from individuals or groups who had suffered losses, and they were paid in such a way—commonly directly to Japanese corporations to cover the cost of supplying the various goods or services which made up the reparations or compensation—as to assist nothing so much as the return of Japanese business to Southeast Asia. Cynics saw commercial motive, rather than actual compensation or reparation, as primary. The areas that had suffered most, especially China, were not compensated at all. Although none of these should properly be seen as reparations or compensation agreements, the Japanese government has nevertheless pointed to them as justification for refusing all subsequent claims.

Two matters that are central to these questions concern the comfort women issue and wartime forced labor. Increasingly, these are the central questions at issue in judicial proceedings too.

Comfort Women

The matter of the so-called comfort women has been widely reported and can only be briefly recapitulated here.[62] Sexual-service facilities were first provided during the 1932 Shanghai incident for the comfort of Japanese occupation forces in China and to avert the tensions caused between the occupying forces and local populations by large-scale rape. They were gradually expanded into a vast organization covering the whole Coprosperity Sphere. The women were seized by force or by deception from villages and towns in Korea, China, Taiwan, Philippines, Indonesia, Malaya, Vietnam, the East Indies (including Dutch women), and even from Japan itself. Some were as young as thirteen. Total numbers are unknown, but a figure somewhere between 100,000 and 200,000 is generally agreed upon. The principle of one woman to every thirty-five soldiers was apparently followed in calculating how many to deploy to the various theaters of war.[63] Koreans were preferred, and probably constituted about 80 percent of the total, because the strictness of the Confucian society in Korea meant that young unmarried women would mostly be virgins, thereby minimizing the risk of venereal disease. In parts of Indonesia (then the Dutch East Indies), however, the women were mobilized by local press gangs and, according to materials released by the Japanese government in 1992, the 282 women working in the twenty-seven comfort stations in South Sulawesi were virtually all local Indonesian women.[64]

Their humanity, even in a sense their gender, was of little relevance to the service required of them. They were treated as goods, to be supplied and used (and, where appropriate, disposed of), and they were commonly known, not by names but by number, a practice that symbolically marked their divestment of humanity, just as the appellation *maruta* (log) marked those destined for experimentation or torture by the Unit 731. Resistance was met with violence, and the comfort women were called upon to service anywhere between ten and fifty men per day, a process that destroyed them as surely as any bullet or bayonet. At the end of the war, the women were either abandoned and left to their fate or were killed,[65] and there is some reason to think there may have been a plan to kill them all. Only a thorough study of materials and of the testimony of survivors will make it possible to know for sure.[66]

No reference was made to these matters in the crimes for which the Japanese authorities were indicted after the war. It is not that the facts were unknown, for the network had been massive and its dismantling and the subsequent repatriation of the women was a major operation. What seems most likely is that crimes against women did not at that time rank highly on the occupation forces' scale of criminality.

In December 1991, a group of thirty-five Korean women who had been sex slaves to the Japanese Army on various war fronts launched an action in the Japanese courts for apology and compensation (twenty million yen each). In September 1993, a second group, this time from the Philippines, launched a similar action, and other groups of women from other countries were preparing to do likewise. Until December 1991, the consistent position of the Japanese government was to deny all knowledge of the matter, or to treat it as a fabrication. Then it pleaded that, although the prostitution business existed, it had been run by private contractors, independent of any government control. When that defense collapsed, the government stance shifted again, to arguing that the women had not been coerced. Each point was conceded with obvious reluctance and only when incontrovertible documentary evidence of official responsibility was discovered and published by independent researchers, and those who had been involved in the capture and transport of the women began to speak out about their roles.[67] During an official visit to Seoul in December 1991, Prime Minister Miyazawa issued a formal apology. In July 1992, the chief cabinet secretary expressed the government's sincere apologies and remorse, but continued to insist that there could be no individual compensation. It was August 1993 before the government caved in on the question of direct official responsibility. Even then, however, its position remained that compensation would not be paid because all such matters had been settled by the San Francisco Peace Treaty of 1951 and by bilateral treaties such as the Japan-Republic of Korea Normalization Treaty of 1965. Faced with the obvious objections that this matter was not taken into consideration in 1965, and that the Japanese government only conceded the existence of the system of slavery and trafficking in women in 1991, and official responsibility for it in 1993, by 1994, politicians and bureaucrats in Tokyo were struggling to find a formula to meet the demands for compensation through establishment of a private fund. (The South Korean government had already begun to pay a pension to the women, even though obviously it bore no responsibility for what had happened to them.)

It is striking that the demands made by women's groups are strongly moral rather than financial in character. Their demands for publication of the full truth (*shinso kyūmei*), backed by public resources, and for punishment of the guilty (however symbolic that might have to be in the 1990s) were paramount. They perceive that a government that colludes in the suppression of truth is morally bankrupt, and they know well that while the official commitment to cover up lasted for forty-eight years, the commitment to openness is only two years old and still to be tested.

All in all, the comfort women story is a grim reminder of the reality of the inner meaning of Japan's sacred war. The exercise was of historical significance: It was probably the largest-scale state-sponsored rape in history. Carefully and soberly organized by clerks in the Japanese Army, who recorded minute details, and then just as carefully covered up by a later generation of bureaucrats (and their political and bureaucratic masters) who knew, but chose not to know, about it, the use of comfort women was not perceived to be a crime by either Japan or the Allies. Gradually, from the perspective of the late twentieth century, it is emerging as a crime of the first magnitude, and the guilt of those who perpetrated it is matched only by those who *either* were blind to it or deliberately covered it up. The complicity between the Japanese authorities who organized the trafficking and abuse of the women on the one hand and the Allied authorities on the other is an aspect of the comfort women issue to which attention is rarely drawn. The Allied complicity of 1945 was compounded during subsequent years, when they enjoyed the cooperation of the Japanese government in mobilizing another generation of young women, this time mostly Japanese, to provide precisely the same sexual services for the occupation forces. By August 18, 1945, three days after Japan's surrender, the attention of local police authorities was being drawn by the Home Ministry to the importance of providing comfort facilities for the occupation garrison, and of mobilizing women, with a preference for geisha, licensed and unlicensed prostitutes, waitresses, hostesses, and other women who "customarily provide various sexual services."[68]

Thus it was that a crime widely known in Japan for over forty years—if for no other reason than for the fact that millions of Japanese soldiers for whom the comfort had been provided returned at war's end to towns and villages throughout Japan—was only written about in relatively obscure books until the late 1980s. It was denied consistently by government spokesmen until they were confronted with irrefutable documents from the archives in 1991, and then was represented as a trade carried out by private contractors independently of the Imperial Japanese Army. Direct responsibility was established beyond doubt only in 1993, slowly stirring the world's conscience. The reluctant concessions from the Japanese government were forced from it by human as well as documentary proof: The women themselves gradually overcame their own sense of shame and began to demand that guilt be acknowledged where it belonged, and former army personnel and civilians began to come forward to give their testimony. The maturation of civil society throughout the region in the post–Cold War era gave new weight to considerations of human rights and gender equality and thereby exposed the ledger of long-unsettled matters from the war of fifty years ago. This also raises moral questions that need to be addressed by proponents of the superiority of the Confucian social order. The generation of politicians that aspired to a role of leadership in the "new" Asia found that they would first have to deal with the legacy bequeathed them by their fathers.

Forced Labor and the Hanaoka Mine Affair

During the war, people were mobilized into the service of the Japanese armed forces on a massive scale throughout the Asian and Western Pacific region. About a million Korean and Chinese laborers were drafted into mines and military installations in Japan; in Southeast Asia, vast numbers were impressed—at least two million for various projects in Java and another 200,000 for the construction of the railway between Burma and Thailand.[69] Whether Chinese rounded up in their villages and sent off to New Guinea or the Solomons, Indians captured in Singapore and sent off to Thailand or Burma, Pacific Islanders transported to remote areas to help construct the new order, Koreans sent anywhere from Sakhalin to the South Pacific: All were abandoned and left to fend for themselves when the war ended. Since the war, all approaches for compensation to the companies concerned or to the

Japanese government have been rejected. The government view is that the mobilization of labor was a legitimate act of state under the 1938 General Mobilization Law, a defense of "legality" that was rightly brushed aside in the Nuremberg trial of the Nazis (and in subsequent trials such as that of Adolf Eichmann). What follows is merely one case study in the huge phenomenon of wartime forced labor.

Kajima Construction Company is one of the giants of the Japanese construction industry. Along with other companies in the same sector, it was active in urging the wartime government to introduce a system of import of Chinese labor, which was then adopted by the Tojo Cabinet in November 1942. From February 1944, a force of 40,000 Chinese workers was imported, allowing Kajima and other construction and mining companies to replace their regular workers. Kajima's Hanaoka mine in Akita Prefecture housed about 1,000 Chinese laborers. On July 1, 1945, they rose up in rebellion against appalling labor conditions, torture, and inadequate food. Five people were killed in the initial outbreak. Those who escaped were quickly rounded up, and 418 of them were killed, including 113 who were tortured to death.[70] The surviving leaders of the uprising were tried, and on September 11 (nearly a month after the surrender), they were found guilty of breaching national security by rioting in wartime and were sentenced to life imprisonment.[71] After the war, the ten major construction companies (including Hazama, Taisei, and Kumagai, as well as Kajima) received a series of "compensation" payments from various Japanese ministries, making up for the losses they suffered—works not yet paid for or works not done because of the rebellion or Japan's defeat in the war.[72] In postwar, democratic Japan, the head of Kajima, Kajima Morinosuke, became a member of the House of Councillors in the national Diet, philanthropist, well-known scholar, and prolific author on Japanese diplomatic history. In 1965, he was prominent in insisting that the abandonment of any compensation claims by China be a precondition for the reopening of diplomatic relations.[73]

In the two-volume official history of the company's 130 years, there is no reference to the Hanaoka rebellion, although the certificate of grateful appreciation received from the army for wartime services such as the construction of the underground complex designed to serve as a last-stand underground Imperial Army Headquarters in Nagano Prefecture (*Matsushiro Dai Hon'ei*) and the Burma-Thailand Railway in Southeast Asia are both recorded with pride. Forced labor of Koreans was used for the former, and forced labor of Australian, British, and other prisoners-of-war, as well as forced labor from many Southeast Asian nations (the so-called *Rōmusha*) for the latter.

In 1989, representatives of the surviving Chinese and their families launched a claim against the company for a public apology, proper commemoration of the victims, and a compensation payment of five million yen each to some 1,000 victims. In February 1994, the former vice president of Kajima, Kiyoyama Shinji, on trial for corruption in the series of General Construction Company or zenekon corruption cases, compared his feelings after four months of detention with those of the Japanese soldiers detained in postwar Siberia or with those of the conscripted Japanese schoolboys who had been sent to their deaths in Southeast Asia—in other words, as an innocent victim. A brief apology was issued in the company name in July 1990, but other requests have been flatly rejected. Kajima continues to protest that it had merely followed national policy, although it was prepared to contribute a small sum toward the cost of constructing a cenotaph.[74]

In terms of the exploitation and ill-treatment of Chinese or Korean workers, Hanaoka was far from being an unusual case. The story of Liu Lianren is, in a way, even more remarkable. Liu was taken at bayonet point from his Shandong village in 1944 and sent to work in the Showa coal mine in Hokkaido. Unlike those at Hanaoka who rose up in rebellion, he fled into the mountains. He escaped in July 1945, just about one month before the end of the war, but he was so terrified that he remained in hiding, living off grasses and nuts, and occasionally descending to the remote coastline to collect seaweed, less afraid of bears than of human beings, and with no knowledge that the war was over, until he was by chance discovered by a rabbit trapper in 1958.[75] When he emerged, not only was the war well over, but Kishi Nobusuke, the Tojo Cabinet's Minister for Commerce and Labor, who had been responsible for the forced-labor program, had become prime minister. When Kishi's government ordered an investigation of Liu on suspicion of illegal entry into the country, Liu published a famous statement of protest and then returned to China. As of the early 1990s, he was still pursuing his case for justice against the Japanese government, and still waiting for a response from it.[76]

The rise of the postwar Japanese construction industry, analyzed in detail in Chapter 1, was based on exploitation of prisoner and virtual slave labor during these wartime years. Not only has no compensation ever been paid to the workers, but compensation *was* paid to the companies when they lost their workforce due to defeat. Thus the companies received a double benefit, suffered little, and have consistently denied responsibility.

Matsushiro Underground Imperial Headquarters

Would Japan have surrendered in 1945 even if the bombs had not been dropped on Hiroshima and Nagasaki? There can be no definitive answer. Nor could a negative answer be seen as amounting to a justification of the destruction of those cities. However, the more that is known about the processes then at work within Japan's ruling circles, the less likely that proposition becomes. As the Japanese defeats in the Pacific led to the inevitability of direct U.S. bombing raids on the mainland (which actually began in November 1944), attention turned to the idea of a last stand, in which countless Japanese would die a glorious death but commensurate losses would be inflicted upon the invading forces. Gathered around the throne, a last magnificent stand, or *gyokusai*, would be undertaken. Full-scale excavation works began in November 1944 on a site in Nagano Prefecture for the relocation of the throne and of the functions of command, administration, and communications. An enormous series of tunnels was burrowed out in an area of some twenty kilometers circumference under the three mountains of Maizuru, Zōzan, and Minagami. It became known as the Matsushiro Imperial Headquarters (*Matsushiro Daihon'ei*), after the adjacent town (and railway station) of Matsushiro.[77] The major works responsibility was assumed by Kajima and Nishimatsu construction companies, and the labor was provided mostly by Koreans. The number of laborers mobilized on this job is not known precisely, but there were over 150 barracks built to house them, and the best estimate is that their numbers must have been about 7,000. It was, of course, known that Japan was gradually withdrawing its key facilities underground toward the end of the war, but the scale of the works only slowly came to be appreciated afterward. Thirty years after the war ended, the Ministry of Construction did a survey that found that there were still tunnels in 3,394 places; many others must have been destroyed in the intervening years.[78] Matsushiro was simply the largest and most important of a vast range of facilities. Still, in 1992, huge new tunnels were being discovered. In the Nara vicinity, a maze of tunnels of some two kilometers in length was revealed, and other documents in the Defense Agency archives detailed excavations at 549 places, most of which have still even to be rediscovered.[79] The exact length of tunnels at Matsushiro is not known, but certainly exceeded ten kilometers. Working conditions were poor and dangerous, supervision harsh, food and medical supplies grossly inadequate. Countless workers died, with survivors recalling that the number of deaths was often five or six per day. The project was due to be completed and ready for use in August 1945, with facilities ready to accommodate the emperor and his retinue, the Imperial Army Headquarters, the government, bureaucracy, and national media. Even as final preparations were being made for this retreat into the mountains[80] and the imminent Battle for the Mainland (what the Americans were referring to as Operation Olympic), and the mobilizing of women and old men with bamboo spears to fight it, the bombs were dropped on Hiroshima and Nagasaki, and by the famous imperial intervention of August 10 the decision to accept the Potsdam declaration (on condition of maintaining the national polity, or kokutai) was adopted.[81] One consideration in the emperor's mind was the impossibility of guaranteeing the safe removal of the imperial regalia— the sacred mirror, sword, and jewel—to Nagano.[82] Even in the interval between the issue of the Potsdam Declaration (July 26, 1945) and the dropping of the atomic bomb on Hiroshima (August 6), the emperor's mind was focused above all on "defense of the imperial regalia"[83] and when he eventually authorized surrender he did so only on condition that his own position be upheld. Perhaps another consideration might have been his growing sense that there was little to fear for his own personal safety in a surrender, since it was obvious to him that the bombing raids had carefully avoided his palace in Tokyo, and there might be much to fear about the eventual outcome of a last ditch stand in the Nagano mountains.

The parallel with the other great wartime construction projects, such as that of the Burma-Thailand Railway on which Western prisoners and Southeast Asian laborers were mobilized between November 1942 and October 1943, is striking: Supervision was ruthless, workers were expendable, targets were absolute; and in both cases the final product was either not used at all (Matsushiro) or used only briefly to carry 65,000 Japanese soldiers to their deaths in the Imphal campaign (Burma-Thailand).[84] Part of the Matsushiro complex was at least eventually put to good postwar use as a national seismological institute. But the project has to be viewed not only as a pointer to the prolonged and catastrophic war that might have raged through the main islands of Japan long after August 1945, but also to the complex debts Japan owes to its neighbor, Korea. Financial compensation is probably out of the question, but the demand for the truth to be recognized and properly commemorated about huge projects such as Matsushiro is fair and reasonable. To a large extent it is also true, as Higaki, the historian of Matsushiro, observes, that the colonial relationship between Japan and Korea was what made it possible for Japan to construct not only Matsushiro, but also many roads, bridges, tunnels, airfields, ports, mines, factories, dams, and other works, even including the National Diet buildings. This, in sum, made possible Japan's postwar recovery and high growth.[85] It is the denial of that relationship as well as the reluctance to meet any individual claims for compensation that has blocked full trust and cooperation between the two countries in the postwar period.

The Shinjuku Bones Affair

A similar case in which the sincerity of the Japanese government authorities in meeting the pledges by Prime Minister Hosokawa and others that the truth will be honestly and responsibly faced arises out of the handling of the affair of the Shinjuku bones. In July 1991, in the course of construction work on a new building for the National Institute of Health in Tokyo's Shinjuku Ward, a large quantity of human remains was unearthed.[86] They were clearly human remains, but consisted of about thirty-five skulls and other bones, rather than whole skeletons. The site was the wartime location of the Army Medical College, established in 1928, and had been state-owned land throughout modern times. The bones were discovered adjacent to the site of the Anti-Epidemic Laboratory, the institution responsible for Unit 731 (or the Ishii Unit, after its commander General Ishii Shirō, whose headquarters were outside Harbin in China) and for other related units elsewhere in China and Southeast Asia. Thousands of Chinese, Russian, Korean, and Western prisoners were killed by this unit, often after horrifying experiments involving freezing or deliberate infection with various diseases. Prisoners entrusted to the Ishii Unit became known as maruta (or logs), a term that served to divest them of humanity and make possible their brutalization. When the bones were discovered at the site of the old hospital, there was naturally a suspicion that they were in some way connected with the unit. The crimes of Unit 731 were covered up after 1945 by occupation orders designed to secure and preserve the secret fruits of its research. When the Soviet court at Khabarovsk put a group of senior officers from the unit on trial, detailing especially their work in bacteriological warfare, the U.S. authorities dismissed the evidence as a fabrication. In due course, it was confirmed by evidence from U.S. archives that emerged under Freedom of Information Act and by the direct testimony of former members of the unit. By the early 1980s, there were serious studies on the unit in newspapers and journals, academic and popular books, and documentary films, and in 1981, even the Ministry of Education had to concede that there had been such a thing as Unit 731, as it had been forced to yield on its attempts to substitute words like "advance" for "invasion" in describing the movement of Japanese forces into China. But the ministry continued to fight—clause by clause—to neutralize or minimize the way the information was presented in school history texts. By the early 1990s, it was still stubbornly resisting evidence of experimentation on live human beings or the actual use of bacteriological warfare against China and the USSR, and the evidence that indicated the involvement in the unit's work, not only of so-called mad scientists such as Ishii, but of the most prestigious professors of the medical schools of the imperial universities. If Tsuneishi Kei'ichi, the leading historian of the unit, is right, what he calls the "Ishii network" (to distinguish the broad infrastructure of the wartime medical-scientific establishment that encouraged and supported Ishii's work from the actual staff working at Harbin and other Chinese or Southeast Asian cities) flourished after the war, and large and sensitive questions about war responsibility remain to be faced within these core professions.[87]

In 1991, the Ministry of Health refused requests from Shinjuku Ward to institute a full investigation and simply ordered that the bones be quickly disposed of. Public protest delayed this, and at the ward's request, an investigation was eventually conducted by a private university hospital, which reported in April 1992 that the remains were of mixed racial origin, came from about 100 different individuals, and showed signs of violence (bullet holes) and surgical experimentation (skull incisions). The ministry still refused to pursue any investigation (to order DNA tests, or searches for documentary or other leads to the identity of the remains), and continued to press to have the bones destroyed. By late 1994, both national and local authorities were in agreement that the bones should be disposed of. Such an attitude fitted ill with the expressed wish of government leaders to achieve sincere reconciliation with neighbor countries and to face the truth about the war; instead, it smacked of the desire to destroy possibly incriminating evidence.[88]

The end of the Cold War seemed not to have had any impact on the way this matter was handled, although the crimes involved were clearly crimes both of World War Two, the cause to which Ishii and his colleagues were devoted, and the Cold War, since its exigencies led the United States to become complicit in the original crimes by covering them up and protecting their principals. It is too late now to do much about the human rights of the thousands of people murdered by the unit, but their families' rights do deserve respect, and there is a strong general public right to know the historical truth about what was done and who was involved in ordering or permitting it to be done. Generalized talk about Japan's desire to settle the issues left over from its wars has to be measured not only in terms of the words of prime ministers on formal state occasions, but also in terms of its handling of small and superficially trivial matters such as the Shinjuku bones.

Abandoned Children (*Zanryū koji*)

A different but equally serious legacy of the war that still remains to be settled by Japan is the matter of the so-called *zanryū koji*, or the left-behind children. These are the children of Japanese settlers in Manchukuo, the area of Northeast China under Japanese control between 1932 and 1945. At war's end, there were over two million Japanese in Manchukuo, 600,000 soldiers, and more than one-and-a-half-million civilians. The latter included not only state officials, policemen, doctors, engineers, scientists, and clerks, but also more than a quarter of a million "settlers" living in frontier-style, fortified agricultural communities. About 1,270,000 eventually escaped back to Japan, 250,000 died of cold or hunger or in violent clashes of one kind or another, and the remainder were captured by Soviet forces and sent to Siberia.[89] In this catastrophe, amid flight, starvation, panic, and occasional group suicide, many children were abandoned, lost, sold for a pig or a bag of beans, or simply orphaned and adopted by some Chinese family. For thirty years after the war, they were officially ignored by Japan. The resumption of diplomatic relations with China in the 1970s made it impossible to continue doing so. But in the 1980s and 1990s, delegation after delegation continued to come to Japan searching for their long-lost families. Newspapers and television published photographs, details of blood grouping and physical characteristics and of any known siblings, pathetic pictures of fragments of old blankets that the infants of fifty years ago had been wrapped in, a few Japanese words or names that had been remembered, and the story, as much as was known, of how the children had come to be handed over to their Chinese foster families, whether on the roadside, in front of a railway station, or outside a Japanese internment camp. By 1994, a total of 4,600 families—nearly 15,000 people—had returned to settle in Japan.[90]

The pitiful and tragic stories told by these middle-aged Sino-Japanese men and women provided a disconcerting reminder of the personal tragedies of the war and constituted another matter still to be settled. In November 1994, the tenth such delegation visited Japan, but the number of those who were successful in locating their families had been steadily decreasing.[91] Despite everything, the gap to be bridged would be likely to prove too much for most of them.[92] In the 1990s, the Japanese government conceded the right of the long-abandoned Japanese to return, whether they had found their kin or not, but there were many problems. The returnees did not speak Japanese, and in middle age, they would not be quick to learn. Their livelihood would have to be assured. Most now had a Chinese family that depended on them, but the Japanese government would only cover the repatriation costs of the *koji* her- or himself, plus one partner and any children younger than twenty. For other family members, immigration barriers were formidable.

Here was a group of Japanese who were the direct and tragic heirs of the failed internationalization of the 1930s and 1940s. Their experience was a sad illustration of the emptiness of the slogans of that time, while offering a moving testimony to the simple humanity that led so many ordinary Chinese to take in and care for abandoned children as their own, regardless of their blood or origin. The response of the Japanese state and society in the 1990s to them would be a litmus test of how different the inner content of the internationalization of the 1990s would be. So far, the slow, grudging, and partial efforts to accommodate the zanryū koji and their families suggested that there was still a strong link between the ideology of the 1930s and that of the

1990s. The Chinese foster parents were now elderly, often financially dependent, and of little if any economically productive potential. The Japanese government has shown no desire to welcome or care for them and little sense of gratitude for their having cared for Japanese children in the collapsed ruins of its generation's new world order. There is little to indicate that the Japanese government wants to treat the zanryū koji as a model or test case for openness and internationalism. As the *Asahi* noted in November 1994, the problem of the left-behind Japanese may be seen as part of the larger issue of postwar compensation that still has to be settled.[93]

Around 1990, the complex moral questions that arise from all of these unsettled legacies of the war began to come under judicial scrutiny as the subject of legal claims, both before courts in Japan and (in the case of the comfort women) international judicial bodies.

Korea

The question of Japanese responsibility for war claims by Koreans or of Japan's colonial record generally was not raised in any form in the postwar trials at Tokyo and elsewhere. Koreans who had been impressed into the Japanese forces and had fought or served entirely as Japanese until 1945 lost their Japanese citizenship with the collapse of the empire and so, while Japanese veterans were the beneficiaries of various pension and welfare benefits, Koreans (and Taiwanese) were excluded. The responsibility for colonialism was not formally admitted until Prime Minister Hosokawa did so in 1993. While the complex matter of claims by North Korea confronts the diplomatic task force that has yet to deal with the normalization of relations between Japan and North Korea, the matters at issue with South Korea are the biggest that Japan has to face. The greatest numbers of individual claimants among both the comfort women and the forced laborers are Korean, while there are also many other claims to do with former Korean soldiers or civilian workers of various kinds impressed into the service of the Japanese war machine. Indeed, it could be argued that the policies of assimilation by imposition of the Japanese language, Japanese names and religion, and the suppression of all the basic elements of what constituted Korean identity, amounted to a strategy for genocide, an attempt to wipe out a distinctive culture and national identity by a combination of massive force and persuasion. The violent abuse of the reproductive capacity of a generation of young women could be seen as constituting a central part of such a strategy.[94]

Between 1939 and 1945, around 725,000 Korean ordinary laborers and 145,000 military laborers were mobilized and sent to mines, construction sites, and factories in Japan, China, Sakhalin, Southeast Asia, the South Pacific, and Korea itself. An additional number, of which there is no precise record, were mobilized for the urgent construction of tunnels, airfields, and other installations in the last year of the war, and there was also no record kept of the number of women and girls who were seized (or "encouraged to volunteer") and sent either into factories or military brothels.[95] Overall, between one and one-and-a-half million Koreans were mobilized. As part of this enormous uprooting of people, the Japanese Government General of Korea sent 150,000 men to serve as laborers in the mines or in building landing strips or other military facilities in Sakhalin. The precise numbers are not known, because it was 1991 before the Japanese government began to search its files for relevant information, such as lists of names, and to share the information with South Korea.[96] At war's end, many in Sakhalin were killed, and it may be that a general massacre was planned.[97] After the surrender, the territory was returned to the Soviet Union: Japanese, and Koreans who were prepared to accept repatriation to North Korea, were repatriated; but some 42,000 South Koreans were abandoned, as South Korea had no diplomatic relations with the Soviet Union, and Japan simply ignored their plight. In other words, until 1945, Koreans were mobilized to serve the Japanese cause and treated as if they were Japanese, and thereafter Japan simply wiped its hands of them. Repatriation to South Korea began very slowly in 1988, after the end of the Cold War, but by 1994, there were an estimated 7,000 Koreans brought there during the war left in Sakhalin, along with 30,000 of their descendants.[98] In August 1990, suits for compensation (ten million yen each) were launched by a group of twenty-one of these abandoned Koreans. The Japanese government began to pay the cost of the monthly charter flights between Sakhalin and Seoul in 1988, and in late 1994, it went somewhat further toward recognizing responsibility by offering to build a dormitory and otherwise help in providing housing in South Korea for the returnees.[99] The matter of compensation, however, remained to be settled.

In December 1991 and February 1992, 35,000 former South Korean soldiers and 1,100 ex-employees of the Imperial Japanese Army filed suit for unpaid wages and compensation in the Tokyo District Court. Other Koreans, who had been taken to work in the Mitsubishi Heavy Industries plant in Hiroshima in 1944 and become victims of the atomic bomb, launched an action for four billion yen in unpaid wages and compensation over their sufferings as forced laborers. They had been unsuccessfully pursuing Mitsubishi with their case since 1968.[100] In November 1991, six Koreans, former conscripted workers for the Imperial Japanese Army who had been tried and convicted as war criminals after the war, plus the family of one man who had been executed, also filed suit in the Tokyo District Court. They claimed they had been unjustly made to bear the war responsibility of Japan (including that of the Japanese emperor), protested against their exclusion from the relief provided by the Japanese government for Japanese soldiers, and sought apology and compensation (130 million yen).[101] Other actions are pending for compensation for unpaid wages by Japanese companies and for other matters such as the victims of the loss (in mysterious circumstances) of the repatriation ship *Ukishima-maru*, which sank en route from Maizuru to Korea on August 24, 1945, with 550 Koreans on board; many suspect the ship was deliberately sunk.

Taiwan

Taiwan was also a part of the Japanese empire until 1945. Many Taiwanese were conscripted as soldiers or in various auxiliary capacities into the Japanese forces in the general mobilization of 1938. Of the 207,183 men sent to various fronts of the war, some 33,000 died.[102] To add insult to injury, most had kept their savings in military post office accounts, which vanished with the collapse in 1945.[103] But, on the ground that they ceased to be Japanese when the war ended in defeat, successive Japanese governments denied any responsibility to compensate or care for them or their families. In 1988, the Diet passed a law that offered two million yen in what was described as "consolation money" to each Taiwanese who had been wounded (or to the families of deceased or wounded veterans). The contrast between that sum and the approximately thirty-two million yen that would have been received by that time in accumulated benefits by a Japanese veteran was marked, although (as the *Japan Times* noted) "the Taiwanese who served in the Japanese Imperial Army were treated as Japanese subjects during the war, and were exposed to the same dangers and suffered the same wounds as Japanese soldiers."[104] In October 1991, the Taiwan Federation of Former Japanese Soldiers and Bereaved Families filed suit in Tokyo seeking unpaid wages from the war and the return of the savings they had deposited in military post offices. In November 1994, the association rejected an offer of twenty billion yen for unpaid salaries as a joke, and in December, the Japanese government made a further offer of thirty-five billion to cover all debts owed to the Taiwanese from the period when Taiwan was a Japanese colony. That offer too was rejected, and Wang Jin-pyng [sic], deputy speaker of the National Assembly and negotiator for Taiwan on the issue, estimated that the actual Japanese indebtedness amounted to sixty times what had been offered, or about two trillion yen ($20 billion).[105]

China

The scale of devastation wrought by the long war was greatest in China. Throughout the war with the Western powers, Japan's main armies, over a million men by 1945, were tied down in China; yet officially it refused (and refuses) to recognize the events of 1931–45 as a war. It was merely the "China Incident." There were around twenty million Chinese casualties, and incalculable disruption and destruction. Nanking and Harbin (or Unit 731) are both names symbolic of particular forms of atrocity, but for people in China itself, particularly the generation that lived and suffered through the war, countless other names are equally evocative, and although a vague sense of the horrors of the war as symbolized in particular by the single word Nanking is widespread in Japan, the concentration on that episode and the focusing of debate around it has fed the impression that this was a brief and particular event, uncharacteristic of the war as a whole. Nothing could be further from the truth, but the record of the China Incident, as the war with China continues to be called, is only dimly known, and many details continue to filter through slowly to historical and popular consciousness. Many of the comfort women and forced laborers were, of course, Chinese, and the left-behind children were abandoned in China, but the substance of the long war of 1931–45 still remains largely misunderstood. The Japan-as-victim moments of the war are far more deeply etched on the popular memory than those of Japan-as-aggressor, and the purity of purpose and splendor of initial ideal remembered while the horrors committed in the name of the ideal are forgotten.

In constructing the paradise of the kingly way in Manchukuo after 1931, Japan confiscated huge tracts of land to establish villages of its own farmer-settlers, conducted successive ruthless military campaigns to crush resistance, pursued massive social engineering designed to relocate the population into fortified villages and so isolate the resistance, and mobilized millions into slave labor battalions to work in the mines or on construction or other military tasks.[106] Mass graves (*wanren keng*, or ten-thousand-people pits) of victims of the Japanese punctuate the landscape, from the one containing 2,500 villagers massacred in the village of Ping-ding-shan near Fushun in September 1932,[107] through those of slave laborers from the mines and construction sites. One such pit held 17,000 victims of the construction of the Feng-man Dam near Changchun; another the 1,000 residents of the village of Laohegou in Jilin who were killed over five days in May 1935 (and which was only recorded in detail in 1994).[108]

From 1937, the fighting spread from Manchukuo into the rest of China. Particularly in the north, the attempt to impose the Japanese will and to root out the Chinese Eighth Route Army's resistance led to the adoption of the strategy of terror known as the Three Alls (Kill All, Burn All, Loot All), and to a lesser-known but probably even more catastrophic attempt, known as the *mujinku* (people-free zone) strategy. The Japanese tried to cut off the guerrillas' support by clearing the population from a vast swathe of countryside, burning their homes, concentrating them in fortified villages, and leaving them surrounded by a free-fire zone.[109] Such was the violence and the upheaval of these years that the official history of Jehol Province notes a steep decline in its population over the twelve and a half years of war.[110]

Among the forgotten or neglected crimes of the war were the Japanese Army's drug trafficking and its development and use of chemical and bacteriological weapons. From 1932 to 1945, in a network of secret installations in Harbin, Nanking, and Tokyo itself, Japan carried out systematic and large-scale research and development of bacteriological warfare techniques for the promotion and dissemination of diseases from plague to anthrax. Live prisoners were used for experimental purposes and disposed of when no longer needed. At least 4,000 were killed at Harbin by the end of the war.[111] Japan also manufactured and stored a large stockpile of other poisonous and illegal weapons in China, including mustard gas, lewisite, and hydrocyanic acid, which it used on several battlefronts in China during the war and then just dumped when the war ended. Chinese sources subsequently found scattered in dumps in the northeast of the country around 2 million chemical warheads and 1,000 tons of poisonous chemicals. In some places, such as Dunhwa in Jilin Province, tens of thousands of weapons were buried, and the containers slowly decayed, killing several thousand people and injuring countless others while leaving China with a huge public-health problem. The questions of possible genetic and environmental damage have scarcely begun to be addressed.[112] Having ignored repeated demands from China that the abandoned chemical weapons be properly neutralized and disposed of, Japan found that it would not be admitted to ratification of the 1993 United Nations Convention on the Prohibition of Chemical Weapons unless it responded, and early in 1995, a Japanese bomb-disposal mission finally set out for China to start cleaning up the mess left behind fifty years earlier.[113]

Where the evidence of chemical- and bacteriological-warfare crimes was deliberately covered up at the Tokyo Trials by the United States (which was anxious to acquire the technology for its own purposes and which thereafter assumed a shared responsibility for the crimes), Japan's narcotics trafficking in China was covered up even longer because of the almost complete success of the military in destroying relevant records. Only from the 1980s, and largely by chance, did materials appear that allowed a picture to be put together of the way in which the Japanese army in China deliberately encouraged the large-scale cultivation and trade of opium. The production, transport, sale, and use of opium, legal (in China) under Japanese rule, was a highly profitable business; mine workers were paid with opium in some cases, and around 315 tons of morphine was refined annually at the Port Arthur plant during the Japanese occupation.[114] The profits from the business were an important source of secret military funding, and addiction was deliberately promoted in order to sap the morale of the Chinese resistance. Jehol Province was the center of the Japanese opium industry, although it expanded as far as Hainan Island. Opium was even secretly imported from Iran. Scholars such as Eguchi Kei'ichi argue persuasively that the scale was such as to justify the use of the term Sino-Japanese Opium War.[115]

Another recent Japanese study tackles the heart of the Japan-as victim psychology—the allied bombing with explosive and incendiary weapons of the innocent civilian inhabitants of Tokyo, Nagoya, and

Osaka, and the atomic bomb attacks on Hiroshima and Nagasaki—by demonstrating that the massive aerial bombardment of civilian populations was actually a distinctive *Japanese* contribution to the history of warfare, the attacks on its cities merely an extension of the indiscriminate bombing with which during the long war with China, Japan had pulverized various Chinese cities, especially the Chinese (nationalist) wartime capital of Chungking.[116] The fascist bombing of Guernica in 1937 during the Spanish Civil War is commonly thought to have marked the first use of aerial bombing of a city, which became known in Europe during and after World War Two as "strategic bombing." But the military affairs critic Maeda Tetsuo reminds us of the Japanese "missing link" in the evolution of strategic bombing: the Japanese bombing of the cities of Chinchow in 1931 and Shanghai in 1932, followed by the similar aerial assaults on Nanking, Wuhan, Shanghai, and Canton in 1937. These were followed by the extraordinarily concentrated bombing of Chungking, which lasted not one day (like Guernica) but three years beginning in May 1939. Over 218 raids caused the direct deaths of around 12,000 people and terrorized the entire urban population, forcing them to live a troglodytic existence in underground shelters for long periods.[117] The Japanese Army and Navy dropped over Chungking a mixture of explosive and incendiary devices (the forerunner of napalm) designed to maximize destruction and terror and erode political will. Immense havoc was wrought in enormous raids for which the Japanese forces mobilized over 1,000 planes over one continuous period of 150 hours in the summer of 1941, to attack a city that had already been reported flattened.[118]

This deliberate use of massively concentrated force against a helpless civilian population is precisely what happened in 1945 when the tactic was turned against Japan by Allied commanders, many of whom were very familiar with what Japan had done in China. Even Hitler, as Maeda notes, had at first been reluctant to license such indiscriminate assaults on British cities as the Japanese command embraced.[119] The Japanese contribution to the evolution of strategic bombing, including the use of incendiary bombs designed to burn cities, has not been widely appreciated. It led from Chungking to Tokyo, then to the many cities of Korea during the Korean War, to Vietnam, and most recently to the Iran-Iraq War, and the same thinking was evident in the targeting of ICBM missiles on cities on either side of the Iron Curtain during the Cold War. The massacre of Chungking does not fit well with the view of 1945 as a time of brutal and unwarranted Allied bombing of innocent Japanese civilians.

In comparison with the devastation wrought in China, the scale of claims for compensation has been minuscule. Memories in China are long, however, and the 230-million-silver-yuan payment (equivalent then to about three times the annual revenues of the Qing dynasty) that was exacted by Japan from the Chinese government as a consequence of its defeat in the relatively small-scale war of 1894–95 has certainly not been forgotten.[120]

Japan did not resume governmental relations with China until 1972, and in the joint declaration issued on that occasion, the Chinese government (like that of Taiwan, the Republic of China, in 1952) renounced any entitlement to war reparations. Since 1991, however, moves to open individual claims to compensation began, and in 1992, a bill was introduced in the Chinese People's Congress in Beijing demanding $180 billion in reparations for wartime damage suffered by Chinese civilians. According to the spokesman for this movement, Tung Zeng, what the Chinese government had renounced was entitlement to state reparation only (which he estimated to be about $120 billion). The entitlement to private claims for noncombatant losses and injuries, including those who were subjected to forced labor, abused women, victims of human experimentation, and victims of bombing losses, which should not be affected by the government's act of renunciation, was estimated to amount to around $180 billion (about nineteen trillion yen). Although this movement has been subjected to pressure from party and government in China, and the bill has not been brought to a vote, it is reported to have been widely circulated and gained considerable support.[121] In April 1995, the first suits by a group of Chinese civilians seeking compensation for inhumane, illegal acts, were filed in the Tokyo courts by the Committee for Chinese Civilians Seeking Compensation from Japan.

To the extent that civil society strengthens and private organizations gain the freedom to organize and promote their interests in China, fresh claims by various groups of victims of the war are bound to emerge, with the victims of Nanking, Harbin, and Chungking prominent among them. While it is understandable that Japanese bureaucrats and politicians should be fearful of the consequences of opening the floodgates to private compensation claims from China, and that it should prefer to keep the issue at the level of a bargaining chip that the

Chinese government will occasionally place on the table to clinch a deal of one kind or another, it is hard to understand, much less respect, the official Japanese position that all such entitlements could have been extinguished by a simple government statement. The commitment to human rights and democracy, and to the principle that civil society is superior to the state, that is adopted by Japan in international forums remains to be tested by the degree of its sensitivity to the justice of these claims.

Hong Kong

The major claim from citizens of Hong Kong relates to the losses of wealth and property suffered during the Japanese occupation from December 1941 to August 1945, particularly as a result of the forced conversion of all Hong Kong dollars into Japanese military scrip (*gunpyō*), which became worthless following the Japanese defeat. In August 1993, a group of seventeen people brought suit for the recovery of 760 million yen in losses resulting from forced exchange of this kind. Even as the action was brought, and in the expectation encouraged by the Hosokawa statements that the post-LDP governments might honor their obligations in this matter, forged gunpyō began to appear and the exchange value of the notes suddenly trebled on the Hong Kong exchange.[122]

Southeast Asia

The Imperial Japanese Army's capture of Singapore and the Malay peninsula at the end of 1941 was followed immediately by violent purges designed especially to root out any possible resistance on the part of the local Chinese communities. Around 40,000 to 50,000 were massacred in Singapore—5,000 was the figure conceded even by the Japanese defense lawyers at the postwar trials—followed by several more tens of thousands of people murdered on the Malay peninsula and sporadic violence continuing throughout the Japanese occupation.[123] Large numbers of men were mobilized and sent to labor battalions throughout the region, including work on the Burma-Thailand Railway, where the casualty rate from disease, overwork, and abuse was particularly high.[124] In the Philippines, the war raged long and violently, leaving an estimated 1.1 million dead (including many killed in mass roundups of guerrilla suspects). Many suffered various kinds of personal and property losses, estimated late in 1945 to have amounted to over one billion dollars.[125] Postwar settlement of claims arising from these occupations was summary and minimal. The Philippines' reparations payment was widely seen as a second wave of Japanese aggression rather than a settlement of war debts.

Throughout Southeast Asia, however, the demand for reparations and compensation was slowly gathering strength in the early 1990s. A group of 300 survivors of the Burma-Thailand Railway workforce is seeking $20,000 each in unpaid wages; massacre survivors in Singapore are preparing their claim.[126] In October 1991, a group representing some 23,000 (out of about 50,000) Indonesians who had served as wartime soldiers, or *heiho*, under the Japanese demanded compensation amounting to about $650 million in unpaid salaries.[127] But for others, the climate was still unfavorable. The inhibition preventing women in traditional Islamic societies from voicing their claim for having been sexually abused as comfort women was strong. The importance of the contemporary economic relationship was seen as paramount by all governments in the region, and media for the expression of private, or civil society interests were still weak (as was shown by the 1994 government order for the closure of *Tempo*, the Indonesian journal that had given strongest support to the claims of former comfort women and Rōmusha). The difficulties faced by aging victims of the war in seeking compensation were highlighted during the visit of Japanese Prime Minister Hosokawa to Southeast Asia in September 1993. The Japanese government lobbied through its Malaysian embassy to isolate the former comfort women from any expression of official support,[128] while Prime Minister Mahathir, anxious to secure Japanese backing for his proposed East Asian Economic Council (EAEC) initiative, publicly urged Japan to put the war behind it and declared that his government would not encourage the pursuit of compensation claims against Japan.[129]

The Pacific Islands

Compensation claims by the inhabitants of the Melanesian islands have been rejected by Japan on the ground that all such matters were settled by the Micronesia Agreement of 1969. However, in reaching this deal, no consideration was taken of the views of the victims themselves, and no reference was made to the aggression that had occurred or responsibility for it. Consequently, the view is widespread that the issue of war still remains to be settled. From Belau, both parliamentary and private organizations pressing the case for compensation from Tokyo have been gathering momentum in the early 1990s, and parliamentary committees of the Republic of the Marshall Islands have begun investigations into massacres by Japanese forces of inhabitants at various atolls early in 1945, from which it is expected that new claims will issue.[130] Among the smallest claims is that by the handful of people of the atoll of Attu in the Aleutians, who were all summarily transported to Japan following the Japanese capture of the islands in mid-1942 and were unable to return until early in 1946 (and even then not to their own island, which had become strategically vital to the United States).[131]

The island of Nauru announced in 1994 that it would ask Japan to open discussions on the matter of reparations. One report estimated that 40 percent of the island's population died during the war, most having been sent to Truk Island, where they were forced to work on the construction of the airfield and other works. The government of the Marshall Islands, independent since 1991, was also reported to be considering action, claiming that they were inhibited from doing so until now by the American administration. Similar moves for compensation for victims of murder and rape during the Japanese occupation in Papua New Guinea were reported.[132]

Western POWs

Although the countries signing the San Francisco Peace Treaty in 1951 formally abandoned any claims to redress, individual victims argue that their governments could not have extinguished their rights to compensation. They quoted the U.N. Human Rights Commission view, that "victims have the right to reparation, rehabilitation and compensation from the state whose nationals have done such deeds."[133] The plight of the 140,000-odd Western POWs has been well documented, perhaps never more vividly and movingly than in Gavan Daws's account of "the truth of life according to a POW." One paragraph of Daws' book summarizes the record:

> The Japanese were not directly genocidal in their POW camps. They did not herd their white prisoners into gas chambers and burn their

corpses in ovens. But they drove them toward mass death all the same. They beat them until they fell, then beat them for bleeding. They denied them medical treatment. They starved them . . . They sacrificed prisoners in medical experiments . . . If the war had lasted another year, there would not have been a POW alive.[134]

Many ex-POWs and former civilian detainees received small "consolation" payments in 1956 and 1961 out of liquidated Japanese assets in Southeast Asia, but the amounts were trivial, about $75 each, and were not regarded as in any way tantamount to compensation. Subsequently, claims have been made against both the Japanese state and private companies, with both denying any responsibility. Japanese companies plead that the wartime labor system under which the POWs were mobilized was proper and legal or that there is no continuity between the wartime and present-day companies (even when run under the same name). In 1993, the British Association of Japanese Labour Camp Survivors, with a membership of 12,000, demanded $200 million compensation and threatened legal action against Japanese companies such as Mitsubishi and Nissan (who benefited from wartime slave labor),[135] and in January 1995, a group representing 21,000 former Allied military and civilian prisoners of Japanese labor camps filed suit claiming violation of international laws banning mistreatment for wartime captives. A separate demand was launched in 1990 with the Human Rights Commission of the United Nations for $25,000 each on behalf of the 6,600 claimants of the Queensland Ex-Prisoners-of-War Reparations Committee, which later developed its claim into one for $A500 million to fund an International Medical Research Institute specializing in tropical diseases as a collective tribute to former prisoners of war.[136]

Uilta and Other Peoples

The plight of the various aboriginal peoples living on the fringes of the then Japanese empire who suffered from the war has taken longest to become known. It took nearly fifty years from the war's end before demands for recognition of their rights and compensation for their wartime treatment began to be voiced. The fate of the Uilta, Nivkh, Ul'chi, and other peoples of the island territory of Sakhalin, the southern half of which was ruled by Japan under the Russo-Japanese War settlement between 1905 and 1945, is particularly poignant. Forced by the Japanese colonial rulers to adopt Japanese names and to speak Japanese, they were subject to the general wartime mobilization under which many young men were conscripted for service as scouts, spies, laborers, or soldiers. When the war ended and Japanese jurisdiction ceased, they were denied any right of "repatriation" to Japan, and some were captured and imprisoned in Siberian camps for up to ten years as Japanese spies. Only since the end of the Cold War has contact been resumed between those who remained in what thereafter became Soviet territory and those who were sent back from their Siberian prison camps to a Japan they had never known, where, to add insult to injury, they were denied any pension or other allowance because they were not deemed "Japanese." They were claiming apology, the right to visit their family graves in whichever nation they happened to be, and compensation in the sum of 200 million yen in pensions or other entitlements for survivors and their families.[137]

What to Do?

While writs against it piled up in the courts and demonstrations and protests continued in the capitals of neighboring countries, the Japanese government studied its options. Public opinion seemed to be inclining toward sympathetic response to the claims. Whereas surveys in 1986–87 found around 85 percent of the Japanese people thinking of the Japanese experience of the war as that of victim (*higaisha*) and only 10 percent of Japan as assailant (*kagaisha*),[138] by late 1993, nearly 60 percent agreed it had been an aggressive war, and well over 50 percent that some form of compensation should be paid.[139] A separate survey found 51 percent support for a positive attitude to the compensation issue, with only 37 percent sticking to the official insistence that all claims should be treated as settled (*ketchakuzumi*).[140]

However, direct payments to individual victims were ruled out as all compensation matters are held to have been settled by the San Francisco Peace Treaty of 1951 and other subsequent bilateral treaties. This position reflects the bureaucratic insistence that the fiscal burden that would flow from any relaxation of this principle would be intolerable. Instead of compensation, it was announced in September 1994 that under a "Peace, Friendship, and Exchange Initiative" a fund of 100 billion yen ($1 billion) over ten years would be set up for the promotion of youth exchanges with other Asian countries, vocational training programs, and joint research projects on war-related historical projects.[141] Compensation would not be mentioned. There was to be nothing from the government itself for the victims, although a private sector fund would be set up with "broad popular participation," that is, donations from citizens, from which "solatium" payments (which in the case of the comfort women might amount to around $20,000) could be made.[142]

It is hard to imagine that such a formula would satisfy anyone, and it therefore seems certain that the problem will continue well beyond the war's fiftieth anniversary. The initial response from the Seoul-based Korean Council for the Women Drafted for Military Sexual Slavery by Japan was to interpret the measures as "the Japanese government's attempt to avoid its legal responsibility toward the former military comfort women."[143] The Korean group continued to insist that all relevant records and information be disclosed, an official apology be issued, and due redress paid directly to the victims, and that the guilty parties be punished. The International Commission of Jurists also released a report in 1994 that found the government of Japan guilty of war crimes and breaches of the 1922 international law against trafficking in women and children. It proposed the referral of the matter to the International Court of Justice and called on the international community to put pressure on Japan to take "adequate measures to rehabilitate and provide full restitution to the women," including housing, medical, and financial aid, and as an interim measure to make individual payments of four million yen ($40,000) to each of the women.[144] This report was also critical of the Allied countries that at the end of the war had done nothing to bring the offenders to trial or obtain reparations for the victims, despite full knowledge of the crimes.

To set in context the $1 billion figure that the Japanese government proposed in 1994 as its final response to the many residual problems of the war, recall that the Japanese contribution to the Gulf War was a cool $13 billion, that about $3 billion is paid *every year* to cover the costs to the United States of maintaining its forces and military installations in Japan, that compensation payments to Japanese atomic-bomb victims have amounted to about $1.3 billion, and that billions of dollars are paid out every year ($17 billion in 1994) to Japanese veterans and their families in pensions and allowances. In 1990, even the 110,000 Japanese civilian detainees in North America, whose sufferings no one would even begin to compare with those of the comfort women and other victims, were paid $20,000 each by the governments of the United States and Canada. The U.S. Congress appropriated $1.25 billion and paid out to "any Japanese of any age . . . who had had to spend as little as one day interned on American soil."[145] A personal letter of apology signed by the president was delivered to each former detainee.[146]

The unsettled issue of victim compensation has become a point at which Japan faces a congruence of moral, historical, political, and legal claims. Fifty years after the events, confusion reigns in Tokyo about how to respond to all this, even about what to call the war. Yet some central points may be stated. Despite the purity of initial intent of at least some on the Japanese side, this was not a just or a good war for Japan, but a colonial and an imperial one, fought in defiance of the rules of battle and involving the imposition of a reign of terror over much of Asia. The reason for the wave of claims now rising throughout the region is basically twofold: the unsatisfactory nature of the actual postwar settlement, which recognized only states and gave priority to the economic recovery of Japan over the rights of victims in order to ensure its cooperation with the West in the Cold War; and the slow emergence of a social order in which human rights and the rights of individuals to claim compensation for the violent, brutal, or terroristic treatment meted out to them by states gradually gains acceptance. It is not that Japan alone does, or should, face such claims; far from it. In due course, as Vietnamese society, for example, is transformed and the same basic human rights are recognized, a series of claims for compensation against the governments of the United States and other countries whose forces invaded Vietnam in the 1960s and 1970s may be expected. Indeed, the moral and legal basis for compensation claims to be launched against the government of the United States by the citizens of Hiroshima or Nagasaki, or indeed any of the Japanese cities subjected in 1945 to strategic bombing, would be exactly the same. Likewise, claims against the government of Japan by its citizens for compensation for denial of their human rights and brutal ill treatment during wartime—which would cover, for example, many of the citizens of Okinawa, or the Japanese children deserted in China just as it covers the abandoned Koreans of Sakhalin—deserve to be recognized in the courts.

In other words, the legal implications of the U.N. instruments on human rights that were adopted in the early postwar years are only slowly being realized. The best guarantee that states will honor them will be the demonstration that they will be punished if they do not. The idea that the agreements between states at San Francisco and elsewhere could be seen as extinguishing the entitlement of countless individuals to compensation for having been treated atrociously by the state forces of 1930s and 1940s Japan reflects the sort of value system, characteristic of twentieth-century nationalism, that gives priority to states over individuals, and that, at century's end, is discredited and in process of yielding to a set of values that give priority instead to the inalienable rights of the individual. The universal principle of the obligation to compensate individuals treated by a state in a brutal way and in breach of basic human rights has yet to be established by legal precedent, but the spate of cases now before the Tokyo courts provides an excellent occasion to try to do so. Closely related, and perhaps even more fundamental, is the principle that acts of state be opened to public scrutiny, the principle of shinso kyūmei upon which all the many complainants of Japan's wartime behavior insist.

Financial considerations are important, but it is ethics, morality, and international law, not money, that is at the core of the problem Japan now faces. What the region has sought from Japan for fifty years is not money but evidence of change of heart. The demand by Japan's neighbors for sincerity in its attitude reflects a common perception that Japan is obsessed with monetary values and has lost the sense of virtue and ethics that some would describe as Asian. Proponents of Asianism are notably silent about the pain and suffering of Asian peoples who, in the name of the abstract principle of Japan's Asianism, suffered so much. In the deafness to particular Asian voices and the preference for windy, abstract general principle, much of the rhetoric of contemporary Japanese Asianism resembles that of sixty years ago.

Whether the actual monetary compensation to be paid to the comfort women and others comes from public or private funds, the important point is that the above principle be made clear and that state liability be admitted or declared by the courts.[147] Alternatively, and given the agonizingly slow procedures of the Japanese courts (where the famous case on censorship of school history texts launched by Professor Ienaga Saburō in 1965 still grinds on), the better solution might be a legislative attempt to achieve a comprehensive settlement of compensation claims, based on a clear statement of responsibility.

The 1990 proposal by Doi Takako, then leader of the Japan Socialist Party and later speaker of the lower house of the Diet, that a formal statement of Japan's responsibility for wartime aggression be endorsed by the national Diet in time to mark the fiftieth anniversary of the end of the war (thereby establishing the basis for a historical and moral consensus within Japan and between Japan and its neighbors upon which a shared future could be planned), was followed by tortuous negotiations and political drama. It took until June 1995 for a resolution to finally be adopted. By then, however, the achievement was hollow, in that the opposition and even some of the governing coalition absented themselves from the vote, and the words of the resolution, while conveying deep regret over colonial rule and aggression, fell short of apologizing, much less compensating for them. The actual fate of the bill was uncertain right up to its introduction upon the floor of the house, and its passage on June 9 revealed more the depth of division and the lack of a real consensus than what had been intended. The coalition was opposed by a formidable alliance between a Dietmen's League with well over 200 members, the War Bereaved Families Association (with two million members), the national headquarters of Shinto shrines (*Jinja Honchō*), all linked under the umbrella of the National Committee for the Fiftieth Anniversary of the End of the Second World War.

The climax of the campaign was a mass rally in Tokyo on May 29, 1995, conducted under the slogan Asian Togetherness Festival (*Ajia kyōsei no saiten*), to "thank the war dead and praise Japan for its contribution to the independence of Asian countries." As if to demonstrate that the war had been fought for rather than against Asia, the heads of state of major Asian countries were all invited. None attended, although a few were represented by their Tokyo diplomatic missions. South Korea angrily rejected its invitation as an insult, and China, Singapore, the Philippines, and Malaysia all declined.[148] Participants must have been aware of the previous gathering of such kind, when the various puppets of the Greater East Asian Coprosperity Sphere had gathered in Tokyo in 1943. The gap in historical understanding between the rally organizers and mass sentiment in neighboring Asia was such that the occasion could only be a kind of tragic farce: tragic in the failure it revealed of Japan's self-professed Asianists to close the gap in perception between them and their region despite the passage of more than fifty years, and farcical in the empty and pretentious absurdity of the highly orchestrated occasion.

Although the campaign fizzled out without attracting support from anywhere else in the region, its domestic spokesmen were undaunted.

They included prominent political figures such as Hashimoto Ryūtarō (who was also chairman of the War Bereaved Families Association), Okuno Seisuke, a former Cabinet member and himself a wartime *Kempeitai* (military police) officer,[149] and Itagaki Tadashi, whose father was executed in 1948 as a Class A war criminal. A petition of protest against the proposed Diet resolution was signed by nearly five million people. The spectacle of the bitterness aroused by the Diet resolution suggested that Japan would continue to have difficulty in being accepted with trust by its neighbors. The reason was clear: For decades, it had been laboring over the appropriate term to insert in statements issued by political leaders or by the emperor on the occasion of various visits to neighboring countries. As University of Chicago historian Norma Field observes of this,

> Such refinement is an exercise in ingenuity, the very antithesis of sincerity. Each word is calibrated, and the inferred process of deliberation appears to confer value on the word. The desired effect of the ensemble—at least to date—is to forestall, preferably forever, the loss of value in the form of monetary payment.[150]

Even fifty years after the events, as Lee Kwan Yew put it, "there has not been an open debate within Japan on its role in the war as there has been in Germany."[151]

Thus, in the courts, parliaments, and media of China, Korea, Southeast Asia, and Japan itself, the question of responsibility—evaded, treated as settled, or set aside for fifty years—has emerged in the late-twentieth century as a major public issue. Japan's participation in any new world order in the late-twentieth or early-twenty-first century will depend on its ability to come to terms with and settle outstanding issues from the failed order it tried to create in the 1930s and 1940s. While old soldiers and neonationalists struggle to hold the line with Nagano that the war was a liberation struggle to free Asia from Western imperialism, that it was fought according to generally accepted principles of warfare (with the same regrettable but unintended civilian casualties), and that, despite the military defeat, Japan succeeded in imparting a vital psychological and material impetus to Asian nationalism and economic growth, that line crumbles as the end of century approaches.

Japan is not unique in the difficulty it experiences in coming to terms with its past, or in having fought aggressive or imperialist wars, or in having committed crimes against the rules of war and crimes against humanity in the course of fighting those wars. But, like all countries, it faces a responsibility that cannot be evaded or diminished by reason of the fact that its criminality is common, and in keeping with the higher aspiration it has entrenched in its Constitution—to be a peace state—it has an obligation to be scrupulous in facing the reality of its past militarism and in addressing the wounds caused by it.

Notes

1. For a recent discussion between two conservative historians who argue that the only appropriate term is "that war" (*ano sensō*), see Itō Takashi and Satō Seizaburō, "Ano sensō to wa nan datta no ka," *Chūō kōron*, January 1995, pp. 26–43.

2. Yoshida Yutaka, "Rekishi ishiki wa henkan shiteiru ka," *Sekai*, September 1994, pp. 22–33, at p. 24.

3. Japanese media reports, May 5, 1994.

4. See full text of the interview in *Sandē Mainichi*, May 22, 1994, and discussion, however different his interpretation, in Sase Masamori, "Nagano hatsugen to kokusai kankaku," *Shokun*, July 1994, pp. 162–70.

5. As pointed out by the military historian Hata Ikuhiko (*Mainichi shimbun*, May 8, 1994, quoted in Honda Katsuichi, "Nagano Shigeto hōshō ni kansha suru," *Shūkan kinyōbi*, May 20, 1994, pp. 8–10).

6. Kunihiro Masao, "Hata shushō no osorubeki kokusai kankaku," *Shūkan kinyōbi*, May 20, 1994, pp. 6–7.

7. In the latter category, Ono Kenji, "Nankin daigyakusatsu no kōkei," *Shūkan kinyōbi*, December 10, 1993, pp. 8–13, and Miyamoto Shōgo, "Jin-chū nikki," ibid., pp. 14–21. For a recent discussion of Nanking and its politics, see Ian Buruma, *The Wages of Guilt: Memories of War in Germany and Japan*, London, Jonathan Cape, 1994, pp. 112–35.

8. Hata Ikuhiko, *Nankin jiken*, Chūkō shinsho, 1988.

9. See *Bungei shunjū*, January 1991. Also Ishihara Shintarō, "Nankin daigyakusatsu no kyokō—rekishi no kaizan o haisu," *Shokun*, July 1994, pp. 156–61; and see discussion between Ishihara and Toh Nam-sen. *Mainichi shimbun*, June 5, 1994.

10. Honda, "Nagano Shigeto," p. 9 (citing sources such as the study by Ono Kenji noted in footnote 7 above). And see also Honda's later articles on Nanking in *Shūkan kinyōbi*, August 5, 1994, pp. 21–31.

11. *Asahi shimbun*, May 7, 1994 (quoted in Honda, August 5, 1994).

12. Various press reports, August 1994.

13. "'Hashimoto hatsugen' dō kangaeru," *Asahi shimbun*, November 16, 1994.

14. Buruma, *The Wages of Guilt*.

15. Steve Cranshaw, "Germany Steels Itself to Deal with War Guilt," *The Age* (from *The Independent*), January 16, 1995.

16. Ishihara Shintarō, in interview with Richard McGregor, *The Australian*, May 27, 1994.

17. Charles Smith, "War and Remembrance," *Far Eastern Economic Review*, August 25, 1994, pp. 22–27.

18. Ben Hills "Why Japan Must Face Its Past," *The Age*, October 4, 1994.

19. President Richard von Weizsäcker, speech during a commemorative ceremony in the Plenary Room of the German Bundestag, May 8, 1945. (English text courtesy of the Embassy of the Federal Republic of Germany, Canberra.)

20. Miura Toshiaki, "Kishi Nobusuke gokuchū nikki," *Aera*, January 23, 1995, pp. 13–15. (This article introduces a new political biography of Kishi, which makes extensive use of Kishi's newly released Sugamo prison diaries. See Hara Yoshihisa, *Kishi Nobusuke—kensei no seijika*, Iwanami, 1995.)

21. Quoted in Fujiwara Akira, "Seijika ni motomerareru 'rekishikan'," *Shūkan kinyōbi*, May 20, 1994, pp. 4–6, at p. 4 (*Kishi Nobusuke no kaisō*, Bungei shunju, 1981, and *Kishi Nobusuke no kaisōroku*, Kōsaidō, 1983).

22. Miura, "Kishi Nobusuke," p. 14.

23. On the Fujio and Okuno statements, see Utsumi Aiko et al., "Sensō shokuminchi shihai hansei no kokkai ketsugi o," *Sekai*, March 1995, pp. 160–67.

24. October 31, 1975, Takahashi Kō, *Shōwa tennō hatsugenroku*, Shōgakukan, 1989, pp. 225–26.

25. R. J. B. Bosworth, *Explaining Auschwitz and Hiroshima: History Writing and the Second World War, 1945–1990*, London and New York, Routledge, 1993.

26. Walter Schwarz, "A History That Won't Go Away," *The Guardian Weekly*, January 8, 1989.

27. Mochida Yukio, "Nachizumu o 'sōkessan' suru—Nishi Doitsu gendaishi ronsō," *Asahi jānaru*, November 6, 1987, pp. 87–90.

28. See Gavan McCormack, "Beyond Economism: Japan in a State of Transition," in Gavan McCormack and Yoshio Sugimoto, eds., *Democracy in Contemporary Japan*, Armonk, New York, M.E. Sharpe, 1986, pp. 39–64.

29. For details, see Norma Field, *In the Realm of a Dying Emperor*, New York, Vintage, 1991, pp. 178 ff. Also Buruma, *The Wages of Guilt*, pp. 249–61.

30. Maruyama Hirotaka, "Odokasareru chihō gikai no genron," *Sekai*, February 1989, pp. 15–18.

31. "Nagano hatsugen wa 'naiteki jiko' no bakuhatsu," Kishida Shū, interviewed in *Asahi shimbun*, May 16, 1994. See also brief discussion of Kishida's theories in this volume, Chapter Four.

32. Fujiwara Akira, "Gyakusatsu wa soshikiteki datta," *Shūkan kinyōbi*, August 5, 1994, p. 12.

33. See, for example, Richard Minear, *Victor's Justice: The Tokyo War Crimes Trial*, Princeton, New Jersey, 1971.

34. Gavan McCormack and Hank Nelson, eds., *The Burma-Thailand Railway: Memory and History*, Sydney, Allen and Unwin, and Chiang Mai, Silkworm Books, 1993.

35. Arai Shin'ichi, "Sensō sekinin to wa nani ka," *Sekai*, February 1994, pp. 187–201, at p. 191 (quoting the analysis of Onuma Yasuaki).

36. Ajia ni taisuru Nihon no sensō sekinin o tou minshu hōtei junbikai, *Jikō*

naki sensō sekinin, Ryokufūsha, 1990. The preliminary session of the "Asian People's Tribunal" (*Ajia minshu hōtei*), which planned to meet in Tokyo in 1995 to consider Japan's war crimes, was held in Tokyo in September 1994.

37. See Takeuchi Yoshimi, "Kindai no chōkoku," in *Kindai Nihon shisōshi kōza*, Vol. 7, Chikuma shobō, 1959, and "Sensō sekinin ni tsuite," in *Gendai no hakken*, Vol. 3, Shunjusha, 1960.

38. See the comments of Gotōda Masaharu, a respected and long-term LDP elder statesman, in " 'Nagano hatsugen' naze kurikaesareru," *Asahi shimbun*, May 25, 1994.

39. Kuno Osamu, "Kempō, kokka, shimin—Nihon no gendai," *Shūkan kinyōbi*, January 28, 1994, pp. 10–19.

40. Inoguchi Takashi, interviewed in *Asahi shimbun*, November 16, 1994. (Inoguchi personally lamented that contemporary Japanese thinking should still preserve such racial distinctions.)

41. See the NHK documentary, "Tōkyō saiban e no michi—nani ga naze sabakarenakatta," August 15, 1992. See also the important texts by Herbert P. Bix: "The Showa Emperor's 'Monologue' and the Problem of War Responsibility," *Journal of Japanese Studies*, No. 18, Summer 1993, pp. 295–363, and "Japan's Delayed Surrender," *Diplomatic History*, Vol. 19, No. 2, Spring 1995, pp. 197–225.

42. With over eight million visitors per year, the Smithsonian is the world's most visited museum.

43. I am most grateful to Laura Hein for a copy of her draft text "The Bomb as Public History and Transnational Memory," for the special issue of the *Bulletin of Concerned Asian Scholars* (which appeared later as Vol. 27, No. 2, April–June 1995), pp. 3–15. My brief account of the Smithsonian issue draws on this and on Sodei Rinjirō, "Genbaku tōka no rekishi to seiji," *Sekai*, February 1995, pp. 131–41. The report by Ken Ringle, "Two Views of History Collide over Smithsonian A-Bomb Exhibit," *Washington Post*, September 26, 1994, is also helpful.

44. According to Sodei Rinjirō, "Yanda kioku o chiyu suru 'hirakareta rekishi' no shiten," *Mainichi shimbun*, February 7, 1995.

45. Sebastian Moffett, "Let Nagasaki, Hiroshima Be the Last—Mayors," Reuter, March 15, 1995.

46. Ohe Shinobu,"Hiroshima, Nagasaki o menzai shita Shōwa tennō no sekinin," *Shūkan kinyōbi*, April 28, 1995, pp. 38–41.

47. Ohe points out that the imperial rescript issued to Japanese soldiers and sailors on August 17 differs from his public statement of August 14 in giving the preservation of the national polity from the Soviet threat as the real reason for surrendering to America, Britain, and China.

48. For excerpts from these protest letters, see both Sodei, "Genbaku tōka," and Hein, "The Bomb as Public History."

49. Hugh Davies, "Enola Gay Row Ends in Resignation," *Daily Telegraph*, May 3, 1995.

50. See Sodei Rinjirō, "Paburikku hisutori to wa nani ka," *Sekai*, April 1995, pp. 38–44.

51. The words of General Curtis LeMay, commander of the raid, quoted in Ben Hills, "Tokyo's Hell on Earth," *The Sydney Morning Herald*, March 10, 1995.

For details, see E. Bartlett Kerr, *Flames over Tokyo: The US Army Air Force's Incendiary Campaign against Japan, 1944–45*, New York, D.I. Fine, 1991.

52. Maeda Tetsuo, *Senryaku bakugeki no shisō*, Asahi shimbunsha, 1988. See also Māku Seruden (Mark Selden), "Tōkyō daikūshū kara 'Hiroshima' e," *Shūkan kinyōbi*, May 12, 1995, pp. 42–45, forthcoming in English as "Before the Bomb: 'The Good War', Air Power and the Logic of Mass Destruction," *Contention: Debates in Society, Culture, and Science*, Vol. 4, No. 4, Fall 1995.

53. Teresa Watanabe, "Japanese Mayors Call A-bomb Attack a Crime," *Los Angeles Times*, March 16, 1995.

54. *Asahi shimbun*, November 13, 1993.

55. *Japan Times*, June 5, 1994.

56. "Doitsu ga haraitsuzukeru Nachisu giseisha e no hoshōkin," *Aera*, May 5–12, 1992, pp. 36–37.

57. Text of the treaty in Utsumi Aiko, Koshida Ryō, Tanaka Hiroshi, and Hida Yūichi, eds., *Handobukku—sengo hoshō* (hereafter cited as *Handobukku*), Nashinokisha, 1992 (shiryō 3).

58. See Jon Halliday and Gavan McCormack, *Japanese Imperialism Today: Co-Prosperity in Greater East Asia*, Harmondsworth, Penguin, 1973, pp. 21–22.

59. *Handobukku*, shiryō, No. 25.

60. Arakawa Shinji, "Mikuronesia," *Shūkan kinyōbi*, August 12, 1994, p. 22.

61. Ibid.; *Handobukku*, pp. 154–57.

62. For a convenient resume, see Kim Bu-ja, "Jūgun ianfu," *Handobukku*, pp. 34–35.

63. Suzuki Yūko cites documents concerning the dispatch of 20,000 women to serve the 700,000 men being sent to the Soviet frontier region during the massive maneuvers known as "Kan-toku-en" in 1941. She notes that recent studies suggest a similar proportion elsewhere. Suzuki Yūko, *Chōsenjin jūgun ianfu*, Iwanami bukkuretto, No. 229, 1992, p. 31.

64. Kimura Tetsuo, "Indonesia," *Shūkan kinyōbi*, August 12, 1994, p. 26.

65. On one such massacre, at Truk Island, see Kim Bu-ja, "Jūgun ianfu," p. 34.

66. See Suzuki, *Chōsenjin* (p. 54) about the oral evidence, which continues to be gathered by teams of usually volunteer women workers.

67. George Hicks, "Comfort Women Haunt Japan," *Far Eastern Economic Review*, February 18, 1993. See also, by the same author, *The Comfort Women: The Sex Slaves of the Imperial Japanese Forces*, St. Leonards, Allen and Unwin, 1995.

68. Suzuki, *Chōsenjin*, p. 53.

69. Nakahara Michiko, "Asian Labourers along the Burma-Thailand Railroad," *Waseda Journal of Asian Studies*, Vol. 15, 1993, pp. 88–107; Murai Yoshinori, "Asian Forced Labour (*rōmusha*) on the Burma-Thailand Railway," in McCormack and Nelson, *The Burma-Thailand Railway*, 1993, pp. 59–67.

70. Two policemen and four company employees were later tried and convicted by Allied war crimes tribunals for torture and killing, but they were released without serving prison terms ("Kajima Refuses to Pay Wartime Forced Laborers," *Japan Times*, October 27, 1994). See also Fukuda Akinori, "Hanaoka jiken" *Handobukku*, pp. 114–17, and Buruma, *The Wages of Guilt*, pp. 275–91.

71. Buruma, *The Wages of Guilt*, pp. 275–91.

72. Matsuzawa Tessei, "Seifu, kigyō, gun sōgurumi no Chūgokujin kyōsei

renkō," *Hanaoka kō—doro no soko kara* (Chūgokujin kyōsei renkō o kangaeru kai, ed.) Vol. 4, pp. 1–17, at pp. 15–16.

73. Fukuda, p. 117.

74. Masuko Yoshihisa, "Hanaoka jiken—Kajima wa ketchaku hakare," *Asahi shimbun*, April 13, 1994. Also, Richard McGregor, "Japanese Corporation Rejects Chinese WWll Compo Claim," *The Australian*, October 26, 1994.

75. Masuko Yoshihisa and Akino Sadaki, "Nigeta yama 33 nenme no tabi," *Asahi shimbun*, October 29, 1991.

76. Fukuda Akinori and Hayashi Rumi, "Kakuchi no kyōsei renkō," *Handobukku*, pp. 118–21.

77. The most thorough account is Higaki Takashi, *"Matsushiro daihon'ei" no kakusareta kyodai chikagō*, Kōdansha gendai shinsho, No. 1209, 1994.

78. Hyōgo Chōsen kankei kenkyūkai, ed., *Chika kōjō to Chōsenjin kyōsei renkō*, Akashi shoten, 1990, p. 11.

79. "Daikibona chika yōsai hakken" and "Gun chika shisetsu wa zenkoku de 549 kasho," *Asahi shimbun*, February 23, 1992.

80. The emperor himself had to intervene on July 31 to settle a dispute between the navy, which favored moving to the Nara tunnel complex, and the army, which favored Matsushiro (Higaki, "Matsushiro daihon'ei," p. 87).

81. Ibid., p. 88–89.

82. *Kido Nikki*, cited in ibid., p. 87. See also Bix, "Japan's Delayed Surrender," p. 207.

83. Bix, "Japan's Delayed Surrender," p. 207.

84. McCormack and Nelson, *The Burma-Thailand Railway*, 1993.

85. Higaki, "Matsushiro daihon'ei," p. 236.

86. The following account draws on the work of Tsuneishi Kei'ichi, the researcher who has done the most to discover the truth behind the bones, and on discussions with Professor Tsuneishi. See, for example, his recent "Gendai no kadai to shite no 731 butai," *Gekkan 731 ten*, 1994, and, in English, "Accusing Bones: The Ishii Germ Warfare Unit and the Japanese Concept of World War Two," unpublished paper of December 8, 1991.

87. See also Tsuneishi Kei'ichi, *Igaku to sensō—Nihon to Doitsu*, Ochanomizu shobō, 1994.

88. Oshima Kōichi, "Sengo hoshō to sensō sekinin," *Gekkan fōramu*, December 1993, pp. 12–19, at p. 18.

89. For details and sources: Gavan McCormack,"Manchukuo: Constructing the Past," *East Asian History*, No. 2, 1991, pp. 105–24.

90. Ono Takamichi, "Chūgoku zanryū Nihonjin no kikoku rasshu," *Asahi shimbun*, November 22, 1994. There were probably still thousands left. A 1991 estimate was that there might be between 2,000 and 4,000 Japanese children and the same number of women (the latter married to Chinese) still left in China ("Kimin," *Asahi shimbun*, November 7, 1991).

91. Ide Magoroku, *Manmō no keneki to kaitakudan no higeki*, Iwanami bukkuretto, Series "Nihon kindaishi," No. 9, 1993, p. 53.

92. *Asahi shimbun*, November 16, 1994.

93. Ono, "Chūgoku zanryū."

94. Kim Il-myon, *Tennō no guntai to Chōsenjin ianfu*, San'ichi shobō, 1976.

95. "Kyōsei renkō," *Asahi shimbun*, November 22, 1991.

96. Usuki Keiko et al., *Handobukku*, p. 32.

97. Hayashi Eidai, *Shōgen—Karafuto [Sakhalin] Chōsenjin gyakusatsu jiken*, Fūbaisha, 1991. See also *Handobukku*, p. 48.

98. Yonhap, "Coming Home to Die: The Plight of Koreans," *Korea Newsreview*, January 2, 1993, p. 9.

99. "Housing to Be Funded for Korean Returnees from Sakhalin," Kyodo News Service, December 15, 1994.

100. "Mitsubishi chōyōkō hibakusha mondai," *Handobukku*, pp. 66–71.

101. Taguchi Hiroshi, "Korean 'Emperor's Soldiers' Who Were Made into War Criminals," *Japan Review*, 1993, No. 2, pp. 20–23. In general, on the "BC" war criminals, Yamamoto Ken'ichi, "Kankoku Chōsenjin BC kyū senpan," *Handobukku*, pp. 52–53, also Utsumi Aiko, "Rengōkoku horyō to Chōsenjin gunzoku," Kankoku bunka kenkyū shinkō zaidan, *Seikyū gakujutsu ronshū*, 1995, Vol. 6, pp. 123–96.

102. Itō Takashi, "Taiwan," *Shūkan kinyōbi*, August 12, 1994, pp. 18–19.

103. Japanese "citizens" were compensated after the war for loss of these accounts, but the Japanese government view was that foreign claims were canceled by the various international agreements following the San Francisco Peace Treaty.

104. "War, Colonialism and Compassion," editorial, *Japan Times*, April 30, 1992.

105. Reuter, Taipei, December 21, 1994.

106. McCormack, "Manchukuo," pp. 105–24.

107. Ohga Kazuo, *Nihonjin wa Chūgoku de nani o shita no ka*, Asahi shobō, 1989, pp. 76–97.

108. McCormack, "Manchukuo," and sources cited there; also Honda Katsuichi, *Chūgoku no Nihongun*, Sōjusha, 1972, pp. 58–92; and for the most recent massacre: Zhongguo tongxin—Kyodo, "Details of Massacre," *Japan Times*, September 16, 1994.

109. Himeta Mitsuyoshi and Chen Ping, *Mō hitotsu no sankō sakusen*, Aoki shoten, 1989. This careful study concludes that by 1941 at least 50,000 to 60,000 homes in over 1,000 villages in a 4,000-square-kilometer "insecure zone" of Hwabei were burned to create a "people-free zone," or mujinku, of around 1,500 square kilometres (p. 134, and pp. 146–47 for detailed map) and by 1945 the total mujinku area had grown to approximately 50,000 square kilometers (p. 148).

110. Ibid., p. 174.

111. Peter Williams and David Wallace, *Unit 731*, London, Grafton Books, 1990; Tsuneishi Kei'ichi, *Igakusha tachi no soshiki hanzai*, Asahi shimbunsha, 1994.

112. On the complaint addressed by China to the U.N. Disarmament Conference in 1992, see "Kyū Nihongun ga hōchi shita kagaku heiki," *Asahi shimbun*, February 28, 1992. See also Awaya Kentarō, "Kyū Nihongun no doku gasu tairyō iki," *Handobukku*, pp. 122–23.

113. Ben Hills, "Japan Seeks Dumped Poison Gas," *Sydney Morning Herald*, January 17, 1995.

114. Ibid., pp. 166–68. See also Okada Yoshimasa et al., eds., *Zoku gendaishi shiryō—(12)—ahen mondai*, Misuzu shobō, 1986, and Eguchi Kei'ichi, *Nitchū ahen sensō*, Iwanami, 1988.

115. Eguchi Kei'ichi, ed., *Nitchū ahen sensō*, Iwanami bukkuretto, No. 215, 1991.

116. Maeda Tetsuo, *Senryaku bakugeki no shisō—Gerunika—Jūkei [Chungking]—Hiroshima*, Asahi shimbunsha, 1988.

117. The Guernica raid is estimated to have caused 1,654 deaths, whereas the Chungking raids of May 3 and 4, 1939, left some 5,400 dead (Maeda, *Senryaku bakugeki*, pp. 141, 167).

118. Ibid., pp. 302, 314.

119. Ibid., p. 432.

120. Tanaka Hiroshi, "Chūgoku," *Shūkan kinyōbi*, August 12, 1994, pp. 16–17.

121. "Towareru sengo hoshō," *Asahi shimbun*, November 14, 1993. Niimi Takashi, "Minkan higai—'Zenjindai' ni dasareta kengisho," *Handobukku*, pp. 134–35.

122. Endō Masatake, "Hosokawa hatsugen de hazumitsuku," *Aera*, November 1, 1993, pp. 36–37.

123. Hsu Yun-cho, Chua Ser-koon, Tanaka Hiroshi, and Fukunaga Heiwa, *Nihongun senryō ka no Shingapōru*, Aoki shoten, 1986; Hayashi Hirofumi, "Marēshia Shingapōru," *Shūkan kinyōbi*, August 12, 1994, p. 27.

124. Nakahara Michiko, "Nihongun ni fumikerareta Marēshia," *Shūkan kinyōbi*, August 5, 1994, pp. 32–39.

125. Takemi Chieko, "Firipin," *Shūkan kinyōbi*, August 12, 1994, pp. 28–29.

126. Endō Masatake, "Zutto iyasarenakatta kizu," *Aera*, November 1, 1993, pp. 38, 39.

127. Ibid., pp. 40–41; "Former Japanese Soldiers to Seek Compensation when Emperor Visits," *Japan Times*, September 23, 1991.

128. Nakahara Michiko, "Mahachīru hatsugen no shingi," *Shūkan kinyōbi*, September 23, 1993, pp. 10–12.

129. Ru Pei-chun, "Ninshiki seyo Nihon no sensō sekinin," *Shūkan kinyōbi*, September 23, 1993, pp. 13–15.

130. Matsui Kakushin, "Māsharu guntō," *Shūkan kinyōbi*, August 12, 1994, p. 23.

131. Takagi Ken'ichi, "Aryūshan rettō," ibid., p. 31.

132. Naomi Hirakawa, "War Victims Grow Louder, More Numerous," *Japan Times*, August 27, 1994.

133. Ibid.

134. Gavan Daws, *Prisoners of the Japanese*, New York, William Morrow, 1994, p. 18.

135. Richard McGregor, "PM Dismisses UK War Payout Claims," *The Australian*, September 16, 1993.

136. Queensland Ex-POW Reparations Committee, *Nippon Very Sorry—Many Men Must Die*, Boolarong, Queensland, 1990; Jane Milburn, "Japanese War Fund May Establish Townsville Tropical Disease Centre," *Campus Review*, September 23–29, 1993.

137. "Kuni ni hoshō yōkyū e," *Hokkai Taimusu*, November 10, 1994; and other articles in Hokkaido newspapers, various dates, November 1994. For a copy of a letter sent to Prime Minister Murayama in March 1995 by one of this group, Kim Yun-shin, see Tanaka Ryō, "Saharin no senjū minzoku," *Shūkan kinyōbi*, May 12, 1995.

138. See Eguchi Kei'ichi and Nakamura Masanori, "Ima Shōwashi o kangaeru," *Sekai*, February 1989, pp. 42–60, at p. 59 (quoting the *Asahi* survey).

139. *Mainichi shimbun* survey of September 1993, quoted in Yoshida Yutaka, "Rekishi ishiki wa henka shite iru," *Sekai*, September 1994, pp. 22–33, at p. 23.

140. *Asahi shimbun*, November 13, 1993.

141. Susan Wyndham, "Japan's Offer Little Comfort To Sex Slaves," *The Australian*, September 3–4, 1994.

142. According to Prime Minister Murayama, speaking in Tokyo on August 31.

143. Hirakawa, "War victims grow louder."

144. " 'Despite Treaties, Japan Owes Comfort Women,' group says," *Japan Times*, November 23, 1994. (In 1993, The South Korean government made a lump-sum payment of 5 million won [about $7,500] to each woman, and also began payment of a monthly allowance toward food, fuel, medical insurance, etc.)

145. Gavan Daws, *Prisoners of the Japanese*, p. 390.

146. Text of George Bush's letter in *Handobukku* (shiryō 44).

147. One suggestion is that Japan's ODA budget, currently around 1.2 to 1.3 trillion yen per year, be diverted to the extent of, say, 50 percent to payment of compensation. Over a period of ten years, this would amount to a sum of between 5 and 6 trillion yen, not enough perhaps to cover all claims, but certainly a substantial basis for a fund (Murai Yoshinori, "The ODA Bid-rigging Scandal," *Ampo—Japan-Asia Quarterly Review*, Vol. 25, No. 4, 1994, pp. 2–4.)

148. "Sengo 50 nen ketsugi shinchōha ga 'kyōsei no saiten'," *Asahi shimbun*, May 30, 1995.

149. For a frank discussion (with British scholar Ronald Dore) by Okuno of his political beliefs, see "Watakushi wa naze 'fusen ketsugi' ni hantai suru no ka," *Sekai*, May 1995, pp. 192–203.

150. Norma Field, "War and Apology: Japan, Asia and the Fiftieth," unpublished draft paper. My thanks to Norma Field for a copy of this paper, forthcoming in *Positions: East Asia, Cultures, Critique*.

151. Quoted in Michael Richardson, "Japan Must Apologize for War, Say Neighbours," *The Australian*, June 5, 1995.

Concluding Remarks

Japan at Century's End

In November 1994, while researching and thinking about this book, I happened to be strolling beside the canal in the Dutch resort of Huis Ten Bosch in Nagasaki Prefecture when I was accosted by a group of students from Gifu Girls' Commercial High School. They were apparently seeking foreigners with whom to practice their English conversation, while at the same time, perhaps with some encouragement from their teacher, attempting to articulate some basic message about themselves and their country. The carefully prepared "Peace Message" card that they thrust into my hand contained the following simple, moving thoughts expressed in their own hands:

> I renounce the war because everyone wants to be happy.
> I am loving peace. Let's stop the war and make a peaceful world.
> Japan is a peaceful country. But now there are little wars which I don't know in the world somewhere. Let's hand in hand in all [sic], and make the world peaceful.

There were a number of other individually signed messages in a similar vein, and they had added a poem, built around the refrain "It's a small world."

When pressed to inscribe my own message in return for my card, I paused for a long moment. The foreigner encounter/English-conversation practice/peace statement was a minidrama that had been enacted countless times in countless different locations, even in my own personal experience of life in postwar Japan. For me to respond in Japanese would have been to disappoint them and to break the rules of the encounter, so our language remained English. But what I wanted to say, and what for a very long moment stayed in my mind, was something like, "For peace and justice in the world, let us consume less and strive to transform the economy into one of zero-growth," or "For the sake of world peace, how shall we confine the insatiable desires of Japan and the other rich nations?" Actually, the book I was writing was in a sense the message they were asking for, although it was scarcely one I could deliver to them there and then. The autumn day was too perfect, the setting of seventeenth-century Holland reproduced by the shores of Omura Bay too unlikely and disarming, to admit of the harshness of a discordant, unexpected note. So I simply wrote for them the banality they were expecting about sharing their desire for peace. In the remote event of any of my young interlocutors ever coming across this book, I would wish to convey to them through it the thought that love of peace and hostility to war is indeed the foundation of morality and social responsibility, but no more than the foundation.

A few years earlier, I had written an essay in which I coined the term "3C" to describe the political economy of Japan, the "3C" being construction, consumption, and control.[1] Since then, the expression, which at the time was to some extent fortuitous and rhetorical, has grown to seem increasingly apt. Enough has been written in this book on the subjects of construction and consumption, but little about control. By control, I am not wishing to imply the sort of systematic, hard repression practiced by a Gestapo or a Kempeitai, but a soft and diffuse mode in which the key roles are played by advertising agencies or by television and supermarket moguls. Their importance stems from their assigned social role of ensuring that economic growth does not slacken. To achieve this, they devise the various programs—the software—to stimulate the demand for goods and services. That is to say, they identify and manipulate human desires, turn them into the taste for particular commodities, and rouse those desires to the point of constituting the markets that sustain growth and profit. Desires are forever created, homogenized, fed, redefined, and recreated, in the course of the construction of an endless cycle of desire, consumption, and waste. The basic rule is that demand must never be satisfied. In this sense, choice is indeed multiplied in modern societies, but the parameters are commonly engineered so that the individual is often left with little more than a choice between brand names, whether of cosmetics or political parties. This mesh of soft control is by no means unique to Japan, but Japanese society is saturated by commercial incitements of a most sophisticated and intense order, whose power is in inverse proportion to people's consciousness of them. Had I attempted to draw an analogy between militarism and commercialism, armies and admen, the peace-loving Gifu girls would certainly have thought me a madman; yet the analogies have to be considered.

In Japan, the approach of the end of the century is experienced with particular pain and unease, because the long quest for the holy grail of modernization and equality of status with the West is over, but, having "made it," people are bombarded with messages urging them to redouble their efforts, to work harder (because of the fierce rivalry stirred by the success of their efforts so far), to import more (to help other countries pay for their Japanese goods), and to consume more, so that the trajectory of growth may be resumed. The object of the long quest of the modern age is chimerical, a bird glimpsed momentarily through the foliage that flew away so quickly that perhaps it was never there in the first place. In no country is social life so structured around the imperatives of economic life, or are people subjected to more pressure to consume. Nowhere is the emptiness of affluence more deeply felt. The faith in modernization began to weaken even as its promised land was being occupied. The disparity between human needs and human desires was becoming patent. The salaryman who had created the miracle of postwar Japan was beginning to see himself as a Sisyphean jogger on the treadmill of infinitely expanding and replicating desire. What the students from Gifu Girls' Commercial High School will have to reflect upon is a much more complex matter than simply peace versus war.

The assumption that social and political health may be measured by continuing economic growth runs deep in all modern societies. Japan has done brilliantly at the game of economic growth, but news of its preeminence being confirmed by one or other fresh statistic—the yen scaling new heights, or Japan's banks or overseas assets or aid budgets attaining or retaining the world's number-one role—no longer elicits even a single round of applause. The deep-rooted dissatisfaction with the workings of the supposedly triumphant market in Japan, and the search for an alternative way in government, business, and society generally (discussed in Chapter 2), gathers strength as the end of the century looms, even if the direction it will eventually take remains unclear.

The goal of attaining something like Japanese consumption levels has driven growth in much of Asia since at least the Vietnam War, and has come to define the kind of future to which people aspire. Japan is thought to have found, deciphered, and put into practice an alchemical formula for growth and prosperity. It constitutes both model and magnet, pulling upon the entire Asian region. Yet it is not possible to replicate the profligacy of raw materials and the carelessness of environmental impact practiced by Japan and the other advanced industrial countries. Japan therefore does not constitute a model, and it should be obvious that neither is there a model to be found in North America or Western Europe. Not only is Japan's affluence deeply problematic, but it pulls the region around it toward social and ecological disaster.

In the body of this book, I have referred enough to the views of representatives of the many Japanese citizen, environmental, or academic groups. If some readers still remain skeptical of their message, let me here refer to the 1995 volumes of the Japanese government's annual *Environment White Paper*. This unlikely official source is steeped in profound concern at the dimensions of contemporary global ecological and civilizational crisis. Somberly, it suggests that the limits of the path of contemporary civilization that originated in the West and had spread through virtually the entire world were already evident in terms of resources and environment, and that technological responses offered little prospect of any solution. Without drawing any specific analogy to Japan itself, it reflected that ancient civilizations, such as the Sumerian, had collapsed because of salinization and reduced wheat crops due to the large-scale irrigation engineering and the cutting down of the forests, among other factors. It stressed the urgency to move to a society based on the use of renewable materials and energy in a sustainable cycle, calling attention to the model of Ainu society, which had preserved its natural ecology and treated the foods taken from rivers and sea as blessings from the gods. The Japanese government's paean of praise for Ainu ecological wisdom was certainly unprecedented. So was the unambiguous sounding of the death knell of the civilization of mass production, mass consumption, and mass waste, although the paper was notably lacking in specific prescriptions for what to do about it.[2] The problems it outlines are the problems that the girls from Gifu Girls' Commercial High School will have to face.

What message might one hope to hear from them to their late-twentieth- and early-twenty-first-century world as they assume citizenship within it? First, one hopes that they will not forsake their insistence on the centrality of peace. The aspiration for a future world and regional order founded in peace is, however, inseparable today from the task of cooperating with their fellow citizens and the people of neighboring countries in first establishing a common past. It may seem harsh to suggest that they, and their innocent generation, should be held responsible for the deeds of a generation they scarcely know, but the moral continuity of the nation state, and the responsibility before history, are taken very seriously by the world community, which expects sincere recognition of the past violence and aggression of Japanese colonialism and imperialism—not as something unique, but as something that is not to be passed over because it was "just like" what the Europeans or Americans did. Such crimes have to be recognized, repented, and compensated, for the creation of a shared sense of the past is a precondition for the creation of a shared future, as has been eloquently demonstrated by the German government as it commemorates the fiftieth anniversary of the fall of the Third Reich.

Second, this generation will have to face the same dilemma as that of their predecessors in yet another sense: how to define its own identity without negating either Asia or the West, while dealing at the same time with the added dimension of the crisis of the South—accelerating poverty and global maldistribution of wealth and resources. The previous generation challenged the non-Asian empires, but did so in the end by emulating them and establishing a Japanese empire in their place, invading and colonizing Asia while posing as its liberator from the yoke of Western colonial rule.[3] The continuing strength of that fantasy even in the mid-1990s was demonstrated vividly by the Asian Togetherness Festival held in Tokyo in May 1995 (discussed in Chapter 6) designed to express thanks to Japan for liberating Asia and offer condolence to those who had made sacrifices to help achieve that goal (i.e., the members of the Imperial Japanese Army). Promoted as a celebration of togetherness, it actually highlighted the psychological and moral gap between the politically influential Japanese, who still believed in the sacredness of the war cause, and the Asia they sought to represent.

Furthermore, the rhetoric of Asianism or neo-Asianism has to face not only the truth about Japan's role in the pursuit of regional hegemony by an earlier generation, but also the contradictory qualities of the contemporary relationship. The discussion on food in Chapter 3 should be sufficient to establish this. Already, Japan's external dependence is such that its people rely for their everyday subsistence on the labor of their neighbors. More and more of the scarce resources of

Asia—especially its arable land and its seas—is being used to produce food for Japan's affluent consumers. It is an outcome logical and virtuous in terms of the global GATT regime in practice and of neoclassical free markets in theory, but both morally dubious and, in the long term, politically and economically misguided. The structuring of economic exchange in which the labor of many in several countries is devoted to the production of food for the (relatively) few in one other country has commonly been described as colonial or imperialistic, rarely as just or desirable. In the sharpened competition for food, especially protein, that is expected in the twenty-first century, this relationship is bound to be questioned.

During the postwar, high-growth decades, Japan withdrew from international public space into "political, moral, and psychological isolationism" in the privatized spaces of high growth.[4] Turning their backs on the whole idea of Asianness, ordinary Japanese citizens cooperated in the pursuit of national wealth and power, their gaze fixed firmly to the East (the United States) rather than to the West (Asia), ignoring the suffering and damage inflicted upon their Asian neighbors and identifying almost exclusively with the victims rather than the perpetrators of the war. The moral amnesia of this posture was reinforced by education practice and policies. All of this has left a legacy of attitudinal problems that today's young generation must face.

There is a further, sad, historical irony in the Japan-Asia relationship: Japan's corporate skills at mobilizing and accumulating are revered almost as much as its former single-minded pursuit of military hegemony was (and is) hated, without the inner connection between the two being grasped. The components of that Japanese model, which insists on the sublimation of social and individual goals to the ends of the corporation, and attaches highest value to the achievement of market share, which is wasteful of materials and practices the routinized, rationalized organization of human life to an extreme degree, does not have much to offer, yet is eagerly studied and applied.[5] Part of the responsibility of young Japanese today must be to try to convey to their neighbors, and to the world generally, the flaws of the model, so that they not be reproduced.

The third, and perhaps greatest, challenge the girls from Gifu will have to face are the problems raised in their own government's *White Paper,* of how to transform their own lifestyles in a way even more profound, and literally revolutionary, than the transformations of their parents or grandparents. Theirs will be the task of meeting the challenge to human survival posed not by obviously brutal or rapacious military force but by their own lifestyle; to transform that will be no less difficult than coping with militarism, and essentially it will have to be done without the help of outside intervention.

The notion of zero growth is not popular in conventional or neoclassical economics. Yet it is not a "green" fantasy but solidly grounded in classical economics, and sensitive to the laws of both the natural and the ethical or moral orders. The problem of the limits and function of growth was considered by the founders of the field of political economy. John Stuart Mill (1806–1873) looked forward to the achievement of what he called the "stationary state," which might today be called the zero-growth state, as something to be welcomed. Writing in 1848, he referred to "the mere increase of production and accumulation" that excites the congratulations of "ordinary" politicians with minds that require "coarse stimuli." His words ring true and wise, and with a particular appropriateness to contemporary Japan, long after he penned them:

> I know not why it should be matter of congratulation that persons who are already richer than anyone needs to be, should have doubled their means of consuming things which give little or no pleasure except as representative of wealth . . . It is only in the backward countries of the world that increased production is still an important object: in those most advanced, what is economically needed is a better distribution.[6]

Increase of wealth is not, and cannot be, boundless, and "at the end of . . . the progressive state lies the stationary state [zero-growth state]." Mill goes on,

> I confess I am not charmed with the ideal of life held out by those who think that the normal state of human beings is that of struggling to get on; that the trampling, crushing, elbowing, and treading on each other's heels, which form the existing type of social life, are the most desirable lot of human kind, or anything but the disagreeable symptoms of one of the phases of industrial progress . . . But the best state for human nature is that in which, while no one is poor, no one desires to be richer, nor has any reason to fear being thrust back, by the efforts of others to push themselves forward.

It is scarcely necessary to remark that a stationary condition of capital and population implies no stationary state of human improvement. There would be as much scope as ever for all kinds of mental culture, and moral and social progress; as much for improving the Art of Living, and much more likelihood of its being improved, when minds ceased to be engrossed by the art of getting on.[7]

Put in such terms by a prophetic nineteenth-century voice (who could have had no more than an inkling of the lengths to which human exploitation of the earth's resources would go or of the countless ways in which human desires might be created and defined as needs), zero growth becomes the goal of all mature economies. Such a prospect need not be bleak. As the 1989 program of the German Social-Democratic Party (SPD) put it, "Those activities must grow which secure the basic elements of life and improve its quality . . . [which] promote self-determination and autonomous creative activities. Those activities which threaten the natural foundations of life must diminish and disappear."[8] The French thinker André Gorz, who has long been grappling with the problem of work in advanced industrial society, identifies the detachment of expanding capital from felt human needs as the root of the pathology of contemporary industrial society, and proposes a better life through reduced consumption, the flourishing of many varied subcultures, and maximum individual autonomy. He calls for a thirty-hour working week, an annual working year of approximately 1,380 hours, further reduced, by the right to a sabbatical year, to about 1,150 hours, and eventually to the 1,000 hours a year which was the norm in the eighteenth-century preindustrial world.[9]

A similar vision for Japan is developed by the eminent Japanese economist Tsuru Shigeto, himself the author of Japan's first postwar *White Paper on Economics,* strategist of postwar economic recovery and growth but critic of its subsequent obsessive pursuit. Tsuru developed further Mill's vision of affluence by drawing the picture of a Japan in which labor power would come to be seen as end rather than means, and reorganized so as to become meaningful and satisfying, and by his thought that the combination of the humanizing of work, the rendering artistic of life, and the fulfillment of leisure might constitute the program for a reorienting of Japan's energies in creative and socially beneficial ways.[10]

This is also, presumably, the direction of the initiatives by the heads of Sony and Canon, by the Keidanren business federation, and by the Research Group within MITI on Sensitive Business (See Chapter 2), although the formulae they generate are bound to incline toward compromise driven by their commercial and bureaucratic interests; they will tend to give priority to reforms that are designed to create new markets, rather than new values.

The thoughts of Mill, Tsuru, and others from the classical and Marxist traditions are taken up and developed by many Japanese economists and social and political philosophers (especially those grouped in the Entropy Society, some of whose work was cited in Chapter 1).[11] In English too there is a considerable literature. One of the best-known writers in this vein is Herman Daly, an economist who is well known as one of the contemporary advocates of the concept of steady-state economics. Daly points out the flaw of conventional studies in economics that treat the economy as a total system in which everything is more or less substitutable, and that fail to give due attention to the operation of natural laws governing what he refers to as "the flow of resources from the larger natural system through the economy and then back into the larger system as waste."[12] "Unfortunately," he says, "the market as a category of economic thought abstracts from the community and the biosphere."[13] This flow process must in principle be contained "within the regenerative capacity of the input side and within the absorptive capacities of the waste/output side." The dilemmas that Daly highlights arise from the fact that while biophysical laws operate to render continuing growth impossible, for political reasons it is not possible to stop it, although he hopes that the latter impossibility will prove less absolute than the former.

Unless the principles enunciated by scholars from Mill to Daly are somehow disproved, Japan's lifestyle and consumption patterns are not sustainable, but in the political immobilism, drift, and economic uncertainty of 1995, the sense of gloom in Japan could scarcely be exaggerated, and these crucial questions play little role in any national political agenda. The mood was described by prominent political leaders and critics in terms of unprecedented severity: as a nation in the grip of "collective depression" (former Prime Minister Miyazawa), or "nihilistic populism" (former Prime Minister Hosokawa), a "deep social unease" akin to that of the time of depression and international instability of the 1920s, which led to fascism and militarism (former Deputy Prime Minister and long-term Liberal-Democratic stalwart, Gotōda

Masaharu), as a "terminally ill democracy" (the prominent critic Nishibe Susumu), or as "a leaderless and identityless" country, neither part of Asia nor able to understand Asia, able only to look "inward, downward, backward" (another prominent critic, Ohmae Ken'ichi).[14] Yet crisis also constitutes opportunity for change. The achievement of the material and technical bases of affluence in contemporary Japan is beyond question, and Japan's greatest wealth is the goodness, generosity, humanity, and intelligence of its ordinary people. The aspiration for change rooted in the popular movements that have struggled for decades against the madness of the Cold War, the excesses of corporate society, environmental degradation, fetishistic consumerism, and now collective gloom and hysteria maintains at the grass-roots level, commonly invisible to the international media, a network of community, cooperation, and conservation, three "C"-words of very different import from those making up the "3C" political economy. They have always pursued the fundamental moral principle that the only sustainable social or political order is that which is equitable. In the midst of the recession of the 1990s, the chain of so-called "Third World Shops" that resisted the conventional wisdom of the absolute importance of cheapness and insisted instead on the principle of fair and just price, meaning *higher* than world-market price, were growing at an extraordinary annual rate of 30 percent.[15] The Japan that is constituted by such networks is more than ready to play an active, open, cooperative role in the creation of a new world order, thereby fulfilling the ideals of the Constitution. The ambition to be a great power interests them little, for they prefer the ambition expressed in the 1920s by the liberal intellectual Ishibashi Tanzan, to be a "small Japan" worthy of pride and respect.

The transformation to which the energies of so many grass-roots Japanese individuals and groups are committed is one that would have the effect of opening and recasting the Japanese identity, so that various ethnic groups, some, like the Koreans, long resident in the country, would cease to feel contradiction between their ethnic identity and Japaneseness, as Japaneseness becomes a civic and moral, rather than an ethnic, quality. The international state of Japan would gradually become, in the words of the political philosopher Katō Takashi, the multicultural, multiracial, pacifist, human rights-championing, "Republic of Japan."[16] The process may take, as Katō recognizes, fifty or even a hundred years, but it is a vision and an ideal no less substantial than that of becoming a great power. In this process, in which some at least of the girls from Gifu Girls' Commercial High School will play roles impossible today even to imagine, I like to think that the erosion of the human, social, and ecological capital of Japan—its true wealth—which during the years of my experience has been the price of prosperity, may be reversed; and that the restlessness of the modern, corporate expansion, hell-bent on convenience and profit, that has so diminished the country I came to know thirty-three years ago, may be rolled back. I do not expect to see the reversal of this trend, but perhaps it shall be my fortune to be reborn in a Japan that could combine the immense beauty I first encountered in 1962 as high growth was beginning, with the wisdom and maturity of a post-growth order based on revived regional communities, openness to the world, economic zero-growth and zero-emission technology, and restoration of the mountains, rivers, and sea.

Notes

1. Gavan McCormack, "Pacific Dreamtime and Japan's New Millenialism," *Australian Outlook*, Vol. 43, No. 2, August 1989, pp. 64–73.
2. Kankyōcho, Ed., *Kankyō hakusho*, 1995. See resume in "Minaose, tairyō shohi no gendai bunmei," *Asahi shimbun*, May 30, 1995.
3. Yoshikazu Sakamoto, "The Fifty Years of the Two Japans," *Medicine and Global Survival*, June 1995 (in typescript version, for which my thanks to Professor Sakamoto).
4. Ibid.
5. Katō Takashi, "Sengo gojūnen to chishikijin," *Sekai*, January 1995, pp. 68–83.
6. John Stuart Mill, "Principles of Political Economy," J. M. Robson, ed., *Collected Works of John Stuart Mill*, Toronto, University of Toronto Press, and London, Routledge and Kegan Paul, 1965, Vol. 3, p. 755. (I am indebted to Professor Tsuru Shigeto, whose citation of passages from this text of Mill drove me back to the fascinating original.)
7. Ibid., pp. 754–56.
8. Quoted in André Gorz, *Capitalism, Socialism, Ecology,* translated by Chris Turner, London, Verso, 1994, p. 32.
9. Ibid., pp. 75, 98.
10. Tsuru Shigeto, " 'Seichō' de wa naku 'rōdō no ningenka' o," *Sekai*, April 1994, pp. 84–98.
11. For a discussion of the economics of entropy, see Herman E. Daly and John B. Cobb Jr., *For the Common Good*, Boston, Beacon Press, 1989, 1994, pp. 194–206.

12. Richard Evanoff, "Steady-State Economics: An Interview with Herman E. Daly," *Japan Environment Monitor*, September 1994, pp. 10–11.

13. Daly and Cobb, *For the Common Good,* p. 51.

14. Miyazawa and Gotōda in *Aera*, May 1–8, 1995, pp. 25, 29; Hosokawa and Nishibe in *Aera*, April 24, 1995, pp. 25, 26; Ohmae in *Chūō kōron*, January 1995, pp. 263–93.

15. Uchihashi Katsuto, *Kyōsei no daichi*, Iwanami shinsho, 1995, pp. 6–7.

16. Katō, "Sengo gojūnen," p. 83.

Index

Abandoned children, 257–59
Aboriginal peoples, compensation
    for, 270–71
Advertising, 288–89
"Affirmation of the Greater East
    Asian War" (Hayashi), 238
Agriculture, 86, 113–45
    cooperatives, 144
    desirability of free market, 128
    domestic stagnation, 124–25
    external market opening, 125
    Japan as model for, 141–45
    Japan's food dependency, 122–26,
      127, 291–92
    market protection, 113
    peculiarities of Japanese, 139–41
    regional patterns in, 132–39
    resource growth in, 121
    scale expansions in, 125
    and world population, 116–22
    See also Farming population
Agriculture Ministry, 124
Ainu (people), 48, 201, 290
Akashi Straits Bridge, 16, 27
Alienation, 18
ANIEs. *See* Asian Newly
    Industrialized Economies
Anti-Epidemic Laboratory, 255
Anti-Western resentment, 162–63
Anzen (credit union), 94
Aoki Hidekazu, 13, 35, 39
Aoshima Yukio, 18, 19
Arms imports, 193
Army Medical College, 255
Arranged marriages, 179–80
Asada Akira, 100
Asahi (newspaper), 179, 215,
    217

Asia
    concept of, 160–61
    distancing from, 155, 160–61
    European hegemony in, 154
    GNP in, 157–58
    government intrusiveness in, 169
    growth rates in, 155–59
    Japan versus, 171–74
    reconciliation with Japan, 162
    as representation of resistance, 167
    supposed cultural traits, 164
Asia and Pacific Trade Center
    (Osaka), 26
Asianism, 162–69, 180, 274–75,
    291–92
    and civilization theory, 169–71
Asian Newly Industrialized
    Economies (ANIEs), 156, 159
Asian Togetherness Festival, 275–76,
    291
Assembly for the Establishment of a
    Sovereign Constitution, 197
Associations of Construction
    Companies, 38
Asthma, 52
Attu (Aleutian island), 269
Aum Supreme Truth (cult), 6, 82
Auschwitz, 242
Australia, 93, 126, 127, 134–38, 166,
    201
    beef industry, 135–36
    drought of 1994, 137
    grain production, 136
    national identity in, 177–78
    rice production, 137–39
Australian Independent Commission
    Against Corruption, 38
Authoritarianism, 164–65

Korean Council for the Women
  Drafted for Military Sexual
  Slavery by Japan, 272
Korean War, 191
Kuala Lumpur, 63
Kuma (Ehime), 104
Kuno Osamu, 239
Kurobe River, 46
Kurokawa Kisho, 61–62
Kyōsei. See Symbiosis
Kyoto, 4, 28, 52, 98
Kyushu, 88

Labor
  movement, 81
  social organization of, 80–81
  See also Forced labor; Unions;
    Work hours; Work week
Labor Standards Law, 80
Lake Biwa, 66
Land-price inflation, 13, 91–92, 105
Land reclamation, 31, 32, 48–50,
  58–59
Land speculation, 57, 91
Laohegou (China), 263
La Port Ski Dome SSAWS
  (Funabashi City), 99
Lawrence, Geoffrey, 136
LDP. *See* Liberal-Democratic
  Party
Leahy, William David, 243
Lee Kuan Yew, 164, 165, 276
Leisure state, 78–106
  international dimension to, 92–95
  and local development, 101–06
  market for, 79–80
  as new growth area, 85
  resort boom, 86–92
  and theme parks, 97–101
Leisure World, 17, 68
Levies, 33, 37–38
Liberal-Democratic Party (LDP), 6,
  35, 38, 56, 185, 186, 202, 214
Lifetime employment, 81
"Limits to Growth, The," 119
Liquefaction, 9
Liu Lianren, 252
Living standards, 78–79, 141–42

Local empowerment, 15, 19, 45,
  101–02, 201–02
London Blitz, 243
Loyalty, 200

Maeda Tetsuo, 265
Maekawa Haruo, 124
Maekawa Report, 58, 124
Mahathir bin Mohamad, 165, 168, 268
Mainland, Battle for the, 254
Makuhari *Messe* (convention)
  complex, 16
Makuhari New City, 61
Malay peninsula, 267
Malaysia, 93, 133, 157, 246
Malnourishment, 117
Malthus, Thomas, 116
Manchukuo, 257, 263
Manchuria, 165
Manchurian Incident (1931), 170
Mangrove forests, 133
Manufacturing industry, 6
Maori (people), 201
Marriages. *See* Arranged marriages
Marshall Islands, 269
Mass graves, 263
Matsui Yayori, 179
Matsumoto Ken-ichi, 167
Matsushiro Imperial Headquarters,
  251, 253–55
Matsushita Kōnosuke, 66
Meat, 122–23, 133–35
Meiji Constitution (1889–1946), 188
Meiji state, 176
Meishin Highway, 12
Metropolitan Waterfront Subcenter
  Project, 18, 59
Micronesia, 246
Micronesia Agreement, 268–69
Military budget, 123, 193
Mill, John Stuart, 293–94
Millennium Tower, 62
Minamata disease, 55
Minato Mirai 21. *See* Twenty-first
  Century Port City
Minimum Access Formula, 114
Ministry of Construction, 11, 33, 34,
  47

Gavan McCormack is Professor of Japanese History in the Research School of Pacific and Asian Studies, Australian National University. He was educated at Melbourne and London universities, with a Ph.D. in History from London University in 1974. He taught at the Universities of Leeds (UK), La Trobe (Melbourne), and Adelaide, before being appointed to his current position in 1990. He has lived and worked in Japan on many occasions since first visiting as a student in 1962, and has been a visiting professor at Kyoto and Kobe universities. He has written a dozen books on aspects of modern Japanese, Korean, and Chinese history. He is well known in Japan (where many of his works have been translated and published) and his work has also been translated and published in Chinese, Korean, Thai, Arabic, and the main European languages.